ÅSA RINGBOM

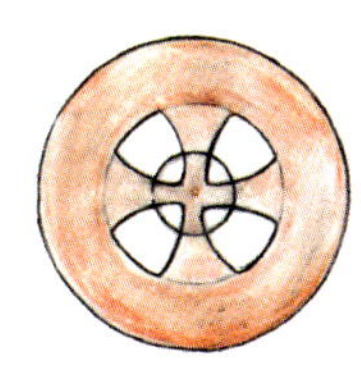

THE VOICE OF THE ÅLAND CHURCHES

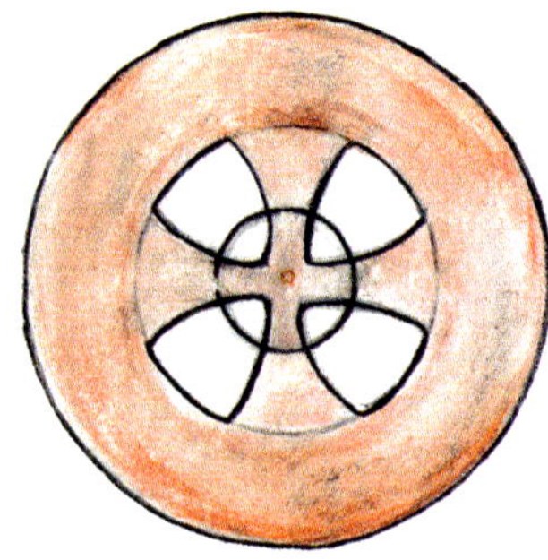

An inauguration cross from the church in Eckerö

An inauguration cross from the church in Eckerö has become the constantly repeated symbol for the Åland churches project. Inauguration crosses, circles inscribing a cross with arms of equal length, have been preserved from most medieval stone churches in the Åland Islands. In principle, inauguration crosses should be found in all churches, and in principle they should belong to the first stage of the construction. According to legal directives the inauguration of a church should follow the identical strict formula in each individual case. It was the bishop who performed the inauguration of the church and on the occasion he should splash holy crisma at twelve different places, one for each apostle. Each point was painted with an inauguration cross on the wall. Additionally, in Åland the inauguration crosses were often inscribed in wet plaster, as was the case in Eckerö. Regardless of the given formula the inauguration crosses can be surprisingly individually executed: they can differ in size, they can be surrounded with concentric circles and they can be discreetly ornamented in different ways. Paradoxically, when the church has gone through a new inauguration after a more substantial rebuilding or enlargement, there can be inauguration crosses of different ages in the same church. At the renewed inauguration of the church, new inauguration crosses frequently supplemented old existing crosses.

ISBN 978-952-5614-42-8 · PUBLISHED BY ÅLAND'S MUSEUM · · FORM: APRIL KOMMUNIKATION · PRINTED BY WAASA GRAPHICS

CONTENTS

Preface

PREFACE

Åländska kyrkor berättar. Nytt ljus på medeltida konst arkitektur och historia was published in Swedish in 2010, aiming at those interested in the Middle Ages in general, and at those who wish to get a firmer grip of the history of the Åland Islands. It also aimed at art historians and archaeologists who want to follow the development of interdisciplinary scientific methods. But equally important was the wish to provide useful information for tourists and to guide those who pay the Åland Islands a visit. It therefore feels necessary to provide the same information in English for visitors from near and afar who want to deepen their understanding and learn more about this region.

I am deeply indebted to William Morgan, professor emeritus of Architectural History, University of Louisville, who has not only checked my English and suggested important improvements to the text, but who also shared my passion for the Åland churches ever since his first visit to the Islands in 1986.

Thanks to optimal arrangements I have been able to share my time as professor in Art History at Åbo Akademi University with a research professorship where I have directed the interdisciplinary project of the Åland churches. It is high time to present what we today believe we know about the medieval churches of the Åland Islands. The following presentation is the result of research conducted since 1990 on the Åland churches. The publication rests on earlier published volumes of individual churches, on research in preparing forthcoming church volumes, on individual articles, and on numerous presentations through the years, where I have focused on different aspects of medieval Åland.

The presentation is threefold. The first part is a wide survey where the architectural development of the churches is described century-by-century, emphasizing artistic highlights. The second part presents the churches in alphabetical order. The idea is that it should function as a tour guide for church visitors. Last, the different interdisciplinary methods implemented in the project - also developed within the project – are described. They form the basis of the medieval chronology of the Åland churches.

Heartfelt thanks go to friends and colleagues who in different ways have contributed in making the research an exciting and meaningful adventure. Stig Dreijer, Head Archaeologist of the Åland Islands, welcomed my intentions to initiate the project.

Together with Bo Ossian Lindberg he paved my way to make it possible. Bo Ossian Lindberg is further thanked for his reconstruction drawings and for inspired discussions on the Åland churches throughout the years. I am also grateful to Augusto Mendes for having carried the main responsibility for the photographic material, and to Ann-Maarit Pitkänen-Darmark for the sketches century by century. In earlier volumes Christina Remmer has described the post-reformation interiors meritoriously. I also owe thanks to the faithful audiences who have followed the development of the research in my numerous presentations throughout the years, organized by the Friends of Åland.

Above all, I am indebted to the interdisciplinary group, who come rain or shine have shared the task of refining and further developing the method of mortar dating, especially Alf Lindroos and Jan Heinemeier. It is both fun and a great privilege to work in such a creative group. No advances could have been made without them. Lately this inner circle has been widened to include Pia Sjöberg and Pia Sonck-Koota, both active within the international part of the project. Also Kenneth Gustavsson, who has followed the project from the very beginning with great interest, belongs to this circle. Those mentioned above have also generously offered to check the text in question.

The interdisciplinary collaboration has further dimensions. Initially Peter Tångeberg dated the medieval wooden sculptures in Åland by stylistic analysis. Collaboration with Peter Klein, who has complemented the dating of sculptures with dendrochronology, demonstrates the accuracy in stylistic dating when performed with expertise.

For different reasons my research has come to focus on dating mortar. One important contributing factor probably lies in my background. My road to school was awe inspiring, lingering as it did along the outer edges of the Limberg lime quarry, the enormous open cast mine in Pargas. The breathtaking abyss on the other side of the fence stimulated thoughts of the history of lime quarrying. My father Bo Nikander was chief engineer at Pargas Kalkbergs' Limited Corporation (later Partek). His international colleagues playfully called him "Mr. Cement of Finland". Numerous times I walked around the cement works with him listening while he described the processes. Roman building technique and pozzolana were other interests that I shared with him. Therefore I dedicate my research to the memory of my father.

To generous sponsors, in gratitude:

The Academy of Finland functioned as an economic guarantee during the first seven years of the project on the Åland churches, gradually to be succeeded by the Åland University of Applied Sciences and the Åland Parliament. All those mentioned above are deeply thanked for supporting research and development of methods within the project. For sponsoring of the important parallel part of the project, International Mortar Dating, thanks go to the Foundation of Åbo Akademi, and once more the Academy of Finland.

For printing this volume financial support has been given by the Foundation of Åbo Akademi, the Åland Museum, the Åland Cultural Foundation and the Swedish Cultural Foundation in Finland.

Bartsgårda July 30, 2011
Åsa Ringbom

Åland

Geographically, the Åland Islands form the westernmost part of the large archipelago between Sweden and Finland. More than six thousand islands, mainly to the east and the southeast, surround the main island. Together with Öland and Gotland in Sweden, Bornholm in Denmark, and Saarenmaa in Estonia, Åland is counted as one of the Baltic Islands. All of the Baltic Islands have a fascinating past, with individual characteristics in art and architecture and an intriguing history, shaped by navigation, trade and warfare.

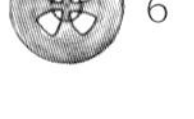

The earliest history of Åland is not known, but when the first written sources start to emerge at the end of the 13th century, the Islands are already counted as part of Eastern Sweden, together with the counties in the Finnish mainland. Ecclesiastically, Åland belonged to the Diocese of Turku at least since the 14th century. Åland together with Finland was part of the Swedish Kingdom until the war between Sweden and Russia in 1808-1809, which ended in Swedish defeat. As a result Finland, including Åland, became a Grand Duchy under Russia. In 1917 Finland achieved independence during the Russian Revolution. The status of the Åland Islands was confirmed by the League of Nations in 1921, when the Islands became a self-governed region, still under Finnish rule.

Why Åland's Churches?

Ever since the age of nine, when I discovered archaeology and egyptology, I have wanted to take an active part in dynamic research one day, and to be able to contribute to clarifying large historical contexts. At the same time I visited Åland for the first time. I was amazed at the prehistory of the Islands, all these burial mounds, so visible in the terrain. This was something entirely new to me - all these churches, so individual and so beautifully adorned, with different stages so clearly discernible.

What was this? What did it all mean? What could burial mounds and churches tell us about the past?

The Åland Summer University was initiated in 1969, which meant that I started my academic career by participating in their course on archaeology, including the excavation of the church in Finström. To witness the discovery of the older wooden church on the site intrigued me even further. This was fun, it was something that I wanted to devote my life to. To find out the chronology of the Åland churches would be an important and exciting task. Studies in archaeology, and later art history, followed. When twenty years later I was able to initiate the project on the Åland churches, it felt like coming home.

At that stage I had already realized that nobody really knew how old the churches were. The lack of written sources also meant a lack of an objective chronology. As the field was open to all sorts of speculations total confusion prevailed. Everybody was skating on thin ice. Individual researchers have had radically different views on the age and the building history of the churches over the years. The dating could vary with many centuries for one single church, depending on which expert was consulted.

The controversial medieval period attracts scholars of all ages. Life was incredibly difficult, and people suffered unbearably from wars and disease. But still, the power and complexity of medieval art and architecture are hard to surpass, not only esthetically and artistically, but also from a technical point of view. The churches were always in focus. They have provided the architectural framework for the mass, for the feasts of the year and feasts of life, for music and liturgy. Through the centuries they have accumulated what was seen as the most beautiful and precious of its time. The all-encompassing hegemony of the Catholic Church made those responsible active participants of life in European cultural centers. They were well aware of the latest news and fashions. Ambulating foreign artists and building masters collaborated with local workshops and builders. Together they created a unique entity reflecting the local medieval society.

The churches are the only buildings in the Åland Islands to have been in continuous use since the Middle Ages. They have constantly been maintained, and they have been objects of the loving care of the parishioners. The inhabitants of the parish functioned as building commissioners, together with ecclesiastic and secular persons of authority. "The farmer builds the church" was the phrase used by the Swedish medieval county legislation. Therefore the churches reflect local creativity and local "Kunstwillen" in contrast to the Åland castle of Kastelholm, which was centrally governed and represented the Royal Power. And for long periods Kastelholm was deserted and in ruins.

There are no medieval sources that shed light on the building history of the churches. Yet the churches themselves, with their fittings and decorative ornamentations, optimally function as an important source of knowledge about the medieval history of the Åland Islands. The Åland churches project was initiated to compensate for the lack of written sources with all available means - scientific, historical and archaeological. Today the project has reached a stage where we can discern the outlines of the whole picture.

Both exterior and interior, as well as the decorative ornamentations, are generally well preserved in the Åland churches. They still hold a large amount of medieval wooden sculptures while the development of wall paintings throughout the entire medieval period can be traced. In addition, most churches have been archaeologically excavated.

In short, we have all the prerequisites to use the churches as historical sources, to let the churches themselves tell the story of medieval Åland. The need for increased knowledge and new information about the present state of research is obvious.

Chapter 1

CENTURY BY CENTURY

THE 11TH CENTURY – HIATUS OR CONTINUATION?

The transition between the Viking Age and the Middle Ages is an enigmatic and insufficiently researched period in the history of the Åland Islands. The continuation in the habitation has been debated, and there are researchers who believe that Åland was abandoned and more or less deserted between ca 1000 to 1200 AD.

It is obvious that a change really did take place after the rich and dynamic Iron Age, when parts of Åland, with innumerable graveyards and house foundations, came close to the Mälaren valley area in central Sweden. The change in burial customs is most striking. During the Iron Age cremation of the deceased was the norm. During the 11th century it seems as if this custom gradually gives way to inhumation of the dead. The odd inhumation burial can be seen in the outer margins of the Iron Age graveyards, but on the whole it seems as if burials in general had come to an end in the Islands. Still, an important sign of continuity in the habitation is the graveyards in the northern part of Åland, today immediately close to functioning farmsteads. Archaeological excavations have further shown that several Iron Age farms were in use way into the Middle Ages. In Saltvik one can mention the ancient hill fortress of Borgboda within surrounding habitation, Kohagen, a dwelling site north of Saltvik church, and Tjudnäs in Sund. Pollen analysis has further shown that agriculture was in continuous use during this period.

It is tempting to interpret the changes in the burial customs as a sign of early Christian influence. But we know far too little about these things. We cannot yet discern any church building activity. One important indication for continuity, however, is the fact that the largest graveyards in each parish tend to be in the immediate vicinity of the churches. That is, the place of central interest for the cult in the Viking Age still maintains the attraction when planning the Christian temple. The thought of a hiatus and a de-population seems more and more unlikely. Future research will hopefully provide more answers. Most interesting in this context are areas immediately surrounding the churches, the individual farmstead Iron Age graveyards and the outer margins of the great Viking Age burial grounds. ■

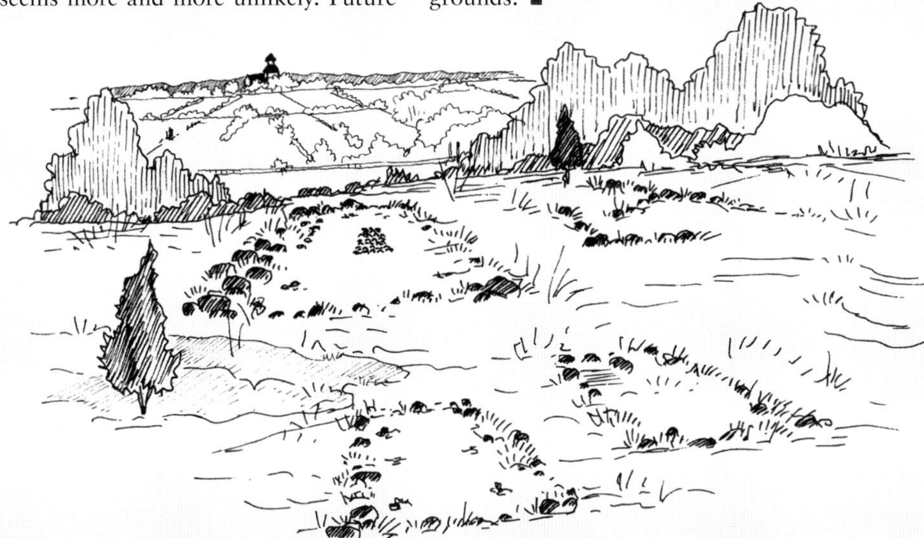

▲ Fig. 1. Kohagen in Saltvik, free sketch of a dwelling site from the transition between Viking Age and the Middle Ages.

THE 12TH CENTURY – WOODEN CHURCHES AND SCULPTURES

Even if we today don't know enough about the 12th century, we can presume that Christianity at this stage was well established in the Åland Islands. We can further presume that churches of the first generation were built in wood. Exactly when these first wooden churches were erected is also unknown. But we have indications of wooden churches erected in the area in the 12th century. Then, due to the land lift phenomenon, the water level was approximately four point three meters higher than it is today. Two distinctly different factors were decisive for the location of the churches: the immediate neighborhood of the greatest pre-historical graveyard, and the vicinity of secure harbors along existing sailing routes. The present stone churches probably have the same location. Archaeological excavations have shown remains of early wooden churches for instance in Finström and in Lemland - signs of early ecclesiastic activity in Åland. A group of early graves, covered by stone slabs, immediately outside and partly under the west gable of the church in Finström, must have belonged to the wooden church. Under the church in Saltvik were remains of Viking Age habitation connected with the largest pre-historical graveyard in the Islands, Johannisberg, immediately to the south east of the church. An earlier wooden church on the site is indicated by ancient burials, again partly stretching under the walls of the present stone church.

The east wall of the church in Eckerö also rests on tightly packed inhumation burials. The existence of wooden churches in the 12th century and early artistic activity in the Åland Islands is confirmed by early coins and ***dendrochronologically**** dated wooden sculptures. ■

** See Glossary, 154-155.*

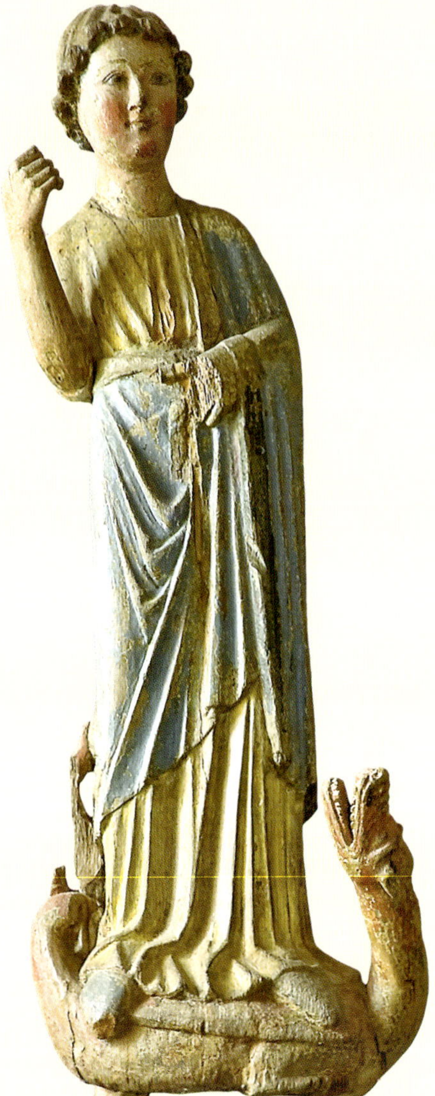

▲ Fig. 2. Saint Michael from the church of Finström.

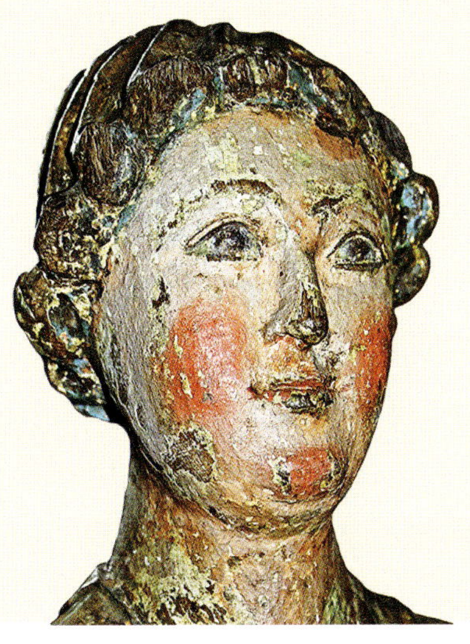

◀ **Fig. 3. Detail of Saint Michael from Finström.**

Åland pine from 1180

In Finström there is yet another example of Romanesque wooden carving - a human head in wood walled into the tower vault in the middle of the 15th century. The head was carved in pine of Åland origin. Already in 1968 Matts Dreijer had the head radiocarbon dated in the Westwood Laboratories, New Jersey. The result was 800±95BP, which after calibration gives a wide tide span 1050 -1290 AD. For a more exact dating dendrochronological analysis was needed. The analysis, performed in 2006 by Peter Klein, Hamburg, showed that the log was felled around 1180, almost simultaneous to smiling Saint Michael. The pine head is probably a fragment of an ornament from the early wooden church on the site.

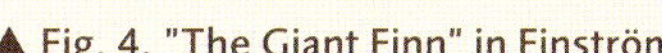

▲ **Fig. 4. "The Giant Finn" in Finström.**

Smiling Saint Michael

This wooden sculpture of Saint Michael from the church of Finström has lost both spear and wings, and his wooden shrine has the wrong location. Earlier research has traced him to southern Scandinavia around 1250 AD. Dendrochronological analysis, however, performed by Professor Peter Klein of Hamburg, has shown that the sculpture was carved in Baltic oak, and that the timber was felled around 1179. This means that Saint Michael from Finström is the earliest scientifically dated wooden sculpture in Finland.

Art historians often talk of the "Gothic smile", an interesting phenomenon spreading all over Europe in the 1230s. Stone sculptures on the west ***façade**** of the Cathedral of Rheims in France are usually mentioned as a source of inspiration and a center of distribution. Strangely enough, sculptures or images of human beings in general have not laughed or smiled since archaic Greece and Etruria in the 5th century BC. After a hiatus of some 1500 years the smile is supposed to have returned in art. The smiling prophet Daniel in the Porta Gloria in the Cathedral of Santiago de Compostela, from around 1170, however, shows that the smile must have occurred earlier, and that it must have been well known. Ever since the ninth century this well-known pilgrimage site has been the long-awaited final goal for innumerable pilgrims. Still today many smiling Romanesque Madonnas are watching the pilgrims along the different routes to Santiago. Smiling Saint Michael, the ***patron saint**** of Finström, shows that this trend reached the north at an early stage. To have such an early sculpture of Saint Michael preserved in this church indicates an early ecclesiastical organization in the Islands. The shrine framing the sculpture is of Åland pine felled in the 1220s. Saint Michael is the first in a long line of imported sculptures that have been finished in Åland. They provide an early example of the interplay between foreign imports and local workshops.

The 13th century – church plans and façades

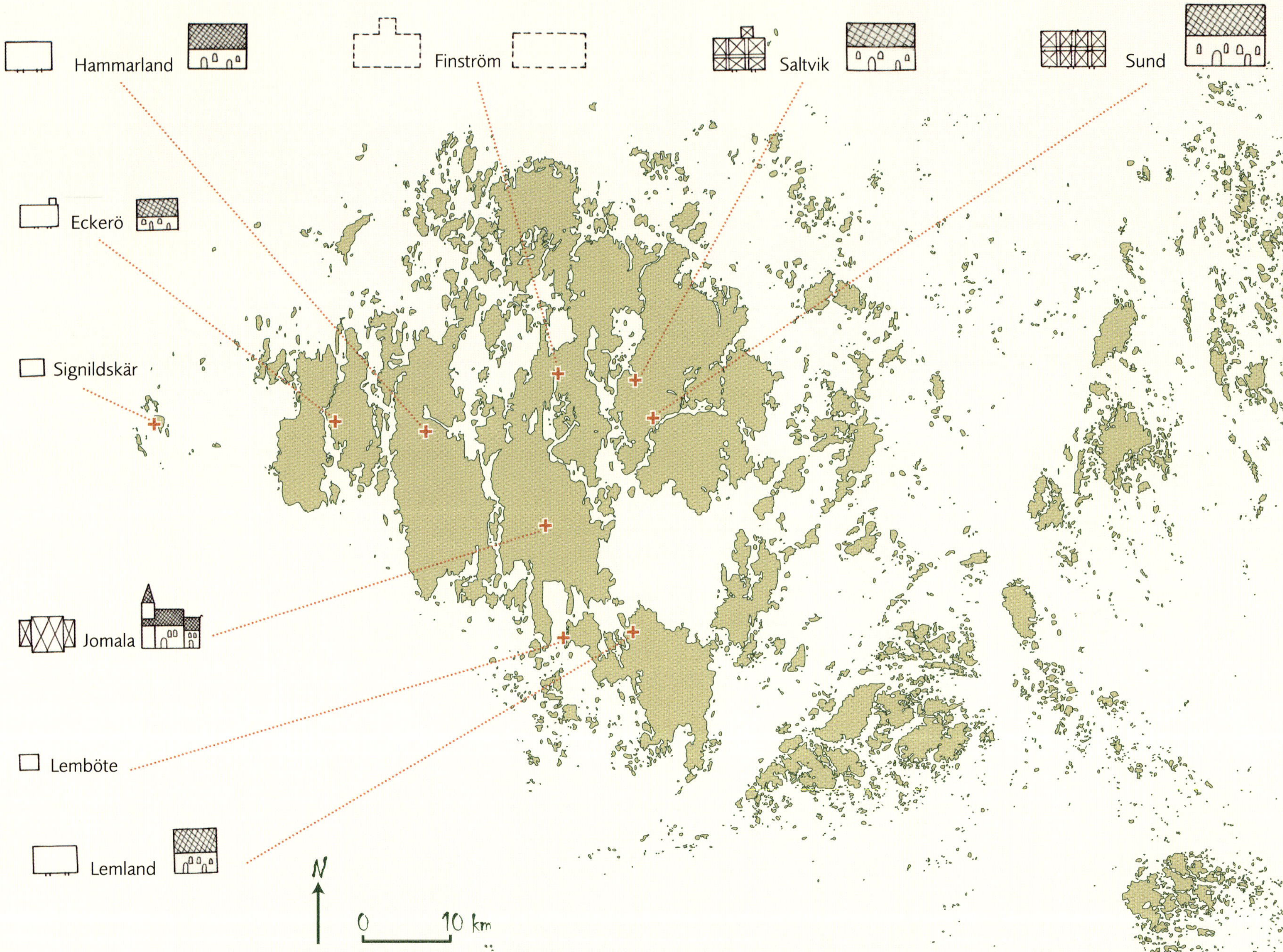

▲ Fig. 5. Åland churches in the 13th century, with plans and exteriors reconstructed in scale, with the coastline from around 1250, when the water level was approximately 3.8m higher than it is today.

THE 13TH CENTURY – ÅLAND STONE CHURCHES TAKE SHAPE

It was not until well into the 13th century that the wooden churches in the area were replaced by stone churches. This marked the beginning of a real building boom in the Islands, with six or seven naves erected within this century. Most of the churches were so called mother churches, or main churches. Some of them had subordinate chapels. The early building history of the chapels is unknown.

Common traits of the first generation stone churches can be discerned with all secondary building stages ripped off (Fig. 5). Jomala church excluded, they all have identical rectangular plans, where the chancels in the east were within the overall rectangular ground plan. The churches faced towards the south, which means that the south façade was the main façade. We notice double portals, both of them towards the south, the main portal further west and the ***priest's door**** leading directly into the chancel. Narrow and highly placed windows were also facing south. Another common trait is the building material, the easily cut local red granite, also called ***"rapakivi"**** (rotten stone).

Loose blocks of local Ordovician limestones were used for the framing of windows and portals, and for the burning of the lime. (The limestone had been brought to Åland thousands of years ago with the inland ice, and spread all over the main island). Walls had facings of granite on both sides and a cavity in the center filled with rubble and mortar. Numerous fragments of scaffolding, still preserved in the walls of the attics, demonstrate that regular scaffolding was used. Today the outer walls appear as large surfaces of selected granite blocks, with grand granite blocks in the corners. Originally the churches were whitewashed externally. Windows and portals were framed by local limestone, probably never whitewashed. Most churches were resting on simple foundations, socles, of red granite. Jomala church was the only one that diverged from the pattern. It has unusual proportions: the plan was almost symmetrical, with all building units, ***nave****, ***chancel**** and tower, wider than they were long. The chancel to the east was narrower than the nave, with a straight eastern wall instead of an ***apse****. Towards the east the chancel wall had three coupled windows forming a so-called trinity group. It seems that the nave at Jomala, with the adjoining chancel, may represent the first mortared stone construction in Åland, dating from the first half of the 13th century. It is also the only church in the Islands with architectural ornamentation in stone. From the original decorative program the so-called Jomala lion and a human head have been preserved, both of them cut in Ordovician Åland limestone (Fig. 6).

Given the limited amount of documentary material - mutually conflicting architectural drawings from 1808 and 1871 - it is hard to visualize the exact shape of the church at Jomala during the Romanesque period. Even if nave and chancel may have been finished already during the first half of the 13th century, it seems that the main part of the preserved ornamental decoration belongs to the time after 1283, at a time when the tower was added and when the pointed arch had been opened between tower and nave. Thus Jomala is the only 13th century church to have had a campanile in the west. It is also possible that the vaulting of the nave, including the pointed arch between the chancel and the nave, belongs to the same Gothic stage.

Jomala church was probably the first stone church in the Åland Islands. Yet it was the church of Sund that be-

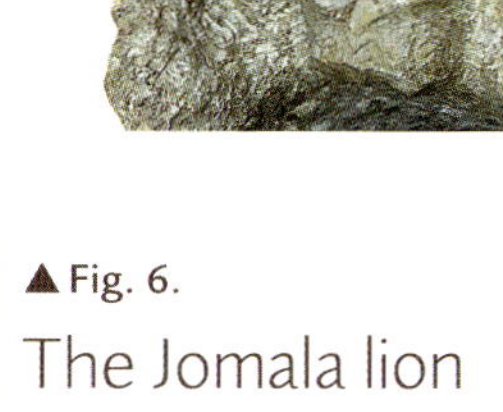

▲ Fig. 6.

The Jomala lion

The so-called Jomala lion, a Romanesque limestone sculpture from Jomala church, represents a lion's head holding a human head in its open jaws. Wide-open eyes stare at the beholder. Sculptures in stone cannot be dated scientifically. Yet, stylistically the limestone comes close to the wood head in Finström (cf. Fig. 4). The Jomala lion was found in the beginning of the 20th century, hidden in a cubbyhole in the church. A horizontal cavity underneath the head suggests that it may have crowned a gable, possibly the east gable truss of the chancel that was torn down in the 1830s.

came the role model for the remaining stone churches in the area (cf. the façades of Saltvik, Lemland, Hammarland, and Eckerö, Fig. 5). Everywhere we can see south-facing main façades, with two portals and highly placed narrow windows. Windows preserved intact from the first stages of the construction can be seen in Sund and in Lemland. They are framed by local Ordovician limestone. Rounded arches crown the window openings. The portals too have a framework of limestone.

Our knowledge of the oldest stone church in Finström remains blurred, and it is quite possible that we may never be able to reconstruct the façades or the plan. Mortar dating analysis from a couple of samples at foundation level gives only vague information about the existence of a mortared stone construction at the site during the second half of the 13th century. The same age is indicated by the odd coins found in the nave and by a larger hoard deposited under the ***sacristy**** floor. Wall paintings from many different stages can be identified on the east wall of the chancel. Four inauguration crosses in the chancel, all individually shaped, must belong to the first stage of the stone church.

The plan arrangements in the early Åland churches also have common features. Again, only Jomala differs from the model. All the other churches, probably also Finström, belong to the ***hall church**** type, which means a church consisting of one nave with a rectangular plan. The double-***aisled**** plan in Sund was only repeated in the church of Salt-

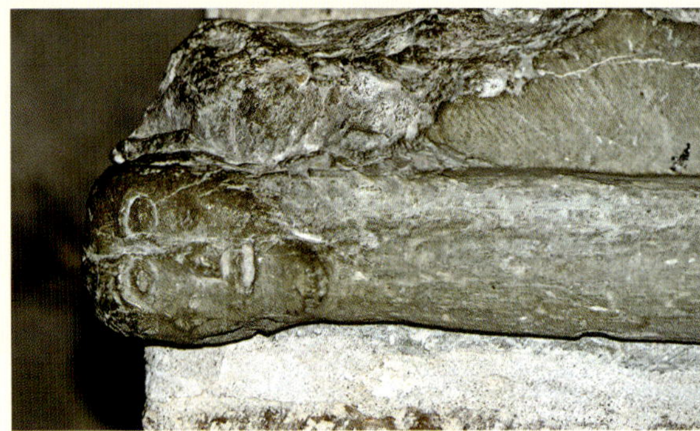

▲ Fig. 7.

Limestone head in Jomala.

The decoration of Jomala also includes a little human head, carved in the corner of a horizontally walled-in slab of limestone, on the northern side of the tower arch. Stylistically the face comes close to the Jomala Lion. The slab is part of the supporting construction for the arch. The carefully finished profiled side is turned down, whereas the upper surface is rough and uneven, possibly indicating a secondary position. According to oral tradition a similar stone head on the opposite side to the south, was destroyed during the Great Northern War (1714-21). Possibly the limestone slab belonged to the first Romanesque stone church of Jomala, and was removed from its original position when the tower was erected in the 1280s.

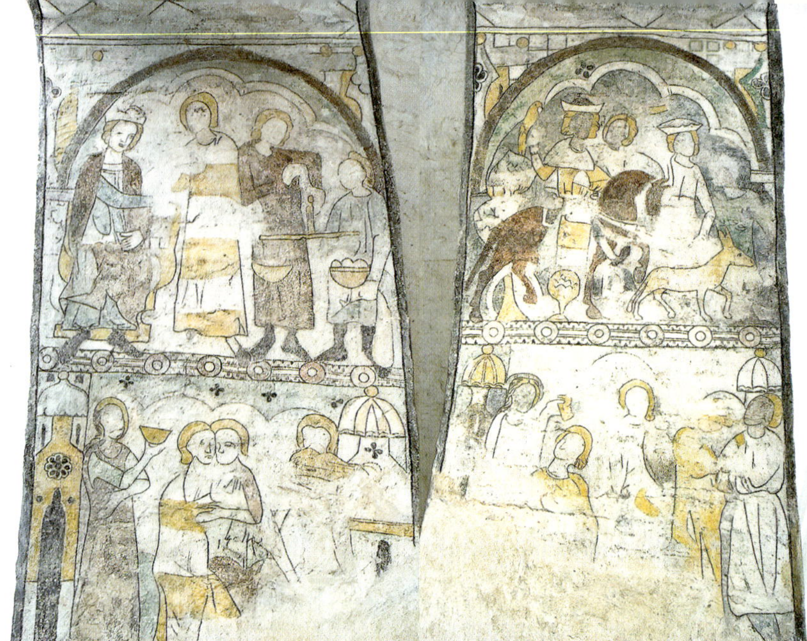

▲ Fig. 8 a-b.

Wall paintings in the tower arch at Jomala

The wall paintings belong to the same building stage as the west tower, i.e., the 1280s. The arch was immediately painted with a totally covering image program representing a courtly knight's tale, typical of the time. The main figure, dressed in a tunic with yellow and white stripes occurs in every scene. The story begins on the top of the southern side (to the left), with the main figure in the center, surrounded by a crowned figure enthroned, and two men dealing with balance scales. High up to the north (to the right), is a worldly scene where a youth represented as a knight with a hunting falcon on his right hand and a hunting dog in front of him, proudly rides out into the world, accompanied by a man and a woman.

A green quinte-foil arch crowns the scene. The background has been shining blue. Behind the knight one can discern two coats of arms, no longer clearly visible. The series continues lower down on the southern side, where the knight embraces a woman. Two persons flank the couple, one to the left who raises a bowl, and one to the right who either carries a piece of meat, or maybe plays a stringed instrument. Towers, crowned with umbrella-like spires, flank the scene. The final scene, opposite in the northern side of the arch, is even more damaged. The fragment indicates another festive occasion framed in by umbrella towers. Five people can be discerned, but the main figure is no longer clear.

The narrative pictorial has been interpreted as the biblical parable of the Prodigal Son. According to the parable, the son, after having received the inheritance from his father, left his home for the world, lived in sin, only to eventually return to his father's house in repentance. Some details do not conform to the parable, such as the father being crowned and enthroned. Also the impressive riding scene is not mentioned, but the same details occur in other pictorial versions of the parable.

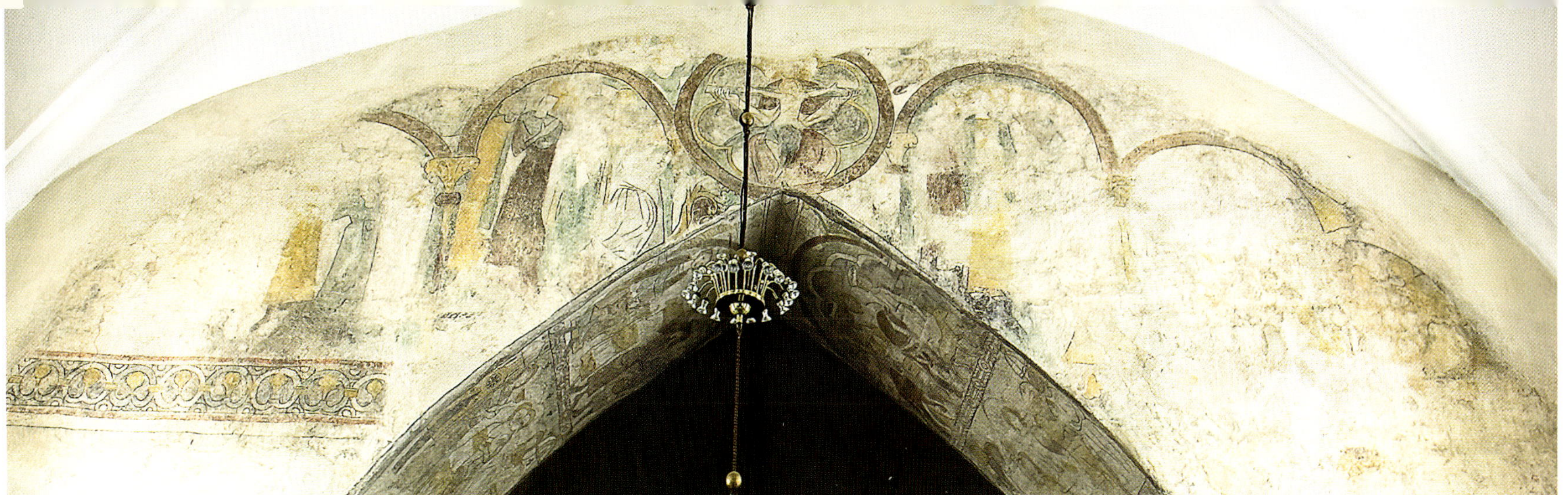

▲ Fig. 9.

The Last Judgment in Jomala church.

Facing the nave, the western gable is covered with a wall painting of the Last Judgment in a rare version. High above in a medallion The Father of Grace (i.e., God the Father holding Christ Crucified in his arms) is enthroned, functioning as Judge of the World. The dove of the Holy Spirit is missing. It was probably torn down together with the vault in the 1880s. It is unusual that the Father of Grace, symbolizing Trinity, should act as Judge. On the left side of the father, the condemned are walking down towards the mouth of Hell. To the right the blessed are moving towards the gates of Paradise. The scenes are architecturally framed with round arches carried by thin Romanesque colonnettes. A vegetative frieze under the narrative is also Romanesque in style. The frieze can be seen in fragments along the other walls of the nave. High up on the northern wall of the nave one can still see traces of the Wheel of Fortune, another popular theme in the courtly and moralizing world of images from the end of the 13th century.

vik. They both have a rectangular plan, and therefore must be seen as a variation of the hall church.

Another remarkable feature is that several of the naves were already vaulted in the 13th century, and that easily worked fieldstones were used in the vaulting of relatively large areas. With plenty of different types of natural stones and easily splinted granite there was no need for bricks. Instead magnificent fieldstone vaults were cast on wooden forms. Imprints of the boards from the forms are still clearly visible in the mortar. The vaults rested on arches parallel to the walls of the nave, further supported by simple profiled ***brackets**** in limestone. The nave at Jomala was vaulted in two wide-spanned bays, whereas the vaults in the double-aisled naves at Sund and Saltvik were carried by a row of pillars along the central ***axis****. Naves without vaults had horizontal ceilings covered with wooden paneling (Lemland and Eckerö). We further know that the horizontal ceiling at Lemland was richly decorated by medallion paintings. Once more, the exact configuration of the nave of Finström remains unclear. Sacristies in stone belonged to the first building stage in Eckerö and Saltvik, where they were individually placed against the north wall of the naves.

We have no knowledge of chapels subordinated to mother churches during the 13th century. However some of the "seafaring chapels" may have been erected at this time. The chapel of Lemböte may belong to the end of the 13th century, and early coins from the chapel of Signildskär far out in the Åland Sea west of Åland, may suggest the same chronology. Different from other medieval stone constructions, the chapel of Signildskär was erected by a dry wall technique, without mortar. This means that the date could not be verified scientifically. Signildskär probably formed a station on the medieval pilgrimage route from Finland via Åland to Sweden. Some seafaring chapels in the Åland archipelago are situated along the so-called Danish Itinerary, the sailing route of King Valdemar, which describes the daily stages between Utklippan in Blekinge (southeastern Sweden) and Tallinn in Estonia. The lost original of the itinerary has been dated to the middle of the 13th century. It documents some early Åland place-names, such as Linaboete (Lemböte), Fyghelde (Föglö), Thiyckaekarl (Kökar). Even if it is tempting to connect some of the chapels with the itinerary, it remains to be proved that the connection existed already in the 13th century. Coins found at Lemböte suggest that this may indeed have been the case.

The size of the churches varies. Largest is the nave at Sund, followed by Saltvik, Lemland and Hammarland. Only the church of Eckerö is smaller than Jomala, which remains the odd man out in this context. As expected, the size of the first stone church at Finström remains a question mark.

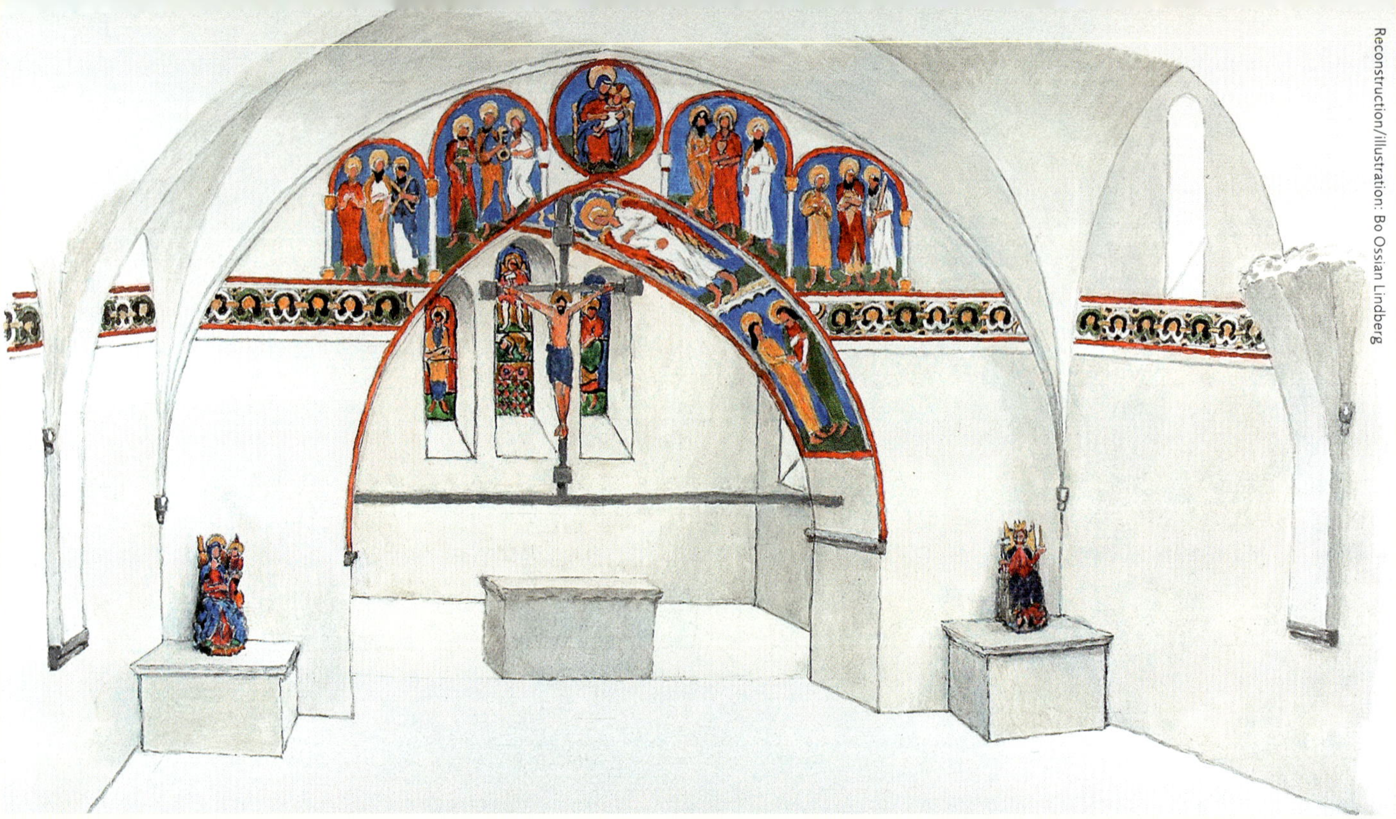

Reconstruction/illustration: Bo Ossian Lindberg

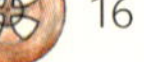

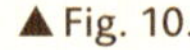

▲ **Fig. 10.**

Reconstruction of the interior of the church of Jomala in the 1280s, eastern view.

Secondarily preserved drawings and written sources make it possible to reconstruct the interior of the church at Jomala the way it looked after 1283, when the tower had been erected and the tower arch had been opened towards the nave (cf. Figures 110-112). The tower arch repeats the forms of the ***triumphal arch****. Flat horizontal slabs of limestone finish the vertical supporting constructions of selected limestone. The chancel is dominated by a big and freestanding high altar. The information concerning the windows (Fig. 110) of the chancel is contradictory. On the one hand a drawing from the beginning of the 19th century documents the eastern wall of the chancel with two windows, on the other hand F.W. Radloff, who in 1795 published his description of Åland, mentions "three windows towards the east, and three windows towards the south" granting enough of light in the church. In such case, we are talking of a Trinity window. Similar separate narrow chancels, without ***apses****, with trinity windows towards the east, can be found in Romanesque Cistercian architecture in Gotland. The south wall of the nave had only one high and narrow window opening.

Through the stained glass of the Trinity window light filtered in to the chancel. Two side altars, facing the congregation, flanked the triumphal arch. The south was devoted to Saint Olof, the patron saint of the church. The northern altar was traditionally a Mary altar. Both ***side altars**** were decorated with wooden sculptures of respective saints. A limestone slab, probably from one of the side altars (Fig. 116) has been preserved. The crucifix of the church also shows influence from Gotland (Fig. 114). The crucifix was probably placed in the triumphal arch, on a ***rood beam****. Today the original cross of the crucifix has been lost. The ends of the cross arms were probably decorated with reliefs depicting the four Evangelists. The original arrangement of the ***choir screen**** remains unknown.

The intensive scale of the colors can be reconstructed from the wall paintings preserved in the tower arch, and the fragments of paintings on the walls of the nave. A total pictorial program in the chancel can also be presumed, even if it does not show in the reconstruction. The wall paintings, so bleached today, were originally shining in bright yellow, emerald green, ruby red and azure blue. But the reconstruction of the wall paintings on the triumphal arch, with the Madonna in the crowning medallion flanked by apostles grouped by three in down-falling arches, is purely imaginary. In this case the idea is to give an idea of the original splendor of the colors and the function of the reconstruction is to present a visual counterpart for the Last Judgment on the west gable (Fig. 9). And we must not forget that the medieval wooden sculptures of the church were all polychrome and gilded. The same goes for the font, also imported from Gotland in the middle of the 13th century. Numerous fragments of stained glass, uncovered in archaeological excavations of the nave, bear further witness of Gotland origin.

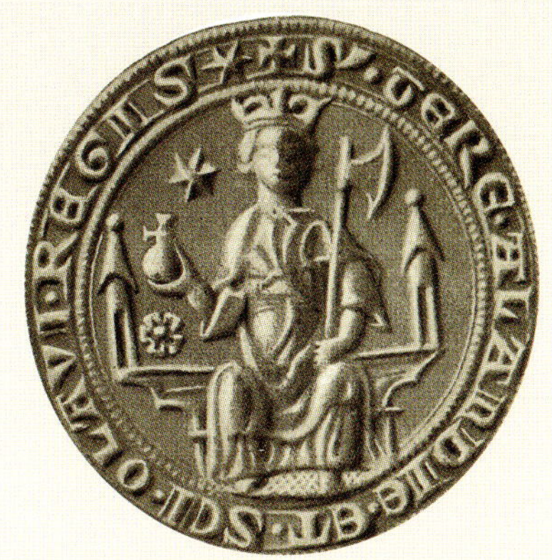

▲ Fig. 11. The oldest version of the Åland County seal, preserved as an imprint, was attached to a document from 1326.

The first generation of stone churches in Åland, except for Jomala, can be seen as an expression of the local taste. A new church type, the hall church with a rectangular plan, still not dominating elsewhere in the surrounding areas, has consistently been realized in the Islands.

Our knowledge of the medieval church interior and the liturgical fittings is satisfactory. The rectangular nave is divided into two parts, the chancel in the east and the western part reserved for the congregation. Only the clergy and the sacristan were allowed in the chancel, where mass and other liturgical ceremonies were conducted. The medieval marking of this division of the nave has been debated. It is however possible that a screen belonged to the setting from the beginning. The congregation was expected to stand during mass. Thus, in principle the churches lacked pews or benches. Pulpits the way we know them today were also lacking. A couple of *ambos**, a type of reading stalls, can be imagined for each church, one on the northern side for reading the Gospels, and another to the south for the reading of the Epistles.

Yet, it remains unclear how frequent ambos were in parish churches in Scandinavia. High altars, in stone, dominated the chancel, usually standing free from the east wall. The earliest altar decorations are unknown. Each church had two additional side altars, one devoted to Mary on the northern side, and the other in the south reserved for the patron saint of the church. These side altars were placed near the chancel, in the congregational part of the nave. Wooden sculptures of the respective saint adorned the side altars. The nave was further divided according to gender, women on the northern side and men to the south. The wall towards the north lacked windows.

Åland stone churches of the first generation were cast in the same form. Yet, depending on frequent secondary additions and varying decorative ornamentation, today's impression is that the churches are highly individual. The decorative program reflects a larger network of contacts in different directions. Relatively dark interiors were filled with colors with paintings covering the entire walls, with stained glass fitted into small and high windows. Wooden sculptures, richly gilded and polychrome, finished the splendor. 13th century wallpaintings of high artistic quality are to be found in the churches of Jomala, Lemland and Sund. To some extent they differ from each other, thus reflecting influence from southern Scandinavia (Jomala), Småland in Sweden (Lemland) and Gotland (Sund).

Magnificent wooden sculptures, such as crucifixes (Sund, Saltvik and Jomala), Madonnas in mourning (Sund) and a remarkable Mary shrine (Kumlinge) were bought to the Islands mainly from northern Germany, from Gotland and from southern Scandinavia. There is recurring evidence that the final joining and assembling of the sculptures must have taken place in Åland. For the crosses and for the joints in different members of the body, local timber has been used. It indicates early artistic activity in the Åland Islands, that is, workshops both for carpenters and for painting.

On the continent liturgical plays were common in the early Middle Ages. Usually the phenomenon has been connected with cathedrals and abbeys, whereas smaller parish churches would not have had the necessary resources to mount such shows. Although it is not possible to definitely claim that liturgical plays took place in Åland parish churches, there are many indications, both in sculptures and in wall paintings, showing that liturgical drama was indeed known in the Islands.

We can further presume that all Åland churches had fonts of limestone, either in the western part of the church, or closer to the chancel. Most of the fonts preserved in Åland were imported from Gotland already by the middle of the 13th century (Saltvik, Jomala, Kökar and Föglö). But we also find fonts of local Ordovician limestone inspired by Gotland. The fonts also contributed to the color scheme of the brightly polychrome interiors. In Sund and Finström - the biggest and at the same time the most prestigious churches - medieval fonts are missing. Bases of a couple of different fonts have been found in archaeological excavations at the church of Lemland.

The patron saints of the churches have gradually been identified. Already at the end of the 1100s Saint Michael seems to have been the patron saint in Finström. Towards the end of the 13th century Saint Nicholas and Saint Catherine of Alexandria are strongly emphasized in Lemland. Eckerö church was devoted to Saint Lawrence, while Saint Catherine of Alexandria was worshiped at the church of Hammarland. John the Baptist was mentioned on a late medieval church bell in Sund, and Saltvik had a Saint Mary church. But by far the most popular saint was Saint Olof (Olav), the Norwegian King. Jomala church was devoted to Saint Olof, and this saint is also mentioned in connection with Lemböte Chapel. The same Norwegian royal saint also had a dominating place in secular Åland, as can be seen from the medieval seal of the County of Åland, preserved in many versions. On stylistic grounds the oldest

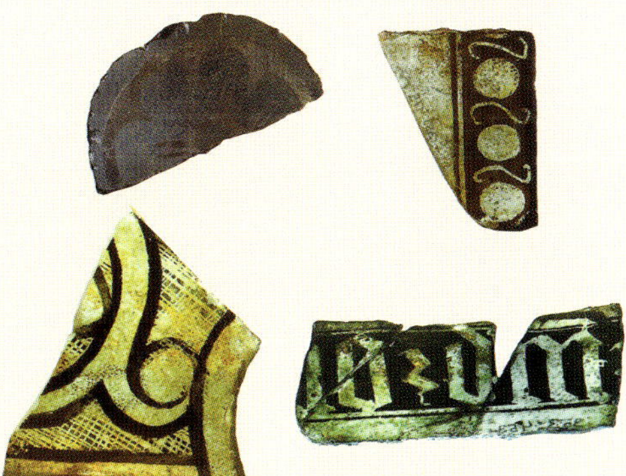

▲ Fig. 12.
Jomala church, sherds of Gotland stained glass, from the 1280s.

version seems to belong to the end of the 13th century (Fig. 11), with Saint Olof crowned and enthroned, with his symbol, the wide-bladed axe.

The early Åland church type developed during the 13th century shows a conscious uniformity all over the Islands and, at the same time independence in relation to surrounding regions. The rich ornamentation, on the other hand, points to southern contacts, towards southern Scandinavia and Gotland.

It still remains to explain why Jomala differed so much from the Åland model. Of course, it may depend on its early age. It is Romanesque in style, such as we know from Cistercian contexts in Gotland, with a separate chancel without an apse, and a trinity window towards the east. One might also speculate that the church may have been privately owned, perhaps erected by the local aristocracy, the so-called Dalkarby gentry, often mentioned in early medieval Åland sources.

Even if a lot remains to be further investigated, one thing seems clear: In the 13th century the farming community in Åland lived in an intellectually alert environment, amidst secular and ecclesiastic gentry. Those who had ordered and taken part in the planning of the exquisite pictorial programs for the churches at Lemland and Jomala were highly civilized people with impressive insights in complicated theological matters and in recent trends in literature on the continent. Nevertheless, a conservative taste can be discerned, particularly in details, as in the choice of decorative friezes. ■

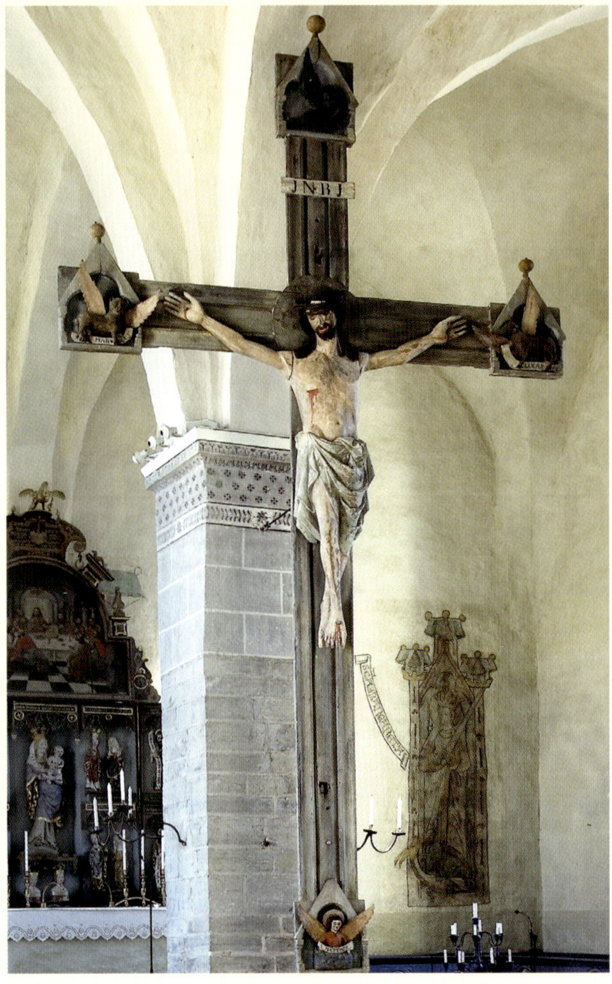

▲ Fig. 13.

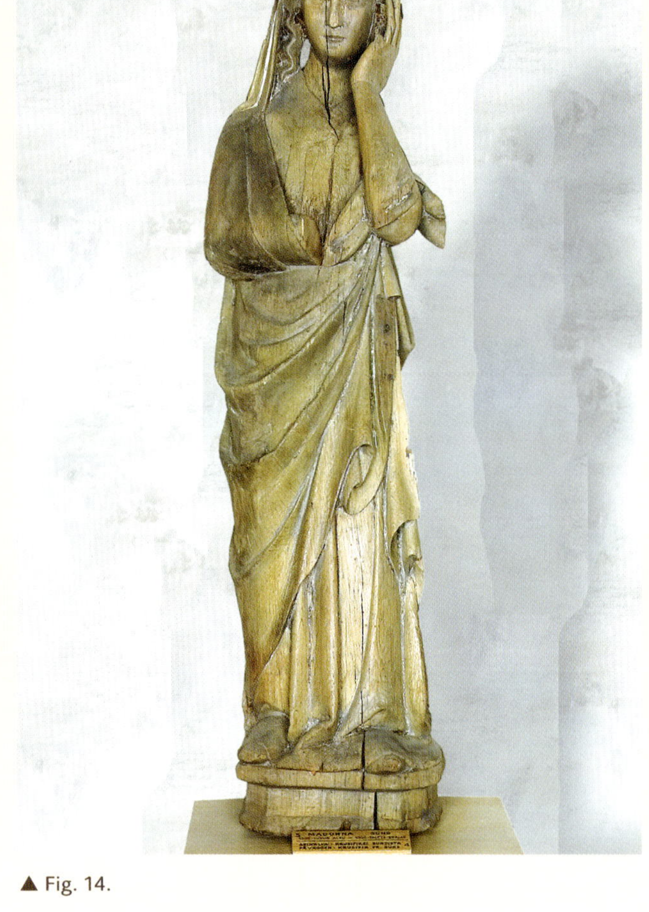

▲ Fig. 14.

Triumphal crucifix from Sund, ca 1250-1260, and Mary in Mourning, the 1260s.

Originally the crucifix from Sund was a ***ring crucifix**** of Gotland type. Together with Mary in Mourning (nowadays in the Nun's Chapel, in Turku Castle) and a Mourning Saint John (now lost), the ring crucifix was part of a ***Calvary group****, with mourning figures surrounding the crucified. The cross of the crucifix belongs to the tallest in a parish church north of the Alps. Dendrochronological analysis has shown that the oak of the corpus of Christ was felled in Northern Germany around 1238-48. The symbols of the Evangelists inside, the aediculas at the end of the cross arms, are also of oak. Probably the Christ figure and the Evangelists were carved in Northern Germany in the 1250s. The analysis further showed that the crucifix included parts of local wood. The cross, 5.06m high, is of elder, while the plugs that join the arms of Christ to the body, are of pine. Also the now lost ring of the cross was of pine. We may therefore presume that the crucifix was ultimately assembled in Åland, and that also the final painting of the sculpture was performed by a local workshop. Mary in Mourning is also carved in oak from Northern Germany, probably in the 1260s

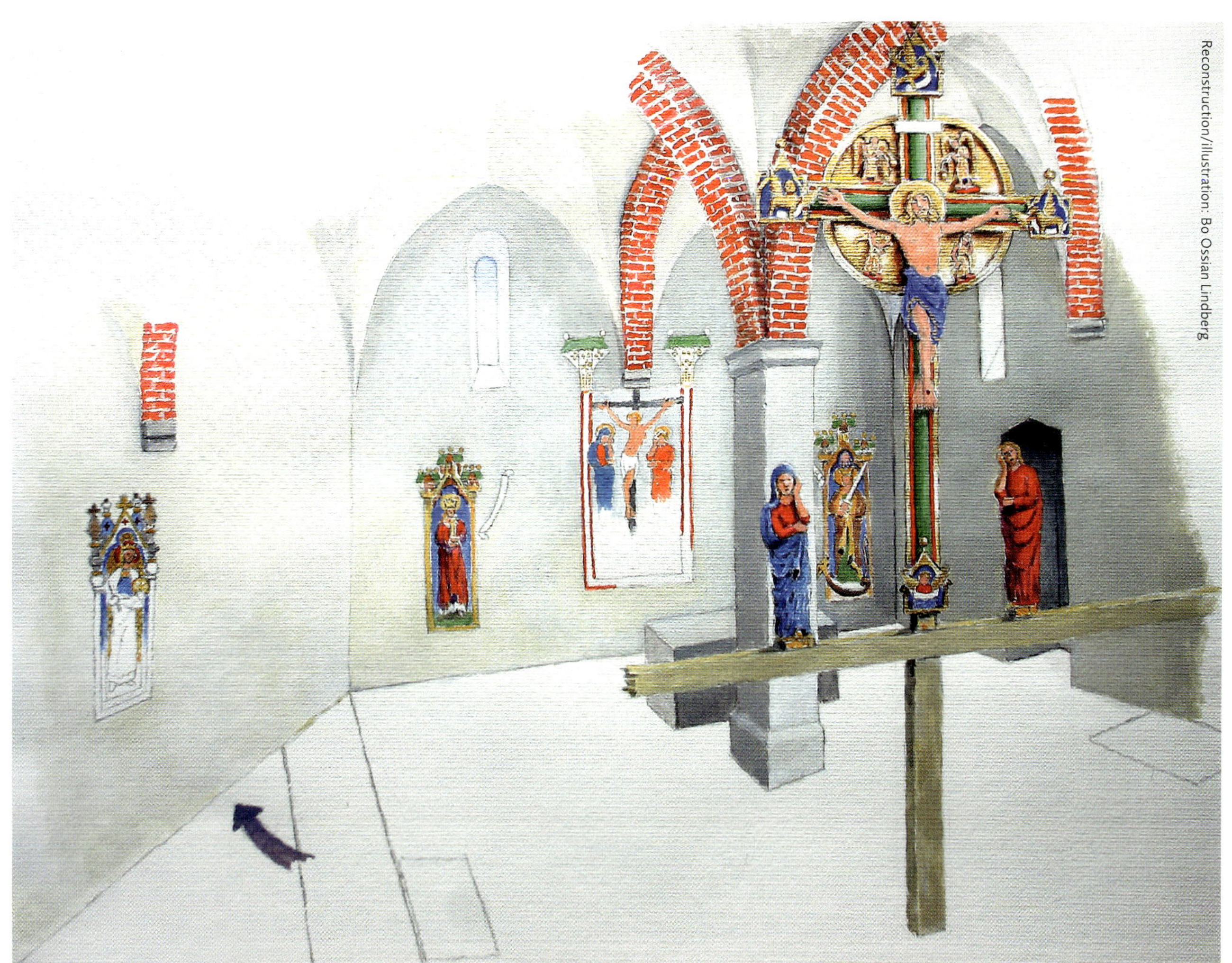

Reconstruction/illustration: Bo Ossian Lindberg

▲ Fig. 15.

Reconstruction of the interior in the church of Sund, at the end of the 13th C.

The original church interior in Sund is easy to reconstruct. Important documentation is provided by the 17th century church archives, in the rich body of sculptures, in wall paintings and in the odd original window opening. In the reconstruction the windowless northern wall is turned open to make Saint Catherine visible. Two side altars are marked in the floor. The church interior of Sund must have been even more impressive in the 13th century than it is today, with the division into two naves and the high elegant vaulting of fieldstones. The proportions between the crucifix and the church interior are in beautiful harmony, and we have to presume that the Calvary group was acquired for the vaulted interior of the church. This interior differs completely from those at Jomala and Lemland, partly because of the graceful *pillars** along the central axis, cut in local Ordovician limestone, partly because of the images of the saints in the wall paintings, with an architectural framework painted on a background in white. In Sund we find isolated saints in full figure rather than pictorial narratives. Some of them illustrate saints, such as the crowned virgins, Saint Catherine of Alexandria and Saint Margaret with their respective attributes, the wheel of torture and the dragon. Saint Barbara, north of the main altar, is a pure reconstruction, not represented among the existing paintings. The saints from Sund belong to the very end of the 13th century, or around 1300.

The surface in the middle of the east wall, between the two chancel windows, was covered by a wall painting representing the Calvary Group, maybe functioning as the original altar decoration. The painting is documented on a photo from the 1930s when the central part of the chancel wall was temporarily visible. In all essentials it repeats the theme from the group of sculptures on the rood beam, marking the limit between chancel and congregation. Even the architectural framework, with the crowning golden nodes on the aediculas at the end of the cross arms is copied. With its large whitewashed surfaces the church interior at Sund must have been much lighter than the other churches. Imitations of brickwork on the arches of the vaults contrasted beautifully against the white background. At the same time it showed the awareness of modern trends. People in Sund knew that brick was the most prestigious new building material. While there was no big need for burning bricks, at least they wanted to give the illusion of a brick construction.

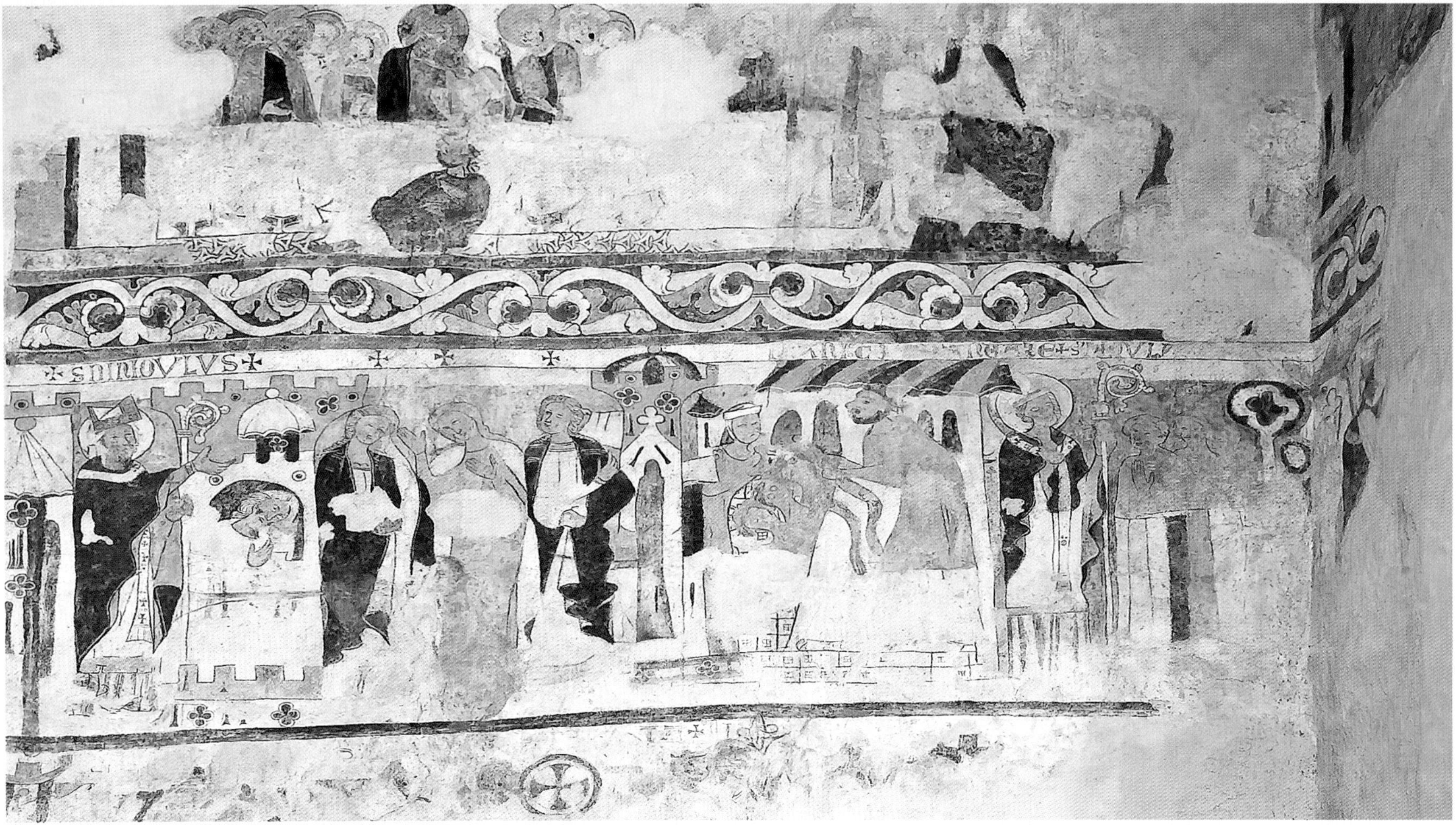

▲ Fig. 16.

Paintings on the northern chancel wall in Lemland.

The chancel in Lemland was totally covered with wall paintings in many friezes on top of each other at the end of the 13th century. The uppermost northern and eastern friezes illustrate the Passion, the sufferings of Christ. The narrative starts with the Last Supper towards the north. Under the Last Supper we find well known scenes and miracles of Saint Nicholas, often repeated in the so-called Plays of Saint Nicholas, liturgical dramas performed in honor of the Saint. The first scene, "Tres filiae" represents the legend of the economically troubled father and his three daughters. To put an end to the economic misery the daughters had suggested that the father should turn them over to a brothel. The father is seen restlessly sleeping by an open window. By throwing three lumps of gold in through the window, Nicholas rescued the daughters from a sinful life.

The following scene towards the right "Tres clerice" illustrates the legend of the three students who were poisoned and killed by evil tavern owners. To preserve the human flesh for future need, the couple salted the lifeless bodies and placed them in a barrel. Once more, the passing Saint Nicholas came to rescue and revived the students. The painting follows the different scenes of the liturgical drama in detail. Yet, we lack final evidence of liturgical dramas actually performed in Lemland. The colors today differ greatly from the original. For instance, the black in the mantle of Saint Nicholas was bright red.

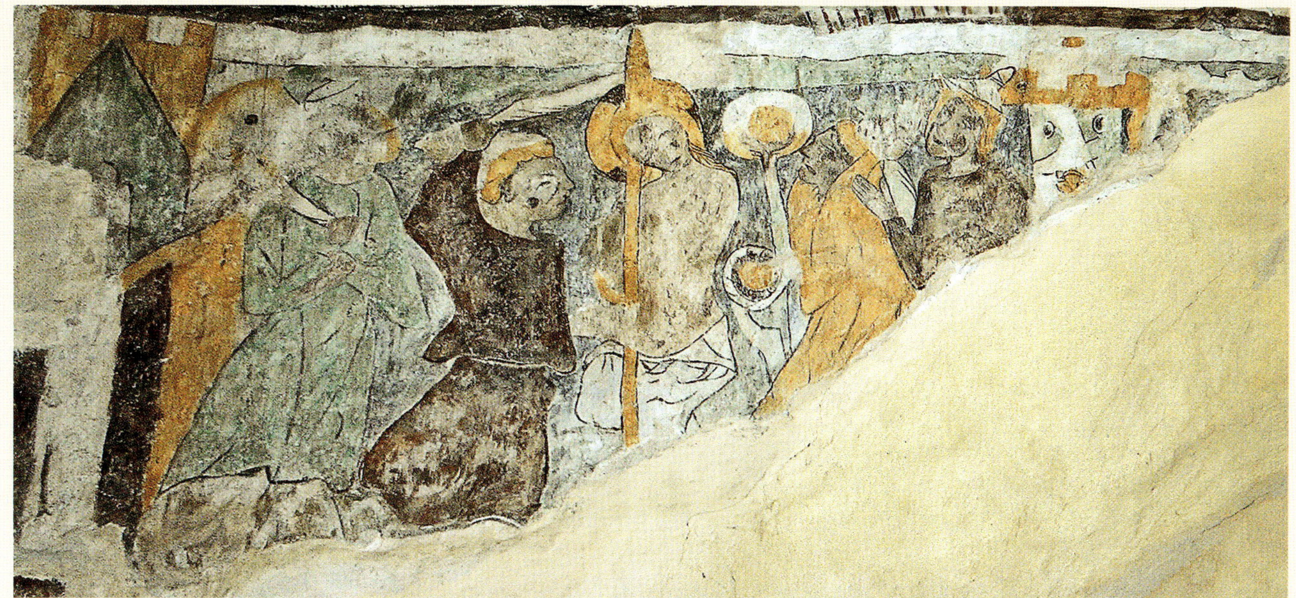

▲ Fig. 17.

The Passion.

The Passion of Christ continues in the uppermost frieze of the eastern chancel wall. Although severely damaged, one can clearly see the Flagellation and the Crucifixion, in beautifully preserved colors. The scene to the far south has often been interpreted as Doubting Thomas. But since the figure depicted so clearly is a woman, the scene has to be seen as a "Noli me Tangere" wherein the resurrected Christ reveals himself to Mary Magdalene. Mary Magdalene first mistook him for a gardener and asked him where he had taken the deceased Christ. Christ said "Mary" thus revealing his identity. Mary was told not to touch him, since he had not yet ascended to Heaven. Towards the north, in the frieze below, we can see only fragments from the Nicholas legend. The southern wall of the chancel has been severely damaged by secondary window openings. However, the inscription "Caterina" indicates that the narrative on the south wall originally included scenes from the life of Catherine of Alexandria. Today we can discern only one scene - a sword directed towards the neck of the crowned virgin saint (Fig. 141).

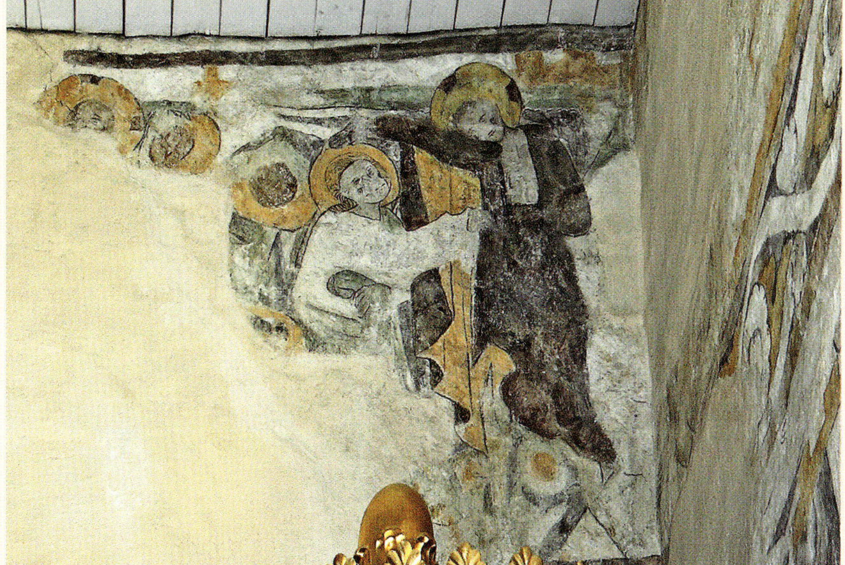

▲ Fig. 18.

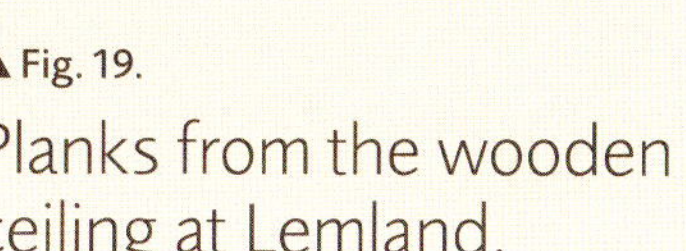

▲ Fig. 19.

Planks from the wooden ceiling at Lemland.

Five dendrochronologically dated planks of pine from the original ceiling at Lemland, with fragmentarily preserved paintings, show that in this case a horizontal wood ceiling with handsomely painted medallions was preferred to a vaulting of the church. The painter has drawn brave outlines - among other things we can discern a monster in profile and a human head en face. The black outlines (partly improved by the conservator) are combined with a color spectrum originally matching the paintings in the chancel wall, in red, green, yellow and blue.

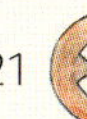

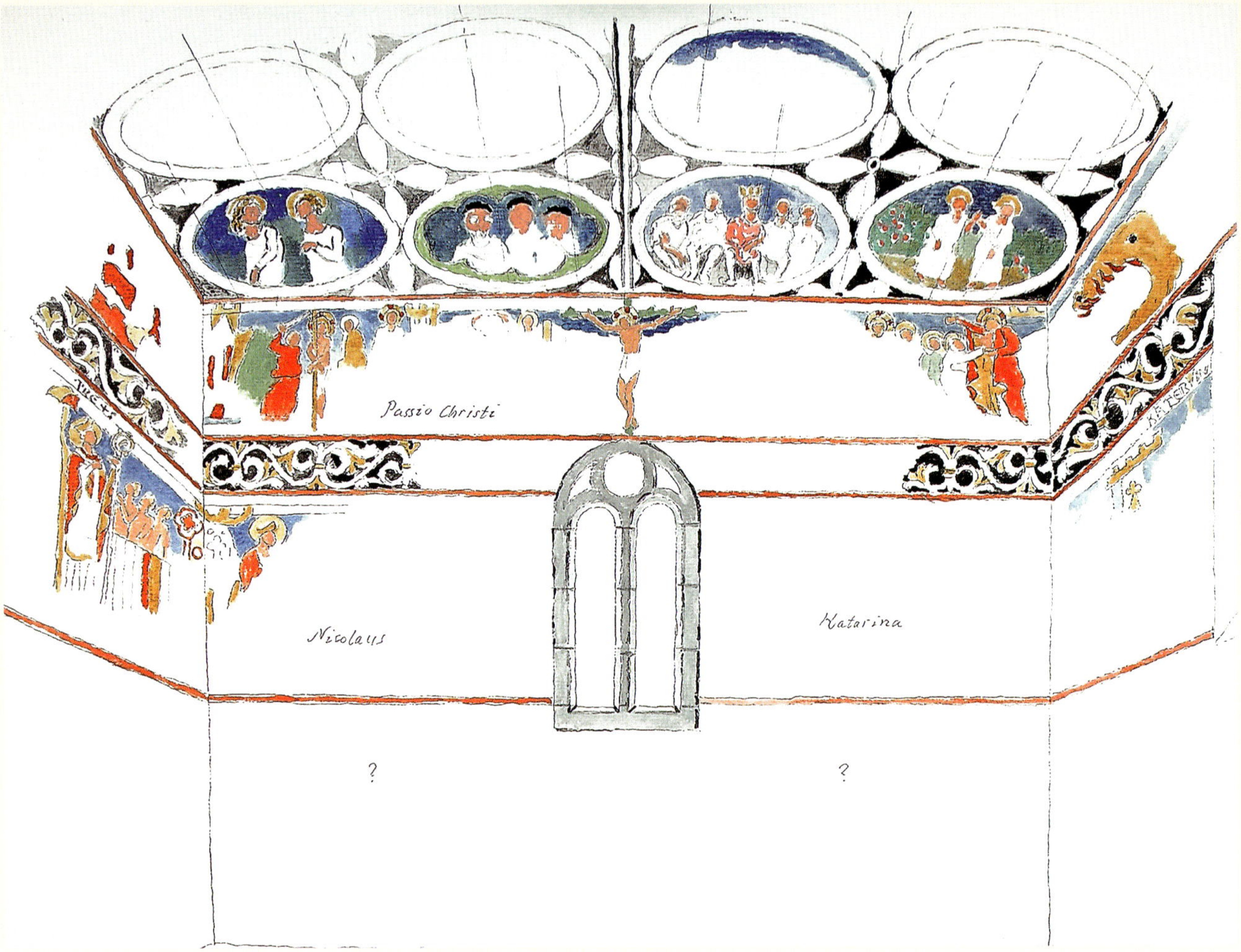

Reconstruction/illustration: Ossian Lindberg

▲ **Fig. 20.**

Reconstruction of the interior of the church in Lemland, around 1290.

The wall paintings, the preserved planks from the ceiling and some originally preserved window openings facilitate a reconstruction of the interior in Lemland church. Thanks to the horizontal ceiling the interior of the nave was high and lofty. The lower part of an eastern chancel window, bipartite and in limestone, was discovered in archaeological excavations. High and narrow windows, lined with limestone, opened towards the south, together with the main portal and priest door. In this nave a whole-covering painting program filled both ceiling and chancel. High reaching wall paintings of the chancel suggest an original horizontal ceiling. The paintings of the chancel are vertically and abruptly interrupted towards the west (Fig. 75), marking the clear division between chancel and the congregational part of the nave. Thus the chancel occupied almost one third of the nave. The division was probably further marked by a screen, of unknown appearance.

Priest and sacristan could enter the chancel directly through the priest's door. The altar arrangement is unclear, but we can presume that the high altar had been free standing also in this case, i.e., it was standing free from the east wall. According to the directives the main altar would have been covered by a lime slab with five inauguration crosses, one in the center and four in the corners of the slab. A small wooden crucifix, still preserved in the church, could have been used as a decoration of the altar. We must further visualize at least two side altars on the border between the chancel and the part of the nave reserved for the congregation, turned towards the west. One in the north devoted to Virgin Mary, and another in the south for the patron saint of the church, in this case probably both Saint Nicholas and Saint Catherine of Alexandria.

The wooden planks, even if fragmentarily preserved, are enough to give an idea of the ceiling of the nave. It was originally adorned with artful large medallions, like those preserved intact in the church of Dädesjö in Småland, Sweden, also dated to the 1290s according to a preserved inscription. The medallions probably covered the entire ceiling of the nave.

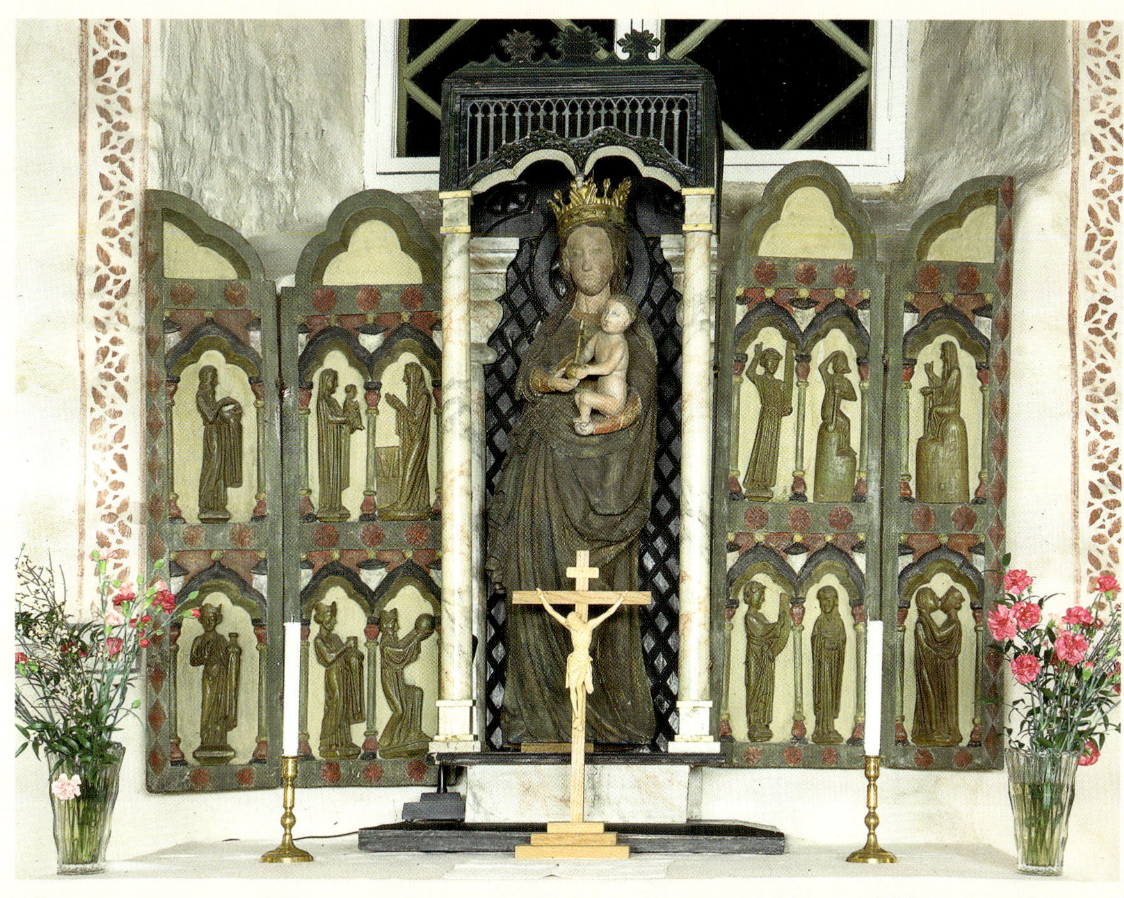

▲ Fig. 21-22.

The Mary-shrine from the church of Kumlinge, from around 1250 AD.

To the right is a detail showing the head of the Christ Child from the original ***corpus****** of the shrine. Today the shrine, in oak, is placed on the high altar of the church at Kumlinge. The shrine has not yet been subject to dendrochronological analysis. Yet it can be stylistically dated to the middle of the 13th century. Wings, elegantly carved in reliefs, flank the corpus of the shrine. When the shrine was closed, with the wings turned against the central part, the trefoil arches of the wings matched the corresponding arches of the corpus. For unknown reasons the original sculpture of the corpus, a Madonna with child, was substituted by a new Madonna figure in the 15th century.

The old age of the Mary shrine has raised questions about the provenance. It has been suggested that the Mary shrine should have belonged to Sund, the mother church of Kumlinge. The reliefs in the wings relates different scenes of the life of Mary: The presentation in the temple of the Jesus Child, the Adoration of the Magi, the Annunciation with the Arch Angel Gabriel and the Virgin, the Annunciation to the Shephards, the Visitation, or the meeting with Elisabeth and Mary kissing in front of the Portal. Originally the central corpus was probably crowned by an image of Heavenly Jerusalem. Only the head of the Jesus Child remains from the Seated Madonna with the Jesus child, originally in the center of the shrine. The neck of the head has a strange cone-like finish (now hidden by the modern base).

The Mary-shrine, including the loose head with a cone-like the neck of the Jesus Child, has parallels in Scania. There are sculptures of seated Madonnas holding the Jesus Child in the lap, with necks of similar form. In those cases where the body of Jesus is intact, the cone-like neck has fitted into a corresponding cavity between the shoulders. Thus, the head of the child was loose. One can visualize the head of the child, shrouded in textiles and carried around in processions, for example in medieval liturgical Christmas plays. The wings of the shrine, which narrates scenes from the childhood of Christ with scenes from the Life of Mary, are reflected in the late medieval wall paintings of the church.

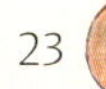

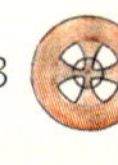

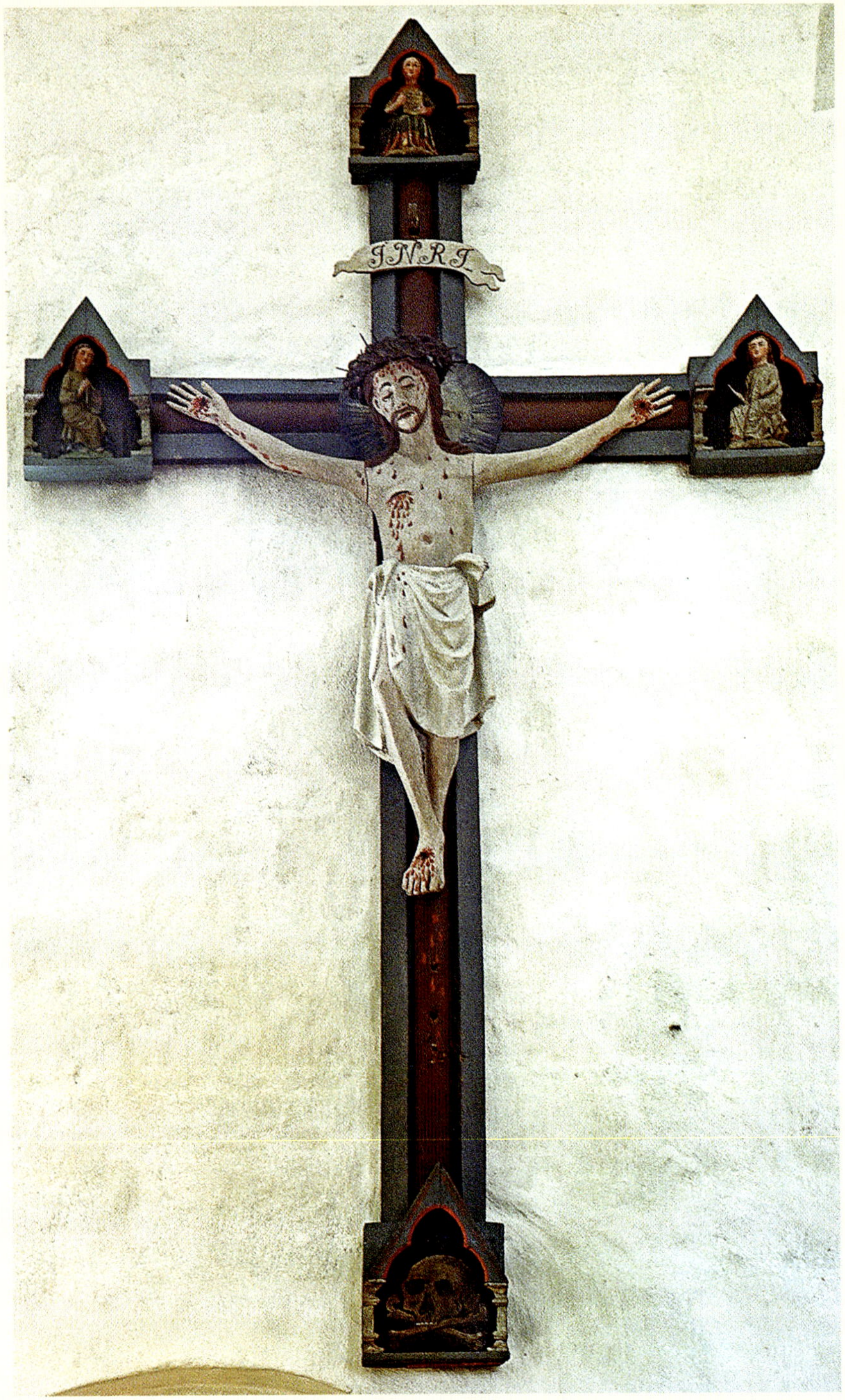

▲ Fig. 23.

The Crucifix from the church of Saltvik, the 1250s.

Even if the Crucifix from Saltvik is smaller and more modest compared to the giant Crucifix from nearby Sund, there are many parallels. They both have aedicula-shaped finishes of the cross arms, in oak. Dendrochronological analysis shows that these crucifixes are more or less simultaneous – the plank of Åland pine strengthening the middle of the cross, was felled shortly before 1250. Also the cross at Saltvik, of aspen, is probably of local origin. Both in Sund and Saltvik the crosses are the results of a combination of imported and local timbers. The final mounting and the painting of the crucifix at Saltvik must have taken place in Åland.

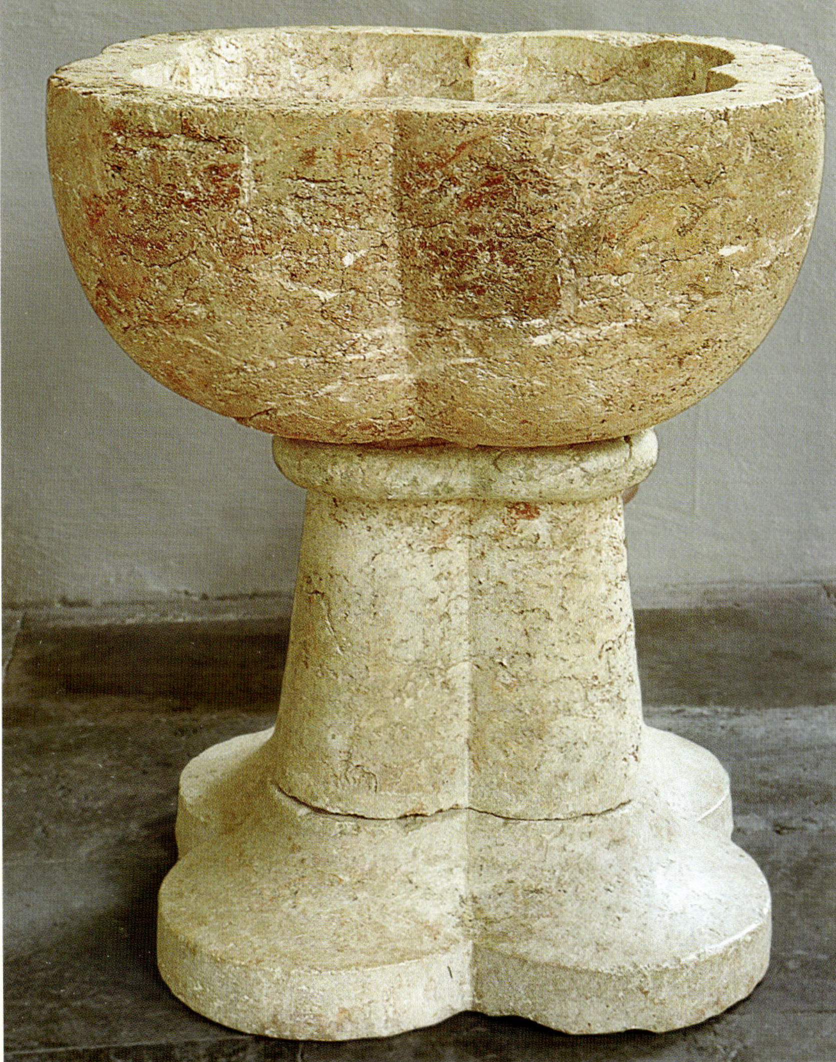

▲ Fig. 24.

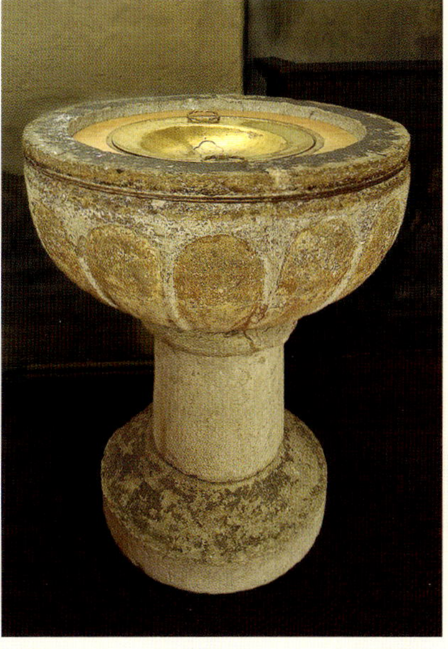

▲ Fig. 25.

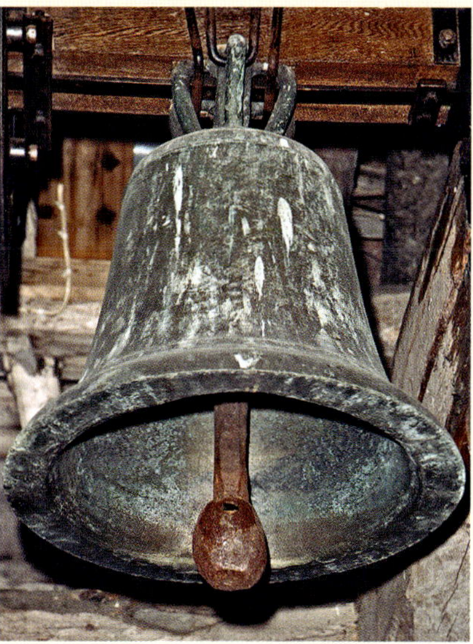

▲ Fig. 26.

The font from the church of Saltvik, the 13th century.

The quatrefoil font from Saltvik is one of the most noted fonts in all of Finland. It is cut in so called Hoburg marble, red shifting marble from Gotland. Stylistically it belongs to 1225-1300 AD. Other Gotland fonts imported from Gotland to Åland in the 13th century are to be found in the church of Jomala, in the chapel of Kumlinge, and in the convent of Kökar.

The font from the church of Hammarland, the 13th century.

This 13th century font from Hammarland church is a rare example of local production. Microfossil analysis has shown that this font (117cm high) has been cut in local Åland Ordovician limestone, modeled on the so-called paradise fonts from Gotland.

The church bell from Eckerö, the 13th century

The 13th century church bell from Eckerö is one of the oldest church bells in Finland. On stylistic grounds it has been dated to the first half of the 13th century. It may originally have been hanging in an earlier wooden church on the same site. Since the clock tower at Eckerö was not erected until the end of the 1460s, one can imagine a separate wooden construction for the bell on the roof ridge of the stone chapel. Since precious metal always was an attractive spoil of war, medieval church bells are rarely preserved. In years of unrest bells were melted down and recast for war materials.

The 14th century – church plans and façades

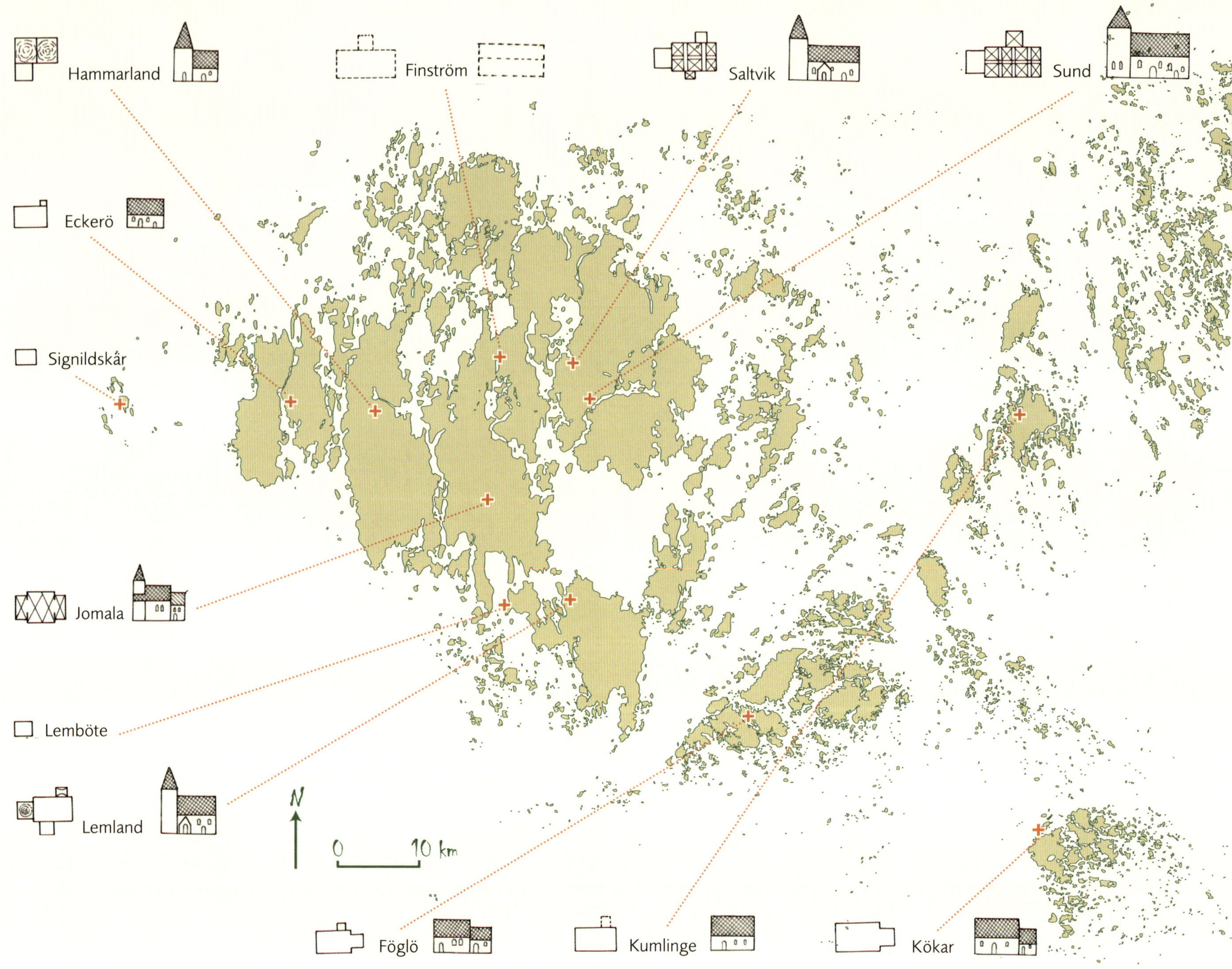

THE 14TH CENTURY – STONE CHURCHES IN THE ARCHIPELAGO, TOWER CONSTRUCTIONS AND FLOURISHING ART TRADE

The 14th century is problematic for research in general. As a result of the Black Death church building is greatly decreased in Europe and in the Nordic countries. The 1340s marked the outbreak of the feared plague, which returned mercilessly at irregular intervals during the remaining Middle Ages. Another problem is the irregular behavior of the calibration curve during this century, meaning that it is not possible to reach exact dating results with radiocarbon analysis, regardless if the material is mortar or wood. Where suitable material for dendrochronological analysis is lacking, one can only define the right century for the individual building construction during this period.

Church building in Åland apparently reached the archipelago at this time. Naves in stone were erected in Kumlinge, Föglö and in Kökar. On the main island church building continued with secondary additions. But above all, the 14th century means the erection of church towers. Earlier it was presumed that all Åland west towers were more or less simultaneous, and that they served fortification purposes. Now we know, however, that they belong to three different centuries. One of the earliest is the tower of Hammarland, unorthodoxly built against the southern wall of the nave. The towers of Lemland and Sund were additions in the west. The tower of Saltvik was erected around 1381. No common political background factor can be traced, and fortification was hardly the reason. These towers most certainly were erected as campaniles.

The earliest porch in Åland was erected in Lemland around 1318. The one in Saltvik followed in the 1370s. A sacristy was constructed against the original northern portal at Sund. The sacristy in Lemland also belongs to the secondary building units from this century.

According to a common decision and a united agreement among both aristocratic and worldly persons in the landscape of Åland mentioned above, with a righteous administrative authority, recommend that one tenth (a tithe) of the catch from the seal hunt, formerly donated to the building foundation in the mentioned landscape, forever should be withdrawn, and directed to the households of the vicars in each respective parish, considering the heavy burden they are carrying because of the visitors.

Medieval sources of Finland, nr 426, translated by ÅR.

The only medieval written source directly concerning the Åland churches dates from 1335. It was Peter, Archbishop of Uppsala, who established the directive of the seal tithes (cited above). The interpretation must be that the churches at this stage were regarded as so near completion that the support from the seal tithes forever could be deferred. Instead the money could be used to strengthen the households of the vicars, who were burdened by too many visitors, probably mostly pilgrims. The correspondence concerning this case was directed to the most distinguished person in the region, Sigurd of Finnaström, vicar of Finström around 1328-42, and Canon at the Diocese of Turku. The letter mentions the building foundation of the churches, but nothing is said of the building material. We now know, however, that most of the naves were finished by 1335, and that was why the financial support could be withdrawn.

The first stone church in Finström is not sufficiently supported by scientific analysis, even if two samples of mortar at socle level seem to belong to the end of the 13th century. More samples need to be analyzed, especially from the lower level of the ***socle****. Even

◀ **Fig. 27. The 14th century Åland churches, with plans and exteriors reconstructed in scale, with the coastline around 1350, when the water level was approximately 3.3m higher than it is today.**

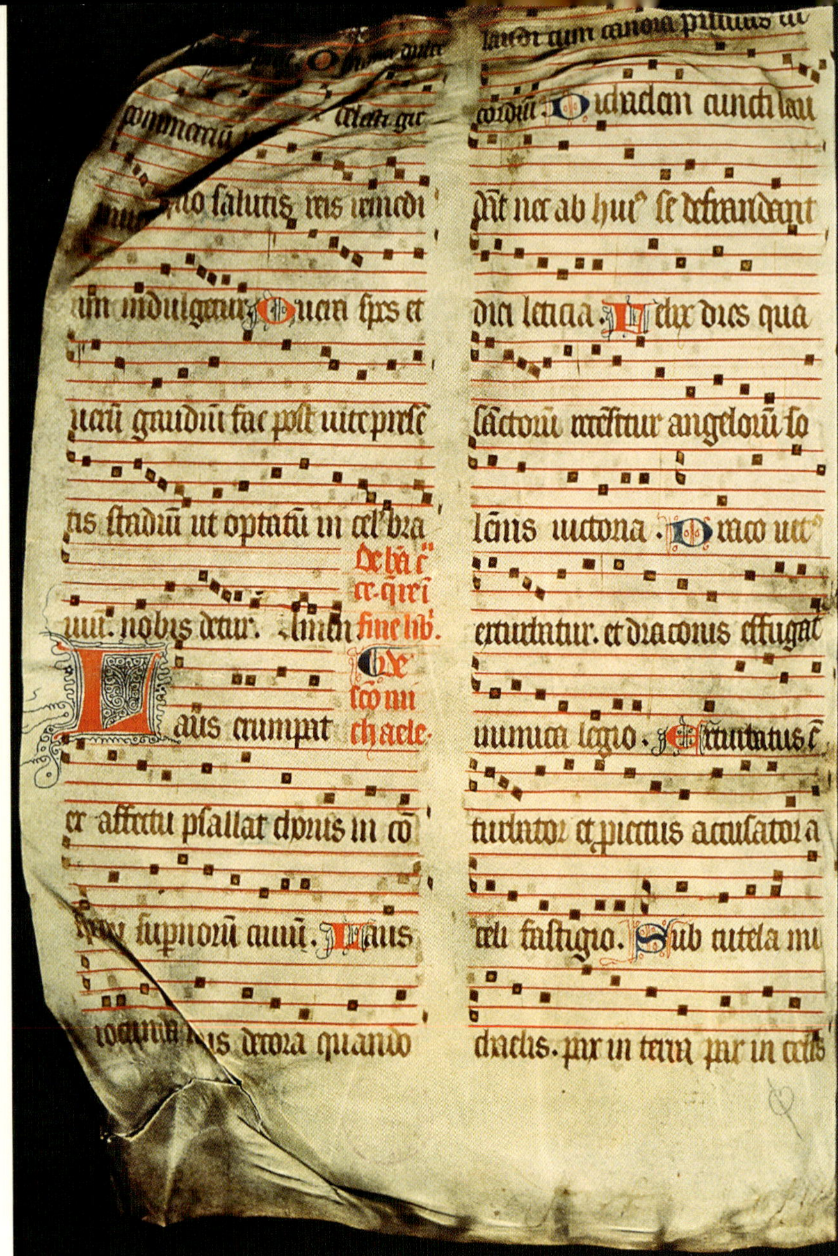

▲ Fig. 28.

"Laus erumpat ex affectu", Saint Michael's sequence from the sequentionarium of Finström.

The red note in the margin, approximately in the center of the page, states that *"laus erumpat"* should be chanted *"Die sco michaele"*, that is, on Michael's day or at Michael's mass on September 29. Here 21 verses praise Michael as the great general, the leader of the united crowds of angels in the fight against the evil symbolized by the dragon. Interestingly enough, Saint Michael is also presented as the dragon slayer among the images in the church of Finström. Laus erumpat is believed to derive from the 12th century. Adam of St. Victor from Paris probably wrote the sequence.

Sequences are defined as long chants for liturgical use. In preserved manuscripts they have both texts and music notation. They were sung at a mass of high festivity, and presented a festive element in the liturgy of the individual church. A collection of bound sequences formed a sequentionarium, a category of books never very common.

Well-preserved medieval liturgical manuscripts are rare in Scandinavia. To know the provenance as well is most unusual. After the Reformation, when the entire Catholic liturgy was to be replaced, these manuscripts were not spared. Since every single parish church owned a large number of these books, it resulted in a complete sacrilege. The confiscated manuscripts were written on durable parchment, of finest calf- or lambskin, which was highly appreciated. Torn from their original context, they therefore continued to exist as book covers in archives and accounts from the 17th century. From Finström we have such a rarity preserved.

The Sequentionary from Finström was discovered in a fragmentary state among the covers of accounts from Kastelholm. According to a secondary note on the last parchment page of a total of seven (with 13 fragmentarily preserved sequences), sequences from this collection was sung in 1560, at a memorial service for Gustavus Vasa in the church of Finström. Today the fragments are preserved in the manuscript department of the Helsinki University Library. Toivo Haapanen compiled a detailed catalogue of the medieval liturgical fragments from Finland. Thanks to his careful documentation, I could later identify four more sequences from Finström. Thus a total of 17 sequences from the Finström collection are known today.

The Michael sequence "Laus Erumpat" described above, suggests that the entire sequentionary was originally intended for Saint Michael's church in Finström. According to the paleographer Anja-Inkeri Lehtinen, it was compiled in Paris some time in the 1320s. By a strange coincidence it was the only sequence found intact, with all 21 verses preserved. Most of the Finström sequences are Mariological, i.e., they are devoted to Virgin Mary, and most of them are of Dominican origin. Interestingly enough, all the sequences from Finström, except for "Laus Erumpat" were later to be included in the Missale Aboense, the liturgical handbook for the Diocese of Turku. Obviously, the requester of the Finström sequentionary was an influential person, probably the already mentioned Sigurd of Finnaström, who at this time was both vicar at Finström and Canon at the Diocese of Turku.

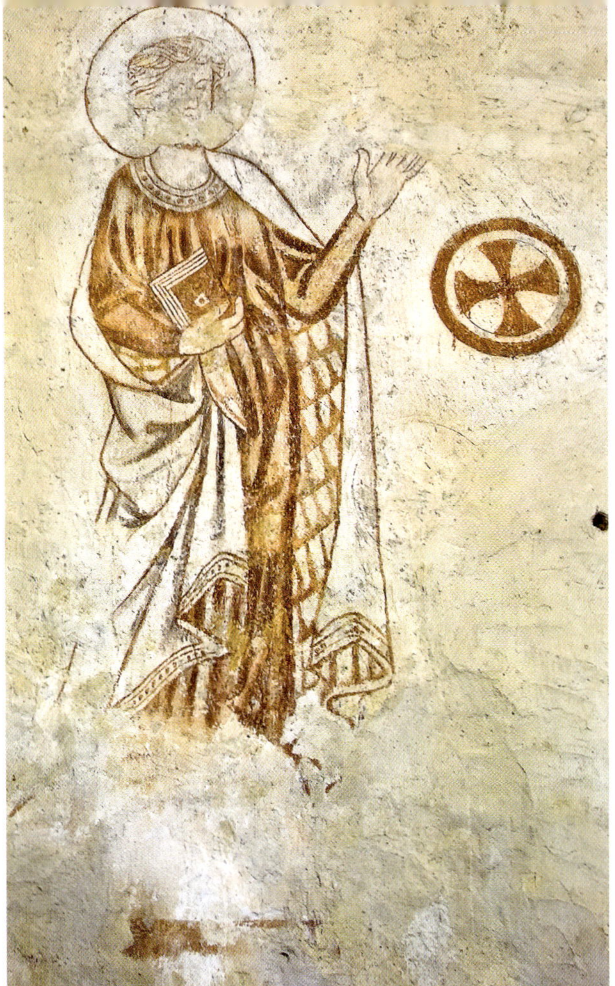

▲ Fig. 29.

Unknown apostle, wall painting in the church of Lemland.

Åland wall paintings from the 14th century are a rarity. Some fragmentarily preserved figures painted in red on white in the western part of Lemland church, may belong to this period. Next to an inauguration cross, holding a book in his right hand, an elegantly drawn figure with a mantle lined with ermine skin, holds the usual attribute for an apostle. One can discern other figures close to three more inauguration crosses. One on the northern wall holds a Saint Andrew's cross, suggesting the remains of a Credo-series, i.e., a series consisting of all apostles, or just a few of them, depicted with an adjoining sentence from the Creed. The paintings from the congregational part of the nave differ radically from the narrative scenes in the chancel. We must imagine another artist and another chronology. These paintings in the western part of the nave probably belong to the beginning of the 14th century.

so, the letter from Arch Bishop Peter from 1335 is an indirect source in support of the building history of the church. At this stage the construction of a stone church in Finström must have been regarded as a finished chapter. The large treasure of coins from the latter half of the 13th century in the sacristy, at a distance of several meters from the foundation of the wooden church, indirectly dates the first stone church. The stray coin from the 13th century was excavated in the nave, but most coins, from the 14th century were evenly distributed over the present surface of the floor, that is, outside the foundations of the small wooden church.

The churches of the archipelago differ from the churches on the main island. With no rapakivi at hand, other local stone materials available were used. Gray archipelago churches represent new types. Rectangular naves were finished in the east by narrow separate chancels both in Föglö and in Kökar. Heavy ***wall-piers**** along the inner walls indicate that the vaulting was of a secondary nature, probably not employed until the late Middle Ages, at the end of the 15th century. At the beginning new archipelago churches had well defined patron saints. Föglö was probably devoted to Mary Magdelene, while Saint Anne, mother of Mary, was patron saint both in Kökar and in Kumlinge.

One of the big question marks is the church of Kökar, along with the surrounding building complex on the island of Hamnö. The Franciscan convent of Kökar was first mentioned in the 15th century. Systematic archaeological excavations of the ancient remains at Hamnö have resulted in a large number of earlier unknown buildings south of the church. Buildings and burials have been subjected to wide and varied scientific analysis, and everything points towards the complex belonging to the 14th century, or earlier. Mortar dating points in the same direction - rather than a Franciscan convent church, the church looks like a normal parish church. This time the nave had a narrower chancel in the east, with no apse. The relations between the earlier habitation and activity and the Franciscan convent on Hamnö, have yet to be investigated.

Another question mark is the castle of Kastelholm. It was first mentioned at the end of the 14th century, but the early chronology of the castle remains unclear. In any case, now at the latest can we presume royal presence and representation of the state in the Islands.

Vicars from Sund appear as strong personalities in the relatively lively correspondence between Åland and the Papal Curia at Avignon. For a short time, the vicar Johannes Peterson even acted as Rector of the University of Paris. He was elected bishop of Turku in 1367. Åland was seen as the eastern part of the Swedish Kingdom, and the Islands were subordinated to the diocese of Turku at the latest around 1330. During this century influence from Franciscans and Dominicans gets more prominent. Remarkable is the fact that the entire Diocese of Turku, including Åland, followed the Dominican liturgy, probably depending on the Dominican Saint Olof's Convent in Turku, and of

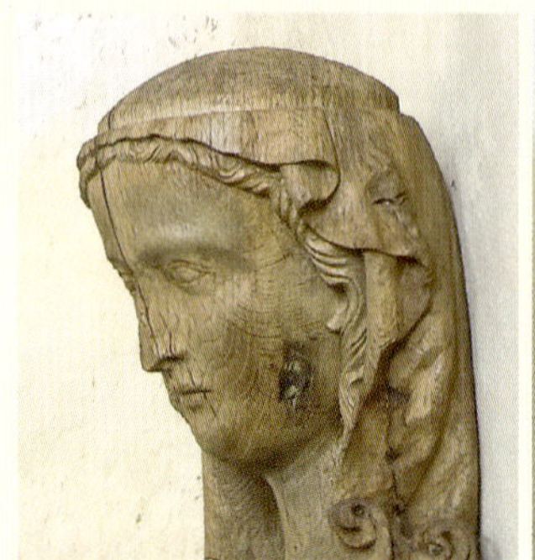
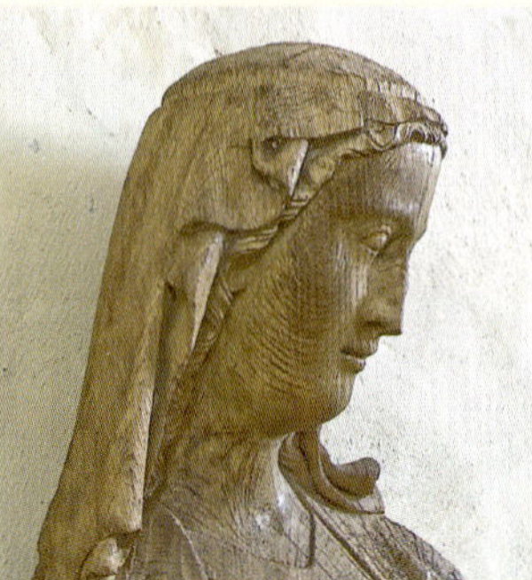

▲ Fig. 30.

Madonna enthroned, wooden sculpture from Lemland, the 1320s.

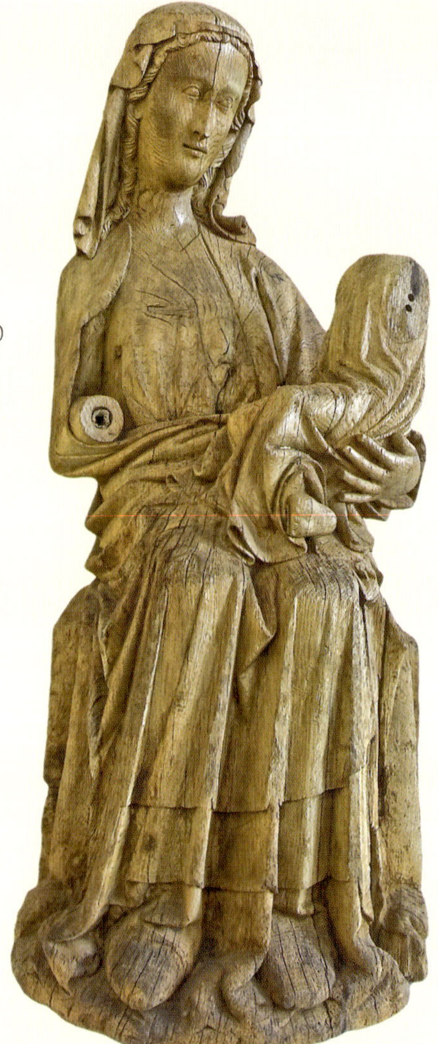

The Madonna from Lemland is one of the most exquisite medieval sculptures in all Scandinavia, dendrochronologically and stylistically dated to the 1320s. Because of the close resemblance to the well-known Madonna from Linde, she was earlier traced to Gotland. But according to Peter Tångeberg, art historian and conservator, she is artistically much superior to the Linde Madonna, and dendrochronological analysis shows that she is carved in oak felled in the Rhine area in Germany. Today the Lemland Madonna is severely damaged. All original polychrome colors have been removed. From her knees down it seems as if somebody had leveled the elegantly falling folds. The Madonna has lost her golden crown, and the Jesus child on her left arm lacks his left arm. Yet the skill of the sculptor is clearly visible, above all in the face of the Madonna. In close up the profile expresses different feelings. From one side she is radiating quiet joy; the other reflects her pre-notion of deep sorrow. Originally the Madonna crowned the Mary altar close to the northern wall of the nave.

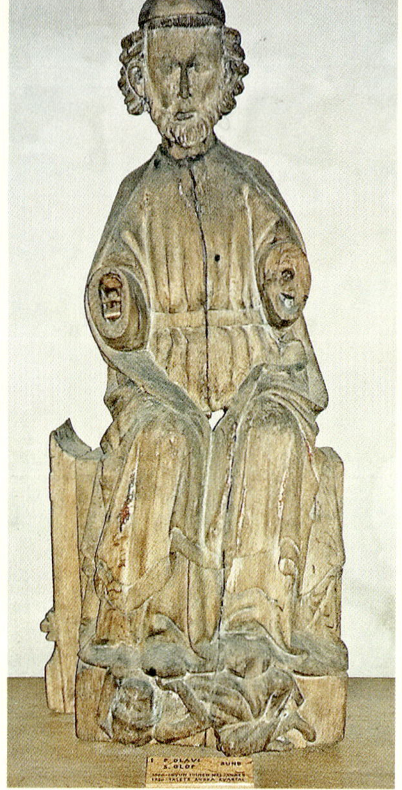

▲ Fig. 31.

Saint Olof from Sund.

Saint Olof, patron Saint of Norway, was a Holy King who in 1030 suffered martyrdom at the battle of Stiklastad. At the same time he was the Patron Saint of Åland, and very popular generally in the Nordic countries. In Åland the cult of Saint Olof was so strong that it later was seen as a threat to the Lutheran church. We have proof from the 17th century that sculptures of Saint Olof (in Hammarland and in Jomala) were to be removed together with his altars. In Sund the Holy King of Norway sits on a throne without a backboard. He has also lost his attributes, the royal crown and the wide edged axe. Under his feet lies his murderer, a diminutive figure, dramatically fighting on his back. This time dendrochronological analysis did not yield a result, and we face the same uncertainty as earlier research when it comes to dating and origin. Yet, in style the sculpture echoes Gotland from the 1320-1330s. Originally Saint Olof probably decorated a side altar in the church of Sund.

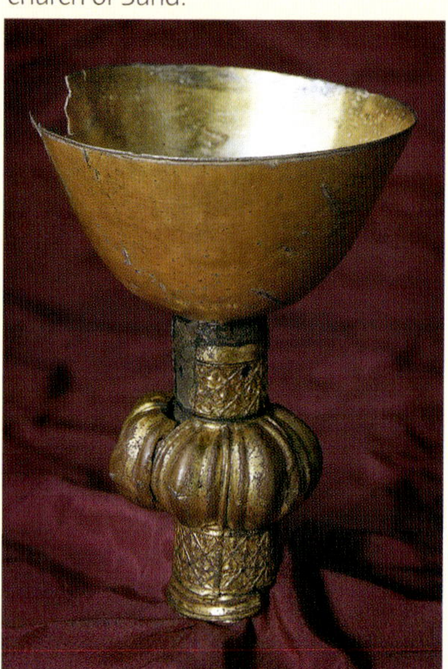

▲ Fig. 32.

Medieval communion chalice from Kökar

A medieval communion chalice, with a bowl in gilded silver and the foot in gilded copper. Surprisingly, at the end of the 1970s, the shining nod, which since 1846 had crowned the spire of the bell tower, proved to be one of the medieval silver chalices of Kökar church. Aron Andersson, the foremost expert on medieval silver in Scandinavia, considered it a Nordic work. On stylistic grounds he placed it in the 14th century, or around 1400 at the latest.

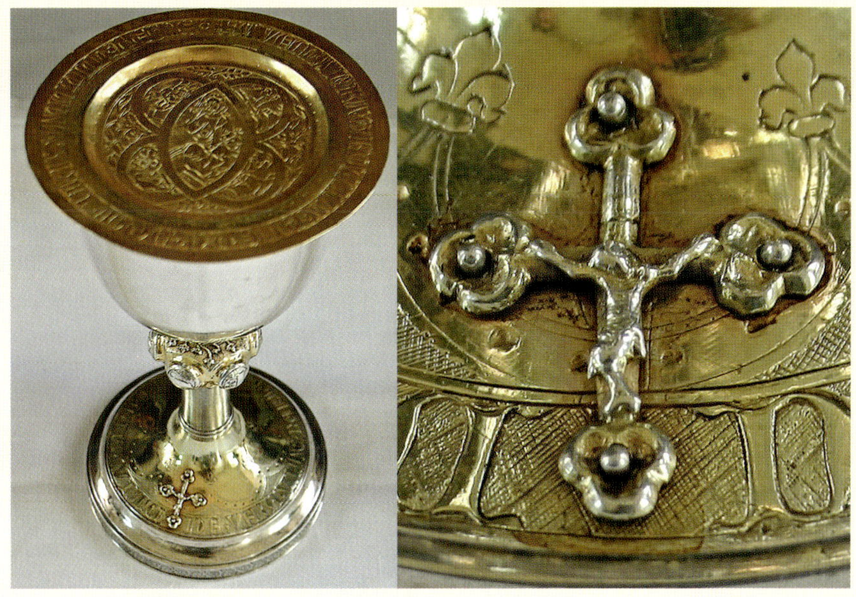

▲ Fig. 33.

Silver chalice and paten from Saltvik, 1346.

The precious silver chalice with adjoining *paten** presents the perfect historical source of information. The paten reveals the year, the donor and the provenance. The bowl of the chalice has been renewed, only the foot is medieval. A Latin major inscription, in English translation, frames the foot: "This vase is the true life". A little nailed crucifix marks the beginning and the end of the inscription. The adjoining paten in gilded silver is preserved intact in its medieval state. The upper part shows Christ in Mandorla, surrounded by the four symbols of the Evangelists. The surrounding inscription in major presents the well-known greetings from Archangel Gabriel to Virgin Mary at the Annunciation: AVE. MARIA.GRACIA.PLENA.DOMINUS. TECUM.BENE. The reverse of the paten is more informative. In English it is as follows:"In the year of 1346 Laurencius Arnberni, Canon of Turku, ordered this chalice for his church in Saltvik". Some years later he figures as Vicar in Sund. The chalice and the paten, of Stockholm origin, are unique in Finland.

individual prominent bishops in the Diocese. Among Åland parishes, Finström is the strongest advocate of the Dominican liturgy, as can be seen from the Finström sequences, partly of Dominican origin and ordered from Paris for the church in the 1320s.

From the 14th century exquisite Åland silver artifacts have been preserved for posterity. The silver chalice from Kökar can be dated to this century on stylistic grounds. Not only are the Saltvik sacramental vessels in silver from 1346 the finest in entire Finland, they are at the same time invaluable for their informative inscriptions. Stylistically the Saltvik vessels belong to the same group as the crucifix from Lemland, and this also goes for the silver chalice from Kökar.

The same activity can be noted in the acquisition of wooden sculptures. Some of the finest sculptures in Åland were acquired during the 14th century, among them the Madonna from Lemland and the apostles of Sund. Older sculptures were "modernized" to adjust to the spirit of the time, i.e. crucifixes were changed to enhance the suffering. Such a modernizing process can be seen among others in the crucifixes from Jomala and Sund, and the practice can be traced in Åland wooden sculptures well into the 15th century.

To stress the pain, faces are remodeled. Mouths are opened and wide-open eyes are shut. Clusters of blood are added to different wounds of the body. Recently acquired crucifixes, both in silver and in wood, reflect the pain through the tortured limbs. The corpus of Christ hangs heavily on the cross, the knees sharply slanted. The face is grimacing; even the waistcloth is changed. Earlier the cloth fell heavily and naturally in deep folds, occasionally from a bigger knot at the waist. Now even the draping of the waistcloth – two straggling folds hanging deep down from either waist – contribute to the indignant atmosphere. Another stylistic change happens during the second half of the 14th century all over Europe, when the suffering is succeeded by the so called "international beau style". This new fashion is also reflected in the sculptures from Åland.

Thus, except for a period of decline in wall painting, there is nothing to suggest the passivity and the economic depression that hit large areas of Europe after the Black Death of 1348. The plague resulted in stagnation in church building and art trade on the Continent during the second half of the 14th century. This was the case for instance in Gotland. After 1361, when Valdemar Atterdag had defeated the Guts in the Battle of Korsbetningen, all activity seems to have come to an end, including the Gotland influence in Åland.

As in Åland, in nearby areas to the east and to the west, ecclesiastic building activity continued uninterrupted during the entire century. Both in Uppland (eastern Sweden), and in Finland Proper (the south west of Finland), the 14th century must be seen as a dynamic church building period. But even if church building and high quality art acquisitions in Åland continued during the entire 14th century, it still cannot compare in quantity with the dynamic development during the 13th century. ■

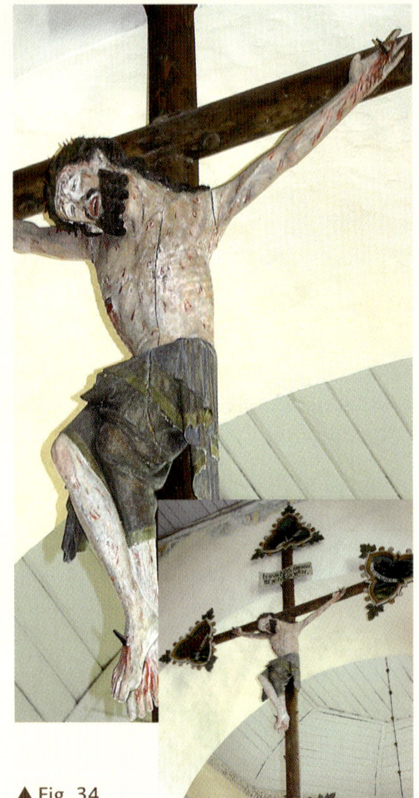

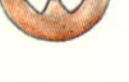

▲ Fig. 34.

Wooden Crucifix, the Church of Lemland.

Also the wooden rood in Lemland points towards the middle of the 14th century. In all essentials it recalls the little nailed silver crucifix from Saltvik. Here the suffering is accentuated to the grotesque, with the grossly twisted position of the Corpus of Christ, and his tortured face. The knees are angled towards the right. By that time a new spiritual center, focusing on suffering and passion, had been created in Cologne. In art history this can be traced in the export of a large number of roods, enhancing the suffering of Christ. In all probability the crucifix from Lemland was acquired from Cologne.

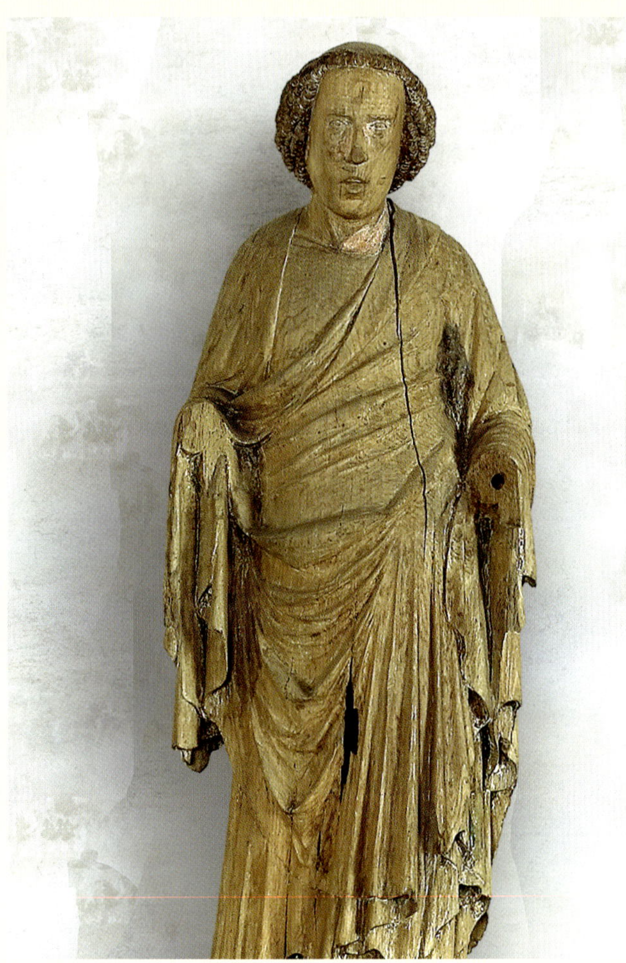

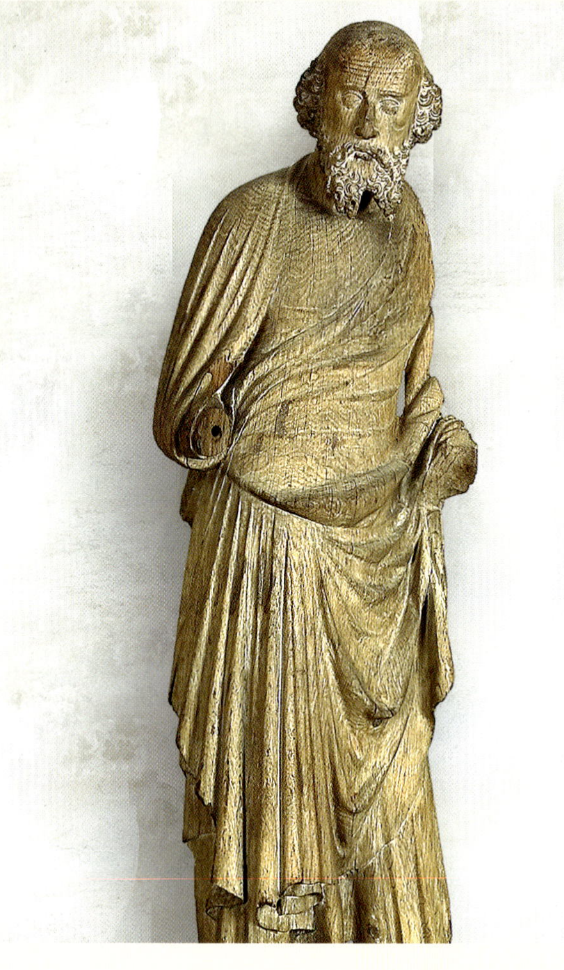

▲ Fig. 35-36.

The Apostles John and Paul from Sund.

Dendrochronological analysis shows that the two apostles from Sund are carved from the same log of oak, felled in Northern Germany around 1380. With gracefully twisted movements they represent the "International beau style". They were created at a time when wooden carving and other artistic activity was low, following the ravages of the Black Death. Artistically the Apostles belong to the most exquisite in contemporary European woodcarving. They are individually shaped, with deep expressions of the faces and elegant poses. Today almost all colors are obliterated. Rich gilding and deep colors in green and blue can still be traced in the innermost cavities of the folds. The sculptures are of natural height. They are relatively shallow, and they have had back planks, now missing. There are still many question marks concerning these sculptures. The acquisition of such prestigious sculptures of the Apostles can have been motivated by the neighboring royal castle of Kastelholm, which at this time appears in the written sources.

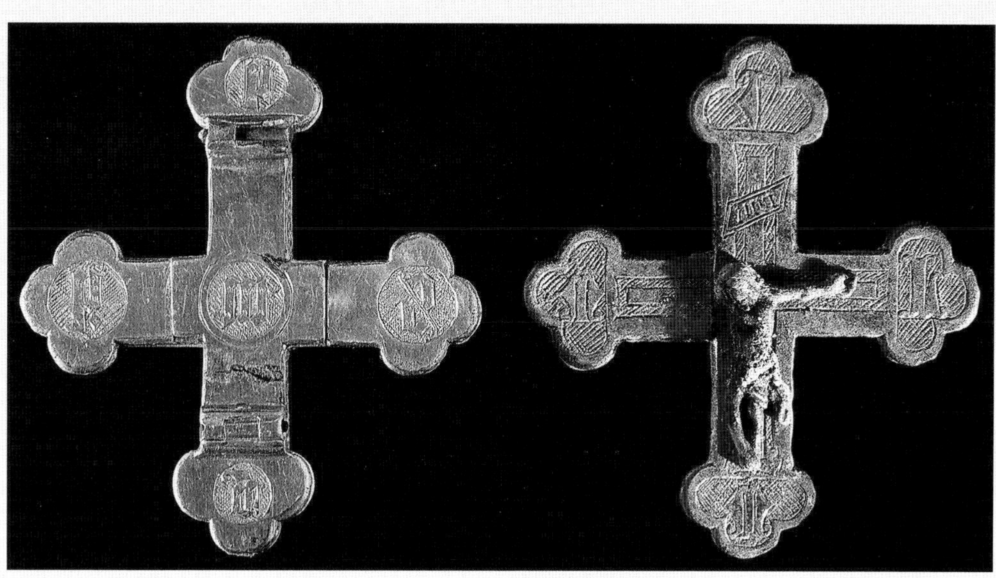

▲ Fig. 37.

Silver reliquary cross from Föglö church

Stig Dreijer discovered the little ***reliquary**** cross from the church of Föglö in 1966 in an archaeological excavation. It had originally been placed in a little wooden box, in a reliquary niche in the medieval altar. When the wooden box had rotted the reliquary apparently fell down into the underlying cavity. At the time of the discovery the silver cross still included the original relics, a couple of bone pieces. The inscription "maria magdalena" on a parchment attached indicates that at least one of the relics belonged to Mary Magdalene.

The reliquary cross, with arms of equal length, in gilded silver plates, has trifoil endings of the cross arms. It measures 60 x 53mm, with a thickness of 5mm. The cross is decorated on both sides. The front is adorned with a crucifix, where the Christ figure, less than 3cm high, stands in high relief. The right arm is missing. The clumsy arm, still intact, stretches horizontally towards the left. The head hangs down towards the right shoulder. Four Gothic majors on the ends of the cross arms: horizontally M and L, vertically J and M, mark the four evangelists: Mark, Luke, John and Matthew. Diagonally across the upper cross arm an inscription in minor reads: inri (Jesus Nasareus Rex Judorum, or Jesus of Nazareth, King of Jews). Both the cross of Christ and the majors on the ends of the cross arms have a crosshatched background. A simple narrow line surrounds the entire cross.

The back of the cross is more simple and decorated only with inscriptions. Here every cross arm is finished by a crosshatched roundel. Horizontally the majors of R and S can be seen against the background. The letters in the vertical direction and in the center of the cross are in minors, from the top down: g, m and b. Matts Dreijer turned to Germany for expert help. According to Doctor Schewe, Art Historian and Theologian from Kiel, the m in the center of the cross should be read twice as follows: "maria grata benedicta" (mary, blessed with grace) and "mater Regis Salvatoris" (Mother of the Royal Saviour).

Matts Dreijer somewhat surprisingly suggests a very late date for the reliquary, to the end of the 15th century or to around 1500. Why he does this is unclear, since Schewe never mentioned the age of the cross. Other scholars have repeated the late date.

Stylistically the Föglö Crucifix is difficult to date, with many contradictory traits. The knee-long voluminous loincloth, falling down in two straps from each side, points towards the 14th century, whereas the legs and the horizontal arms belong to the beginning of the 15th century. The cross is hardly late medieval. Towards the end of the 15th century the crucifixes had a totally different image – the loincloth gradually became shorter, turning into a tight fitting cloth folded around the hips.

Size and material makes the Föglö reliquary comparable to the communion silver from Saltvik, securely dated to 1346 (Fig. 33). The crosshatched background of the text is the same, as is the Gothic major. The Gothic minor of the reliquary represents the "littera textualis formata", which according to Professor Outi Merisalo does not change significantly during the 14th and 15th centuries. Both crucifixes have trefoil endings of the cross arms, but that in itself is not datable, Even if it is difficult to give exact dates for the Föglö reliquary, it is obviously more recent than the chalice and paten from Saltvik.

Today, after prolonged disputes between the Åland Museum and Föglö parish, the silver reliquary adorns the altar in Föglö church, encapsulated in a protective shell of plexi-glass.

The 15th century – church plans and façades

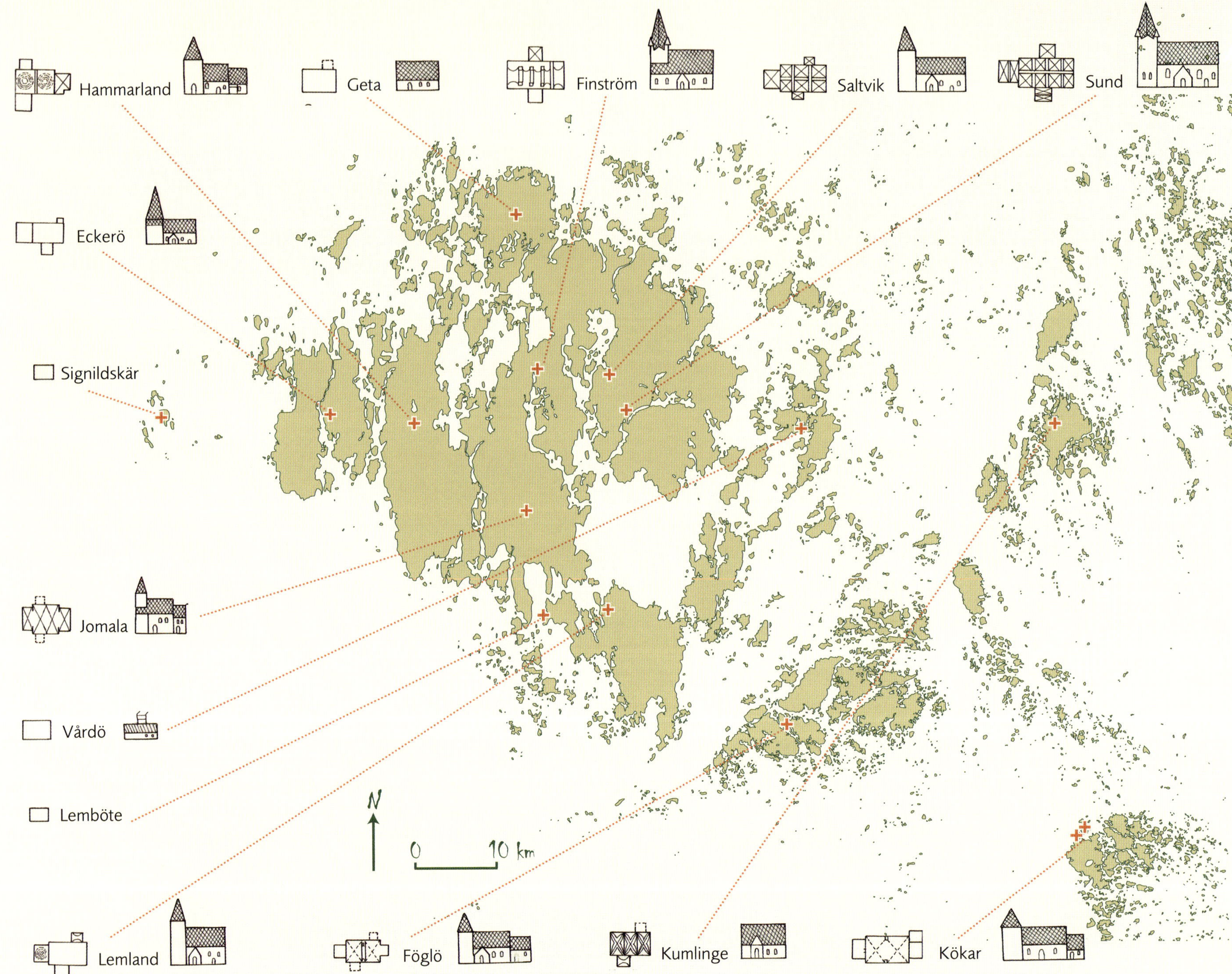

THE 15TH CENTURY – ECONOMIC BOOM

By the second half of the 15th century, the Islands were endowed with 14 churches and chapels, constructed in stone. The chapel churches in Geta and Vårdö represent new buildings. Wooden churches were sufficient for the remaining chapelries. It is still unclear when the first wooden chapels were erected in Sottunga, Lumparland and Brändö. Yet sources from the 16th century describe them as old, with Catholic interiors, suggesting medieval origin.

Bricks do not enter the picture until the 15th century in Åland church building. They become of current interest with the vaulting of the naves in Saltvik, Föglö, Kumlinge and Kökar. Only in Kumlinge has the brick vault survived intact. In Saltvik the earlier two naves were repeated in the renewed vaulting. Two thick pillars in the central axis of the nave carried brick vaults. The narrow longitudinal arches, or the cavities the walls made in preparation for the earlier field stone vaults, were heightened. Both at Föglö and in Kökar, the secondary brick vault rested on separate pillars along the walls. The vaulting in Kumlinge is different. No wall pillars or cavities in the walls were planned. Instead transitional arches carry three star vaults across the nave. Brick brackets anchored in the walls carry the arches. Further brick brackets are to be found in the inner corners of the nave. In the ***star vaults**** at Kumlinge the meeting points of the ribs are marked by circles. Thus, in the head of each vault five little rings are created. With a positive frame of mind the rings can be interpreted as the symbols of the five wounds of Christ, in the same way as in the headgear of the Birgittine clothing.

Yet, the main emphasis during the 15th century was focused on the church of Finström, which must have gone through a complete transformation, both to the exterior and to the interior. This happened in connection with a secondary vaulting of the nave, this time, nota bene, of fieldstones. Also the nave at Finström must be seen as a variation of the wall pillar church, in a solution lacking correspondence elsewhere in the Baltic area. Through the triumphal arch at Finström, the present stairs to the pulpit originally served as

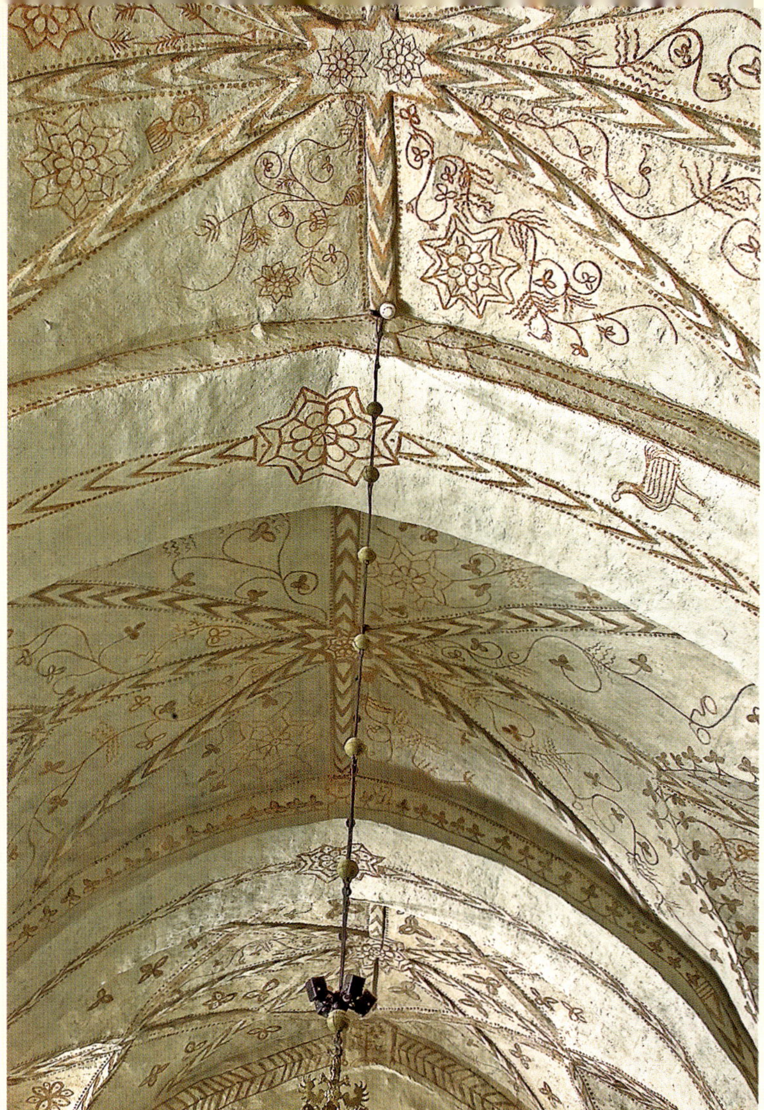

▲ Fig. 39.

Vault paintings and the vaulting system in Finström.

The vault paintings from the 1450s differ from other paintings in the church. They represent the westernmost point for the so-called "primitive" wall paintings from southwestern Finland. Another master painted them, and they form the only Åland example of this style. All the rib reliefs are lined and decoratively ornamented, embracing an illusion of a carrying ***rib vault**** system. In addition to awkwardly drawn decorative elements, with intertwining foliage combined with trefoil clovers, the keystones of the transversal arches are marked with big stars. Smaller stars are spread all over the vaults. Primitively drawn human figures and birds signal an enigmatic message. ▶▶

◀ Fig. 38. The Åland churches in the 15th century, plans and exteriors reconstructed in scale, with a coastline 2.8m below the the present water level.

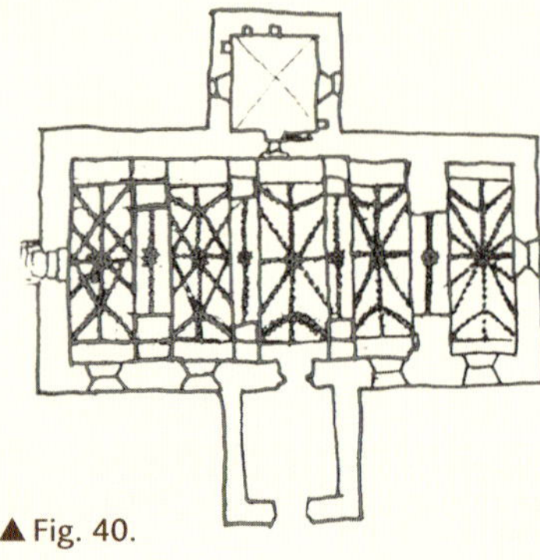

▲ Fig. 40.
The vault system in Finström church.

Two medieval cogs are depicted, one in the triumphal arch and the other as part of the only scene by this artist which can be iconographically identified. This is "The sailing cruise of Saint Olof" on the northern wall of the nave, close to the sacristy portal, where the crowned Norwegian national saint is reproduced with his attribute, the wide bladed axe.

Many questions still remain concerning this group of wall paintings from the southwest of Finland. Surprisingly enough the diocese in Turku must have sanctioned them, although they probably represent some deeper symbolism. The star decoration, for instance, is very logical in a vault, symbolizing the vault of heaven. According to Bo Ossian Lindberg the stars in Finström symbolize much more than that. He thinks that they depict the Three Stars and the Seven Stars, which during the Middle Ages symbolized the Old and the New Testament, identifying the old and the new law.

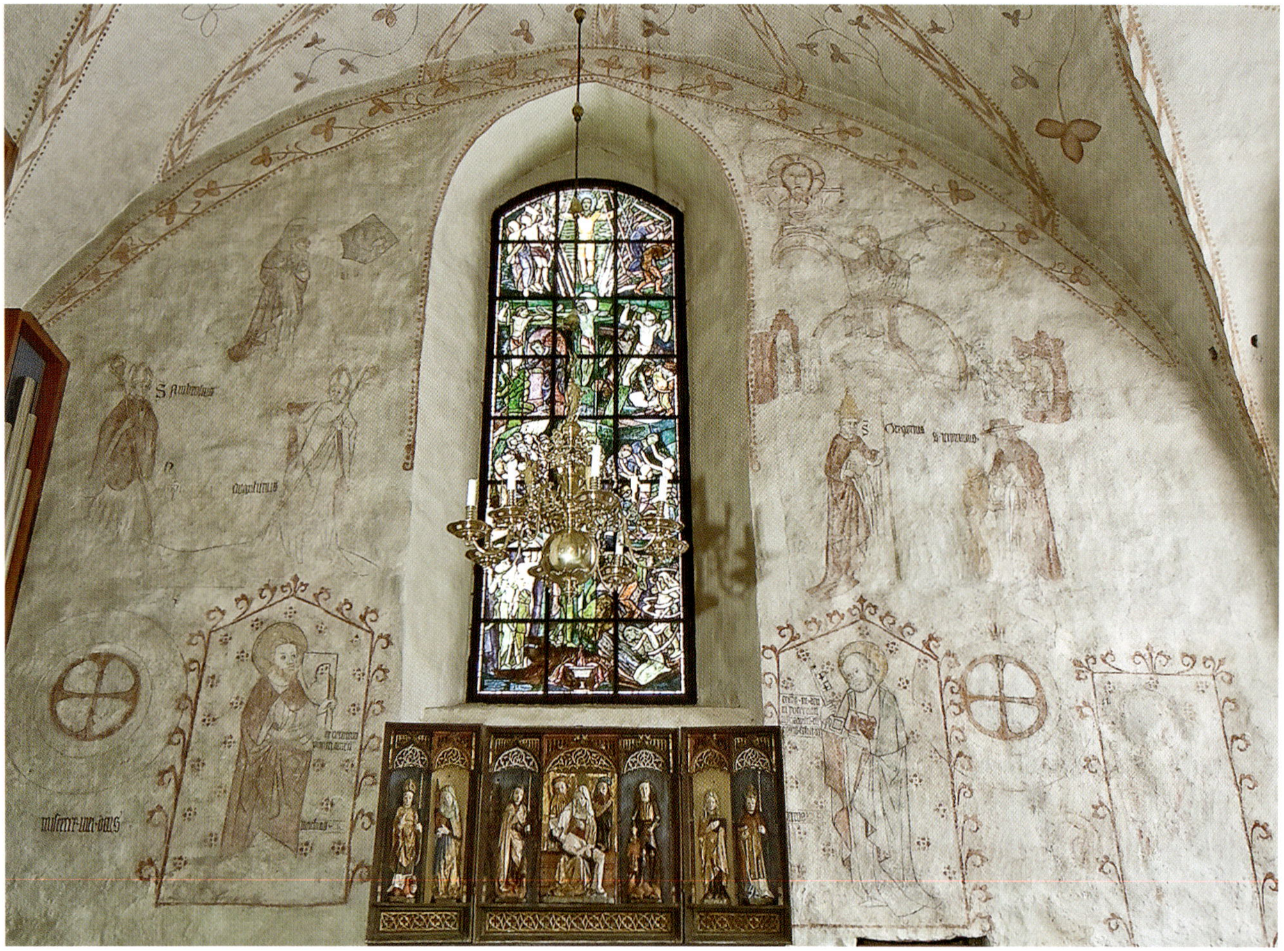

▲ Fig. 41a.

Wall paintings in Finström.

The wall paintings of the eastern chancel wall in Finström belong to many different stages. Several different artists can be discerned. To the earliest stage belong the large inauguration crosses, with the outlines drawn in the still wet plaster and surrounded by many concentric rings. Nearby, to the south on the same wall, it is possible to discern an indistinctly drawn face of Christ, framed by a cross halo. It belongs to the same stage, also drawn in wet plaster. High up on the wall, the Last Judgment is reproduced in a strange position, between the chancel window and the vault. The motive is reduced to the face of Christ with a cross halo. From the mouth of Christ the lily of grace reaches out towards the blessed, and the sword of righteousness points towards the condemned. The Redeemer sits on double, reduced, rainbows. Large areas of the wall are filled with a uniform group, dated by the coat of arms of Olaus Magni to 1440-1450, when he was Dean at Turku Cathedral. This group belongs to the artistic high points in Finnish wall painting. It includes Saint Anne, close to

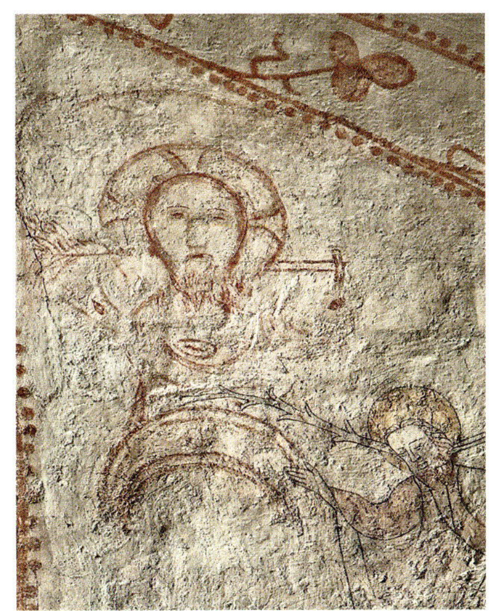

▲ **Fig. 41b.** Detail of the eastern chancel wall, the older version of the Last Judgment.

the coat of arms, north of the window, and a renewed and more complete version of the Last Judgment on the opposite side. Above all it includes the four Church Fathers, horizontally filling the central part of the chancel wall. The same hand also painted the Apocalyptic Madonna on the northern wall, close to a now lost altar of Mary. The high altar, finally, is flanked by large figure paintings of the apostles Peter and Matthias in a totally different style, and crab ornaments frame them. The apostles form the beginning and the end of the Credo series, which can be followed all around the nave.

On the pillar surfaces, facing the nave, the Credo series continues. Other surfaces are filled with other individual saints. They are all framed in by crab ornamentation, even if a different artist can be traced here too.

stairs to an ambo. The wave of secondary vaultings in the region was initiated at Saltvik around 1430. In the middle of the 15th century followed the vaulting of Finström, whereas the vaults at Föglö and Kumlinge probably belonged to the end of the century.

Now was probably the time to erect porch and sacristy in Jomala, set against existing portals in the south and north. Porches became common only during this century, and they were added to the naves in Finström, Eckerö, Sund and Kumlinge, probably also in Föglö. At this stage sacristies had been built in all churches. The first sacristy in Geta was wooden. A lower and narrower chancel was added to the nave at Hammarland around 1430. Two of the best-preserved west towers in Finland are in Åland, at Finström and Eckerö. They were erected almost simultaneously at the end of the 1460s. Copying the tower of the Cathedral in Turku, the tower of Finström was crowned by a spire with four ***turrets**** at each corner. The wooden constructions of the tower spires at Finström and Eckerö are still intact, and thus present rare examples of medieval wooden constructions in our country. The tower at Sund was modernized accordingly, modeled on Finström. Rather than adding western towers to the nave, the chapel congregation at Geta erected a separate wooden staple. The most recent tower of all is apparently to be found in Föglö, from around 1500.

The new economic boom apparently hit Åland in the middle of the 15th century. It can also be discerned in wall paintings and in wooden sculptures. Now those churches that had been substantially transformed, as in Finström, Kumlinge and Hammarland, were equipped with whole-covering paintings on walls and vaults. These paintings had no equivalents in nearby areas. In Finström several different artists can be traced, most of them probably working simultaneously. Enigmatic vault paintings differ radically from the wall paintings of the nave, where the paintings also fail to give an impression of unity.

Unity, however, is well represented in the pictorial program of Kumlinge. Female saints dominate the paintings of the vaults, the southern wall of the nave by the childhood of Jesus and the life of Mary, and the northern by the Passion. In this case we must imagine one single artist who finishes a carefully planned ***iconographical**** program. When the chancel had been added to the nave at Hammarland, intertwining decorations, continuing on to the elegant cupola vaults, covered earlier paintings imitating brick walls on the transversal arch. In the chancel the ornamentation of the vaults continued over the walls. From a Credo series the only remaining apostle is Judas Thaddeus, on the northern chancel wall. The secondary vaults of Saltvik (torn down in the 19th century) were covered with wall paintings. They are hard to visualize since only single details are mentioned in passing in later descriptions, such as "Arma Christi" or "The Man of Sorrows", and the Church Fathers. Earlier 13th century wall paintings at Jomala, Lemland and Sund, remained untouched, even if these churches had also gone through secondary alterations. Renovated churches with vaulted and enlarged naves had partly new inauguration crosses painted to commemorate the new inauguration of the church.

Everywhere the sculptural ornamentation was complemented by new acquisitions, along with older sculptures. Above all, the 15th century is the age of altarpieces and reredoses, a completely new type of object, now becoming increasingly popular everywhere in Europe. Altarpieces earlier unseen were ordered to the main altars of the churches, magnificent ***triptychs**** with side wings that would open in its entire splendor during the liturgical feasts of the year. The altarpieces were usually adorned by sculptures of the patron saints. Side altars, too, were equipped with new wooden sculptures. Once more, Finström church is remarkable in having at least four images of Saint Michael - one painting and three wooden sculptures. During this period the artistic contacts continue east towards the Baltic countries and the land of the Prussian order. The cooperation between foreign deliverers and local workshops also continues, especially in locally made shrines for the saints.

From an iconographical point of view Finström also stands closer than other Åland churches to the Cathedra Aboensis (Turku). Saint Henrik, patron saint of the Cathedral and the national saint of Finland, is enhanced in the pictorial program. Olaus Magnus, Dean of the Cathedral during the 1440s, had his coat of arms depicted on the eastern chancel wall. The Dominican connection, already noticed with the sequentionary, is further accentuated by the wall paintings with the Credo series, but above all by the painting of Peter the Martyr, one of the foremost Dominican saints next to Dominic himself. The strange "primitive" vault paintings in Finström have their closest parallels in southwestern Finland. Finström clearly emerges as the main church of the Islands.

Gradually more Ålanders are mentioned in the medieval sources. They are participating in pilgrimages to expiate their crimes. From a church perspective the squire Kort Harvigsson from Kodbolstad (Bolstaholm) in Geta is of special interest. Through marriage he had acquired substantial wealth. He died childless, and his will from 1484 enhances the consideration for ecclesiastical values. Many Åland churches, such as Finström's Saint Michael, Saint George's chapel in Geta, Saint Anne in Kumlinge and the convent at Kökar were enriched through his donations. For 50 marks of land to the chapel of Saint George in Geta, the vicar of Finström was asked to deliver mass annually for Kort's poor soul. If not, the donation would be nullified, and used for a mass altar for evening prayers and alms.

Fashionable above all in the 15th century was the cult of Holy Birgitta of Sweden. It swept all over Europe, and showed the enormous power connected with the only canonized Swedish saint. In Sund we hear about a true miracle – a drowned boy regains life when his parents are praying to Holy Birgitta. In Åland the cult leaves traces in numerous Birgitta sculptures and in wall paintings. In Lemland Holy Birgitta became the third patron saint next to Catherine of Alexandria and Saint Nicholas of Myra. The new altarpiece includes them all. In Brändö the wooden chapel of Saint James was probably erected during this period. It belonged to the mother church of Kumlinge. Saint Matthias, the new stone chapel at Vårdö, was erected to make churchgoing easier for the congregation during wintertime and in bad weather. The chapel of Saint George in Geta, also a stone building, belongs to the same stage as the big rebuilding of the mother church in Finström.

Building activity during the 15th century is evenly proportioned throughout the entire century. No signs of war and unrest can be discerned in architecture or in art acquisitions.

▶ Fig. 42.

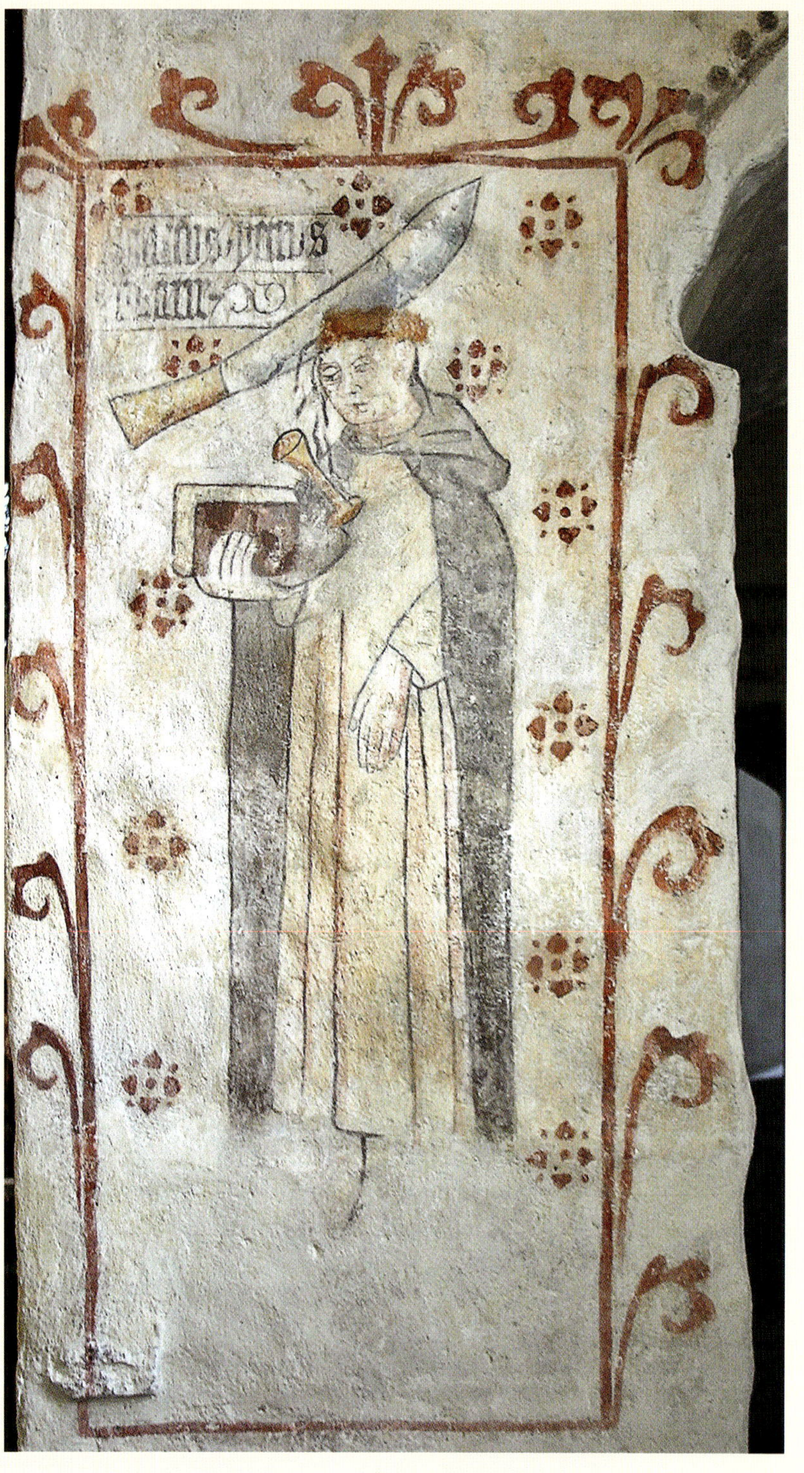

Finström church, Peter the Martyr, ca 1450.

The west wall of the pillar on the left of the main portal represents one of the most important saints of the Dominican Order, Peter the Martyr, who was sanctified in 1252, soon after his martyrdom. He fought untiringly against the heretics in northern Italy and wanted a martyr's death. During a forest walk he successfully managed to attract his killer, who stabbed him with a dagger in the breast, and cut him in the head with a sword. According to the preserved minutes of the court, Peter happily cited the Credo before his death. According to the old regulations of the Dominican order from the 13th century, Peter the Martyr came next to Dominic himself, the founder of the order. The rule of the Dominican Order states that every Dominican church should have one portrait of Saint Dominique and one of Peter the Martyr. Even if the entire Diocese of Turku was Dominican, Peter the Martyr is to be found only once within the Diocese, in the church of Finström.

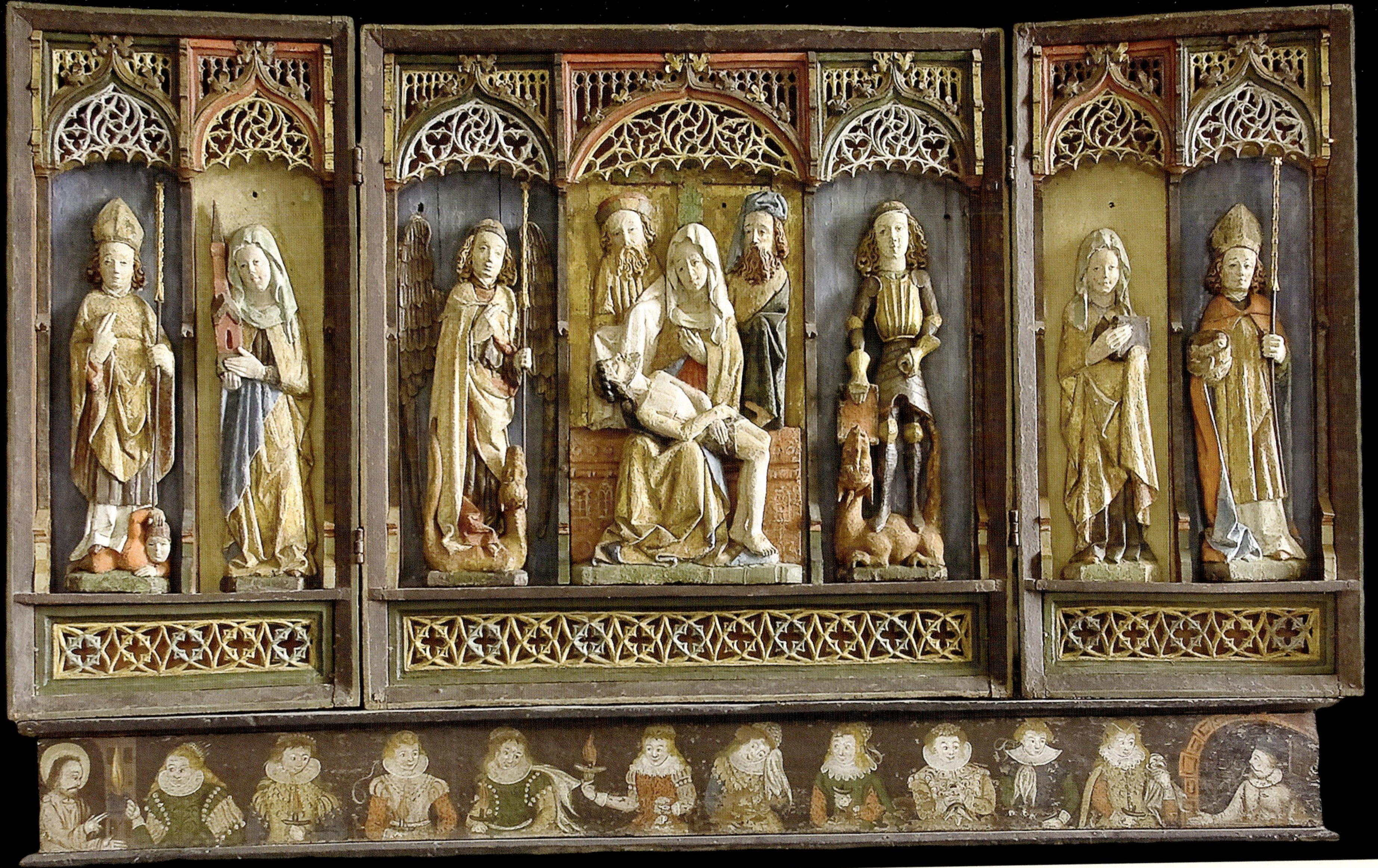

▲ Fig. 43.

The Altarpiece, Finström, from the 1460s, is unusually well preserved.

It was acquired for the new inauguration of the church. Dendrochronological analysis of the oak in the constructive parts gives a plausible date to the time after 1461. The sculptures of linden tree cannot be dated, but the pictorial program of the altarpiece is very informative, showing that it was manufactured for Saint Michael's church in Finström. The archangel Michael and Saint George, two similar heroic saints, who are found several times in the church, both in sculpture and in the wall paintings, flank the central *Pietà** of the corpus. The wings are filled with Swedish saints, to the left Bishop Henrik of Turku and Ingrid of Skänninge (earlier interpreted as Saint Gertrud) to the right Holy Birgitta of Vadstena and Sigfrid of Växjö. The new identification of Ingrid of Skänninge, Saint of the Dominican order and founderess of a convent in Sweden, further enhances the Dominican element in the church of Finström.

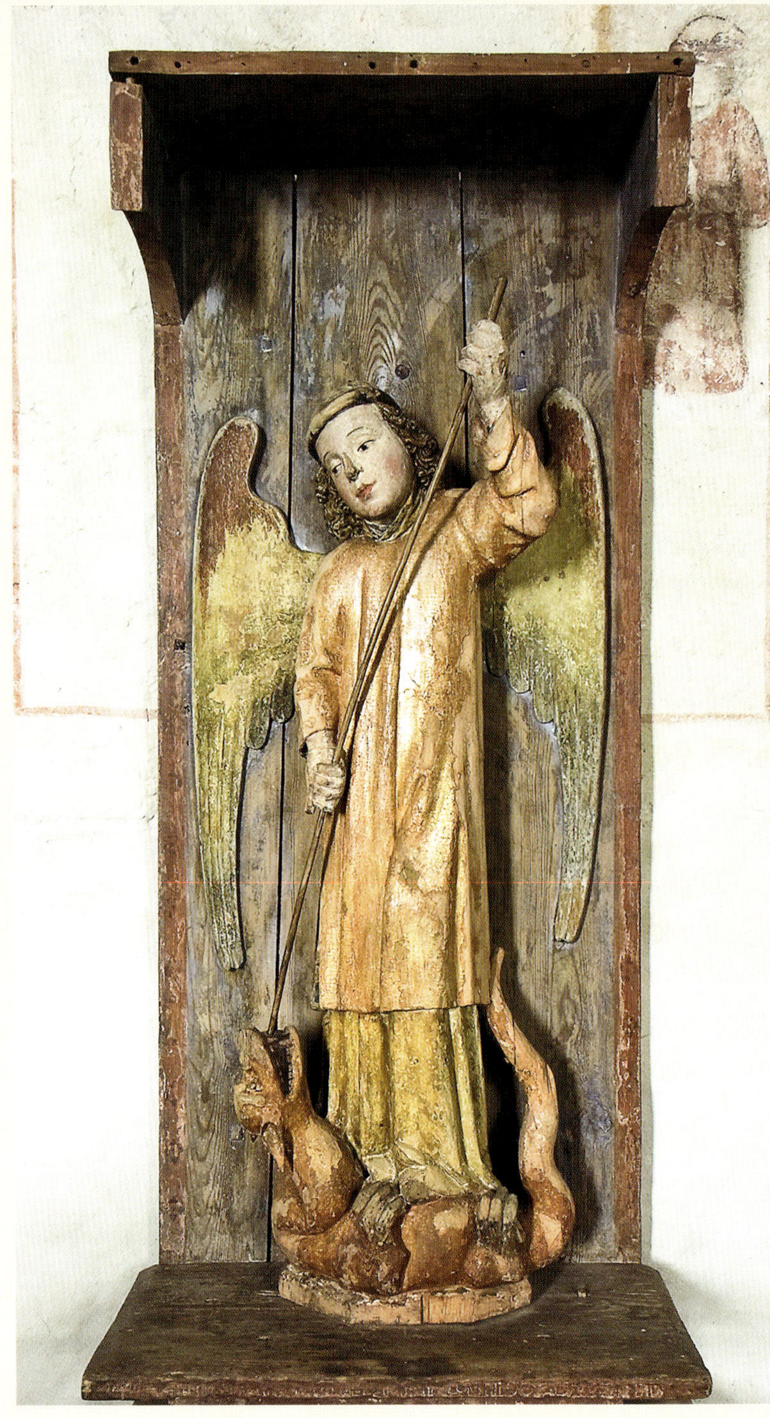

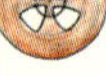

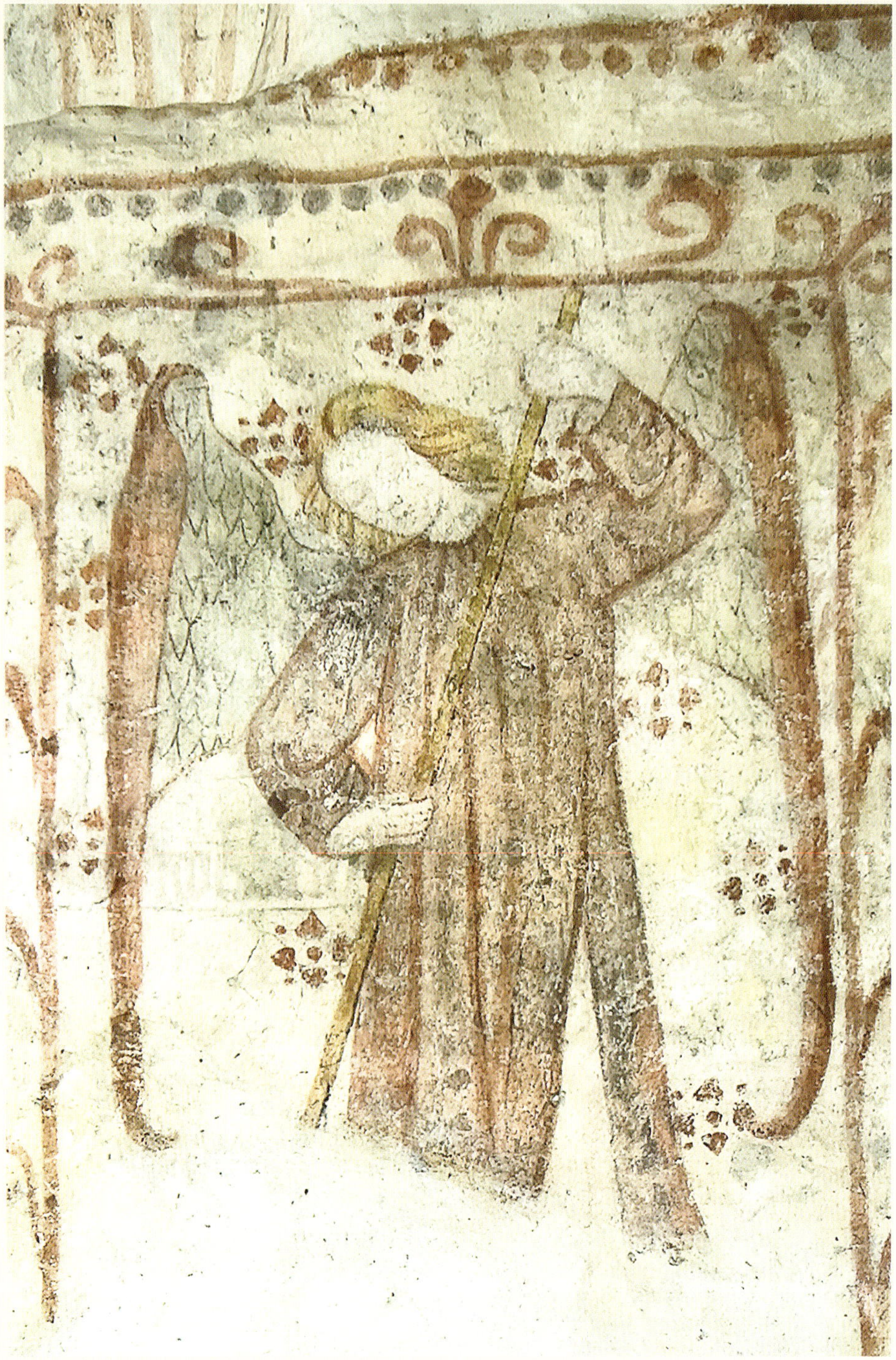

◀ Fig. 44-45.

Saint Michael in Finström, wooden sculpture and wall painting, around 1450.

Yet another wooden sculpture representing the patron saint was acquired for the re-inauguration of the newly vaulted church. This time Michael himself is carved in non-datable deciduous wood, but dendrochronological analysis of one of the wings shows oak of Baltic origin, felled sometime in the middle of the 15th century. It further shows that the framing shrine consists of Åland pine, also from around 1450. What is remarkable this time is that the wings of Michael are fastened to the shrine, not to Michael, and that wood from the very same oak has been used for the door in one of the sacristy niches. This is yet another example of close collaboration between imported work and local workshops when it comes to medieval wooden sculptures in Åland.

Just inside the south portal, immediately to the right, the same Michael is found again, this time in a painted version. Here we can talk of a wall painting portraying the new sculpture of the Patron Saint. The dragon at his feet is missing, but the body position is the same and so are the colors.

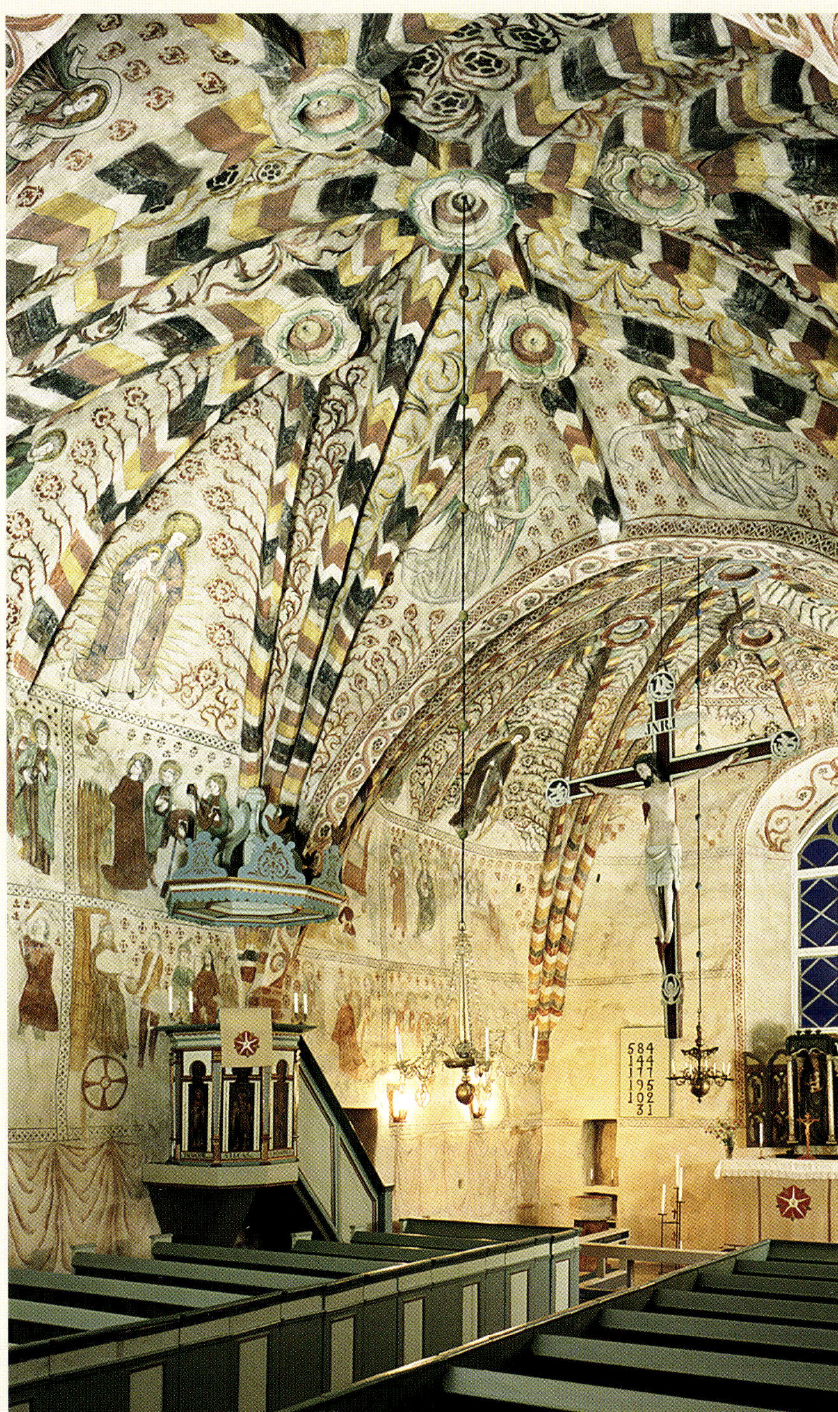

▶ Fig. 46.

The church of Saint Anne, Kumlinge, interior towards the east.

The interior at Kumlinge has not changed significantly since the Middle Ages. Excluding the benches and the pulpit, most of it is intact, although the windows of the church have been enlarged. A re-grouping of the windows must have taken place already at the time of the vaulting of the nave. The church consists of one nave vaulted in three bays. Ribs form stellar vaults with five rings at the meeting point of the ribs. The brick vault has not yet been analyzed for dating.

The wall paintings in the church of Kumlinge, covering the entire interior, have no direct parallels in neighboring areas. Rather than having them whitewashed as in the other Åland churches in the 17th century, Dean Boetius Murenius ordered them to be refreshed, or improved. However, the paintings in the vaults were later badly damaged by soot and fire during the Great Northern War, when Russian soldiers lit open fires in the church. The walls of the nave had been whitewashed, and are therefore better preserved. On the south wall follow scenes from the childhood of Christ and the life of Mary, in several narrative series arranged on top of each other. The Mary shrine from the 13th century, today on the high altar, may have been a source of inspiration. A Vera Icon is depicted above one of the original south windows - literally, the true image of Christ imprinted on a cloth, or Veronica's sudarium. The motive recalls the Birgittine convent in Vallis Gratiae (Naantali), where it keeps turning up in many different versions. The northern wall represents the Passion of Christ, mixed with miracle scenes, like the "Harvest Miracle" occurring during the Flight to Egypt.

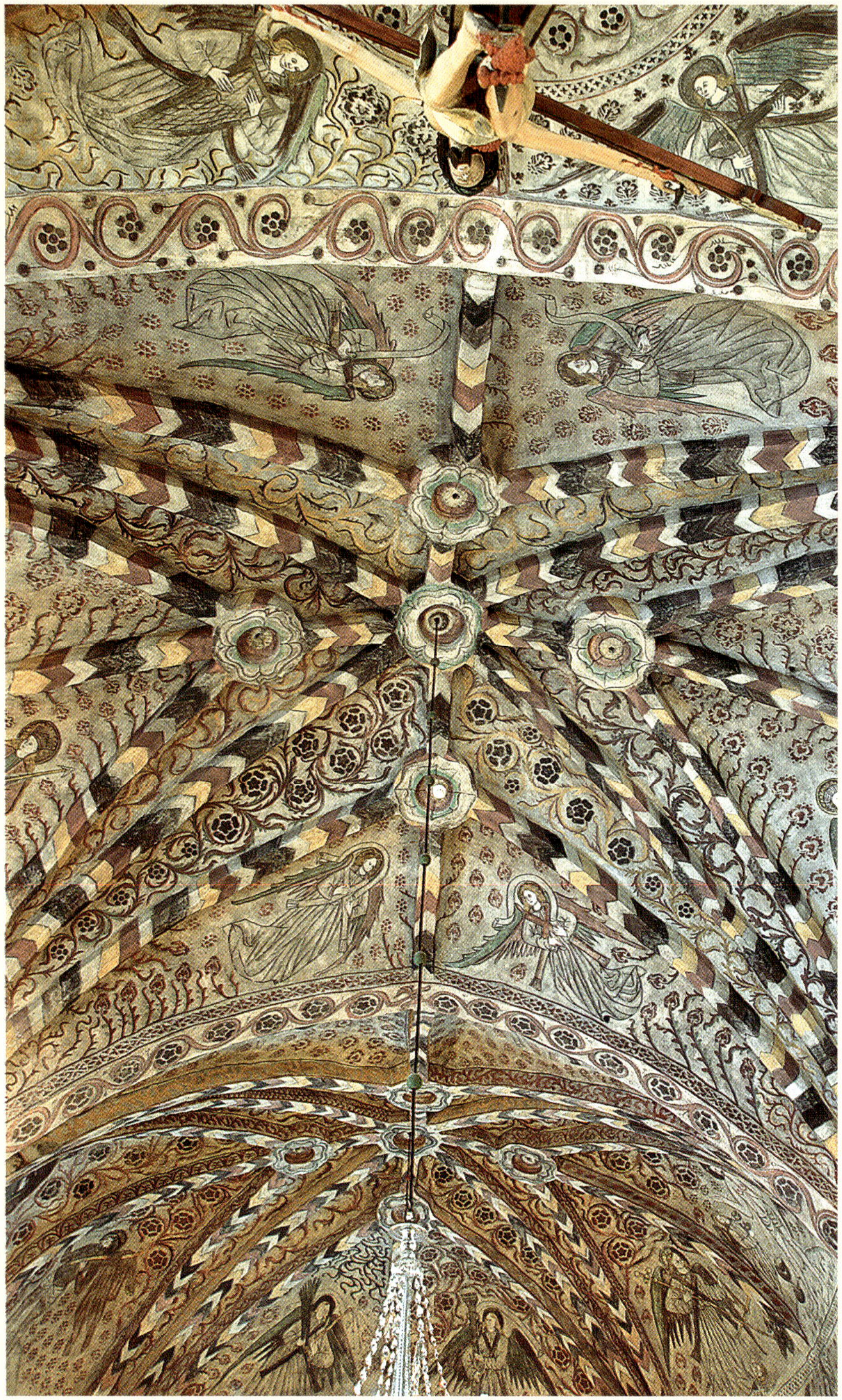

◀ **Fig. 47.**

Kumlinge, paintings of the vault.

The brick vaults at Kumlinge are as yet undated, but on stylistic grounds the vault paintings can be dated to 1480-1500. They are dominated by a rare female world. Except for the Apostle Bartholomew, only female saints are looking down on the beholder, among others the Apocalyptic Madonna and Saint Apollonia. The ribs are ornamentally enhanced. Intertwining foliage and stereotyped flowers surround the female figures. The pictorial program is unusually homogenous, the same artist being responsible for the whole interior. Figures are painted in fast and wide pencil strokes. This time it is tempting to think that the paintings might be the result of a donation, maybe a votive gift, in gratitude donated to the church by a woman. Sixten Ringbom suggested this interpretation.

We do not know any direct parallels to the paintings at Kumlinge. They differ radically from late medieval wall paintings in Finström and in Hammarland. In Kumlinge, both the foliage and the figures are drawn with a stiffer hand. The same is true when comparing the paintings to the so-called Kaland-school in southwestern Finland, with wall paintings signed by Petrus Henriksson, around 1470-80s. Compared to church paintings covering entire interiors in the rest of Finland, like those at Lohja and Hattula, dated to the beginning of the 16th century, the Kumlinge paintings are executed more carefully. Stylistically the paintings at Kumlinge may come closest to the well-preserved pictorial program in the Franciscan convent church at Rauma, north of Turku.

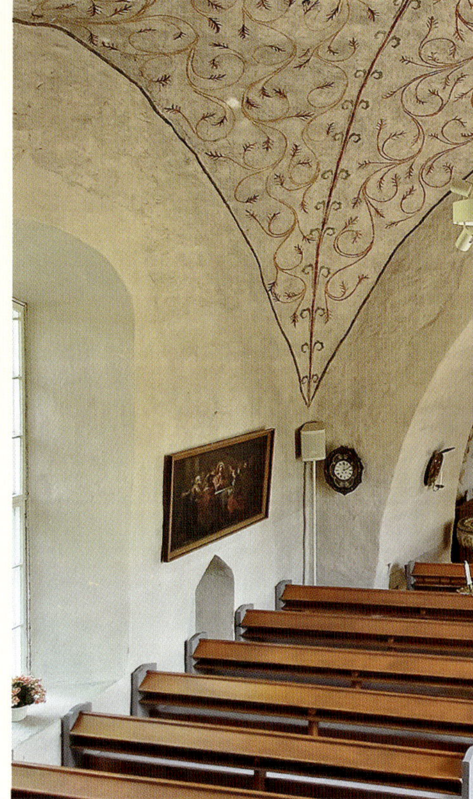

▲ **Fig. 48.**

The church of Hammarland, interior towards the east.

When at last the new chancel was finished, time had come to completely ornament the interior with new intertwining foliage. The cast cupola vaults of the nave and the cross vault of the chancel were filled with uniform wall paintings, painted by the same master. In the process, earlier paintings of imitated brick walls on the ***transverse arch**** of field stones, and in the framing of the original east windows, were painted over, maybe together with other early paintings The Apostle Judas Thaddeus, with his scroll attached on the northern wall of the chancel, suggests that this church may have had yet another Credo series (cf. Fig. 104).

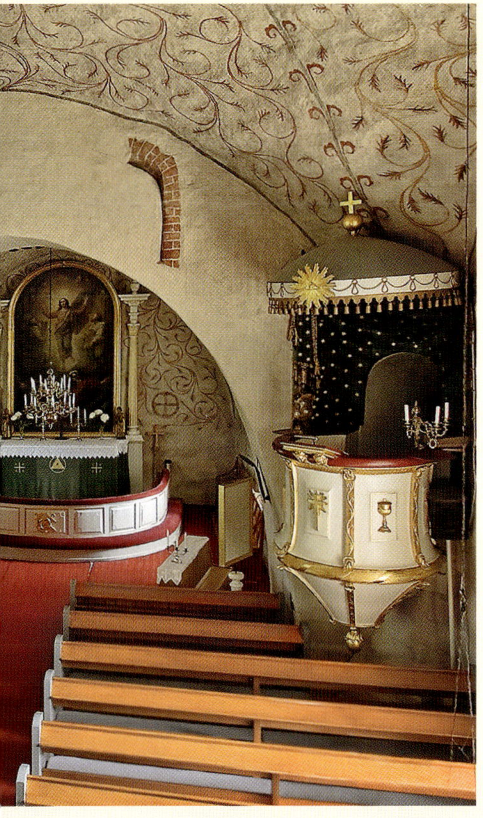

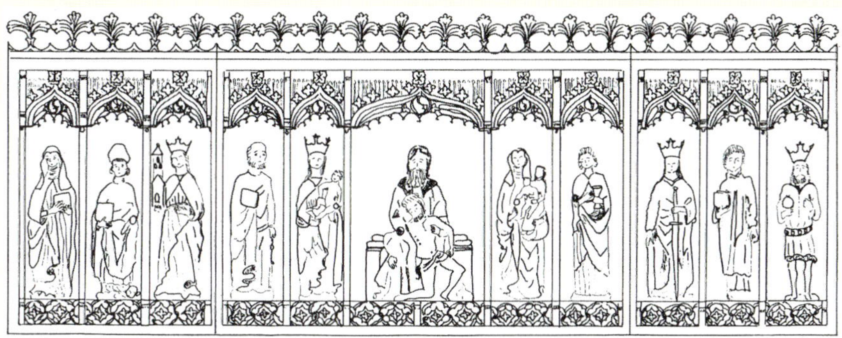

▲Fig. 49.

Reconstruction of the altarpiece at Hammarland.

The medieval altarpiece from Hammarland, around 1440, was deliberately destroyed at the beginning of the 19th century. The order came from Vicar P.U.F. Sadelin who wanted to redecorate the chancel in a strict Lutheran manner. Later the sculptures were sold, thus vanishing in different directions. Only three of the sculptures remain in the church today. The altarpiece can, however, be reconstructed with great accuracy: an elongated and horizontal altarpiece, especially ordered from northern Germany, adorned the main altar of the new chancel. A scene representing the Father of Grace, where the enthroned and crowned God Father holds Christ, descended from the cross in his arms, dominated its corpus. Mary and Saint Anne flank the scene, whereas the side wings were filled by the patron saint of the church, Saint Catherine of Alexandria, apostles and mainly Nordic saints.

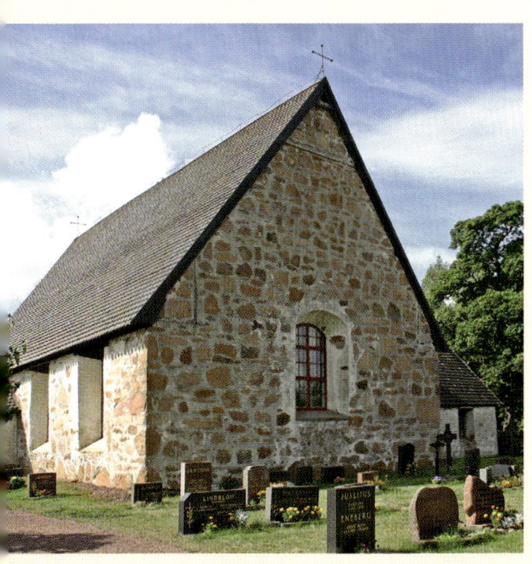

◀Fig. 50.

The chapel church of Geta, exterior from the southwest.

The massive building campaign in the middle of the 15th century at the mother church of Finström, also included the chapel in Geta. Scientific dating suggests that Geta chapel was erected at the same time as the church of Finström went through its total transformation. The timing fits very well in with a letter of indulgence, written by a number of Cardinals on February 3 1463, for the benefit of Finström Church and Saint George's chapel in Geta.

▲Fig. 51.

Vårdö chapel church.

The smallest stone church in Åland is the chapel at Vårdö, devoted to Saint Matthias. The original exterior of the chapel is clearly visible in a map from the 1640s. Instead of a western tower a covered construction for the hanging of the bells was placed in the middle of the ridge. It was resting on four poles. The low chapel had a timbered sacristy against the eastern part of the north wall. The dating of Vårdö chapel church rests on scientific dating of several different materials. Contemporary written sources are missing, but the existence of a medieval stone chapel on the site is supported by later sources. In the 1590s there is a mention of a crack in the wall in the east gable, and in 1636-66 Dean Boetius Murenius describes a chapel with its Catholic interior still intact, with "papal flags" and all sorts of "images". He did not know when the chapel was constructed. He claims that no living person could remember when this had taken place, but that it must have been considerably younger than the mother church at Sund. A substantial enlargement of the chapel in the 1780s, and a western tower added at the beginning of the 19th century, has radically changed the chapel, both inside and out.

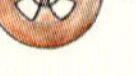
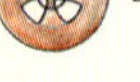

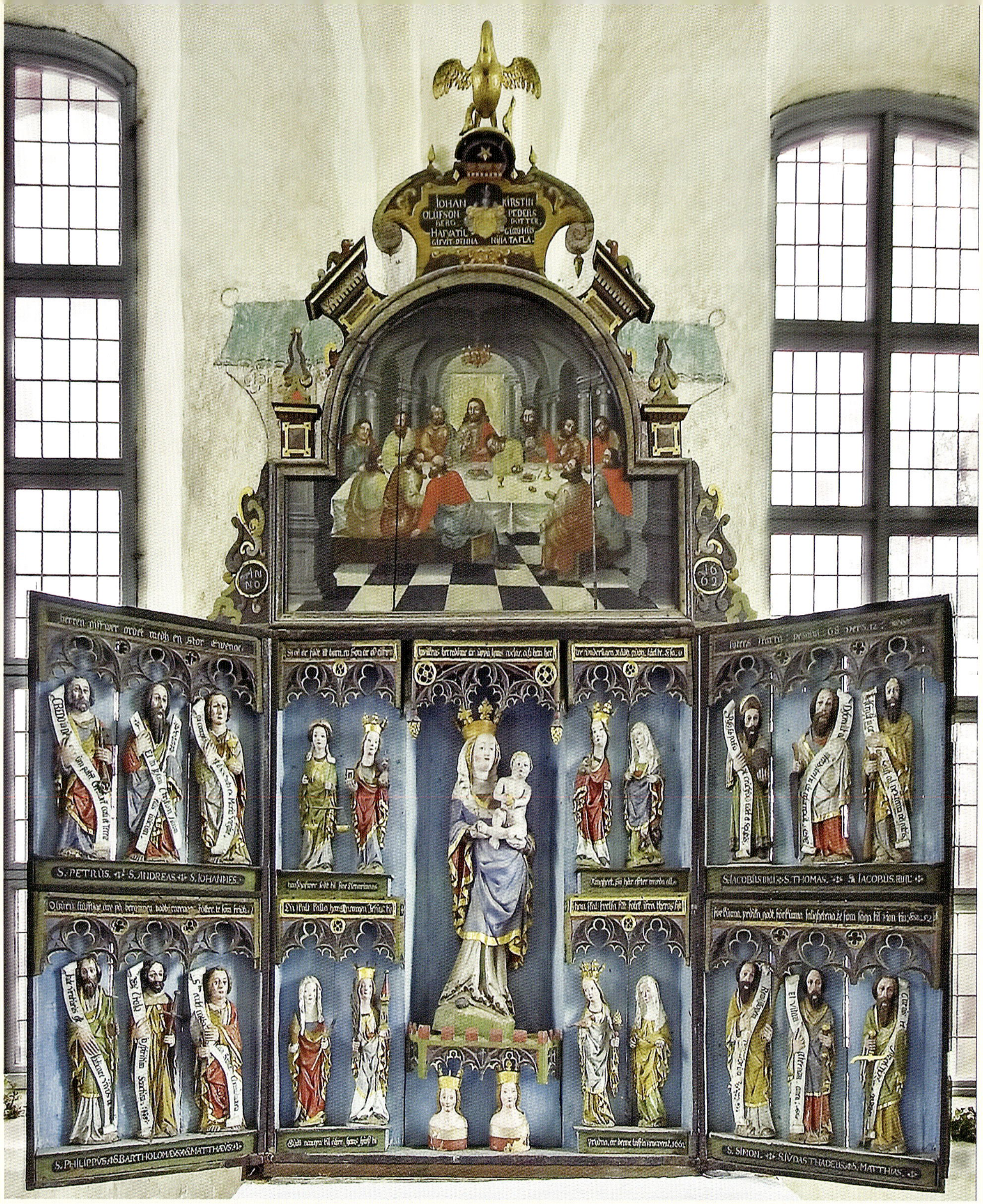

◀Fig. 52.

The altarpiece from Sund (ca 1440).

The original altar decoration in the church of Sund is not known, but the painting of the Calvary group on the wall behind the altar may have served this function (cf. Fig. 15). The impressive altarpiece, which adorns the altar today, was acquired some time in the middle of the 15th century. A niche, narrowing inside, the architectural construction of the altar, and characteristic features of the sculptures suggest delivery from the Baltic countries or from the German Order, in present day Poland. Here nothing indicates collaboration with local workshops. Female saints dominate the corpus of the altarpiece. In the corpus four crowned virgins, i.e. Margreth, Catherine of Alexandria, Dorothea and Barbara, flank the crowned Madonna with the Jesus Child and four other female saints in turn flank them. The side wings are filled with the twelve apostles with the sentences from the creed on scrolls. Thus they represent the Credo series. One can further note that the pictorial program of the altarpiece partly repeats the motives from the earlier wall paintings and sculptures of the church. Other Åland examples of altarpieces acquired from the area of the German Order come from Lemland, Saltvik and Jomala.

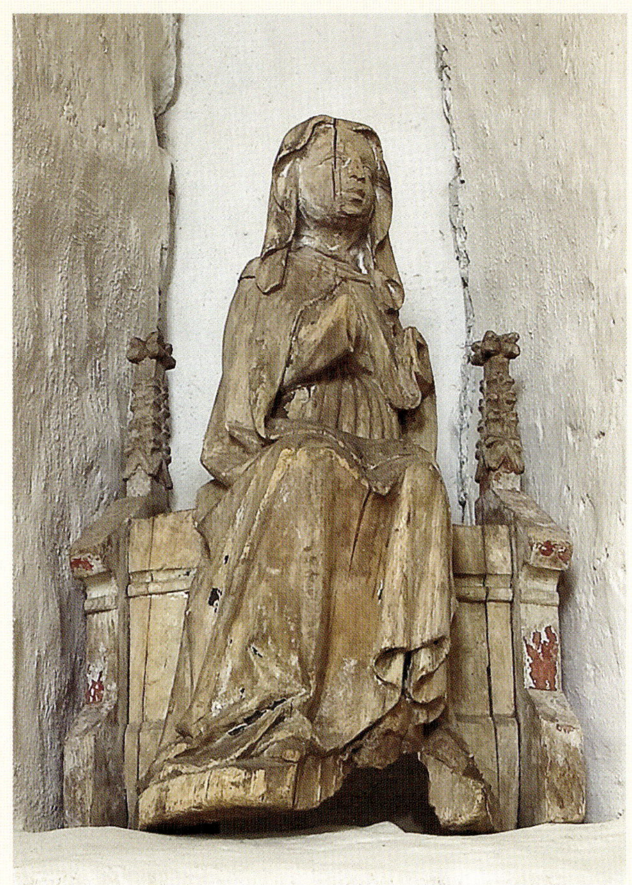

▲ Fig. 53.

Holy Birgitta of Sweden, wooden sculpture from Lemland, from the 15th century.

The wooden sculpture of Holy Birgitta is an example of the Birgittine cult sweeping over the whole of Europe in the 15th century. Earlier the church of Lemland was supposed to have been devoted to Holy Birgitta of Sweden, but it is more likely that she was included among the earlier patron saints, and that the church thus had three patron saints. The altarpiece where Birgitta is sharing space with Saint Nicolas and Saint Catherine of Alexandria indicates that this could be the case (cf. fig. 59). The strength of the Birgittine cult in Åland is further confirmed: every single altarpiece acquired to the Islands during the late Middle Ages, included images of Saint Birgitta, regardless of provenance. Lemland is one of four Birgittine churches in Finland, including the Birgittine convent church in Naantali.

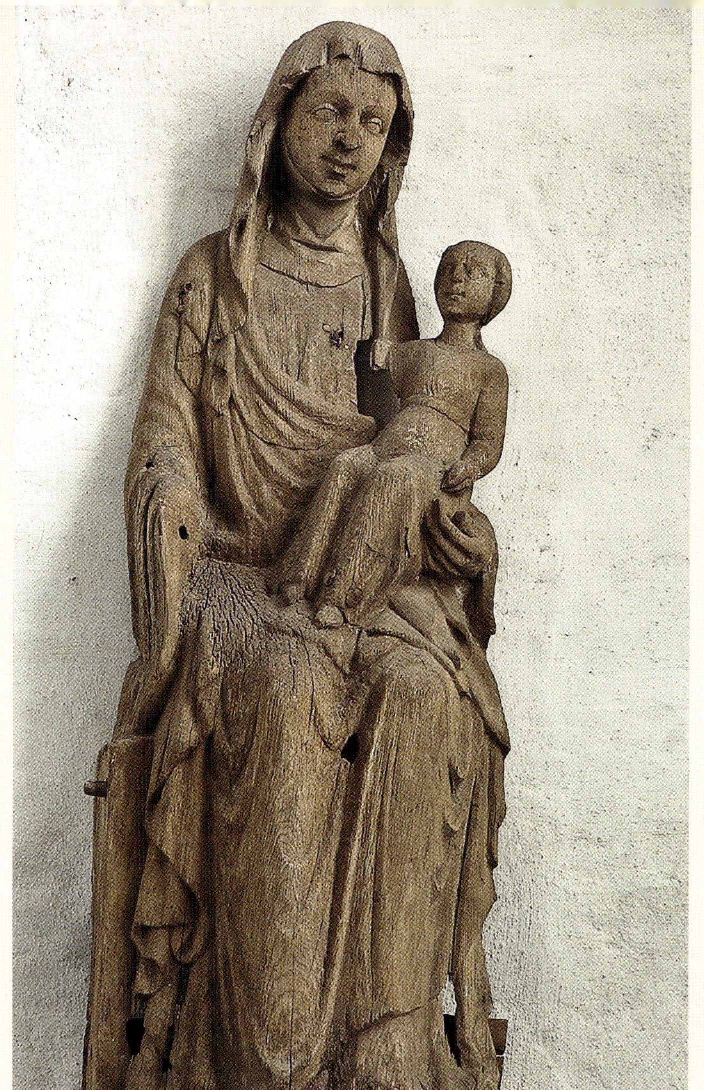

▲ Fig. 54.

Madonna transformed into Saint Anne, Jomala.

Saint Anne, a wooden sculpture from Jomala, is yet another Åland example of modernized sculptures in the Middle Ages. Originally this sculpture represented an elegantly carved Madonna, crowned and enthroned, with the Jesus Child on her left arm. She probably adorned the original Mary altar on the northern side of the triumphal arch. During the late Middle Ages somebody, using a blunt knife, transformed her from a Queen of Heaven into a coarse female figure. At the same time she got a new identity. Hereafter she is identified as Saint Anne, or as she is called in Art Historical vocabulary "Annaselbstdritt". This time, however, the traditional third generation, the little Jesus child in the lap of Mary, is missing.

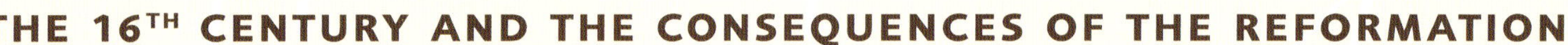

THE 16TH CENTURY AND THE CONSEQUENCES OF THE REFORMATION

The Reformation came to Sweden and Finland in the 1520s, on the initiative of Gustavus Vasa. The new Lutheran faith replaced Roman Catholicism, which for centuries had dominated all aspects of life. It is often thought that this also meant the end of Catholic art, that medieval wall paintings were whitewashed and that wooden sculptures were destroyed. In reality nothing of the kind happened in Åland.

Compared to the rest of Europe, Sweden and Finland have a large treasure of images preserved intact from the Middle Ages. The reason is that the newly Lutheran Sweden took another line of action in this matter than did other reformed countries. Johan III, son of Gustavus Vasa and King of Sweden 1568-92, was married to the Catholic princess Catharina Jagellonica from Poland, which influenced the King's attitude towards Catholicism. Rather than confrontation he looked for mediation between different faiths. Concretely Archbishop Laurentius Petri expressed this in new church regulations, where the importance of continuity in the church organization was enhanced: Destructive and iconoclastic mistakes from other areas should be expressly avoided; instead old traditions should be honored.

In Åland, as in other parts of the Swedish kingdom, there was no ***iconoclasm****.

What happened as a result of the Reformation was that churches with their decorations and medieval fittings were not maintained and fell into decay. The Franciscan convent at Kökar was closed. The Lutheran vicar moved into the old refectory north of the convent church, which was left to decay so much that the congregation had to erect a simple timbered chapel south of the church on the churchyard area.

Because the ecclesiastical liturgy was about to be completely transformed, liturgical manuscripts were subject to systematic destruction. However, fragments of valuable and strong liturgical books, written on parchment, were to survive as covers for accounts in the new administration. Usually the fragments lack provenance, i.e., it was not known which church they came from. Among the accounts from Kastelholm are fragments from churches all over Finland. It is therefore quite remarkable that a secondary inscription on one of the fragments could result in the identification of seven parchment folios as belonging to the church of Finström, where they had been used during a memorial service for Gustavus Vasa's burial in 1560. On that occasion

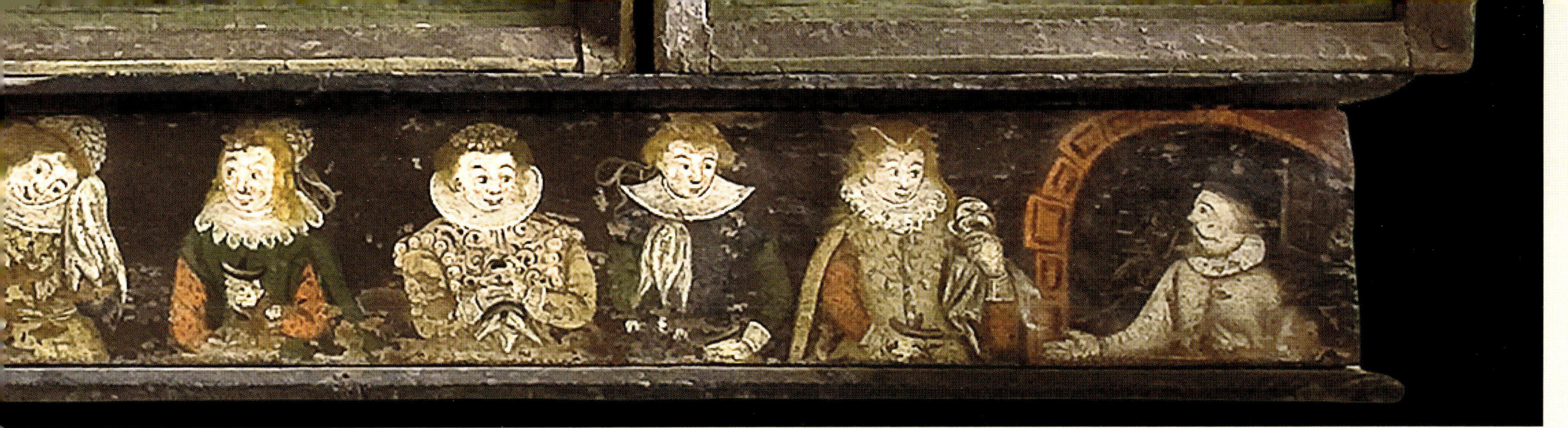

▲ Fig. 55.

The predella under the medieval altarpiece in Finström.

in Finström they still used their Dominican sequentionary from the 1320s. One wonders if Gustavus Vasa turned in his grave!

Otherwise there are no written sources concerning the churches, but the situation seems to have been generally chaotic. Decay and neglect prevailed everywhere. In the Lutheran liturgy the sermon was of central importance. Therefore occasional pulpits and pews were acquired for the churches, so that the congregation could listen to the sermon while seated.

The kingdom suffered constantly from the lack of cash and material for warfare, which in turn resulted in a general confiscation of metal. Both church silver and church bells were confiscated, thus facing the same sad fate as the liturgical manuscripts. The precious metals were melted down to feed the royal bursary, and metals from the church bells were recast for canons and other military purposes. Traces of church construction and repairs in the 16th century are occasionally seen in dendrochronological analysis. For instance, it seems as if some ***roof trusses**** in Geta chapel had been replaced at the end of the century. ■

A predella is the elongated horizontal substructure of an altarpiece. The paintings on the predella at Finström are in many ways unusual. The obviously secondary layer of paint represents "The Wise and the Foolish Virgins", according to the parable (Gospel of Matthew, 25:1-12) about ten maidens waiting for the bridegroom, symbolizing Christ. Five of the virgins face north, with their lamps lit, turning towards the cross-haloed groom/Jesus, seated in a vaulted space. The other five virgins towards the south have no light in their lamps. The parable thus tells us about the importance of being well prepared for the coming of Christ.
For those virgins who waited for Christ, with their lamps lit, the gates to Heaven were wide open. They could enter Heaven together with Christ, whereas the gates remained closed for the foolish maidens with no light in their lamps. Parallel to the "Last Judgment" the parable of "The Wise and Foolish Virgins" has been an important symbol of justice. Ever since the 12th century the motive has often recurred in the decorations of church portals and church façades. The parable has also been used in liturgical drama. In Finström, the wise and the foolish virgins of the reredos can also be linked to the "Last Judgment" which recurs twice on the eastern chancel wall. The virgins of the predella are painted in typical Renaissance style, however, with all ten virgins elegantly clothed in contemporary dress.

Even if some of the foolish virgins wipe their tears with a handkerchief, they seem as happy and pleased as the wise virgins. The model for the elegant worldly tempter in the far south is not to be found in the text of the parable. Yet he does exist in the pictorial program of the Gothic cathedrals, for instance in Strasbourg. The predella has not been conserved, which means that we know nothing about the paintings hiding under the Renaissance version, most likely another earlier version of the same theme. Even if the exact time for the over painting remains unclear, we can establish that the style is unique of its kind in Åland, where no other paintings or works of art remain from the latter part of the 16th century.

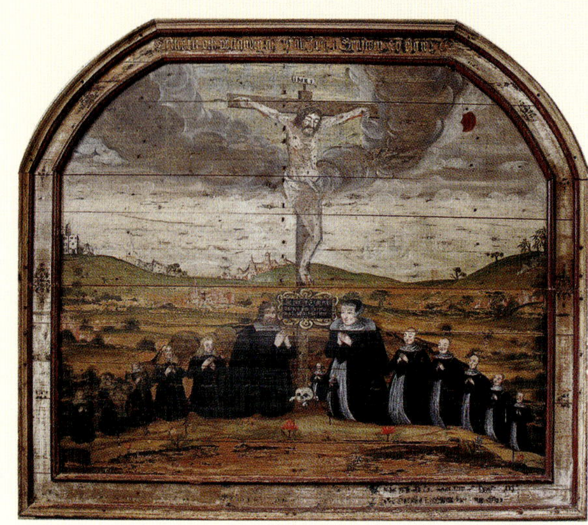

THE 17TH CENTURY – GREAT POWER ERA AND SEVERITY

Åland in the 17th century is unusually well documented thanks to *Acta Visitatoria*, the visitation records of Dean Boetius Murenius from 1636-66. And they do not only concern ecclesiastic matters. The records illustrate Åland in a very versatile and penetrating way. Murenius describes social and health care, the school system, culture and civilization, and further he documents the incredible decay prevailing in the Islands when he took office. The churches were in a terrible state, and vigorous efforts were needed to return to order. Indirectly this means that church building and any art acquisitions must have been neglected ever since the Reformation.

We can follow the building of new wooden chapels in Sottunga, Brändö and in Lumparland, which in each case replace older medieval wooden constructions. In Kökar a temporary wooden chapel was erected, south of the convent church. The fittings of the churches were renewed according to the new demands of the Lutheran church. Medieval side altars were removed (in Hammarland, Saltvik, Jomala and Geta) and with them some images of saints. Saint Olof especially was not popular with the ecclesiastic authorities, while Saint George was favored. Proper pews and galleries, screens and pulpits replaced provisional arrangements from earlier days. The church of Sund was damaged in a devastating fire in 1678, when the church bell from 1430, devoted to John the Baptist, melted down. The medieval wooden sculptures survived miraculously. Boetius Murenius had no tolerance with Catholic textiles: "papal flags" should be destroyed systematically. The painter Mårten Johansson, favorite artist of the Dean, got most of the ecclesiastic commissions, both wall paintings and paintings on cloth or panel. Much of his work was also purely decorative. Many of his works are still preserved, several of them signed with his characteristic handwriting.

It is no coincidence that some of the most important works of art from the 17th century belong to Saltvik church, where Boetius Murenius was vicar. During his time a Protestant painting program covered the interior of the church. Today only occasional fragments survive. Saint George seems to have been especially favored by Murenius. Several times he ordered images of Saint George to be repainted and prominently placed in the churches. He also had completely new images of Saint George commissioned. Generally speaking, Saint George was the Catholic saint who best survived the reformation in Sweden and Finland. "The Last Supper" became the prominent motive for new and renewed altarpieces during the 17th century.

The whitewashing of interiors of churches was initiated at the end of the century, but not for religious reasons. The walls simply needed cleaning. Most sculptures were repainted and thereafter replaced in their original positions. Not even sculptures in bad shape, rotten or dirty, were destroyed. Instead they were placed in the "rubbish chamber" of the church.

Generally the interiors became more severe and colorless, coats of arms and epitaphs now embellished the walls. Screens in galleries and pulpits were subject to decoration. The first organ of the Islands was commissioned for the church in Sund in 1671, and this church in general has quite remarkable art pieces of high quality from the 17th century.

At the same time we must remember that this century in Åland, like elsewhere in Europe, had a dark and frightening side – it was the time of witch persecutions. Often the clergy took an active part in this cruel drama, however, not Boetius Murenius. ■

◀ Fig. 56.

The church of Sund, votive painting from 1671.

Today this votive painting hangs in the porch of the church. It was painted by Abraham Myra (oil on panel, 2.45 x 2.75 m), and it depicts the vicar Bryniel Magni Kiellin surrounded by his family. It is the only Åland example of the so-called memorial paintings from the 17th century, forming a direct succession to the medieval donor's portraits.

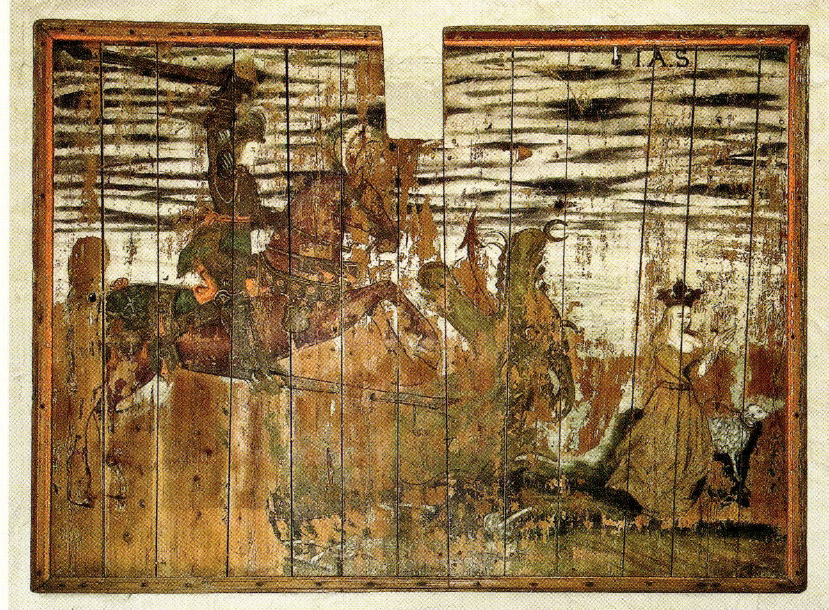

▲ Fig. 57.

Saint George and the Dragon, Saltvik church.

The painting representing Saint George and the Dragon in Saltvik was painted in 1659 by Mårten Johansson (oil on panel, 2.38 x 3.10m). At present it hangs on the northern wall of the tower. It was commissioned by Boetius Murenius to be a copy of the famous Saint George and the Dragon in the Great Church in Stockholm, representing the finest of European wooden carving. That equestrian statue, uncovered on New Year's Eve 1489, is a politically loaded work of art, where Saint George symbolizes Sten Sture senior after the victory in the battle of Brunkeberg. Together with the medieval group of Saint George in Finström church (Fig. 83), this painting in Saltvik presents an important documentation of the original arrangement in the Great Church. The Åland representations demonstrate that the princess originally kneeled in front of Saint George, turning her back to the Saint, and that the present arrangement in the Great Church is not accurate.

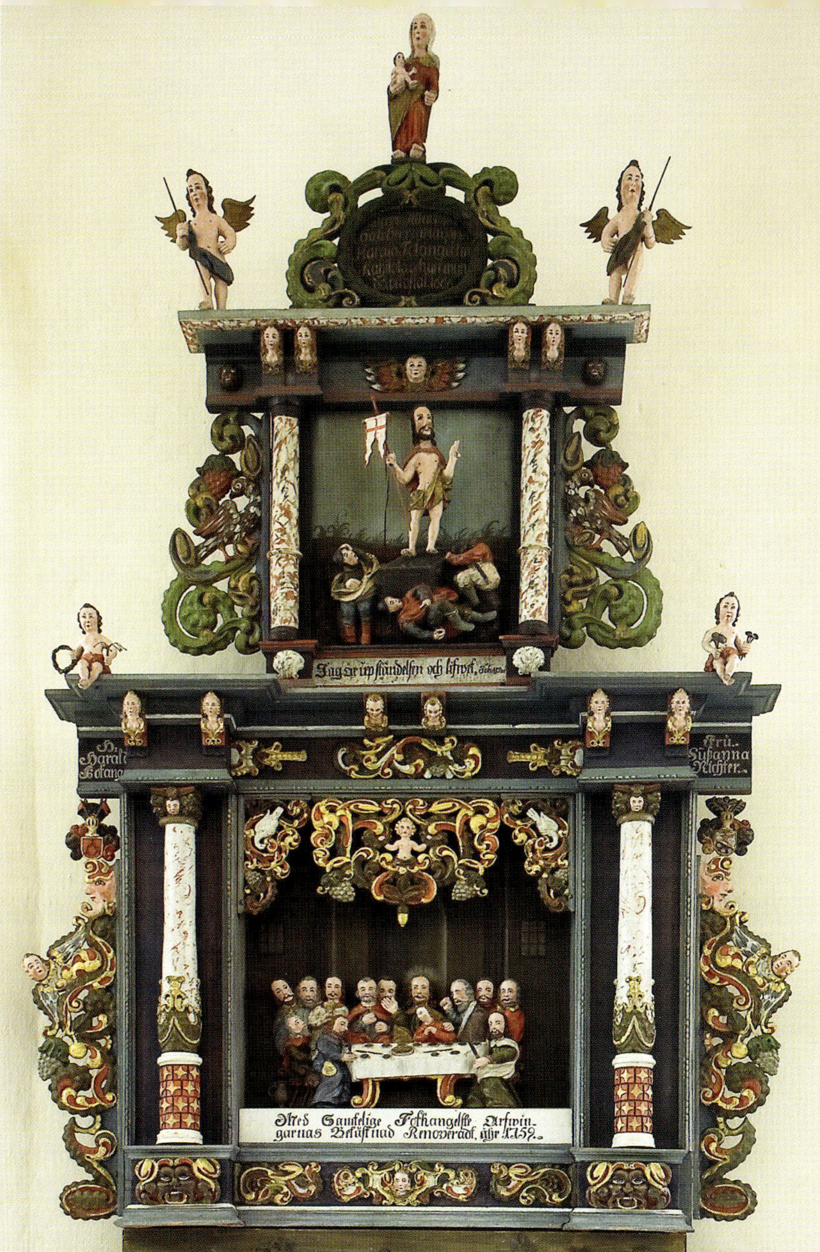

▲ Fig. 58.

Post-Reformation altarpiece in the church of Saltvik.

The church of Saltvik received this altarpiece in 1666 as a donation. The magnificent altarpiece was carved by Mathias Reiman from Turku, and was painted and gilded by Mårten Johansson. Major Harald Footangel of Germundö was the donor. The altarpiece, Baroque in style and two floors high, is carved in relief. The lower part represents The Last Supper, the upper the resurrection of Christ. The architectural framework is rich - with ornamental ***columns**** and ostentatious flourishes and mannerisms such as angels and putti.

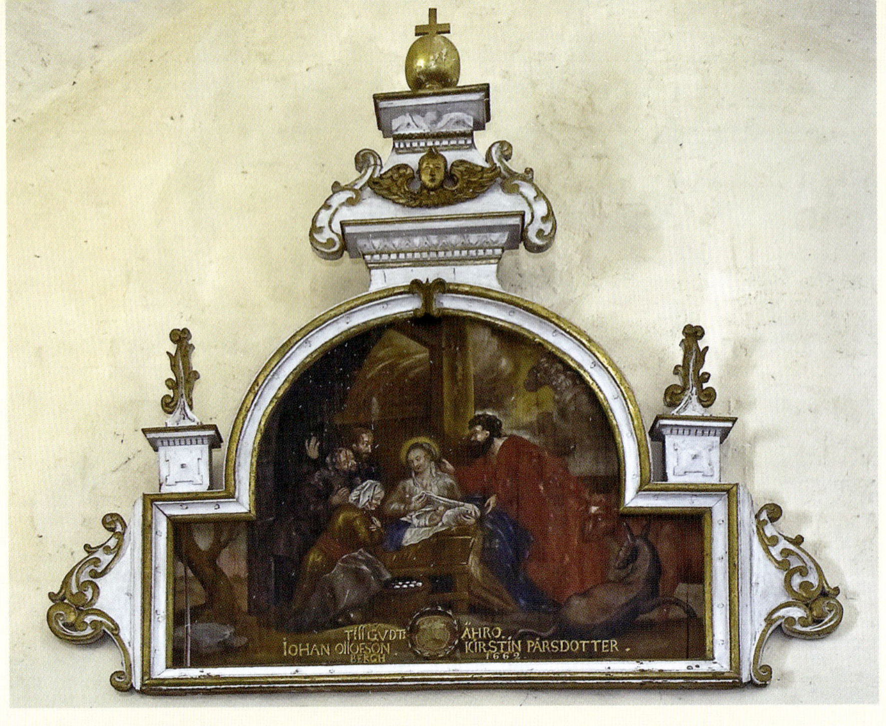

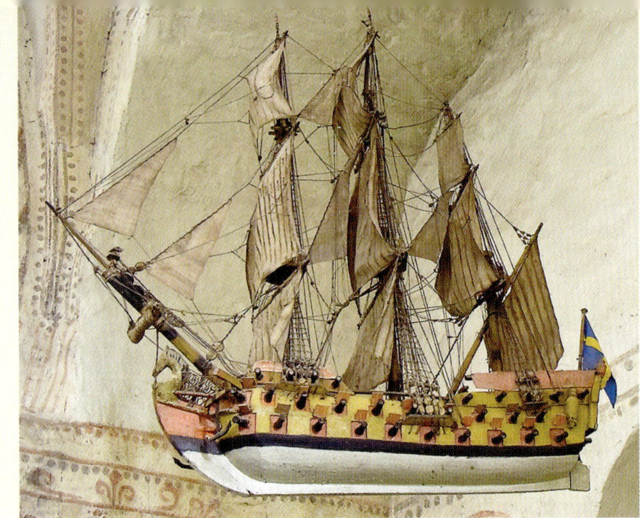

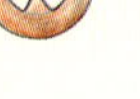

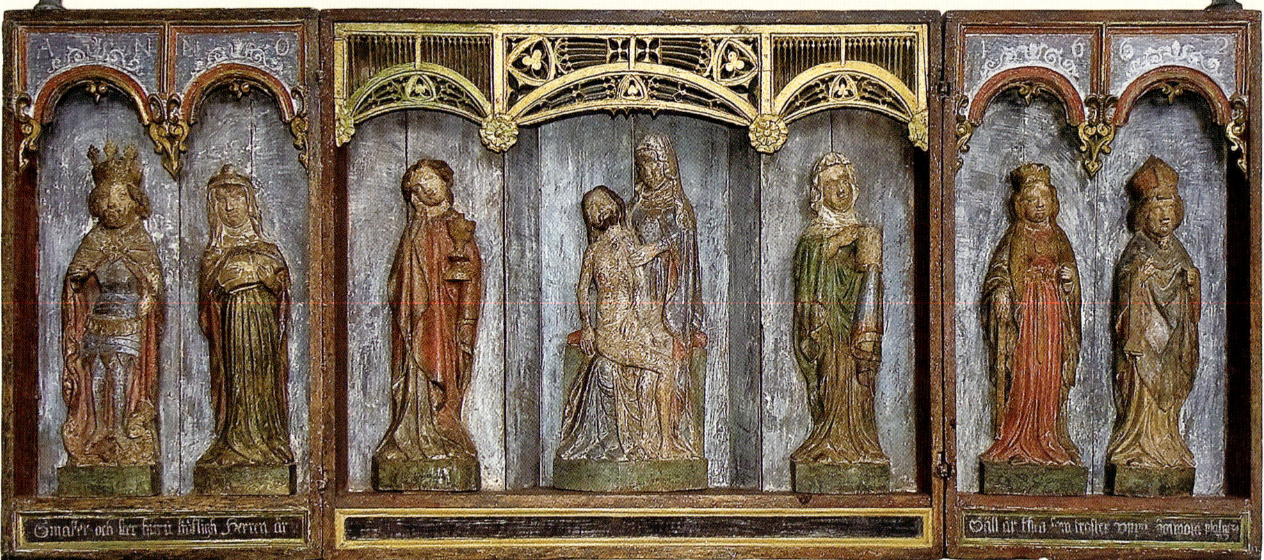

▲ Fig. 59.

The medieval altarpiece from Lemland, modernized in the 17th century.

According to the spirit of the time, the medieval altarpiece was equipped with a crowning segmental image representing The Last Supper, now removed. The donors were the couple Kristin Pedersdotter and Johan Olufson Berg (later Bergenstjerna) from Haddnäs. This couple donated a similar addition to the altarpiece in Sund, and they were generally well known as generous donors to other Åland churches.

▲ Fig. 60.

Church ship from Finström.

This ship from the church of Finström from 1688, donated by the marine officers from the northern part of the parish, is one of the oldest in the Islands. This time it really is a question of a votive ship, which means that it was given in gratitude as a gift. The donation was made after surviving an accident at sea, after being rescued from drowning and a happy return to the harbor, or it could simply be a way to pray for a blessed journey. Usually church ships have been seen as a Post-Reformation phenomenon, but there are indications that they could have belonged to the medieval fittings. During his visitations to single parishes, 1636-1666, Boetius Murenius time and again repeats that the "old, dirty and rotten ships" should be either cleaned or removed. The church accounts further show that the ships were not always votive offerings. The congregation often paid them "for the decoration of the church".

THE 18TH CENTURY - UNREST AND ENLIGHTENMENT

War and unrest were the reasons why the 18th century in Åland was not very significant for church building and church art. During the Great Northern War, 1714-1721, most of the Åland population was driven into exile, and the Islands were left unprotected against the marauding Russian troops. People endured enormous hardships, and the churches suffered greatly. Church archives include very detailed information about the vandalism and the heavy burden of the rebuilding after the peace treaty. A couple of dissertations concerning Åland were published in the 1730s, with some documentation about the churches that is hard to interpret. After the war the wooden churches of Sottunga and Lumparland were rebuilt from the foundations. Things were hardly finished before another war threatened in the 1740s. This time there was less damage, but the economy did not allow any big accessions.

The medieval church bells, not earlier destroyed by fire, disappeared during the Great Northern War, when they were stolen and melted down. Therefore most of the Åland church bells belong to the time after 1730.

The biggest transformation happened at the end of the century, when burials inside the church gradually ceased. The gentry and the clergy took the first initiatives in this direction. The reasons were primarily hygienic. In summer the bad smell was unbearable, and the job with eternal grave digging inside the churches was inconvenient. From now on the graves were laid in lines on the churchyard, carefully avoiding the "evil" northern side. The interiors of the churches were regularly whitewashed. A general increase in the population meant that the churches became too small. Everyone who was supposed to be present at mass could not fit into the church. Vårdö chapel church was enlarged in the 1780s, according to drawings made by the court architect Olof Samuel Tempelman, from Stockholm (Fig. 166). ■

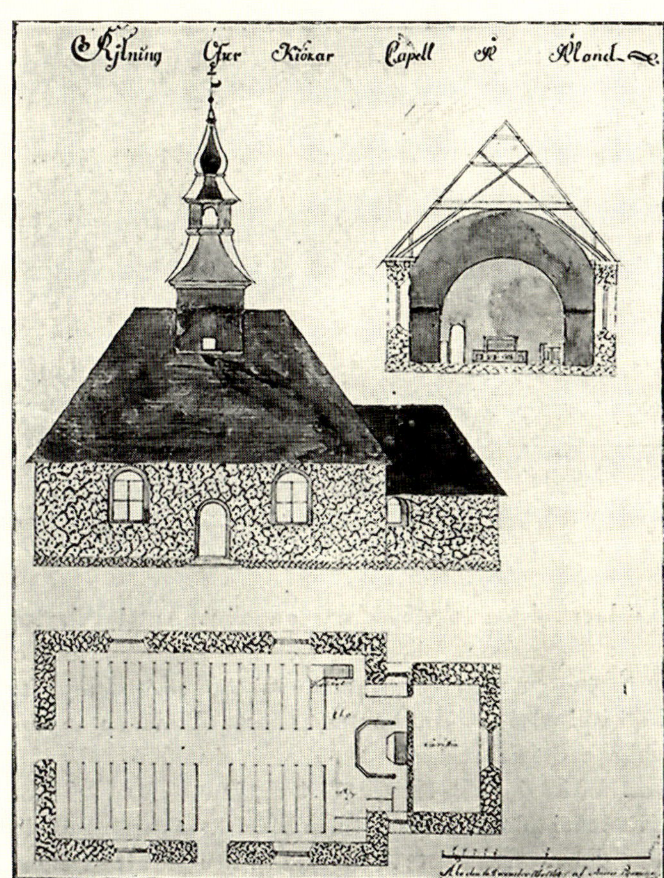

▲ Fig. 61.

Drawing for a stone church in Kökar, ca 1782.

At last it was time to replace the temporary wooden chapel in Kökar from the 17th century with a church in stone, erected on the foundations of the convent church. The carpenter Anders Hartlin-Piimänen designed this transformation drawing. Following a change of architect the church was erected according to another plan, more modern with a tripartite chancel. The wooden churches in Sottunga and Lumparland follow the same plan. The new stone church at Kökar was finished in 1784.

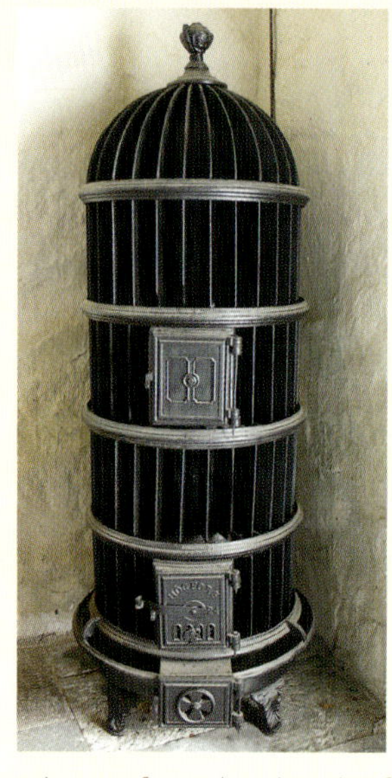

▲Fig. 62. Iron heater from the church of Saltvik, later part of the 19th century.

THE 19TH CENTURY – DEMANDS ON LIGHT AND HYGIENE DEVASTATE MEDIEVAL CHURCH INTERIORS

Before the 19th century the Åland churches in general did not undergo big changes. But the 19th century was the time for transformation on a large scale. Partly the churches were seen as too small, and partly the attitude towards light and hygiene had changed profoundly, with devastating results for the church architecture. Some of the churches, like Föglö and Jomala, were radically rebuilt, whereas others were subjected to harsh treatment when windows were opened in the earlier windowless northern walls, and when earlier windows were enlarged. This is how many valuable whitewashed wall paintings were lost forever, without even being documented for the future. Medieval vaults were torn down in Saltvik and in Jomala, whereas Föglö church practically changed appearance altogether. In Jomala and Saltvik original gables were pulled down to give place for new chancels. A new wooden chapel was erected in Brändö.

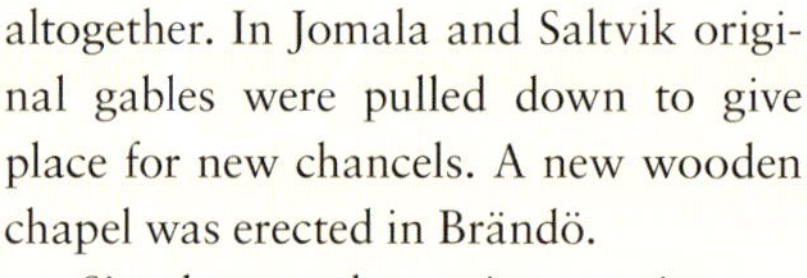

Simultaneously an interest in prehistory and the Middle Ages was awoken. Luckily for Åland research, Finlands's foremost medieval scholar Reinhold Hausen, had strong ties to the Islands. He had family roots at Germundö in Saltvik, and he spent all his summers in the area. From 1871 on his invaluable and well-illustrated documentations and publications he highlighted many important parts of medieval Åland. 1871 also marked the first art history expedition to the Islands arranged by the Finnish Antiquarian Society, with the aim to document every single church.

This also caused a new interest in medieval Åland among Finnish museums, and many remarkable acquisitions were made by the Historical Museum of Turku. On the other hand a need to modernize the church interiors was gradually felt. The old and large altarpieces were replaced by new altar paintings, painted on canvas, ordered from well-known artists such as Robert Wilhelm Ekman and Victor Westerholm.

It was not until this century that the convenience of the members of the congregation was a major issue. Gradually a discussion concerning the heating of the churches was initiated, something that had never been an issue before. One can easily imagine the freezing congregation in wintertime during long sermons in ice-cold churches. To begin with the discussion only focused on heating the sacristies, but towards the end of the century iron heaters were acquired for all the naves in the Islands. ■

THE 20TH CENTURY – CHURCH ARCHAEOLOGY, DOCUMENTATION AND RENOVATION

Architecturally Finström church is the one to have best survived the rebuilding zeal during the 19th century. No windows were opened towards the north. The existing windows of the church were enlarged, but no new windows were forced through the walls.

When, once more, it was time to whitewash the interior at the beginning of the 20th century, experts were hired to examine the church walls. In 1903 the architectural student Carl Frankenhaeuser initiated the uncovering of the wall paintings according to a method he had learnt at Ringsted church in Denmark. That is partly why Finström church today appears as the best preserved medieval building in the whole of Finland. This applies to both exterior and interior, both wall paintings and wooden sculptures.

The interest in the building history of the Åland churches, already awoken in the 18th century, grew in intensity.

During the 20th century bigger changes in church architecture generally was avoided except for the concrete vaults in Saltvik. Rather the focus was laid on restoration, heating and general electrification. In connection with the restorations the churches were archaeologically investigated and for individual churches the Åland Board of Antiquities prepared detailed plans for maintenance. All of this contributed to a more stable foundation for building historical research.

Until the inauguration of Saint George's church in Mariehamn in 1927, Mariehamn ecclesiastically belonged to Jomala. However, since the church of Mariehamn, designed by Lars Sonck, lacks medieval roots, it is not included in this survey.

As a historical source it illuminates the 20th century in Mariehamn, and should therefore, together with other modern church buildings and chapels, be treated in connection with the architecture of the town, and that is a different story. ■

THE ÅLAND CHURCHES AND THE SURROUNDING WORLD.

The differences between the Åland churches and Gotland, Uppland, Estonia and the Finnish mainland are remarkable. There is, unfortunately, not enough space here for a complete characterization of the churches of those surrounding areas.

Åland is in no way the most densely built of these other Baltic areas. The 90 churches in the Gotland countryside stand much closer to one another. Medieval Uppland has more than 180 stone churches. Also in Finland Proper the churches were erected close to one another. Even so, the total number of medieval stone churches in sparsely populated areas in Finland remains small.

The quality of church building and church art in Gotland ranks among the highest in medieval Europe. Because of the unbelievable richness accumulated on the island ever since the Iron Age and the monopoly in the trade on the Baltic Sea, the Gotland churches were well taken care of. Church building there was already under way in the 11th century. To begin with the churches were erected in wood, in stave and in timber-framed construction. Nevertheless stone building was initiated very early, and an eternal wish for enlarging, improving and embellishing can be traced in a regular homogeneous pattern all around the island. The use of stone sculptures in church decoration is beyond comparison, and the same is true of stained glass, wall paintings, fonts and wooden sculptures. Stylistically everything is unmistakably Gotlandish. West towers are the rule, as are priest's doors leading into the narrower and lower chancels. Several of the churches have two naves, and fieldstones were used in the vaulting. Yet everything in Gotland ended abruptly, when the Black Death struck, and when Valdemar Atterdag, the Danish king, in 1361 raided and destroyed the countryside. Gotland never really recovered from these tragedies; art and architecture came to a standstill. Compared to the earlier splendour, what was achieved in the late Middle Ages was of poor quality. In Gotland there are hardly any porches. Otherwise, all west towers and porches are, as in Åland, secondary in relation to the nave.

The Uppland stone churches are more varied. There church building also started early, even if the late Middle Ages seem to dominate. From an introduction with relatively simple small Romanesque churches, hall churches also emerge during the latter part of the 13th century, alongside with churches with separate narrow chancels. There was a larger variation in the plan solutions. No regular pattern in church building can be discerned, as in Gotland. No abrupt breaks can be seen, in church building or in church art. Western towers are not common, nor are two aisles/naves. Bricks are important building materials since the 13th century. Without exception the vaults in the naves are in brick. Fieldstone vaults are to be found only in small spaces, such as sacristies or separate chancels. Whole-covering wall paintings belong to the 15th century.

At present the chronology of the stone churches in medieval Finland is under discussion. But regardless of this we can conclude that there are distinct differences between churches in the Finnish mainland and those in Åland. Generally it seems that the stone churches on the Finnish mainland are slightly younger than the Åland churches. They are generally larger, and the three-aisled rectangular church is predominant. Brick is usual in vaulting and in the upper parts of the gables. West towers are unusual. Fieldstone vaults in the naves are not found, nor Gothic wall paintings.

Åland also had rich contacts with Estonia during the Middle Ages. Some medieval churches in Estonia, especially on the island of Saarenmaa, resemble the Gotland churches. Influence from Saarenmaa, can possibly be traced in the cupola-like vaults in the nave of Hammarland church. ■

CONCLUSION

Even if much yet remains to investigate, and even if details certainly will change and be adjusted, the total picture is gradually emerging. Most important is that we now stand on a more stable foundation as far as the chronology of the churches is concerned. Within the Åland Churches Project we have participated in a challenging and promising development of the method to date non-hydraulic lime mortars. Now the testing of the method continues in other topographies and other chronologies.

It is still unclear when the first generation of wooden churches was erected in the Åland Islands. Stone churches, however, belong to the 13th century, and only Jomala can present an example of Romanesque stone architecture, with strong Gotland features in the details. Could it have been a privately owned church? In no case does it influence the other Åland churches stylistically. Six mother churches were erected on the main island, including Eckerö, during the latter half of the century. Right now it seems as though Sund presents a model for the other churches. Even if Sund represents a church with a rectangular plan, not found in Gotland, the church is entirely impregnated by a Gotland style in architecture, painting, sculpture, and in decorative details. Even if the two early churches, Jomala and Sund, are so different from each other, they both reflect strong influence from Gotland, both in architecture and in art.

The influence from Sund can be traced in the other churches. It concerns relatively small churches, different variations of the hall churches with rectangular plans including the chancel. The churches are south bound, both main portal and priest door facing south. High and narrow window openings, lined with local Ordovician limestone, also face south. The vaulting in two naves in Sund was repeated only in Saltvik, where fieldstones were also used in the vaulting. Also horizontal paneled wooden ceilings can be found. The early stone church of Finström cannot be reconstructed.

Of all the Åland churches during the 13th century, it is only the church in Jomala that presents a different plan. In neighbouring areas, as for instance in Uppland, where the hall church is found more or less simultaneously, it was by no means dominant. More common were churches with narrower chancels, often ending in apses, and these were gradually changed into hall churches. There is a hypothesis that the rectangular hall church represents a simple plan influenced by Franciscans and Dominicans.

In general it is difficult to point at direct models for the Åland churches. Architecturally the 13th century dominates, but the quality is high also artistically. High-class wall paintings from the end of the 13th century in three different churches, so close to one another, are almost unheard of in our latitudes. Exquisite wooden sculptures were imported from abroad, not to mention the overseas acquisition of stained glass and fonts.

The finest wooden sculptures were imported even earlier, by the end of the 12th century. Of stained glass, apparently once rather common on the Islands, today only a few shards remain. The rich wall paintings point to contacts to the south, towards southern Scandinavia and Gotland. With wooden sculptures one can also discern Åland workshops, active already at the beginning of the 13th century.

The economic boom forming the base for dynamic church building and ornamentation must have depended on extensive trading and export. Such commercial activity included above all building materials, such as timber and burned lime, and food, mainly fish. Flourishing markets were to be found nearby, both in the west and in the east. This was the time of the foundation of Stockholm, probably also of Turku.

In the 14th century church building reached the outer islands. Art trade continued to flourish. No stagnation can be seen, except perhaps in wall painting. Western towers and other secondary-building units were added to older naves. Nothing suggests that Åland at this stage was struck by the Black Death, except that the influence from Gotland ended. Many prominent Åland vicars and other personalities appear in the sources, and contacts to the Papal Curia in Avignon were lively. But when it comes to information on the churches news is still scarce. In spite of valuable art acquisitions, the 14th century cannot compare with the dynamic 13th century. It is often claimed that Kastelholm castle belongs to the end of the 14th century, when it is mentioned in historical sources for the first time. But it is better to be careful – before the building has gone through systematic ^{14}C AMS-analysis of the mortar, and any possible encapsulated splints of wood, Kastelholm lacks an objective basis for dating.

Åland during the 15th century is marked by continued good economy. Architecturally the focus was on the rebuilding of Finström church and new stone chapels in Geta and Vårdö. The churches of Saltvik, Eckerö and Föglö, possibly also Kökar, were secondarily vaulted in brick. West towers were continuously erected, as at Finström, Eckerö and Föglö. The influence from Turku Cathedral is very strong in Finström. The 15th century is the time of large altarpieces, and of whole-covering wall paintings.

We are slowly reaching our goal. The chronology of the Åland churches begins to take shape, and the churches can tell their story. Yet important parts are still missing. To understand what happened during the enigmatic period 1000-1200, we need to focus on house foundations from the Iron Age, attached to graveyards nearby, and the areas surrounding the churches. This research, too, will be of great interest and will all further strengthen the story of a remarkable collection of churches. ■

Chapter 2

CHURCH BY CHURCH

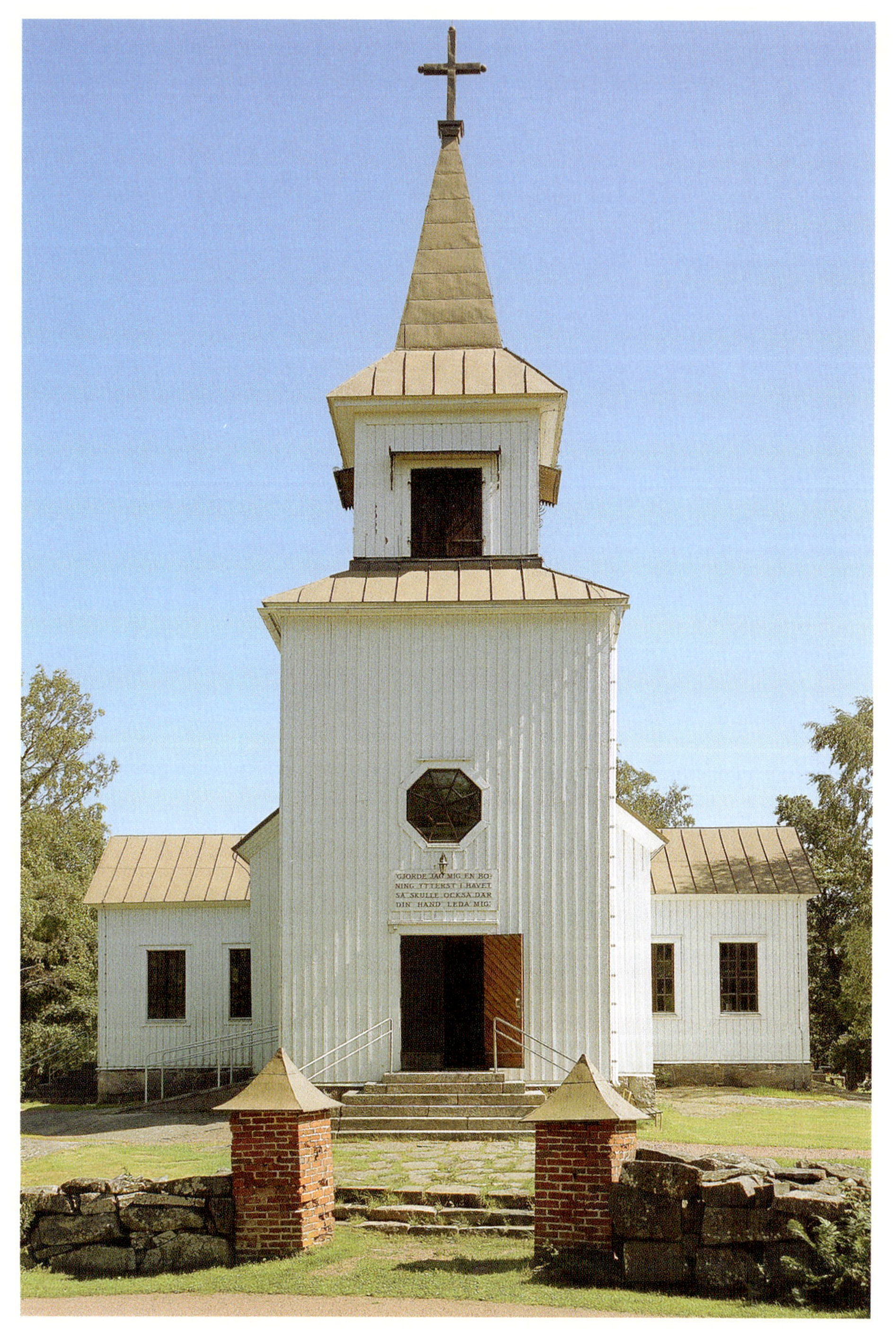
GJORDE JAG MIG EN BO-
NING YTTERST I HAVET
SÅ SKULLE OCKSÅ DÄR
DIN HAND LEDA MIG

BRÄNDÖ CHAPEL

Saint James's Chapel in Brändö belongs to Kumlinge mother church. The present wooden church, probably the fourth chapel in Brändö, was dedicated on October 22 1893.

It was erected in isolation from other habitation, by the northern shore of the main island of Brändö in the eastern archipelago. The new building was adjacent to an earlier bell tower. The builder in charge and building surveyor was David Lönnroth from Uusikaupunki.

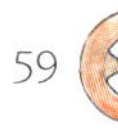

THE EXTERIOR

The white painted church is roofed by galvanized sheet iron. It has a cruciform plan, with subordinated cross arms closer to the chancel. The dominant east-west axis is further accentuated by the sacristy to the east and the tower to the west. Fourteen windows of equal size are evenly distributed along the façades. The main entry, the west door of the tower, is crowned by a small round window. The tower has a square plan narrowing stepwise upwards. It rises in full scale above the roof of the church where it narrows down to form a superstructure for the hanging of the bells. The sound openings face all four cardinal directions. The spire of the tower, crowned by a cross, has a steep pyramidal roof, with sloping brims flaring at the edges.

GROUND PLAN

The plan of the church is shaped like a cross with a dominating longitudinal axis and subordinated *transepts**. The sacristy finishes the eastern *cross arm** and to the west a narrow bell tower is added to the main axis.

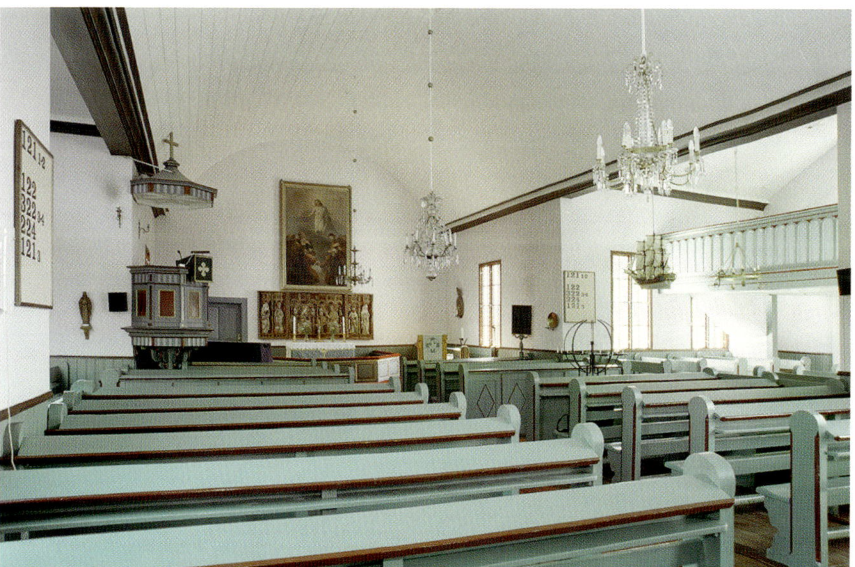

▲ Fig. 64. Brändö church. Interior towards the east.

◀ Fig. 63. Brändö church, exterior from the west.

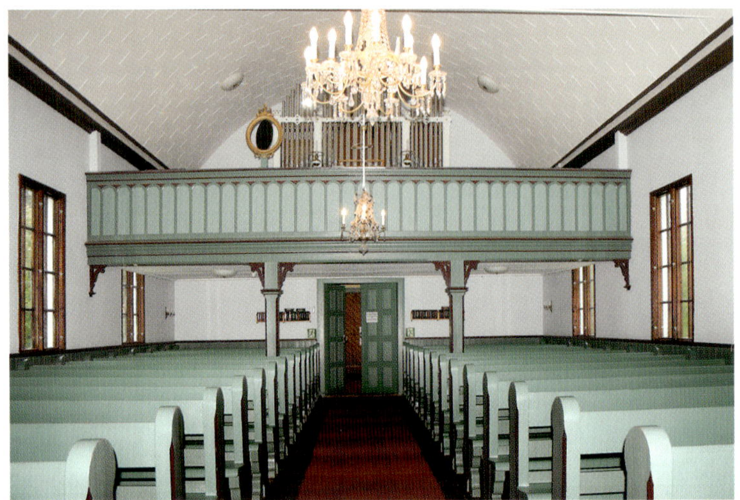

▲ Fig. 65. Brändö church, interior towards the west.

THE INTERIOR

The interior is spacious and light, with a cool color scheme in gray and greenish blue. The longitudinal axis also dominates the cross arms in the interior (with a surface of 163 square meters). The subordinated cross arms are shorter and not as tall. The difference in height is noticeable, since it varies between 6.2m in the longitudinal axis and 4.2m in the cross arms. The ceiling of the longitudinal axis has a barrel vault, while the cross arms have a double pitched ceiling. The chancel occupies the space east of the cross arms. The pulpit, probably carved by Johan Sipelius in 1746, sits in the northeastern corner of the cross arms. The eye catcher is the eastern chancel wall with its double altar decorations - the original medieval altarpiece placed under the big altar painting of the Ascension of Christ, painted in 1883 by Alexandra Såltin-Frosterus. The cross arms contain galleries, while the organ gallery is placed against the west gable wall.

BUILDING HISTORY

The chapel of Saint James in Brändö is first mentioned in connection with the confiscations of Gustavus Vasa in 1544, when the chapel lost a copper bell. Yet an early inventory from 1631 mentions "two Bells, one very small. An altarpiece, somewhat old".

The simple medieval wooden chapel was documented in a visitation in 1637:

The chapel was completely rotten and the entire interior is unskillfully built. It was decided that it should be rebuilt, that it was to be 30 ells long and 18 ells wide, as soon as the mother church had been renovated externally and internally. In the meantime improvements have to be made on roof and floors, the inner door has to be removed, the long beam across the middle of the church must be cut further down, since boys have been hiding behind it, the bell from the altar must be moved to the rear, the windows improved and bird droppings cleared from the entire church, along with all the debris that fills her.

The new wooden chapel was not erected until the end of the 1640s, further north and in a dryer place. The chapel was prefabricated in Saltvik, from selected pine timber. It measured 14.75 x 10.67m, with an inner height of only 2.4m. Porch and sacristy were part of the plan, both measuring 3.50 x 3.50m, and barely high enough for a tall upright man. The roof was covered with birch bark and wedged boards. A new church bell was acquired in 1685. An interesting note indicates that a new altarpiece was to be acquired. Simultaneously the congregation should "get rid of the old images, standing here and there in the women's benches, as for idolatry," probably referring to the medieval altarpiece. Already in 1688 there were complaints that leaking roofs were destroying the chapel.

In 1749 the prefabricated chapel was replaced by a new wooden church in Brändö. The building master was Mats Sipilä from Turku. Johan Sipelius did all the carpentry. This time the church had a cruciform plan, with an entrance to the west and south and a sacristy as an extension of the cross arm towards the north. After substantial repairs in the beginning of the 19th century, the visitation records and inventories reveal an attractive entirety.

The church measured just over 20m from east to west. The ceilings of the cross arms had wooden vaulting. Out of a total of 15 windows, two larger ones marked the chancel, at the end of the eastern cross arm. The center of the cross was crowned by a lantern, with four minor windows. The interior coloring was blue. According to the inventory from 1840 the pulpit was "Berliner blue" with black mirrors and gilded framework. It was crowned by a sky in light blue. The church had three galleries, all Berliner blue with light mirrors framed in yellow. The interior of the church was mottled (marbled) in 1840. The ceiling was painted white. New pews from 1837 were provided with numbered doors, painted in Prussian blue. Even in the sacristy the windows were Prussian blue and the inner walls mottled. The altar and the altar ring had the same blue coating. The church doors were green. The painter Hellsten came from Uusikaupunki.

Wooden paneling covered the exteriors of the walls. Everything was

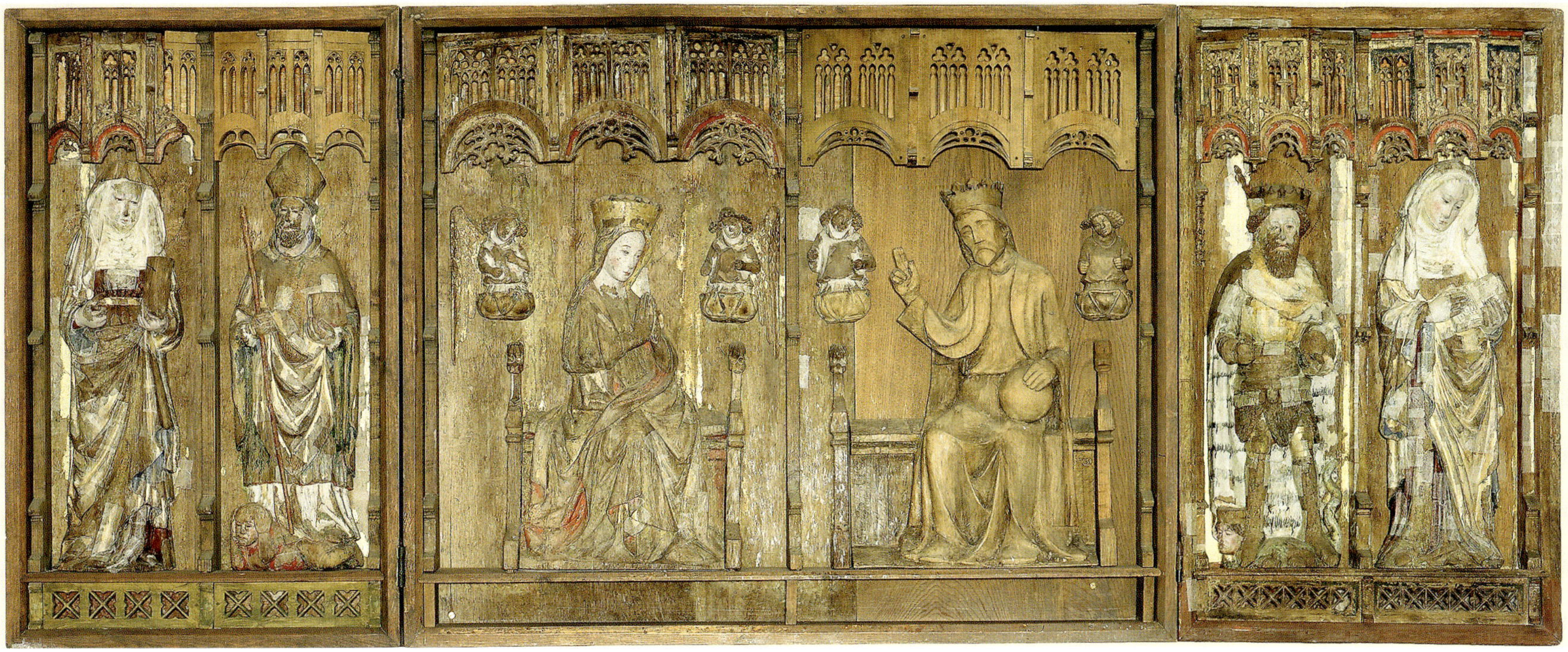

▲ Fig. 66. An Altarpiece from the middle of the 15th century, depicting the Coronation of the Virgin, is the only medieval inventory left in the church.

painted red, including the wooden roof. The church had a freestanding 7,6m tall belfry in framed timber, also in red. The exterior of the belfry was paneled and shingled. The inventory mentions a little cast bell, fastened to the chancel wall by a little wooden tower, probably identical to the little bell mentioned already in 1631. The medieval altarpiece had survived in "two pieces of wooden tablets above each other on the altar, and another ditto on the chancel wall". Another church bell was acquired in 1845.

Because of the marshy location a new building was planned in 1874. A drier place for the church had been selected already in the 1640s. Lack of space was another urgent issue. After an inspection the new building was moved to the stony slope by the older belfry.

INVENTORY

The altarpiece, of astoundingly high quality, was acquired from the Lübeck area in the middle of the 15th century. In the last restoration it regained its original medieval appearance. The coloring is preserved only in parts. The altarpiece is formed like a triptych, with a corpus flanked by side wings, which could be opened or closed according to liturgical needs. The corpus presents the coronation of the Virgin, where the queen-like seated Madonna is being humbly crowned by her son, likewise crowned. The figures are surrounded by angels hovering on the clouds. The side wings are dominated by saints popular in Scandinavia. They are, from the left, St. Mary Magdalene, with her ointment vessel, Henrik, the national saint of Finland, Olav, the national saint of Norway, and finally Saint Birgitta of Sweden. All figures are crowned by openwork ***baldachins****.

The same iconography, i.e. the Coronation of the Virgin in the corpus, surrounded by Scandinavian saints in the wings, reoccurs in the Birgittine convent church of Naantali. Two bells hang in the west tower of the church, one from 1685 and the other from 1845. ■

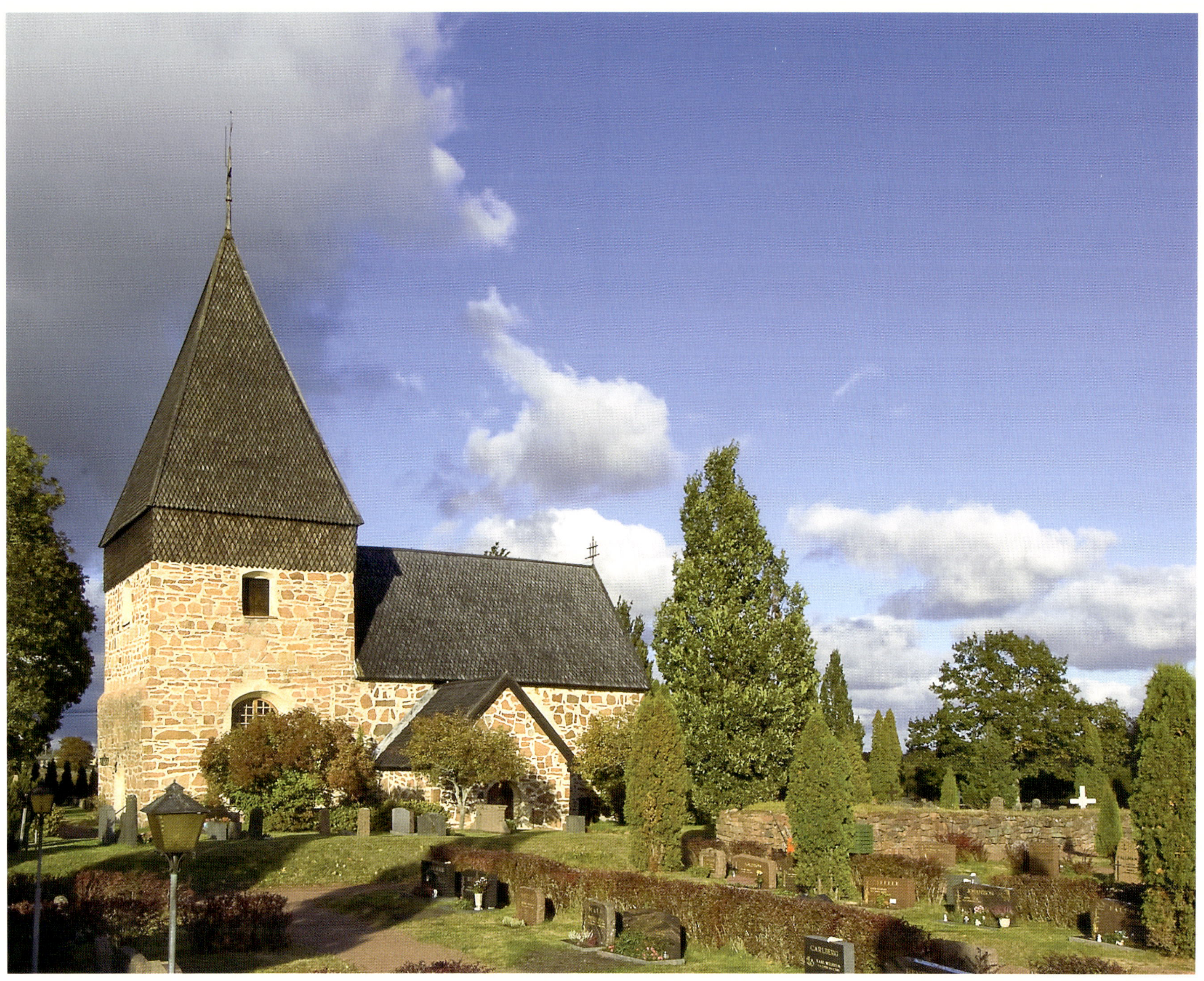

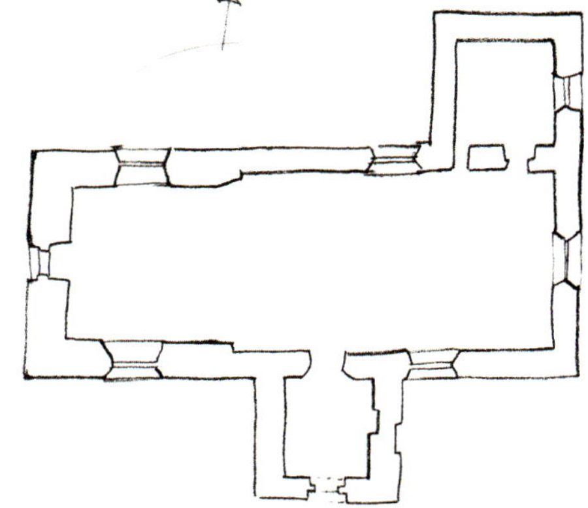
▲ Fig. 68. Eckerö church, ground plan.

ECKERÖ CHURCH

Eckerö parish, the westernmost part of the Åland archipelago, is separated from the main Åland island by the strait of Marsundet.

The nearest Iron Age burial ground lies just north of the churchyard. Less than a kilometre north of the church runs the old postal road, which probably functioned as a pilgrimage route westwards from Finland during the Middle Ages. Eckerö church, one of the smallest in the Islands, is consecrated to the Roman martyr Saint Lawrence (Laurentius). The unusual decoration on the east gable symbolizes a grill, the saint's instrument of torture; he was martyred by grilling in AD 258 immediately outside Rome.

THE EXTERIOR

Like the other Åland churches, Eckerö church is built of Åland red rapakivi granite. It lacks a visible outer socle. The nave is comparatively low and small, with an outsized west tower, built as a direct continuation of the north and south walls of the nave. The main entry to the west is in the middle axis of the tower. A high pyramidal hood crowns the relatively low tower. Both the hood and the upper part of the tower are covered by tarred shingles. The eastern façade of the nave shows archaic features, like high and pointed granite slabs put up along ground level, and the form of the walled-in remnants of the outermost roof truss in the eastern gable. The chancel window facing east is nowadays a walled-up blind window. The other exteriors have big window openings facing north and south. Vertical joints of the wall show that the tower was built later, and that it is resting on the west gable of the nave. Also the porch towards the south, with a shallow niche in the eastern wall, is later than the nave. The eastern wall of the sacristy forms a continuation of the eastern chancel wall.

GROUND PLAN

The present ground plan gives the illusion of a rectangular nave of unusually long proportions, with a sacristy in the northeast corner and a porch towards the south. However, from the thickness of the walls, approximately 1m, we know the original dimensions of the nave. It was a rectangular hall church measuring in the interior 13.4 x 7.4m. The western gable wall is missing. The west tower, with considerably thicker walls, was erected as a continuation of the nave.

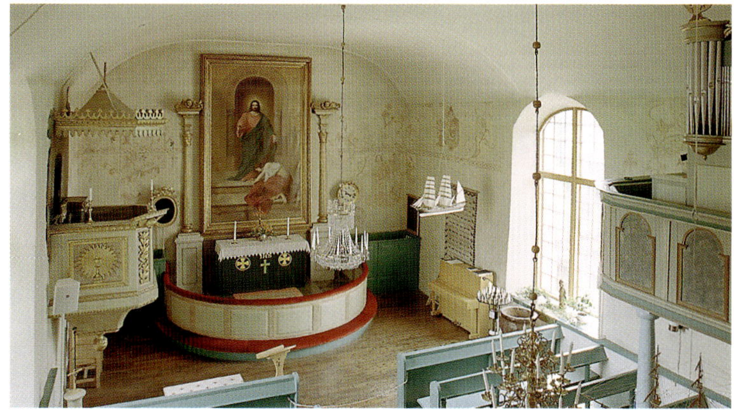
▲Fig. 69. Eckerö church. Interior towards the east.

◀ Fig. 67. The church of Eckerö, exterior from the southwest.

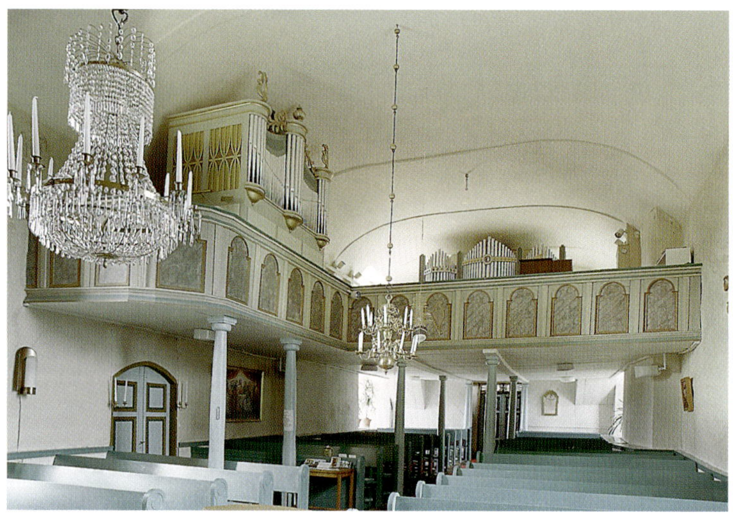

▲ Fig. 70. Eckerö church. Exterior towards the west.

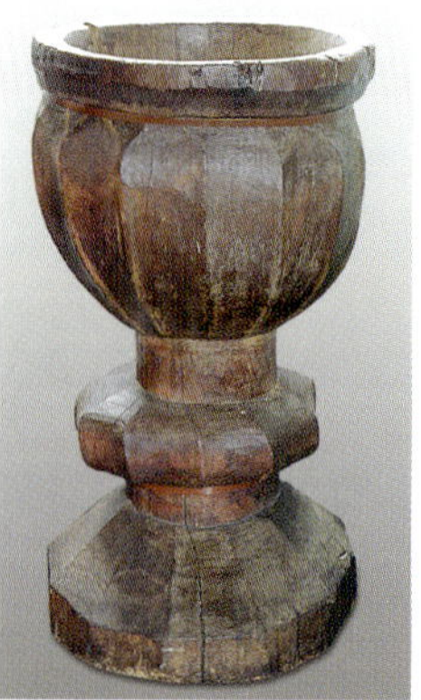

▲ Fig. 71. Eckerö. Medieval wooden font.

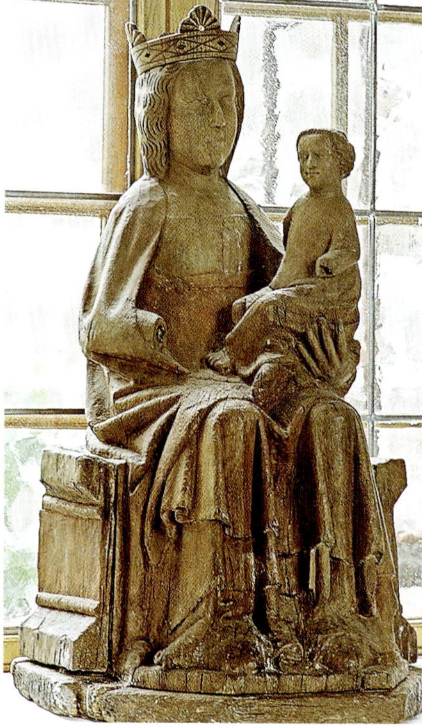

▲ Fig. 72. Eckerö. Madonna enthroned, oak.

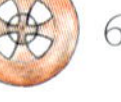

THE INTERIOR

In spite of its humble size the interior of the church in Eckerö gives an impression of space and light. Light floods into the church through unusually high and wide window openings towards the north and the south, and in the ground floor of the tower. More space was gained by removing the west gable of the nave. In the interior thus the nave and the ground floor of the tower merge together into one single space. The preserved inner corners of the original western wall of the nave are hardly noticeable. A flat wooden vault forms the ceiling. The organ gallery fills up the western church space. The pulpit that can be reached directly from the sacristy through a passage in the wall, dominates the northern wall. Placed unusually far to the east is the north sacristy portal. Its flat arch is crowned by an original inauguration cross. The present altar painting, Christ and the Sinful Woman, ordered from the artist B. Reinhold in 1876, hides a walled-in chancel window. An original priest door into the chancel is indicated by an imprint in the plaster east of the south window.

A late medieval wooden font, shaped like a cup, stands in front of the south window. The font is briskly cut from one single trunk of pine. The outer surface of the cup is polygonal, forming fourteen sections. Different layers of fragmentarily preserved wall paintings depicting figural paintings and decorative foliage cover the walls of the nave.

Among the medieval sculptures a Madonna from Gotland is especially noteworthy. It dates from around 1300, and it is situated on the windowsill towards the north. It was later altered to fit the spirit of late medieval times. The wooden crown is a modern addition. A well-cut little crucifix hanging on the north wall also belongs to the 14th century.

BUILDING HISTORY

Bracteates from the beginning of the 13th century and a compact layer of older burials under the east gable of the nave indicate that there was an older church on the site. It was probably in wood. The Romanesque church bell, the "little bell" still in use in the west tower, can be dated on stylistc grounds to the first half of the 13th century (Fig. 26). It probably belonged to the wooden church.

The first stone church in Eckerö, a nave with a little stone sacristy in the northeast corner, was erected at the end of the 13th century. At first

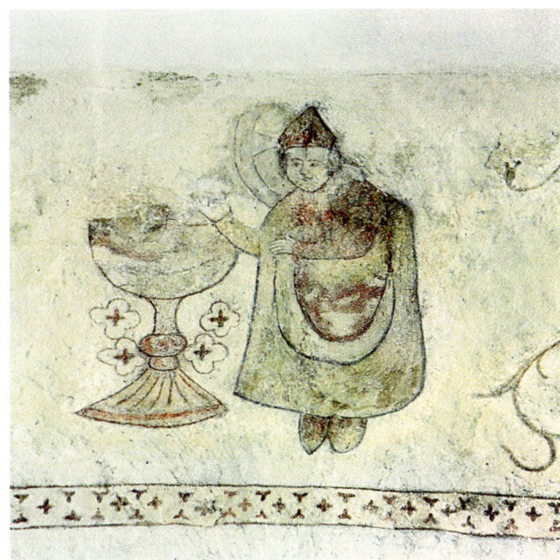

▲ Fig. 73. Eckerö. Bishop and font, wall painting.

the interior was dark, with a few narrow and high-placed windows and a horizontal wooden ceiling. The church had two entries from the south, the main portal further west and the priest door into the chancel. The position of the priest door suggests that the chancel occupied about a third of the nave. An original portal in the eastern part of the northern wall is preserved. It led to a minute sacristy of 2.5 x 2.5m. A circular window is mentioned, probably situated in the west gable wall. Three individually shaped inauguration crosses in the chancel probably date from the first consecration ceremony of the stone church. No major changes in the building can be traced from the 14th century. Some time at the beginning of the century, however, the Madonna enthroned was acquired from Gotland. She probably adorned an original Mary altar by the northern wall. The little crucifix, nowadays hanging on the northern wall, also belongs to the 14th century.

In 1467 the west tower was erected, with support from the western gable and the western end of the walls of the nave. Of the same age is the winch used for the construction, still preserved in the tower. The whole tower, including the wooden hood with its complicated supporting constructions, has been preserved intact from the medieval period, and thus, together with the tower of Finström church, forms one of the oldest preserved wooden constructions in Finland. At first, when the tower lacked a western portal, it was reached from inside, from a narrow door in the western gable of the nave. A narrow window faced south on the ground floor of the tower. The early 13th century church bell was hung in the tower, at a higher level than today. Sculptures of the martyrs and Samaritans Erasmus and Sebastian were acquired. But they are of different wood and different provenance, and therefore cannot be seen as a pair. The altar was also decorated with an altarpiece now missing. Later sources imply yet another wooden altar, probably one of the side-altars.

The wall paintings of the nave are from the late Middle Ages, and in several different layers upon each other. A font is depicted among the fragmentarily preserved paintings, high on the south wall. This painting can be regarded as a portrait of the cup-shaped wooden font from the church, which dates from the end of the 15th century.

During the first half of the 16th century the porch was erected against the original main portal. An inner niche in the east wall of the porch indicates that the room may have served as a chapel. The outer niche of the same wall may have been the framework for a wall painting, maybe in connection with the reputation of the church as an offering church. The intention to vault the porch was never realized.

THE POST-REFORMATION PERIOD

After the Reformation in the 1520s some of the liturgical vessels were confiscated. According to the new Lutheran liturgy a pulpit was installed, but otherwise neglect and disrepair prevailed. The changes performed during the 17th century are generally well documented. The church was substantially repaired after the period of neglect in the 16th century. New pews were acquired. A gallery was erected along the west gable, and a new pulpit was placed close to the south wall. The choir screen was renewed and two church ships are mentioned.

In the beginning of the 18th century the nave got its present wooden barrel vault. During the Northern War (1714-1721) the church suffered great damage. The medieval reredos was destroyed, and massive repairs were required in the interior. Two different artists are mentioned, Jonas Bergman, who repaired the altar painting, and Gustaf Pilou who painted the gallery screen.

The 19th century was a time for substantial changes. The windows were then enlarged gradually to their present proportions. A new altar painting of the Last Supper was acquired. In 1837 the small sacristy was torn down, only to be replaced by the present more spacious one. At the same time the west gable of the nave was removed and the church room was enlarged considerably. Space was assigned for a new gallery further towards the tower. In 1908 the chancel window was walled in.

In connection with a larger renovation in 1952 Eckerö church was archaeologically excavated. ■

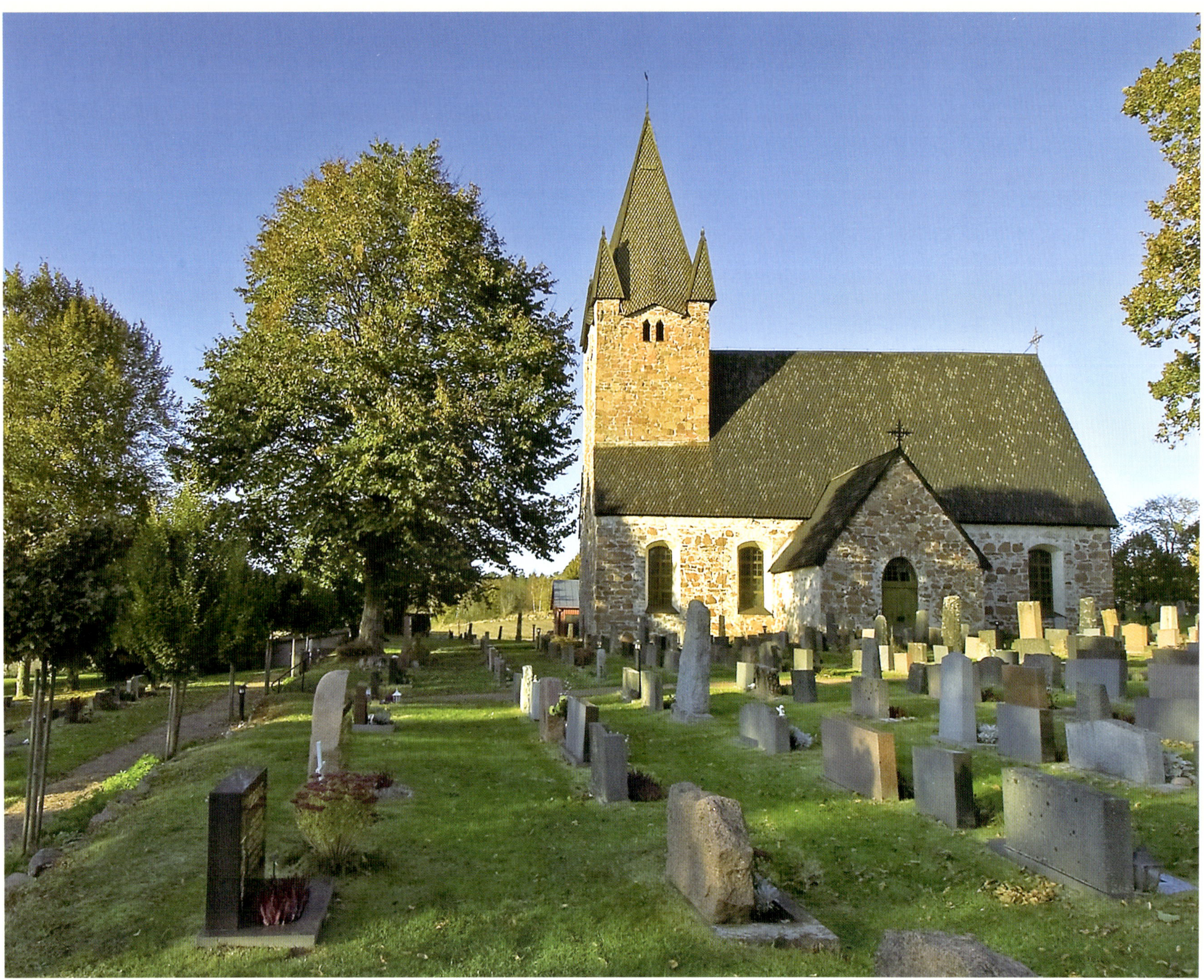

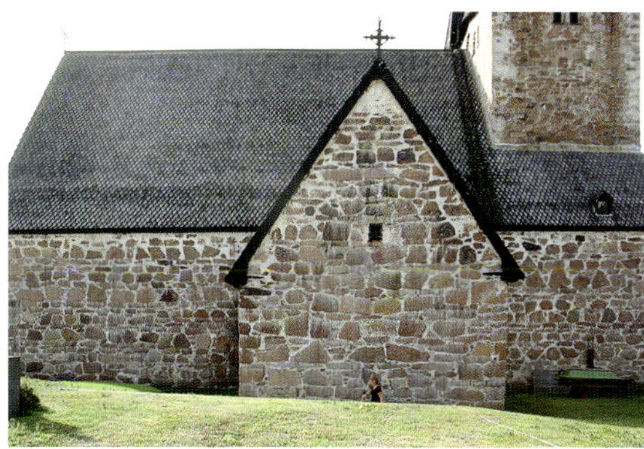

▲ Fig. 75. Finström church. Exterior from the north.

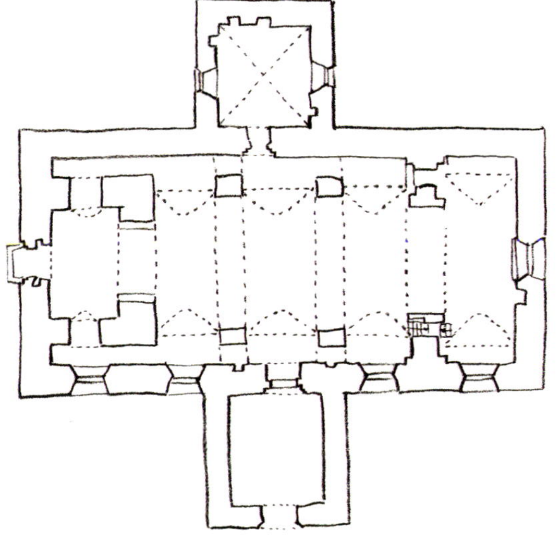

▲ Fig. 76. Finström. Ground plan.

FINSTRÖM CHURCH

Among the Åland mother churches St.Michael's Church in Finström is the only one not to have been built adjacent to the largest Iron Age grave field of the parish. Instead it is mysteriously embedded in deep earth slopes facing north and northeast.

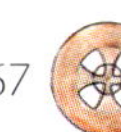

The parish of Finström is centrally located on the main island, surrounded by Jomala, Hammarland, Geta, and Saltvik. The parish is cut by several waterways, with a long coast facing Färjsundet and Ödkarbyviken in the east. Back when the lake Kyrkträsket still could be reached via the Ämnäs straits, the church was situated on an inner bay of the sea, with a well-sheltered harbor.

THE EXTERIOR

The church of Finström is the best preserved medieval building in Finland. This goes for both exterior and interior. The church is not yet fully investigated, and there are still many question marks. The nave has a rectangular ground plan and is built in rapakivi, but otherwise it differs from other Åland churches. It lacks the usual simple step-like socle and the separate priest door from the south into the chancel. Nor is the masonry identical. Rather than selected small stones framed by chains of bigger blocks in the corners, there is a distinct pattern with regular shifts. Two layers of bigger stones alternate with smaller horizontally arranged blocks of granite. Four identical large windows face the south, regularly flanking the porch in the center of the façade. A high chancel window dominates the eastern gable. The church of Finström is one of the few in all of Finland to have kept its windowless north wall intact. Here the horizontal shifts are interrupted by the sacristy, again centrally placed in the façade. The north gable of the sacristy suggests a secondary heightening. The silhouette is characterized by a steep angle of the roof and a pointed spire, surrounded by four smaller turrets. An unusual solution can be seen in the erection of the tower. Normally, the tower would be erected as a separate building unit in front of the west gable of the nave; here, the tower is drawn into the rectangular plan, where it rests on the western part of the nave vaulting.

GROUND PLAN

The church has a nearly cruciform ground plan, with the sacristy and porch placed roughly opposite each other on the northern and southern walls of the nave. Rougher wall pillars under the tower show that the tower was included in the planning of the vaults. Joints in the walls clearly show that the porch is secondary to the nave, but when it comes to the sacristy, the building sequence is not so clear. Contradictory signs point to different directions. The rectangular nave is one of the largest in the Islands, with an inner floor of 283 square meters (outer measures 28.9 x 14.4m). The portal of the porch also functions as the

◀ Fig. 74. Finström church. Exterior from the south.

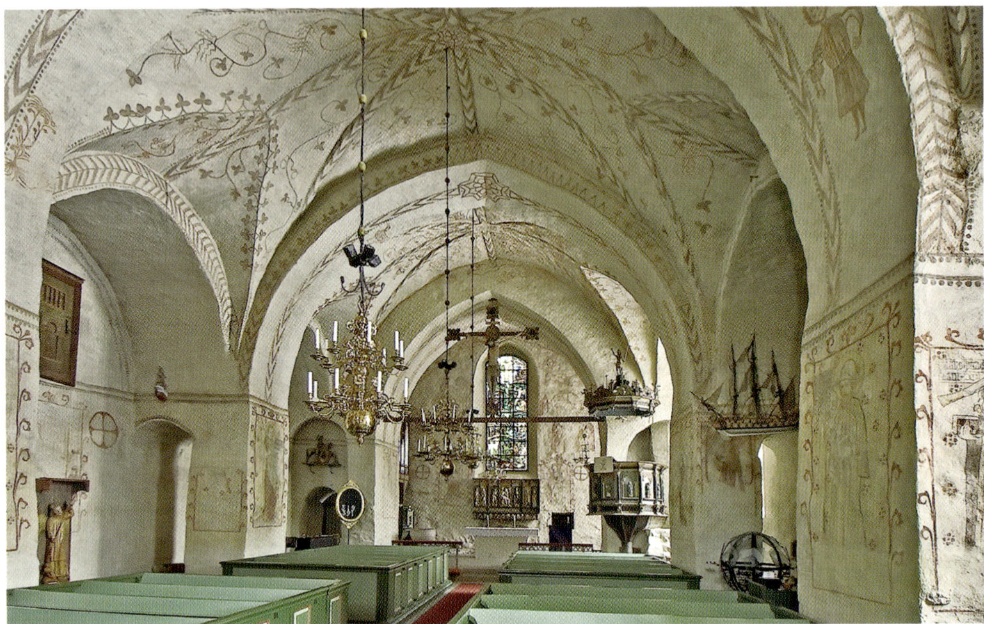

▲ Fig. 77. Finström. Interior towards east.

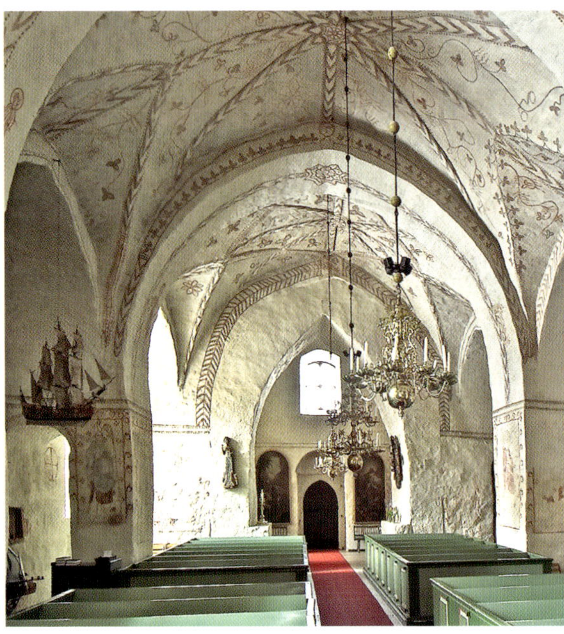

▲ Fig. 78. Finström. Interior towards west.

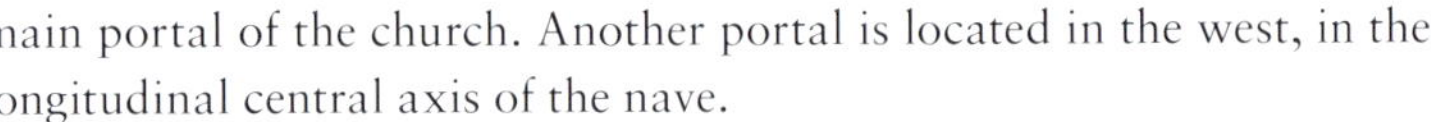

main portal of the church. Another portal is located in the west, in the longitudinal central axis of the nave.

THE INTERIOR

The lack of windows facing north, in combination with well preserved, all-covering wall paintings and the unusual vaulting contribute to the warm and devout atmosphere of the interior. Only a minimum of changes were made during the renovation in the 19th century. Existing windows were cautiously enlarged. A rich painting program that had been covered by layers of whitewash on walls and vaults was carefully restored, and the number of preserved wooden sculptures is unusually high. An early medieval side-altar remains intact, as does an early medieval burial slab of limestone, trapezoidal in shape. The vaults in Finström lack parallels. They are roughly cast in fieldstones in four ***bays****, dividing the nave into a wide central nave flanked by narrow aisles or galleries.

The vault of the central nave stretches like a ***barrel vault**** along the central axis, flanked by barrel vaults from the aisles, set at right angles. These barrel vaults, originally separated from each other, were united by secondary openings, or narrow side passages, cut through the wall pillars. Thus, rough freestanding square wall pillars were formed to take the weight off the heavy transverse arches. The connection between transverse arches and the wall pillars is awkward. Four niches with rounded arches in the triumphal arch, two facing the altar and two towards the congregation, indicate a possible concentration of side altars to this area. The pointed arch under the tower is part of a secondary supporting construction for the tower, which partly hid existing paintings on walls and wall pillars.

Ribs enhanced in low relief show the wish to create an illusion of star vaults with ribs. Under the plaster of the ribs occasional brick stones can be found. The ribs are completely decorative without supporting function. Rather than forming a structural network, they break when meeting the ribs of the aisles, ending in empty spaces in the middle of the vaults. Sometimes they are broken up by draining holes.

The vaulting is different in the wide triumphal arch between nave and chancel and inside the chancel. It is smoother and more even. The ribs, without reliefs, are an illusion painted directly on the smooth plaster. Trefoil decoration lingers smoothly along the vault.

THE HISTORY OF THE CHURCH

When the area in front of the west portal was excavated in 1949, a uniform group of early medieval graves was unveiled. The dead had been

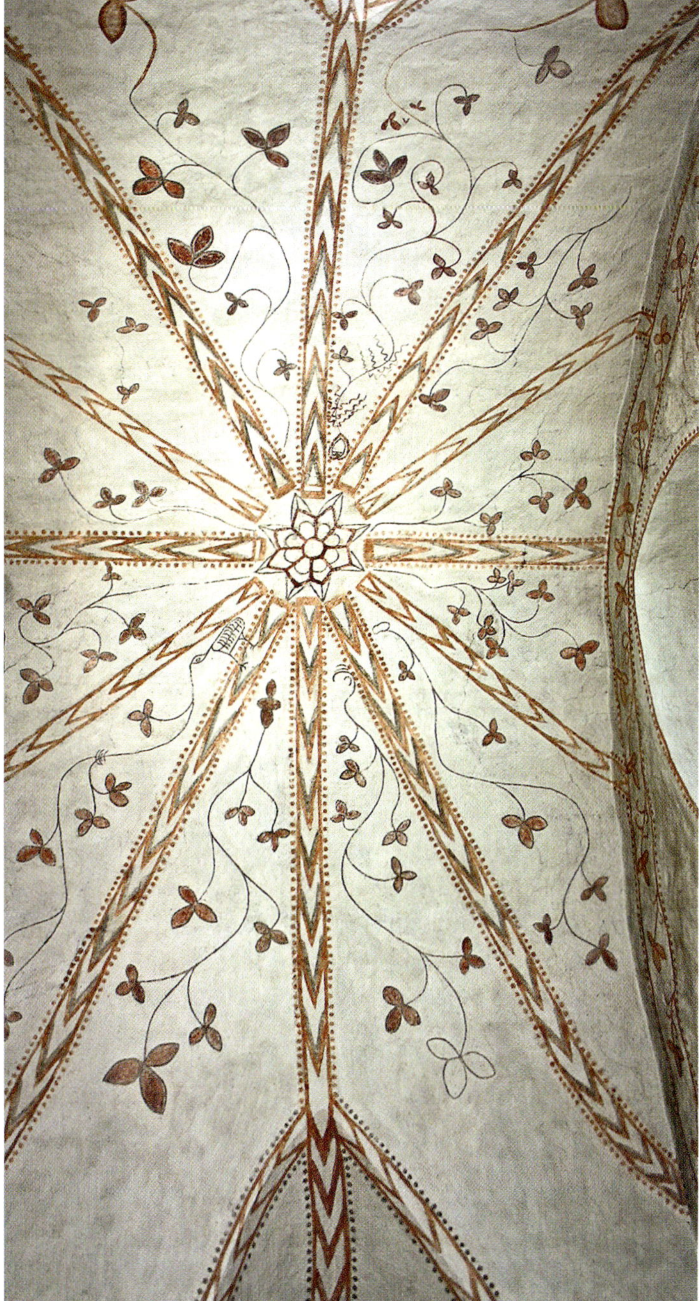

▲ Fig. 79. Finström. Detail of the chancel vault.

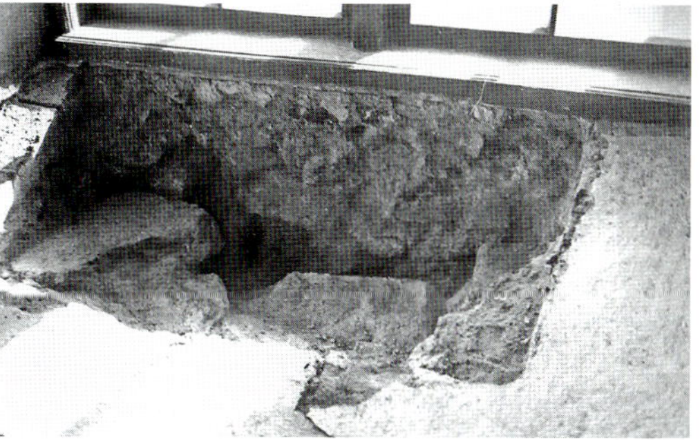

▲ Fig. 80. Finström. Lengthways crack in the south wall of the nave, 1950.

laid in coffins of stone slabs, with their bones partly under the present west gable.

Excavation reports from the archaeological investigations in 1950 mention a crack lengthways along the south and north walls, approximately 70cm inside the inner wall surface. Matts Dreijer, county archaeologist, and Hugo Eriksson, building master in charge, interpreted the crack as an indication that the oldest stone walls could have carried a lighter wooden construction, i.e., that the nave was covered by open roof trusses or a wooden vault. They claimed that the walls from the first stone church still remain in the inner walls of the rebuilt church, that they measured around 70cm in thickness and that they reached a height of 3.20m. The walls would have gained in thickness around 90cm in the secondary vaulting, reaching a thickness of 1.60m. Unfortunately, these observations cannot be verified, but if they are correct, then the original walls would coincide with a painted dotted line which can be followed around the entire interior, except for the chancel.

In archaeological excavations in 1969-70, the stone foundation of a smaller church (around 14 x 8m) was uncovered inside the church. Preserved wooden sculptures of Saint Michael, a human head, and the odd

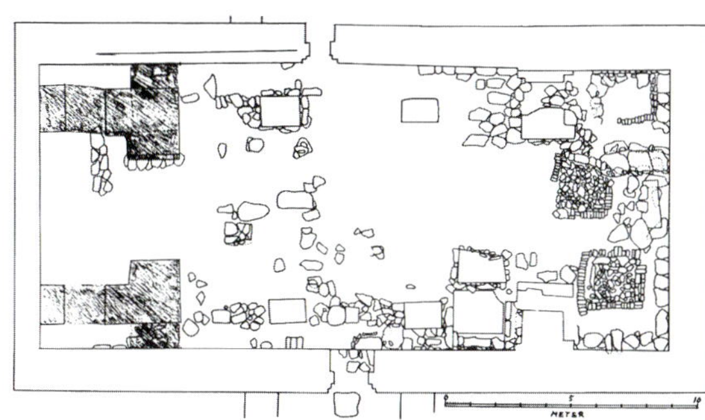

◀ Fig. 81. Excavation plan of Finström church, 1969-70.

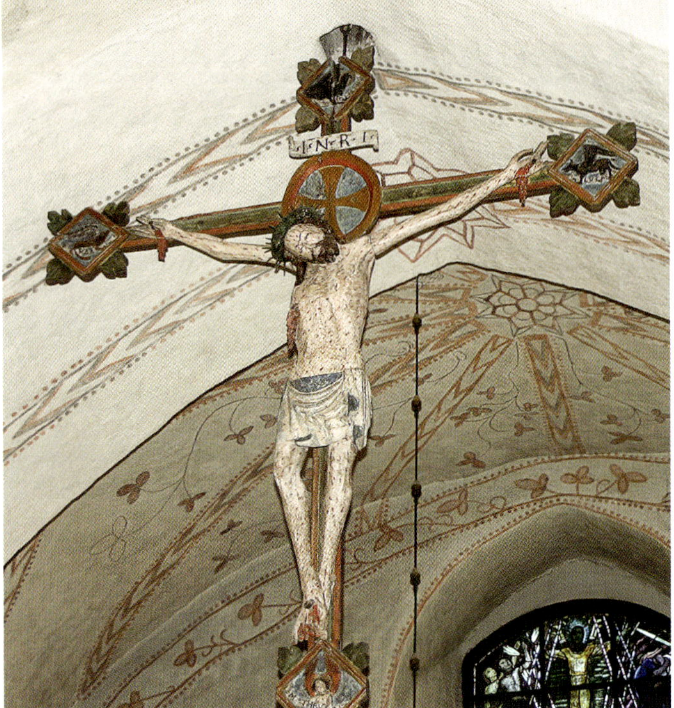

▲ Fig. 82. Finström. The Crucifix.

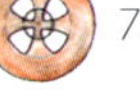

coin, all date this wooden church to the 12th century. The burials mentioned above presumably also belonged to the wooden church.

This time it is the evidence from archaeological artifacts and historical sources rather than natural sciences that indicates that the first stone church in Finström, unvaulted and with a lower sacristy, was erected approximately simultaneously with other mother churches in the Islands, at the end of the 13th century. Also, a large hoard of coins was hidden in the sacristy some time in the 1280s. It is important to note that the lower part of the sacristy is joined with the northern wall of the nave, and that the hoard therefore belongs to the first stone church. Unfortunately, nobody understood to take mortar samples from the foundation level in the nave and in the sacristy in the archaeological excavations in 1969-70. Today it is considerably harder to reach original mortar, since the floor area after the excavations was covered by a thick layer of concrete; the stone floor is laid on top of this concrete cover. Inside the church some coins from the 13th century were found, but most of the coins belong to the 14th and 15th centuries. The size and shape of the first stone church remains unclear. Fragments of limestone mullions and stained glass were found in the excavations.

During the 14th century Finström church strengthened its position in the Islands. Energetic vicars with excellent ecclesiastical networks were responsible for that. The first vicar of Finström to be mentioned is Sigurd of Finnaström (around 1328-42), canon in the Diocese of Turku, confidant of bishops and archbishops. He represents the Islands in the correspondence concerning the seal tithes in 1335-6. An important decision made in this connection was that the seal tithes, used earlier for funding the building of the parish churches in the islands, from now on should be assigned to the vicars in order to support their households. The source concerning the seal tithes is one of the strongest indications that a stone church had already been built in Finström, and that it was seen as relatively finished. Therefore no new building plans were on the agenda. It was probably the very same Sigurd of Finnaström who acquired the new liturgical song book, the sequentionarium, from Paris (p. 28, Fig. 28). From now on Finström church stands out as the foremost representative of Dominican influence in Åland. In the 14th century many more vicars from Finström are mentioned. In 1325 King Magnus Eriksson states that certain parishes within the Diocese of Turku were to be regal, among them Finström.

Thus the Swedish crown now had full patronage over the parish of Finström, roughly at the same time as Grelsby Manor, a few kilometers south of the church, was transferred to King Magnus. Through the transaction the previous owner could expiate a crime for homicide. From now on Grelsby Manor is called the King's Manor. According to information from 1375 the revenue and income from being vicar in Finström did not exceed 18 gold florins annually.

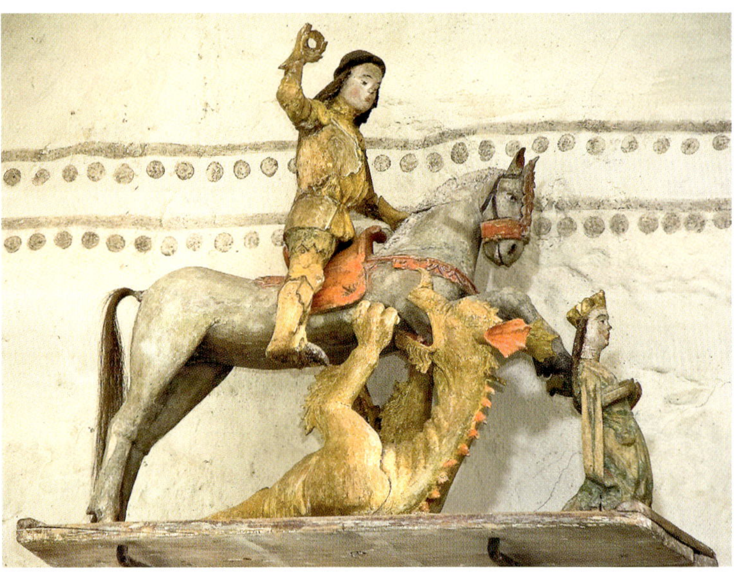

▲ Fig.83. Saint George and the dragon, wooden sculpture.

The middle of the 15th century meant a radical building activity in the church. Dendrochronological analysis shows that all building units were involved, and that it took place during an intensive and dynamic building period which lasted from the 1440s to 1467. This dating of the upper parts of the nave, both in the exterior and the interior, have been confirmed by ^{14}C AMS analysis of mortar. In spite of speculations cited above, we do not know how much remains of the original stone church after this transformation, but apparently the changes were substantial. The façades also changed with the windows matching the new vaulting system.

The great transformation scheme started with a heightening of the sacristy in the 1440s. The vaulting of the nave took place around 1450, a few years later the porch was erected against the south portal, and as the last step of the extension the west tower was constructed in 1467 on top of the westernmost bay of the central nave. The conspicuous spire at Finström, surrounded by four turrets in each corner reflecting the tower in Turku Cathedral, was later to be a source of inspiration to Sund.

The medieval high altar was larger and "more disporportionate" than it is today. It was standing free from the eastern chancel wall. Finström is one of the few churches where you can still see traces of a medieval ambo. The staircase of the present pulpit, through the triumphal arch, belongs to the original arrangement.

The crucifix of the church, stylistically dated to around 1430, still hangs in the triumphal arch. In the south aisle, in front of the triumphal arch, one of the medieval side altars remains intact. The north side altar, consecrated to Mary, has been torn down.

A faithful copy of the equestrian statue of Saint George, from 1498 in the Stockholm Great Church, was executed for the church of Finström. The bottom piece is however older, dendrochronologically dated to the middle of the 15th century. The princess is kneeling in front of the equestrian group, with her back turned against the hero saint. Today the group is placed above the original Mary altar on the northern side of the triumphal wall. Christ is standing on the south side altar, as the ***Man of Sorrows**** showing his wounds. In the sacristy we find a wooden sculpture of highest artistic quality, depicting the Swedish national saint Erik.

THE WALL PAINTINGS

Many different stages can be discerned among the wall paintings on the eastern chancel wall. The inauguration crosses in the chancel are among the oldest, with concentric rings inscribed into the wet plaster. Below the south inauguration cross on the eastern chancel wall there is a faintly drawn face of Christ, also with inscribed outlines.

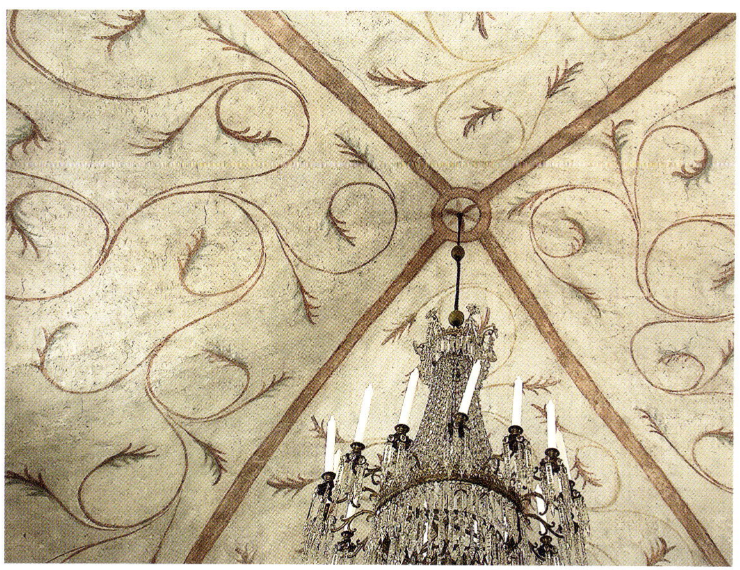

▲ Fig. 84. Finström. Intertwining foliage ornamentation covering the sacristy vault.

After the rebuilding at the middle of the 15th century, the church was covered with wall painting. Even if the time differences are insignificant, it is possible to discern many different masters. The finest paintings, probably also the earliest of the group, comprise the sequence of the church fathers on the chancel wall. Saint Anne is furthest to the north, flanked by the Last Judgment towards the south. The "Maria in Sole", the enthroned Madonna surrounded by sun-rays and sitting on the crescent moon above the original Mary altar in the north, was probably also painted by the same master.

The Credo suite where individual apostles with their text bands represent different parts of the creed has been painted on the walls facing in towards the nave, beginning with Peter south of the high altar and concluding with Matthias north of the high altar. Many apostles from the suite have been covered and damaged by later interference in the church. Individual saints like Michael, George, Henrik, the Dominican saint Peter the Martyr, Gertrude, Catherine of Alexandria, and Birgitta of Sweden ornament other surfaces of the walls.

Apart from the chancel, a line in grey with double dots marks the border between wall surface and vault. The vault has been painted in the so-called primitive Western Finnish style by a different master. The stars of the sky, Orion's belt and the Seven Stars, may symbolize the old

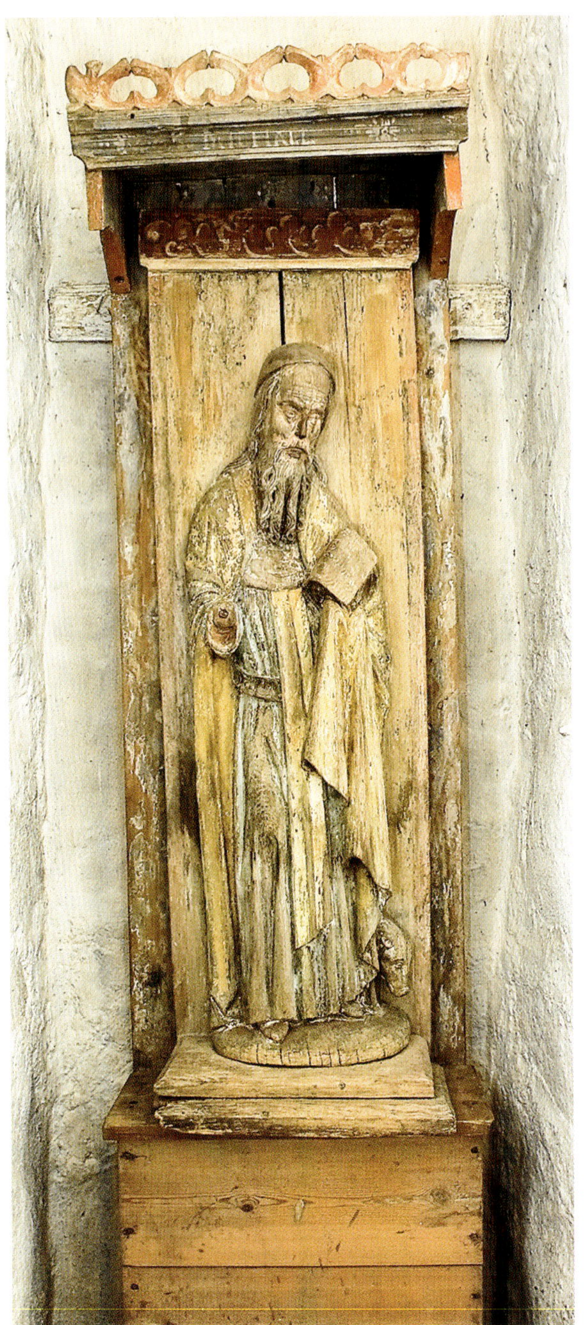

▲ Fig. 85. Saint Anthony, carved in oak from northern Germany.

and the new law according to the Book of Job.

THE SCULPTURES

A large number of the medieval wooden sculptures still remain intact in situ. Two of them belong to the end of the 12th century - smiling **Saint Michael** and the so-called **Giant Finn** secondarily walled into the tower vault (cf. Figs. 3. and 4). Other sculptures were acquired only after the extensive rebuilding of the church in the 15th century, among them a new **Saint Michael**, by the sacristy portal, was ordered for the new inauguration of the church. He is framed by a shrine in Åland pine from the same period. (cf. Fig. 44).

Saint Anthony, dendrochronologically dated to the 1450s, is hidden in the far west of the south aisle. The framing shrine, of Åland pine, is contemporary. Note the double framing of the saint. The outer higher shrine, also of Åland pine, dated to around 1230, originally belonged to the Romanesque sculpture of Saint Michael. Consequently, the shrine of Saint Michael, somewhat younger than the sculpture, is not in its proper location.

The reason for the big rebuilding of the church in the middle of the 15th century is unknown. But it is obvious that Finström during the 15th century further strengthened its close relation to Turku Cathedral. It is confirmed by the coat of arms belonging to Dean Olaus Magni on the eastern chancel wall. The same close relation is shown by the turrets of the tower, obviously inspired by the church tower in Turku. We further have iconographical parallels in Saint Henrik, the patron saint of the Turku Cathedral, found in Finström both as a wall-painting and as one of the sculptures in the reredos. The sculpture of Saint Anthony in Finström is a faithful copy of a similar sculpture in Turku Cathedral, etc. At the same time the Dominican influence is strengthened in the images in the church.

THE POST-REFORMATION

In 1548 Finström church lost a gilded silver monstrance in the confiscations of Gustavus Vasa. After the reformation there were only few architectural changes. The maintenance of the wooden sculptures continued unbroken. Dean Boetius Murenius ordered the sculptures to be repainted and placed according to the wishes of the vicar. To manage the weight of the tower, the underlying vault had to be supported by a stone construction with a pointed arch, probably erected in the early 16th century. The inner walls of the church were whitewashed for the first time in the 1660s. During the 17th century the medieval high altar was replaced by another erected tightly against the east chancel wall.

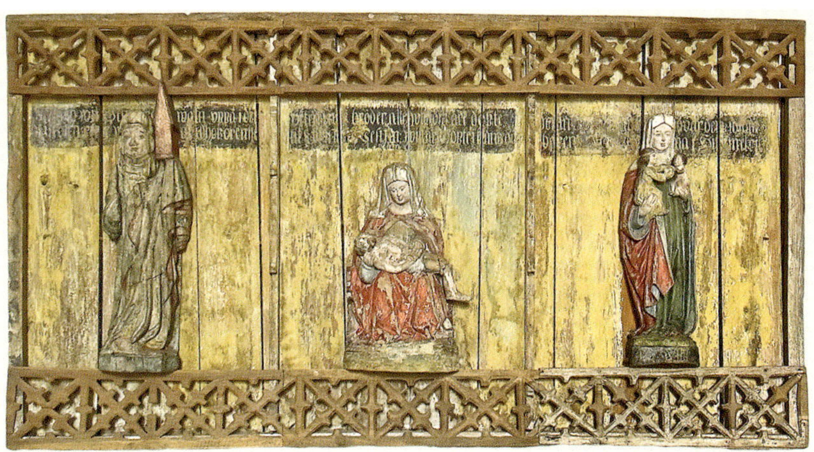

▲ Fig. 86. Baptismal piece, compiled from earlier sculpture in the 17th century.

There is a rarity among the 17th century decorations in Finström church – a Baptismal piece composed by older wooden sculptures from at least two different altarpieces (Fig. 86). Maternity is enhanced. To my knowledge it is very rare to have liturgical objects as a collage of medieval components in the Post-Reformation era. The Pietà in the center is flanked to the right by a female saint usually identified as Saint Gertrude, and by Saint Anne to the left. Dendrochronological analysis of the boards in the background gives a date in the middle of the 17th century. The handwriting in the almost invisible background text reveals that it is by Mårten Johansson.

Pulpit and pews were also installed at the same time. Gradually also galleries were needed for the increasing population. In 1704 it was time to replace the pulpit with a new one. The church's first organ came as a donation in the 18th century. During the 1830s the south windows were enlarged and the chancel window was elongated. In the beginning of the 1900s the medieval wall paintings were carefully rescued under layers of secondary whitewash by the architect C.F. Frankenhaeuser. By using new methods he had learnt in Denmark, he succeeded in revealing the wall paintings in Finström almost unharmed in their medieval state. In the 1920s the conservator Oskari Niemi continued in the same spirit to uncover the rest of the medieval wall paintings of the church.

In 1969-1970 a substantial archaeological investigation was performed, before restoration works started. In the process the organ gallery was removed. The organ received a new location against the north chancel wall. ■

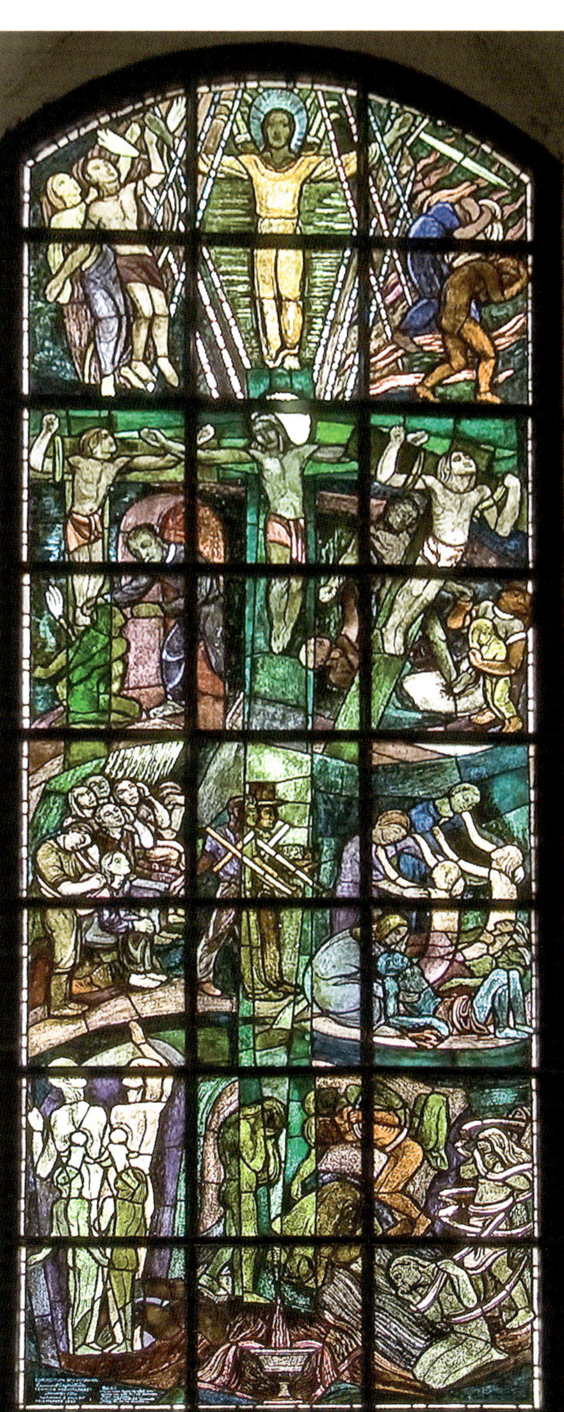

◀ Fig. 87. The modern stained glass window in the chancel, "The World Conciliation" by the artist Lennart Segerstråle, was installed in the old chancel window in 1947.

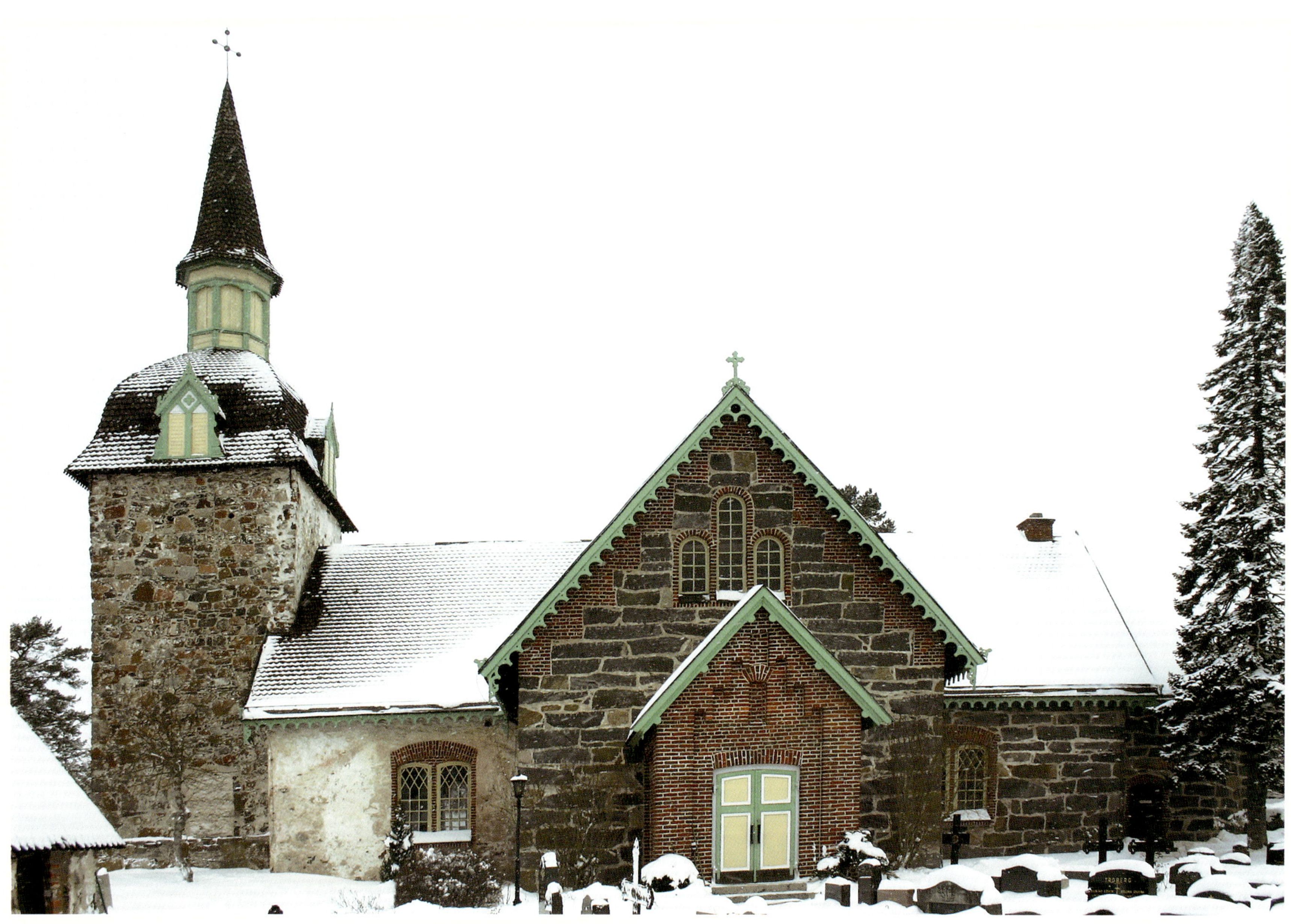

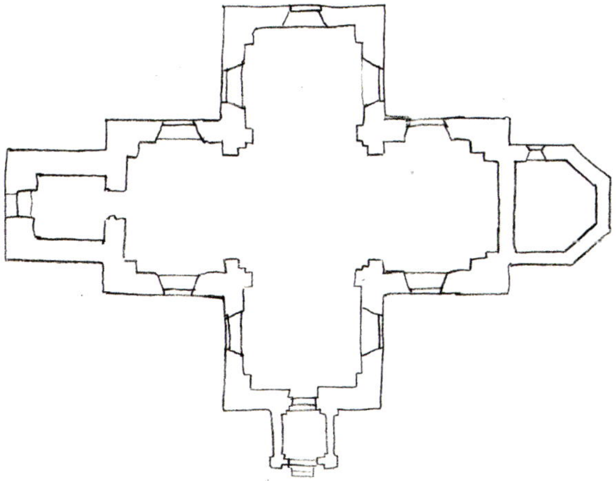

▲ Fig. 89. Föglö church. Ground plan.

FÖGLÖ CHURCH

Föglö church, probably consecrated to Mary Magdalene, is located by the water at Kyrksundet. "Fyghelde" is mentioned as one of the harbors between Linaboete (Lemböte) and Thiyckekarl (Kökar) in the so-called *Danish Itinerary*, written in the middle of the 13th century.

Today the chapels of Sottunga and Kökar belong to Föglö mother church. But this has not always been the case: during the Middle Ages Sottunga was the only chapel under Föglö. The spacious churchyard with well preserved gates is surrounded by an impressive stone wall, where the marks of the farms providing the stones still can be seen. The church is not yet fully investigated, but the present state of research is described here. The present church is the result of a radical rebuilding in 1859-61, according to drawings signed in 1857 by the well-known Turku architect Georg Theodor Policron Chiewitz.

THE EXTERIOR

The exterior of the church differs from other Åland mother churches. Instead of selected stones of red granite, rapakivi, we see great gray granite blocks with big drilling holes from the quarrying, a technique unknown in the Middle Ages. A narrow west tower in red granite, with large windows framed by bricks, is connected to a church shaped like a cross with equal arms. The style is Neo-Gothic, with windows and portals framed by bricks. In the western cross arm, closest to the tower, the remains of an earlier church in red granite can be seen. Even traces of a demolished porch is visible from the south. All cross arms are penetrated by large double windows with decorative diagonal mullions at the top. The southern entrance is built into a brick extension in front of the south cross arm, while a polygonal extension to the east forms the sacristy. A decorative fret-sawed cornice runs around all cross arms. The entrances at the south cross arm and the west portal of the tower serve as the main entries to the church. A narrow door leads directly to the sacristy from the south.

GROUND PLAN

The cruciform ground plan includes the chancel in the eastern cross arm. A narrower and lower sacristy –an extension of the chancel– has a tripartite finish towards the east. A tower in the west connects to the

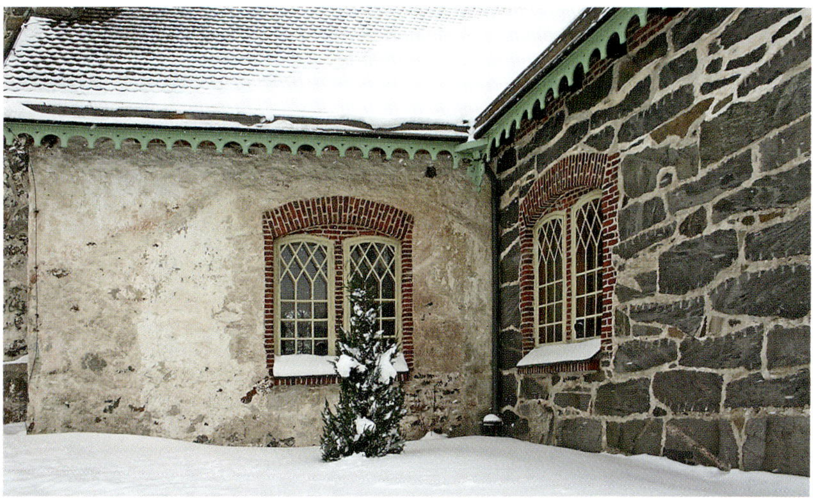

▲ Fig. 90. Föglö church. The south façade, detail.

◀ Fig. 88. Föglö church, exterior from the south.

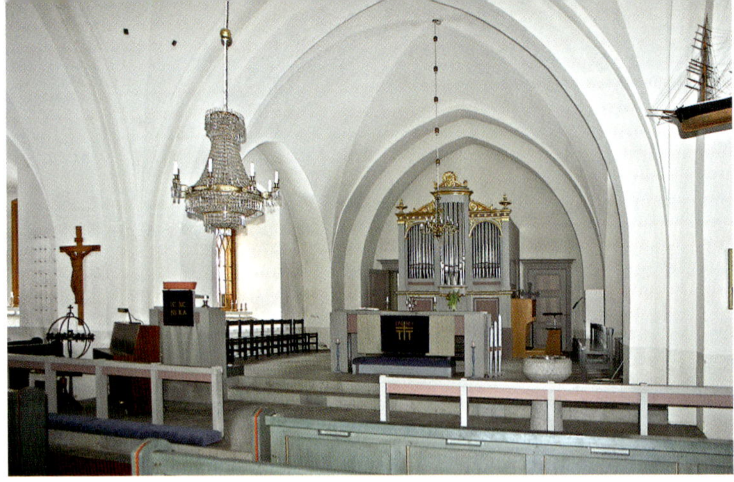

▲ Fig. 91. Interior towards east.

west cross arm of the church. The church has two entries: the central main portal in the west wall of the tower, and an entrance from the churchyard in an extension in the south cross arm.

THE INTERIOR

The light and undecorated interior gives a cool and plain impression. There is a high white ***cross-vault**** in the centre of the cross while the high altar in the east projects far towards the centre of the cross. The chancel in the eastern transept is on a higher level a few steps up. The coloring is modest with whitewashed walls and vaults and the church has a floor of sandstone from Öland. There is nothing in the architecture reminiscent of the medieval church. On the contrary, the fixtures are radically modern, with altar, reading pulpit, and altar round in an ascetic design from 1968. The pews, which were also renewed then, are painted in a dark bluish green. The architect in charge was Erik Kråkström. The altar is ornamented by a medieval reliquary cross in silver, probably from around 1400. It is framed in a protecting case of plexiglass.

BUILDING HISTORY

The design of the old church is well known. It is partly shown on the old seal of the church where the southern façade is seen (Fig. 92), partly by unrealized plans for alteration made by P.J. Gylich in the 1840s (Fig. 93). Additional documentation was received from archaeological excavations in 1966 and 1967.

Föglö church originally had a single nave with a narrower chancel in the east without an apse. A little sacristy had been built against the eastern side of the northern long wall, while an unusually big porch was connected with the western part of the southern wall. A high double window let in the light from the south and there were no windows to the north. The nave was the oldest part, while sacristy, porch and west tower were added later. The narrow chancel is enigmatic: coins from the 14th century suggest that it belongs to the same period as the nave. Yet, in the excavation report the chancel deviated from the main axis and lay diagonally towards the northeast in an unnatural way. Matts Dreijer's explanation that a rock to the north was in the way seems highly unusual. Neither visitation reports nor building surveys from the 1600s until the rebuilding mention that the chancel was in any way different, while problems with the sacristy walls were scrutinized. A more likely explanation could be that the walls of the old chancel were moved in the process of rebuilding.

This older church shows characteristic Åland traits: it was built in rapakivi with windows and door openings framed by limestone, and a priest door led directly into the narrow chancel. The nave was divided into two cross vaults of brick. The secondary vaults rested on heavy columns along the walls.

Remains of the medieval altar were uncovered in the chancel. It was erected immediately against the east wall (Fig. 94). In connection with the enlargement in the 1860s the altar was leveled down to a height of 75cm above untouched earth. Dreijer estimated the original altar slab to be ca 150cm x 110cm. The height of the altar, including the slab, was estimated to be 76cm above floor level. In the excavations a carefully mortared niche was discovered deep inside the altar, against the east wall. Bricks in three layers lined the cavity (18 x 18cm, 20cm deep), which was covered by two flat sandstone slabs. The niche was for hiding relics. An exquisite silver reliquary cross was found in a crack under the hiding place (Fig. 37). Originally it had been laid down in a little wooden box with pieces of metal work. A medieval altarpiece and a crucifix are mentioned among the early inventories.

During the Northern War (1714-21) the church was "wretchedly devastated and totally burnt" by the enemy. Substantial repairs awaited walls, vaults, roof, windows, and doors. Also the upper part of the church tower was rebuilt and the bells were re-hung.

According to an inventory from 1838, the church measured 53 ells (more than 31m) in length, and 15 ¾ ells (9.3m) in width. The height to the ceiling was 9 ells (5.3m). The floor in the nave and chancel was laid in Gotland sandstone. Three of the six windows belonged to the nave, i.e., the two coupled windows to the south lengthened downwards in 1839 and one in the northern wall. Two window openings belonged to the chancel, while one window to the south lit the ground floor of the tower. Two galleries filled the western part of the nave, the gallery for the men against the western gable, and the other for the women towards the north.

The east wall of the chancel was covered by an altar painting from

1759 by Jonas Bergman. The motifs were the Last Supper and the Suffering of Christ in Gethsemane. Walls, vaults, windowsills, doors, galleries and pews were painted, but not the window frames.

The sacristy measured 7 x 6 ¾ ells (roughly 4.1m x 4m), with an inner height of 4 ¼ ells (2.5m). It had a wooden floor and a window towards the east, and no system for heating. The only passage to the attic of the nave was an opening from the sacristy. The exterior was whitewashed, the shingle roof recently tarred and well maintained. After a burglary in the sacristy in 1838 the parish council started discussing different options: the church was either to be enlarged or replaced by an entirely new building. The congregation was totally against the building plans, activated by the vicar Matthias Forsberg. When plans for an enlargement were initiated in 1841, the church was in good condition. Still, for bigger celebrations it was considered "less spacious".

In 1847 the county architect in Turku, Pehr Johan Gylich, delivered his drawings mentioned above, with a plan to prolong the church further east. Czar Nicholas I granted a respite of 12 years for the new building, and at that stage drawings by Chiewitz were already at hand. The result was a drastic rebuilding, where most of the medieval nave, including chancel, sacristy and porch, were demolished to give way for a new, and for Åland completely new church architecture, in 1861.

A century later, in 1966-1967, the church was archaeologically excavated. The results were exceptionally rich. In addition to the spectacular reliquary cross and the medieval altar foundation, 53 medieval coins were found, 17 of which date from the 14th century. The oldest coins were spread all over the chancel and the nave, many of them immediately close to the medieval altar. Remains of heavily burnt stained glass were also excavated. Among the debris from the destruction of the old church was plenty of plaster from the vaults. Fragments of red plaster show that the church had had painted walls. After the excavation the church underwent basic repairs under direction of architect Erik Kråkström. In the process the medieval altar along with the foundation walls were covered with concrete, which complicates further investigations. In 1968 the church was re-inaugurated.

INVENTORY

- **Cross shaped silver reliquary** (Fig. 37).
- **The little bell** from the 15th century, with master marks from Stockholm preserved, still hangs in the tower.
- **An older altarpiece** from 1795 depicting the *Last Supper*, by master painter Jonas Bergman, hangs on the cross-wall, above the southern portal.
- **The altarpiece**, depicting the *Last Supper*, by the Court Painter R.W. Ekman in 1861, has been placed on the western cross-wall after the most recent renovation.
- **The organ**, placed in the very front of the church, behind the high altar, was built by Kangasala Organ Factory in1970. The older organ façade from 1864, however, encases the new organ.
- **A modern wooden crucifix**, carved by the artist Dick Häggblom, hangs in the north eastern corner close to the reading desk. It was donated to the church in 1986. ■

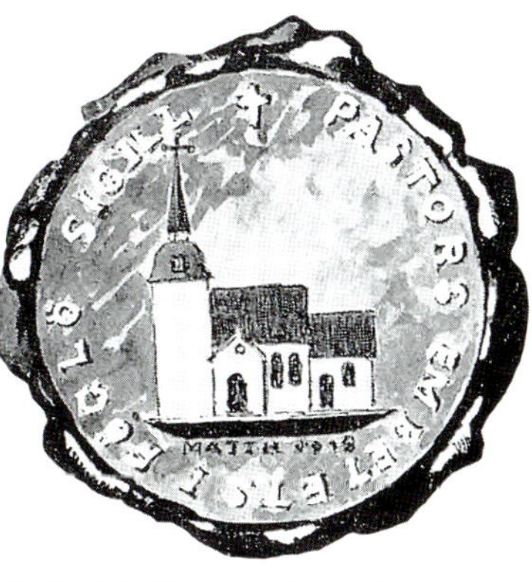

▲ Fig. 92. The church seal from the beginning of the 19th century.

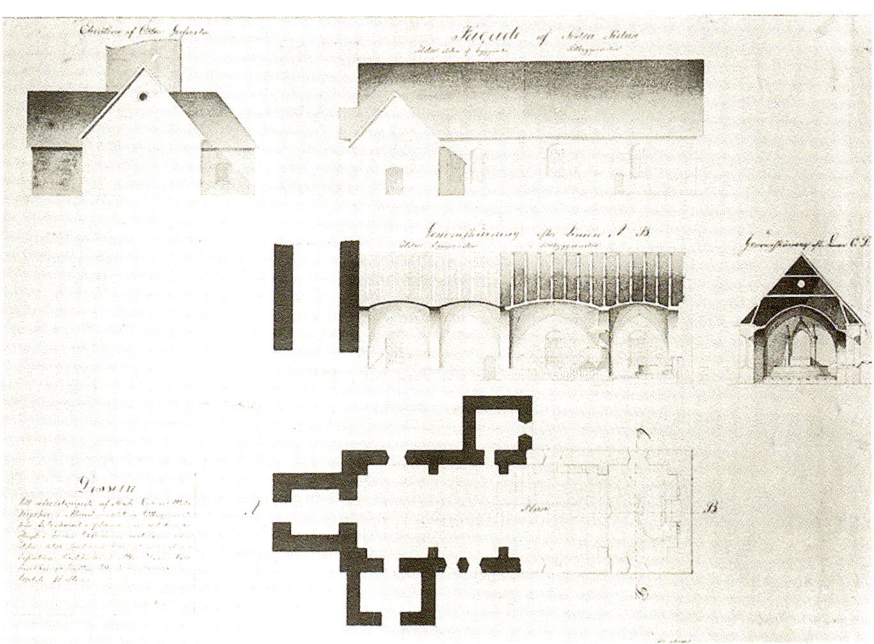

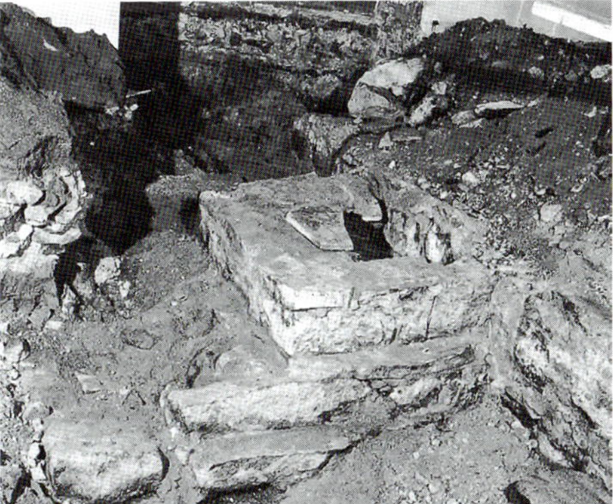

▲ Fig. 93. Drawings for changed building plans from 1840. P.J. Gylich.

◀ Fig. 94. The medieval altar of the church, erected against the east chancel wall, discovered in archaeological excavations in 1966.

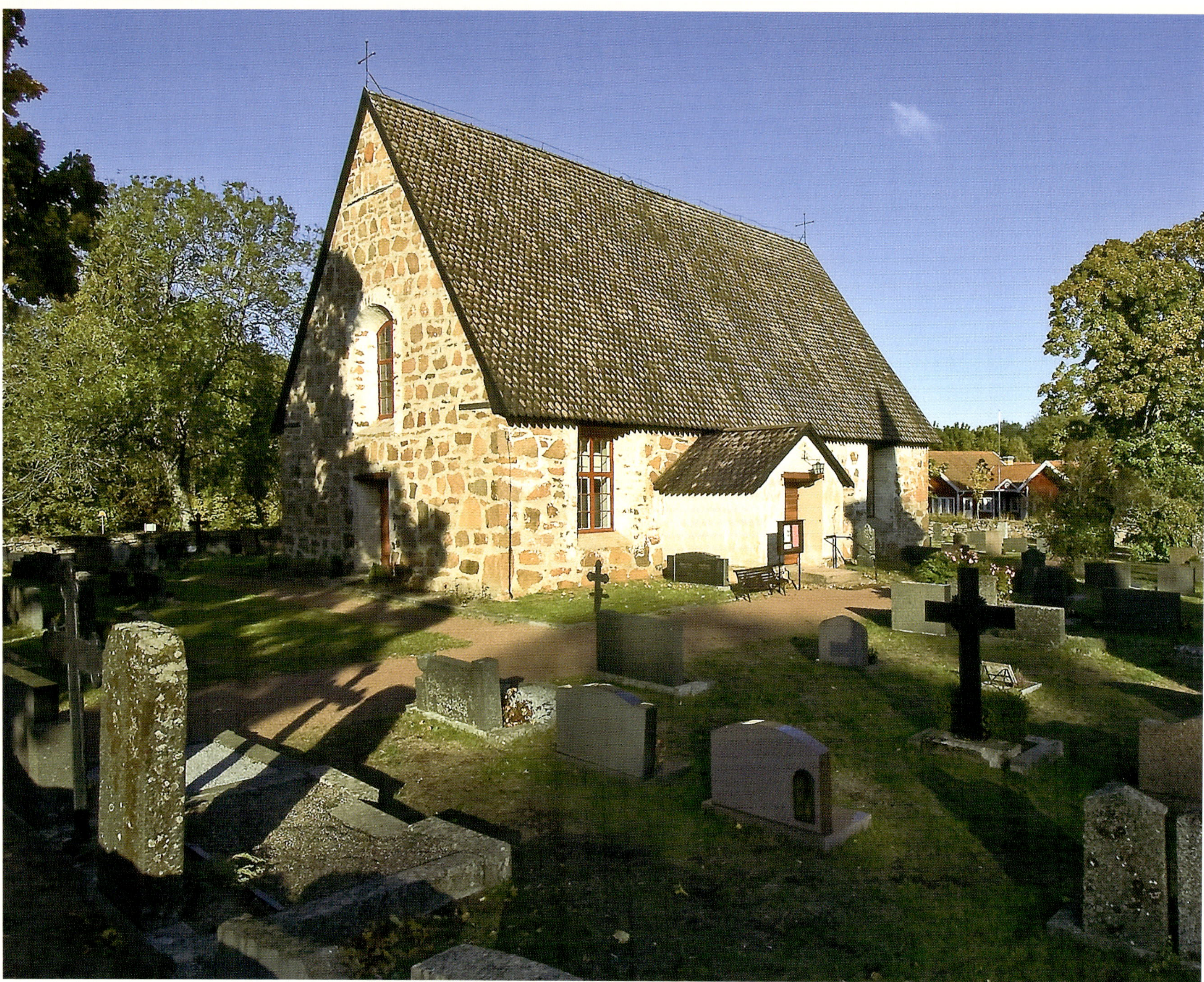

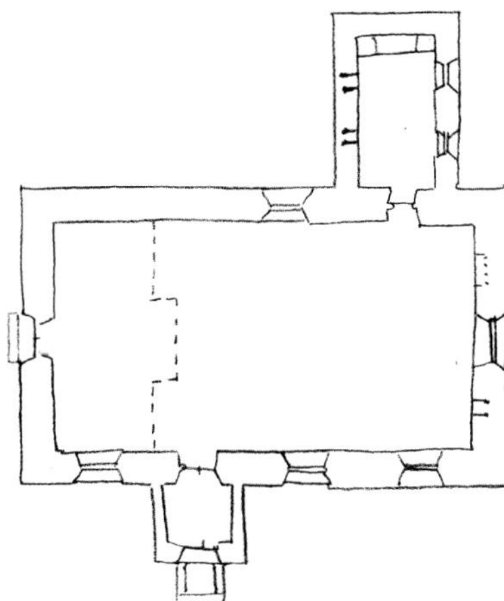

▲ Fig. 96. Geta church. Ground plan.

GETA CHURCH

Saint George's chapel church, centrally situated in Västergeta, belongs to the mother church of Finström.

THE EXTERIOR

Geta Church is a single-naved hall church built of Åland red granite. The tarred, steep saddle roof is covered with shingles. There are windows on all walls. A large chancel window breaks through the eastern wall. On the western gable, the window is higher up, above the entrance. Towards the south there are three big windows, reaching up to the roof, while one window opening faces the north. A porch of brick has been built against the western part of the south wall. The low and spacious sacristy is on the eastern side of the north wall. It was not built in connection with the nave. Instead of a west tower, a detached bell-tower stands beside the church wall, south west of the church. The grave chapel south of the church was built in the 1820s for the Brummer family from Bolstaholm.

GROUND PLAN

The church has a rectangular plan, with inner measures about 17 x 9m. There are two different entrances to the church, one in the middle of the west gable, and one through the porch in the south. A third door in the northern wall opens up towards the sacristy, whose inner measures are about 6.2 x 3.1m. Two windows of the sacristy face east.

THE INTERIOR

Many big windows together with a high wooden barrel vault give an impression of light and space. The chancel wall is dominated by an altar decoration in four parts which almost covers the chancel window. A low painting representing the Last Supper on the altar is crowned by two high and narrow paintings depicting the Adoration of the Shepherds and the Flagellation of Christ. On top there is a long and narrow composition representing the Ascension. The altarpieces were donated by Jacob Rusch and his wife Brita Rothof from Snäckö in 1685. Close to the sacristy portal is the pulpit from 1842 made by Isak Boman, carpenter from Geta. It represents high-class Empire style with much gilding and a striking blue sky covered with stars.

Two coats of arms on the chancel wall representing the family Gyllenflög from Bolstaholm date from 1671 and 1699 respectively. The sacristy also has a wooden barrel vault. The portrait of Captain Nils Åman (1684 – 1758) of Bolstaholm and Möckelgräs is kept here.

BUILDING HISTORY

Together with Finström Church, Geta Chapel was granted indulgence in 1463, and in 1487 Bertil, the Chaplain of Geta, received a donation from Kort Hartviksson from Kodbolstad (today Bolstaholm). These historical sources can be supplemented with scientific analysis. According to dendrochronology, there were a couple of extensive alterations of the roof construction, one at the end of the 16th century and the other in the 1820s. Only one of the ***wall plates**** could dendrochronologically be dated to the time after 1450. The medieval origin of the wall plate

◀ Fig. 95. Geta church. Exterior towards southwest.

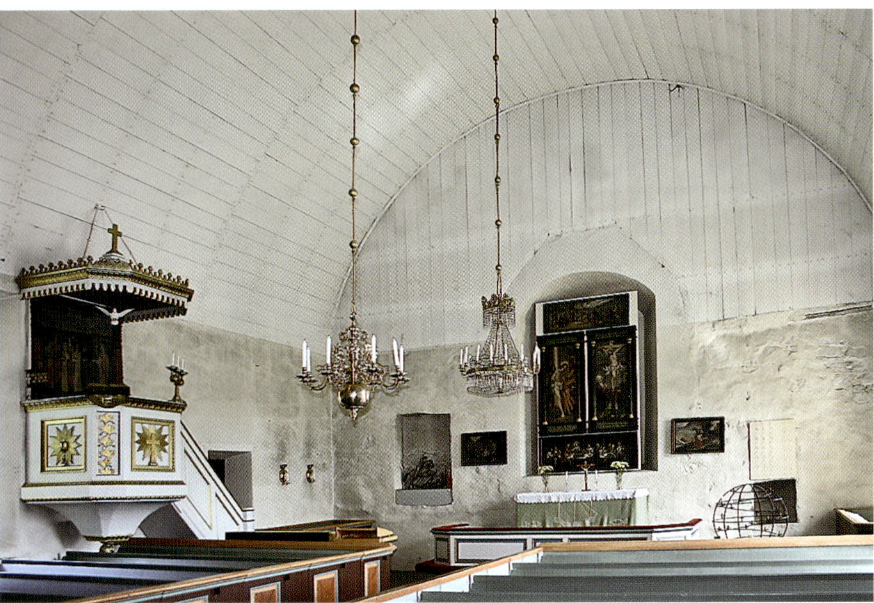

▲ Fig. 97. Interior towards the east.

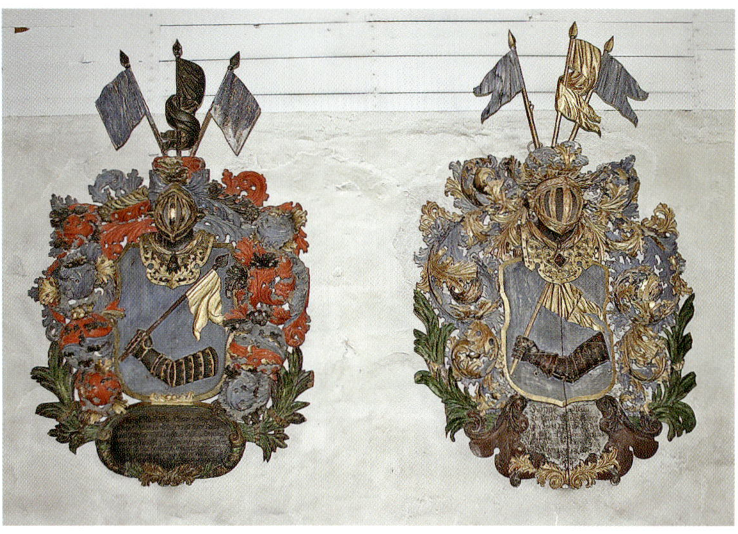

▲ Fig. 99. Coats of arms on the northern wall.

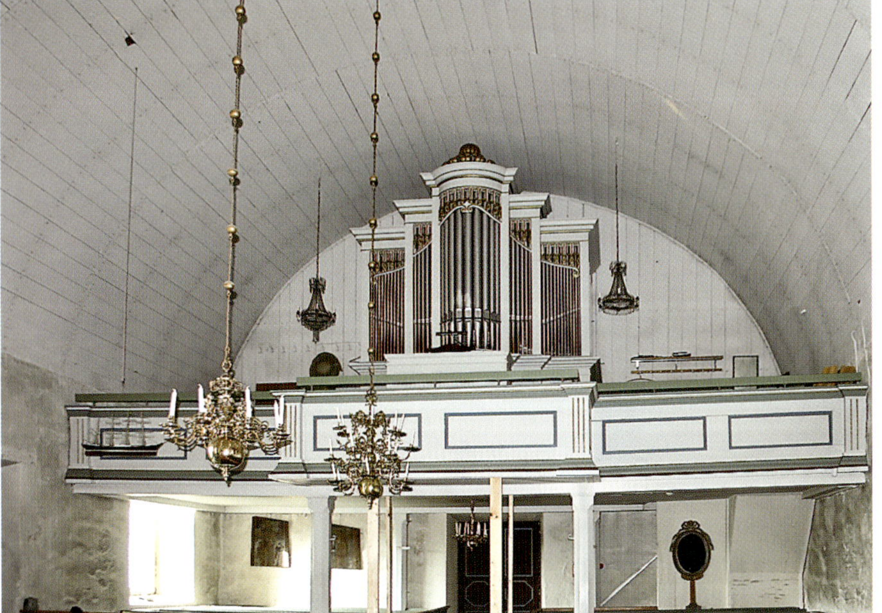

▲ Fig. 98.Interior towards the west.

has later been confirmed convincingly through scientific methods, among them mortar analysis.

The medieval interior of the chapel has also been described by Boetius Murenius in the 17th century. He talks about the neglected interior, with "three repulsive stone altars and other debris" which had to be removed, likewise "papist banners around the altar and the sanctus bell of the chancel". Against the south wall the chapel had a little porch of wood, towards the north a stone sacristy of unknown size. The altar had a wooden altarpiece, which together with a crucifix, and an equestrian group of Saint George and the Dragon had survived from the Middle Ages. The paneled ceiling was horizontal, the windows were fewer in number, and only half the size. The bells were provisionally hanging in a simple construction of loosely joined beams in the churchyard.

THE POST-REFORMATION PERIOD

In the 17th century a number of alterations were made. Three new windows were cut through the wall, which meant that all south windows were enlarged. Another window was opened in "the rear of the church". The roof was renewed. The church received a "new interior" consisting of new pews, a lectern, a bishop's chair, a pulpit and a baptismal font. The medieval altarpiece was cleaned up, as were Saint George and the

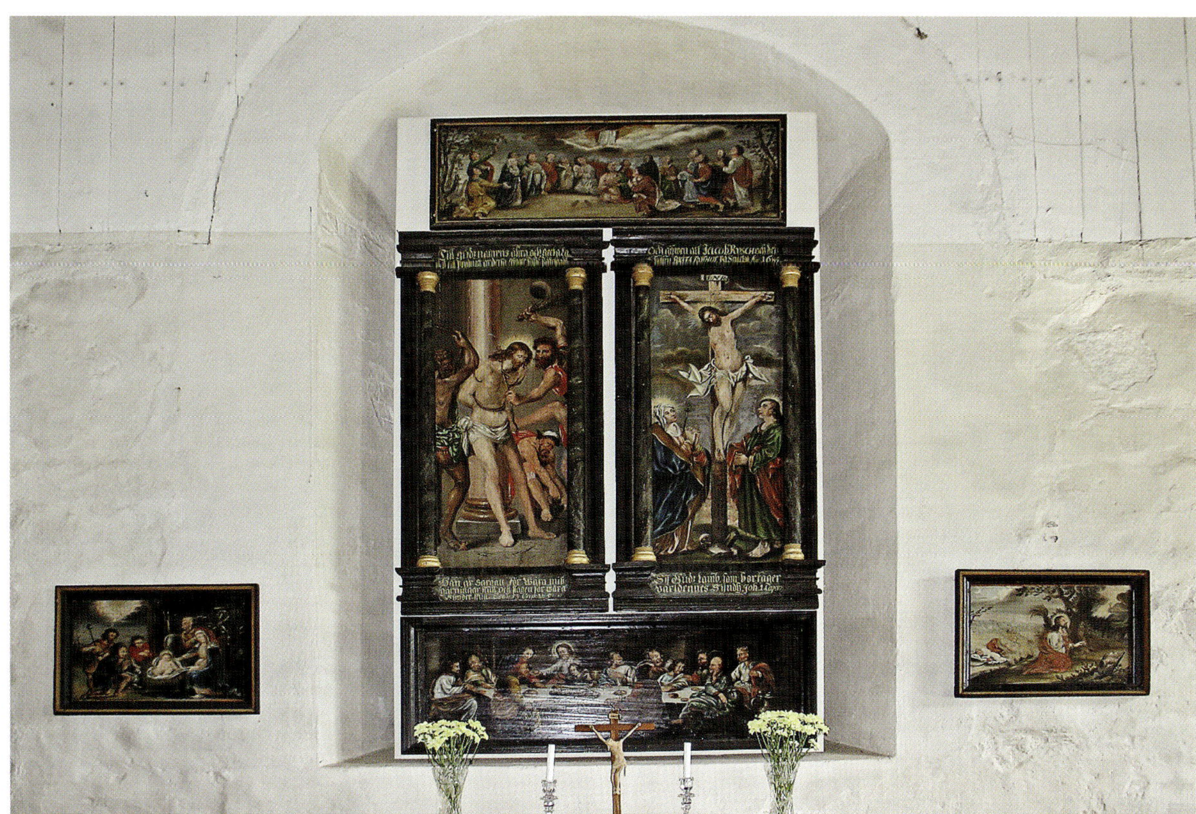

◀ Fig. 100. The altar arrangement in six parts:
1. the Ascension, Christ surrounded by 18 people and Mary.
2. the Last Supper
3. the Adoration of the Shepherds
4. the Flagellation of Christ
5. Christ in Gethsemane
6. the Crucifixion, donated in 1685 by Jacob Rusch and his wife Brita Rothof from Snäckö.

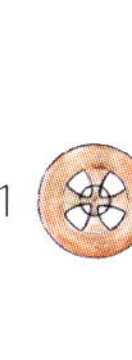

Dragon. The inner walls were whitewashed and the crucifix was hung on the wall. No medieval wall paintings were documented under the plaster. Instead there were fragments of paintings from the Post-Reformation period. Large donations were received from the aristocracy in Bolstaholm, Möckelgräs and Snäckö. The arrangement for hanging the bells was renewed in 1685.

In 1704 a new ceiling was discussed, a wooden barrel vaulting, with reference to what had recently been done to Eckerö Church. No barrel vaulting took place at this stage. Soon afterwards costs for the enlargement of the sacristy were included and a substantial amount of material had been used. The textiles of the church were badly damaged during the Northern War. In a note from 1777 it is said that the chancel railing should be removed, because it prevented the congregation from seeing both the altar and the board of numbers. Around that time the interior, that is the gallery and the altar desk, was painted by Jonathan Lindström. A new bell was donated to the chapel by Captain Nils Åman in 1749.

As everywhere, the 19th century also meant more extensive changes in Geta. The general ideal, also among the Åland churches, was that the interiors of the churches should be bathed in light; they should give the impression of airiness and hygiene. Internally, the walls were whitewashed. The ceiling got its high barrel vault in 1828, at the same time as the windows were enlarged so that they reached their present size. The windows in the gable walls were also renewed and enlarged. A new brick building substituted the little wooden porch. Externally the joints were given new plaster. The bell tower was rebuilt and repaired in many stages and the lower part of the belfry was used to store material. The precinct wall in stone was built in the 1850s.

In the 1930s minor renovation programs were initiated in the church. The conservator Oskari Niemi documented existing wall paintings. At the same time a new bell tower was discussed. The porch also underwent renovations. In 1965-66 the church was restored on a larger scale under direction of the architect K.R. Lindgren. Lindgren designed new pews for the church, while the conservator Veikko Kiljunen uncovered what was left of the Post-Reformation wall paintings. ■

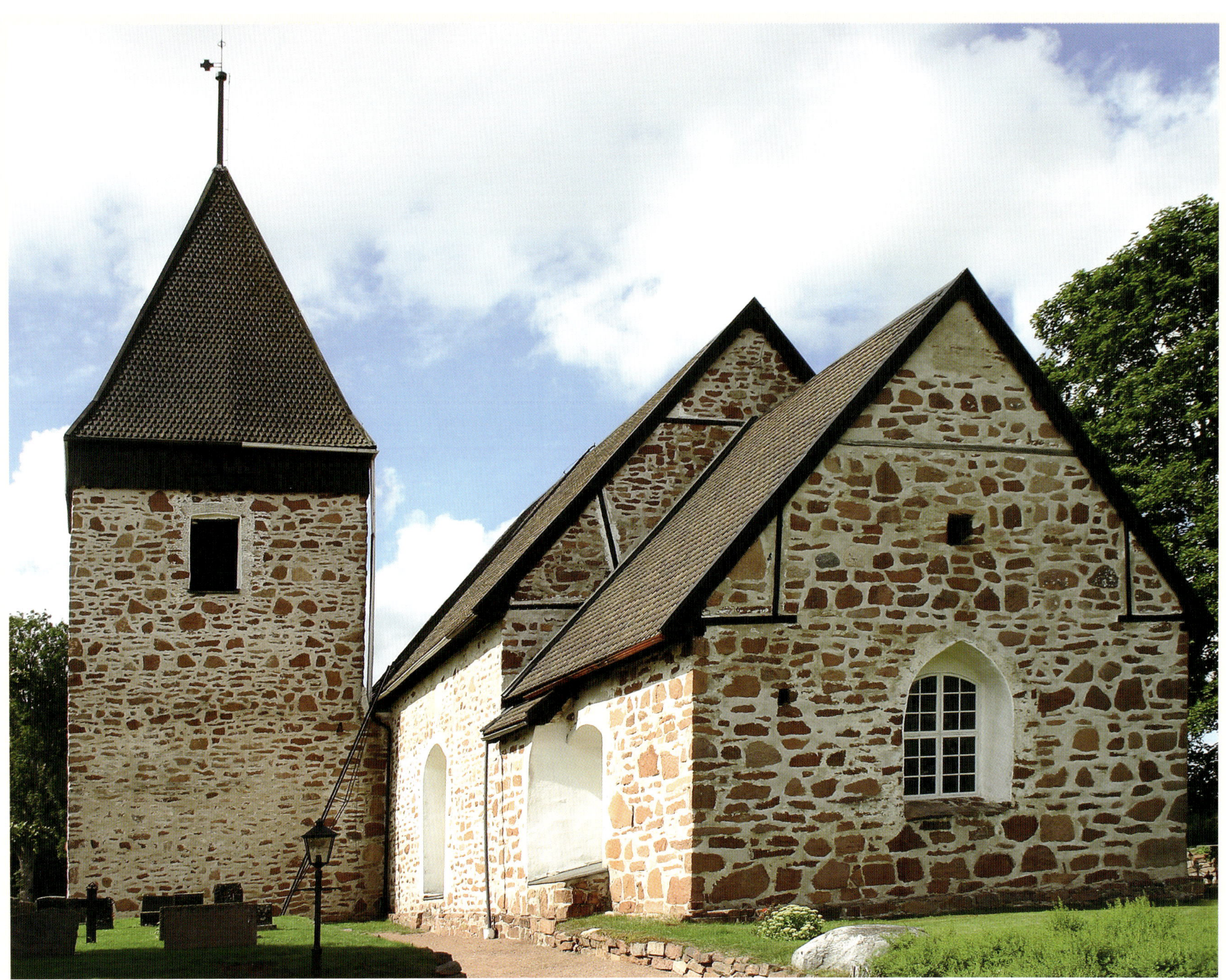

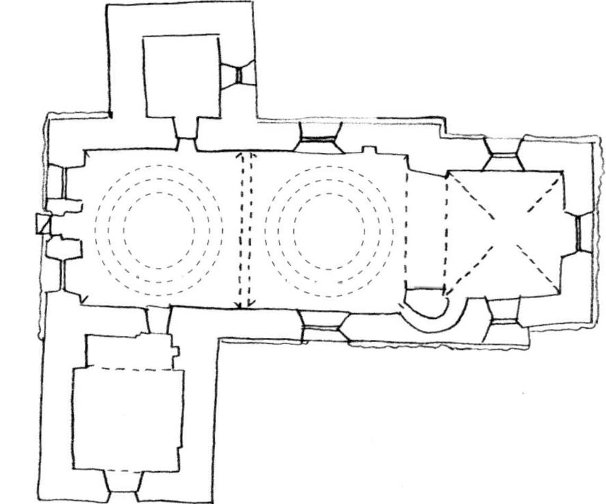

▲ Fig. 102. Hammarland church. Ground plan.

HAMMARLAND CHURCH

Hammarland Church, consecrated to Saint Catherine of Alexandria, is one of the mother churches of Åland, with Eckerö as an subservient chapel.

The church was built close to a little lake to the north, with an outlet into a bay and further out into the sea. The church lies along the old postal road, which is probably identical to the medieval pilgrims' road from Finland further out in the world. The largest graveyard in the parish, "Kjusarn", lies immediately west of the church, surrounded by well preserved and picturesque church stables.

THE EXTERIOR

The church has a skyline in three steps, the highest point being a pyramidal tower built against the western part of the southern wall of the nave. The nave is second highest, and the lowest part is the narrowing chancel building to the east, built against the eastern wall of the nave, the original chancel wall. The exterior of the church thus shows many different stages of building: secondary units directly connected with the nave can be discerned. The building material is the local Åland red granite, rapakivi. In the nave the stones are small and the façades are framed by larger granite slabs in the corners. Except for a short part along the southern wall, a simple stepped socle runs along the whole nave. The windows are consistently large, and roughly hewn through the walls. The south façade of the nave shows traces of many alterations. Obvious *joints** show that both tower and sacristy are secondary additions. The location of the tower, against the south wall of the nave and in direct line with the west gable, is most unusual. Also, the sacristy against the northern wall lies unusually far to the west. The joints between chancel and nave are not that obvious. Without a visible joint, the nave continues further east into a high and narrow wall. The wall is roughly executed and ends abruptly in the east. The entrances are one portal in the southern wall of the tower and another in the western gable of the nave.

GROUND PLAN

The ground plan shows a rectangular hall church (inner measures 16.6m x 8.3m) divided into two squarely vaulted bays connected by a transverse arch. Against the nave a tower, a narrower eastern chancel, without an apse, and a sacristy have been erected. The placing of the tower to the south is rare. It has been placed against the original main portal in the southern wall of the nave. The sacristy portal, roughly opposite the south portal, is placed unusually far west for Åland. Thus the sacristy, too, lies unusually far to the west. Yet another portal is found in the middle of the western gable. To the south, in the joint between the nave and the chancel, there is a mysterious construction, or "a block in the wall" of unknown original function. Today it houses the

◀ Fig. 101. Hammarland church. Exterior from the southeast.

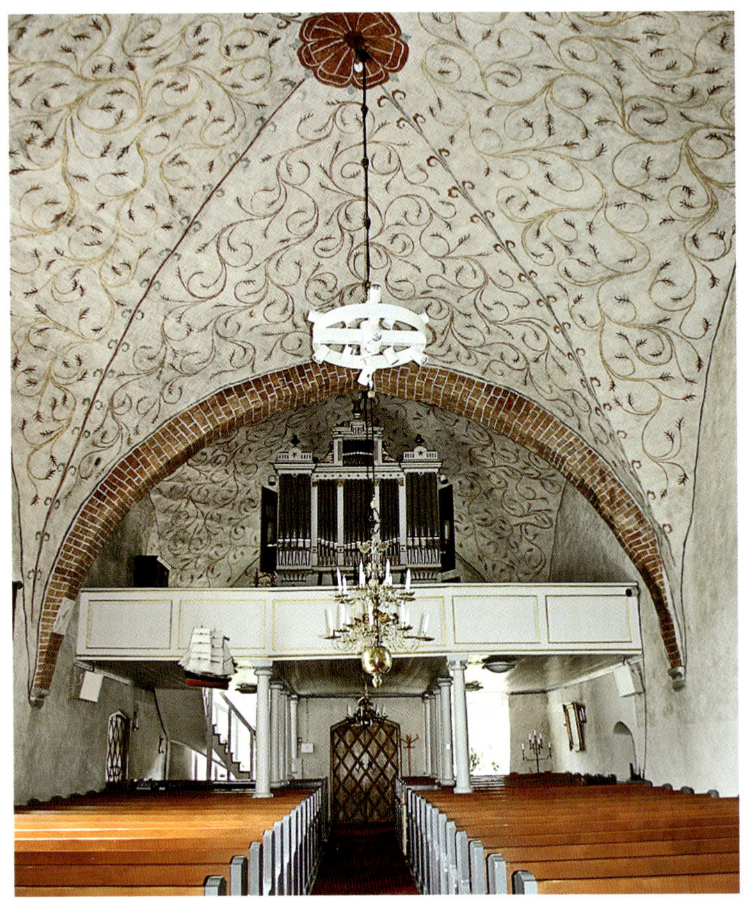

▲ Fig. 103. Interior towards the west.

stairs to the pulpit. Another narrow staircase in the south wall reaches up to the attic of the chancel.

THE INTERIOR

The interior of the church is harmonious and proportional. Here we can see all the different building stages, also visible in the exterior: a single rectangular nave, with secondarily added tower, chancel, and sacristy. The nave is obviously the oldest part. It is divided into two bays, with a transverse arch in between. The bays of the nave are covered by elegantly cast cupola vaults of concentrically arranged fieldstones. The vaults start low down along the walls, reaching considerable height at the top. The transverse arch between the vaults, which is also made of fieldstone, has been covered by a painting giving an illusion of a brick wall. The arch rests on simple profiled brackets in limestone. The vaults are completely covered by medieval multifoliate ornamentation in green and red. The brick imitation recurs in the framings of two walled-in windows situated high up to the east. Under them the nave opens up towards the chancel through a low triumphal arch. The chancel vault differs from the vaulting of the nave in that field stones have been arranged as a cross vault with clear *groins** and angled corners. The ornamentation in the chancel covers the entire vault as well as the walls.

West of the northern window, immediately close to an inauguration cross, is the only figural painting in the church: Saint Judas of Thaddeus, seated with a double cross and an associated text band. He is the only one of the twelve apostles preserved from a Credo-suite. Wide and high windows to the south and north are complemented by three window openings in the western gable. Two of them flank the west portal, and the third, asymmetrical in shape, is placed higher up in the central axis of the church.

The unusual location of the tower can be explained at least partly: it has been erected against the original main portal in the south. Correspondingly, the location of the sacristy far in the west can be explained: it was erected against an existing north portal.

BUILDING HISTORY

In Hammarland no traces of an earlier wooden church have been identified. The first stone church was erected in the second half of the 13th century. The vaulting was finished somewhat later. Once more, it was originally a hall church with the chancel area included in the eastern part of the rectangular plan. A priest door, nowadays walled in, led directly into the chancel from the south. The brick imitation on the transverse arch and the double windows in the east wall of the chancel belong to this first building stage. The exterior of the same windows can be seen from the attic of the chancel as well as two round-arched and highly placed windows with limestone framing in deep window niches. To the west, the church had only one opening high up, formed like a quatrefoil of Åland limestone. The other window openings were high up in the southern wall. There were no windows facing north.

The tower was erected in the beginning of the 14th century. The reason for choosing to build the tower against the original main entrance may have been bad foundation conditions in front of the west gable. Another reason might have been a wish to avoid blocking a wall grave in the western wall of the church, indicated by later sources.

The ground floor of the tower had a double function. It was both

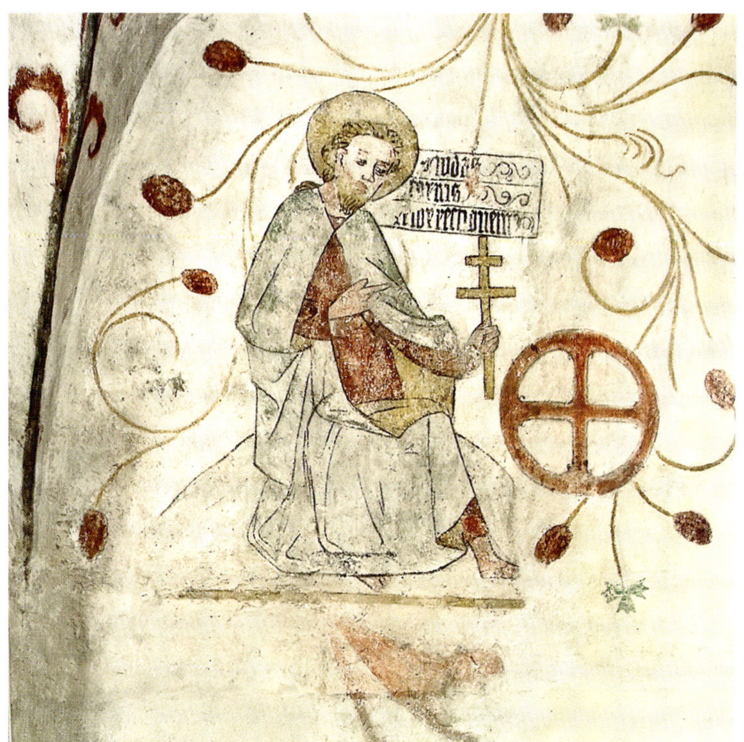

▲ Fig. 104. Wall painting representing Judas Thaddeaus, detail.

porch and chapel with a large stone altar consecrated to Saint Olof. The nave was enlarged in the beginning of the 15th century with a new chancel, narrower than the nave, and with a straight east wall. During this building period, however, a devastating fire occurred in the attic of the nave. Flaking field stones above the vault bear witness of the disaster. Indirectly the fire can be dated through dendrochronological analysis of the new roof trusses, which in the 1440s replaced those that had burnt. Because of the fire the roof of the chancel was not finished until the 1460s. The sacristy belongs to the late Middle Ages.

After the chancel part had been added in the middle of the 15th century both the nave and the chancel were painted with wall-to-wall multifoliate ornamentation. The medieval triumphal arch between nave and chancel was round arched and much narrower than it is today. In the middle of the opening hung the church crucifix dating from around 1440. The altarpiece was destroyed and the sculptures spread in various directions, but it can still be reconstructed with considerable certainty: a long altarpiece ornamented the new altar in the chancel. The centre part is dominated by a scene representing the Father of Mercy, where the enthroned Father holds the deposited Christ in his arms. The scene is flanked by Mary and Anne, the apostle Peter and John the Evangelist. The left wing was filled with Saint Birgitta, Saint Henrik and Saint Barbara. In the right wing follow Saint Catherine of Alexandria, Saint Lawrence, and Saint Erik. The church ordered the altarpiece from northern Germany, around 1440.

THE POST-REFORMATION PERIOD

Immediately after the Reformation the church was neglected. Hair-raising stories have survived of how the porch functioning as a charnal house, containing several hundred skulls. The hood of the church was renewed in the 17th century, but the medieval pyramidal form was preserved. The portal through the western gable was hewn up in the beginning of the 18th century. No essential architectural alterations were, however, made until the first half of the 19th century, when existing windows were enlarged and new windows were made to the north and in the western gable. In the same process the triumphal arch to the chancel was enlarged.

Archaeological excavations directed by the architect Alarik Tavaststjerna were initiated by 1913. In connection with the excavation the church was renovated and medieval wall paintings were uncovered. Another large restoration and cleaning took place in 1960, when the old iron heaters were replaced by a new hot air system, which a few years later gave way to central heating. In the autumn of 1987, the interior once more faced a well needed cleaning.

INVENTORY

- **The baptismal font**

A so-called 'paradise font' of Gotland type, but of local Åland limestone, dates from the latter half of the 13th century (Fig. 25).

- **The bishop's chair**

The bishop's chair, fragmentarily preserved, against the northern chancel wall, was acquired in 1650. The painting in the front mirror represents the priest Aaron, brother of Moses, and an Old Testament predecessor of the bishopry.

- **The crucifix**

The crucifix from Hammarland church was sold in 1888 to the Turku Historical Museum. It now hangs in the Nun's chapel in Turku Castle. Originally it filled the triumphal arch in the church, standing on a transversal beam. Stylistically the crucifix can be dated to the beginning of the 15th century. ■

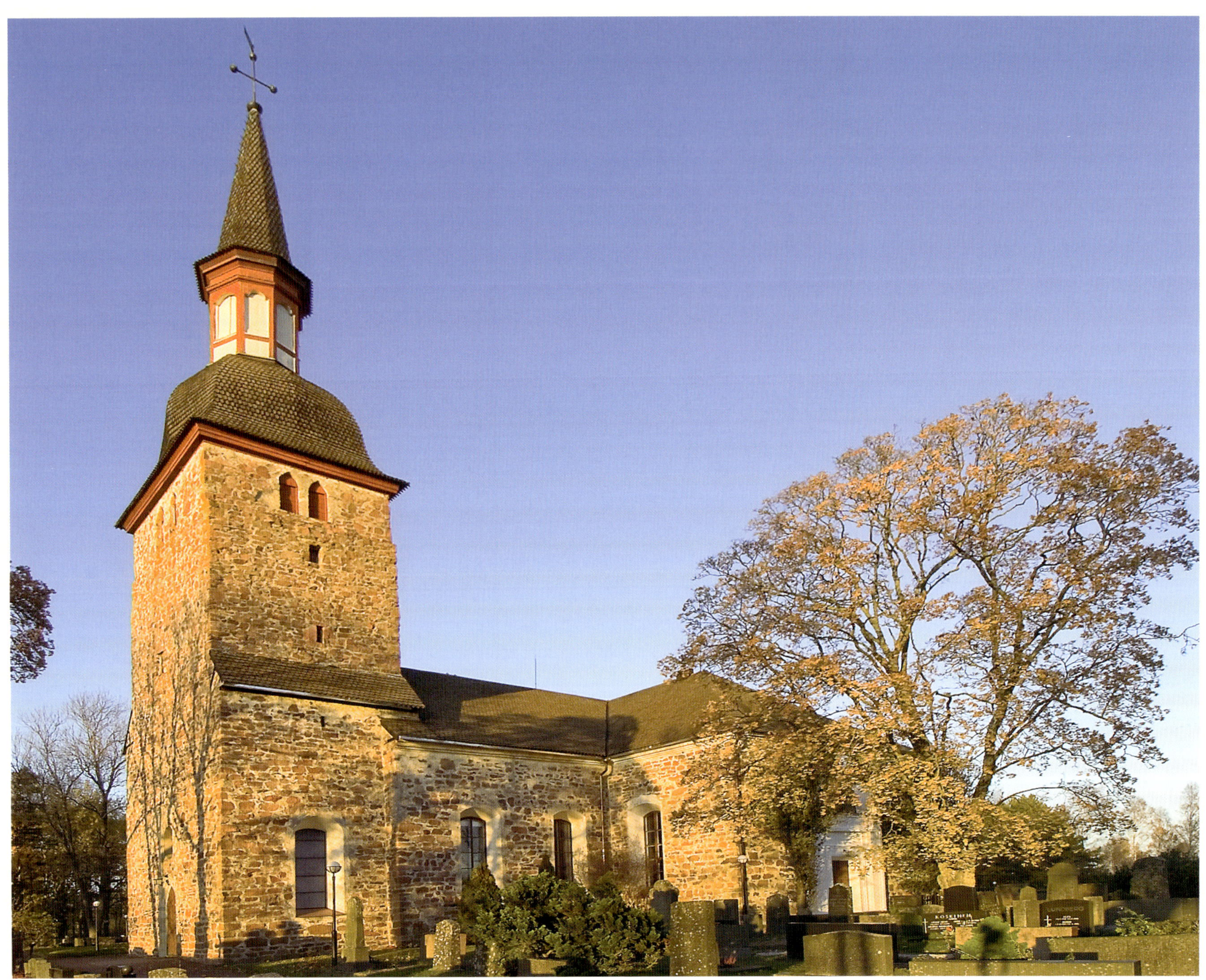

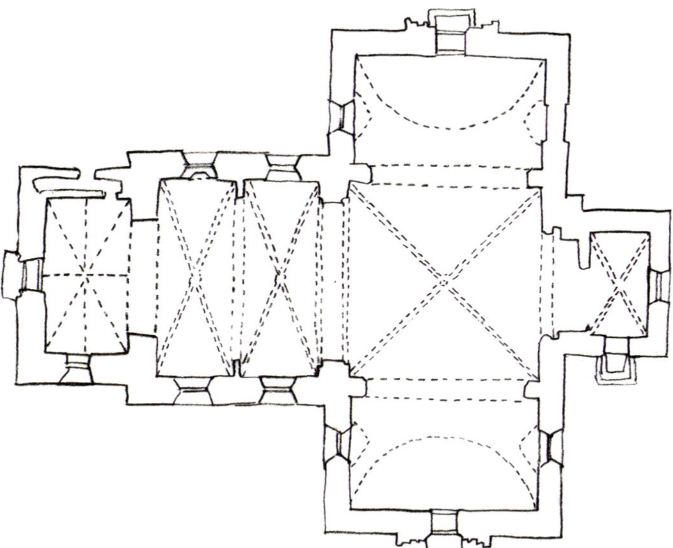

▲ Fig. 107. Jomala church, ground plan.

JOMALA CHURCH

Saint Olof's church in Jomala is centrally located in Åland, immediately adjacent to the largest Iron Age graveyard. It was erected in the middle of Jomala plain, which is abundant in limestone, but without direct contact with the sea.

Yet the church tower serves as a characteristic landmark for seafarers from afar. It has generally been seen as one of the oldest stone churches in entire Finland. In ground plan, proportions, and in the use of stone sculptures in the decorative program, it radically differs from all other Åland churches.

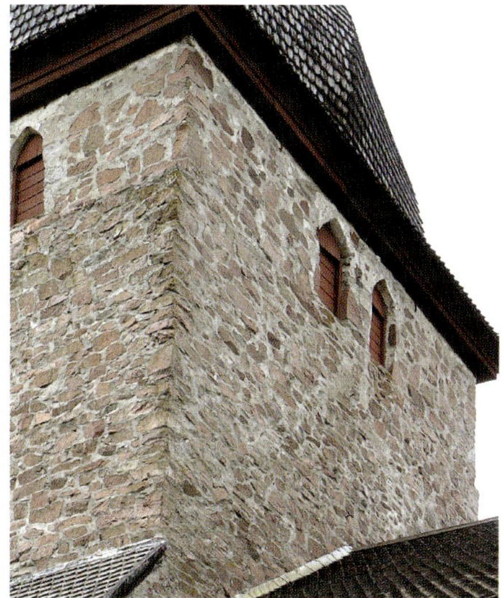

▲ Fig. 106. Jomala church, detail of the east wall of the tower.

THE EXTERIOR

Already on the exterior Jomala church reveals a complicated and multifaceted building history with a number of secondary interferences. Traces can be seen of both demolitions and later additions. The church is built of selected small stones in local red granite (rapakivi), mixed in with plenty of local ordovician limestone. The limestone is to be found in the walls, in the corner chains, and as decorative framework in the west portal of the tower.

The high west tower has shingle covered "shoulders" cut off against the nave. On the eastern wall of the nave the original roof angle of the nave can be traced (Fig. 106). It is evident that the original roof was both taller and steeper, and that the shoulders of the tower were adjusted to it. The wide body of the building, or the transept in a north-south direction, which has been added to the nave in the east, today has the same roof height as the nave after the demolition. Uniform stepped cornices underline the likeness. Nor does the masonry of the transept differ all that much from the original walls of the nave. But the framing of the portals towards the north and the south indicate the beginning of the 19th century. Also the eastern addition, the sacristy, with bricks in the upper part of the gable, stands out as a feature foreign to Åland church architecture.

The northern and southern façades of the nave show traces of walled-in portals in the south and the north, placed axially opposite each other in the western part of the nave. Large window openings have later been hewn through the northern and southern walls.

◀ Fig. 105.Jomala church. Exterior from the southwest.

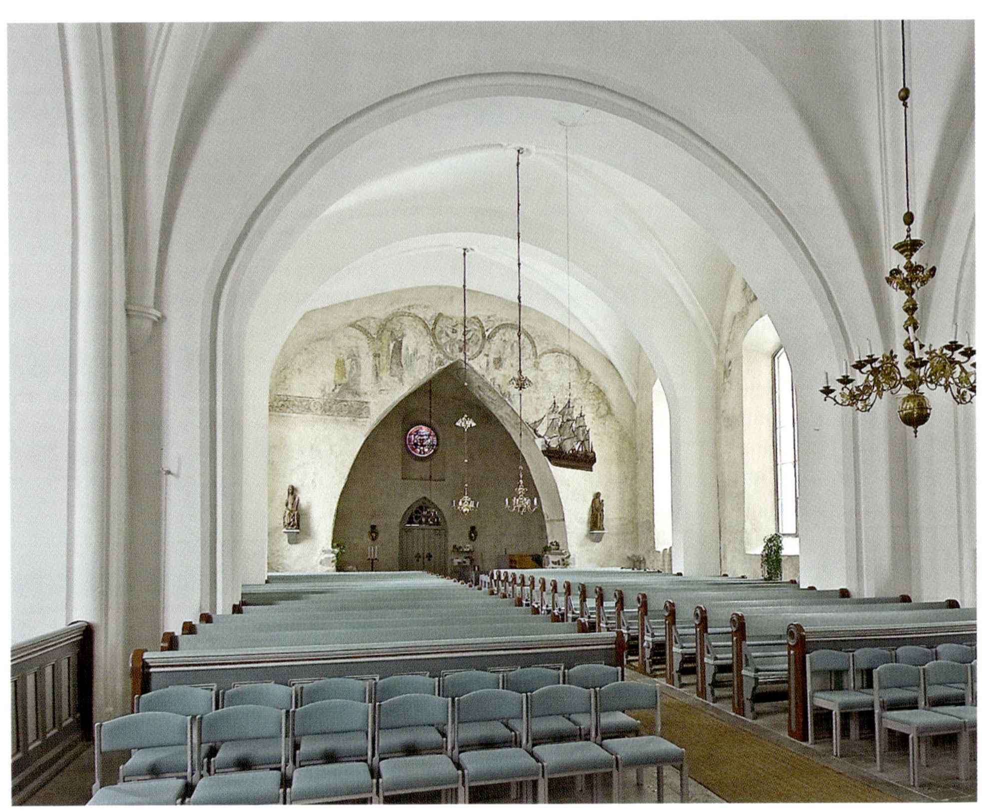

◀ Fig. 108.Jomala church. Interior towards the tower arch in the west.

GROUND PLAN

Jomala Church has an unusual T-formed ground plan. A nave of 9.3m x 10.9m, where the width exceeds the length, is finished in the east with a transept oriented north-south. The west tower is connected with the nave, and in the extension of the nave to the east the church ends up with a sacristy, with a separate entrance from the south. The ground plan is the result of the radical interference and building alterations made during the 19th century. The western portal of the tower and the portal in the southern transept form the main entrances to the church.

THE INTERIOR

Inside the church the various building stages can be clearly discerned (Fig. 108, and Fig. 109). The changes of the 19th century with smooth and bare wall surfaces to the east are markedly different from the medieval parts of the original nave and the west tower. The medieval part of the church to the west gives a warmer impression, and fragments of high-class lime paintings can still be seen on the pointed arch of the tower, on the west gable, and on the north and south walls of the original nave. The arch of the tower rests on solid supports of limestone, covered with wide, profiled limestone slabs. A strangely placed human face sculpted in limestone remains in situ on the northern shelf of the vault. (Fig.7). The face is sculpted in the corner of a horizontally placed slab of limestone. Yet rough chisel marks on the upper surface indicate that the position may be secondary - the lower surface is beautifully profiled and neatly edged. A rough broken surface on the corresponding limestone surface on an opposite southern slab indicates that there may have been a similar stone carving. The interior also shows traces of walled-in southern and northern portals. The uniformly cast vaults in both transept and nave show that they belong to the same secondary building stage which can further be seen in the attic of the nave. The demolition of the original vault and the lowering of the roof are very clear. In the process the walls of the nave were also leveled and with them the largest part of the large attic openings towards the north and the south. Only the roughly cast tower vault remained intact in the process.

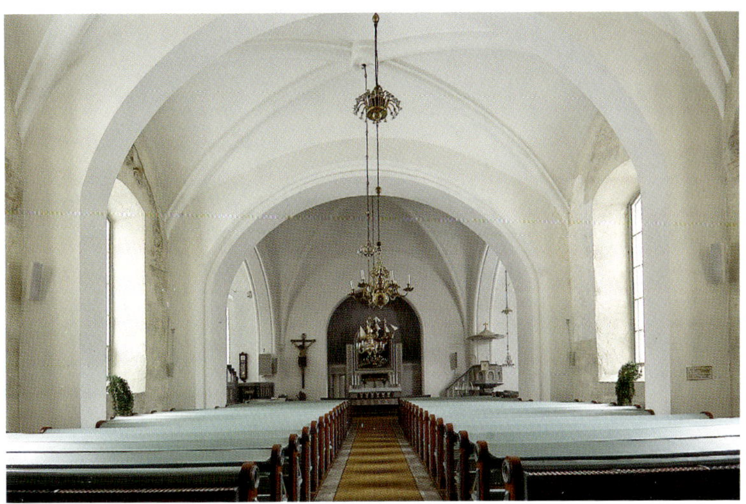

▲ Fig. 109. Jomala church. Interior towards the east.

THE BUILDING HISTORY

The building history of Jomala church is not yet fully investigated. Archaeological excavations on the site revealed no traces of a possible older wooden church. But there were plenty of signs of ecclesiastic activity during the beginning of the 13th century, i.e., during the Romanesque period. The decorative limestone sculptures, the so called "Jomala Lion" (Fig. 6) and the little human face (Fig. 7) secondarily placed in the northern supporting construction of the tower arch belong to this stage. We do not know exactly what this potential Romanesque church looked like. But we do know that it had an appearance totally different from the other Åland churches and from other contemporary churches in general.

The church was already considered too small in the 1600s. To deal with the problem an alteration plan was drawn in 1808 at the Royal Superintendent's Office in Stockholm. The drawing, which was not realized, is still preserved (Fig. 110). It provides valuable information concerning the church, indicating how it appeared before the great architectural changes in the 19th century. As a historical source, however, this drawing is problematic. In addition to the planned double galleries in nave and chancel, it includes suggested changes around windows and portals. Yet it gives a trustworthy picture of the church, of what it must have looked like in the 1280s, with the west tower finished and the original chancel without an additional apse in the east.

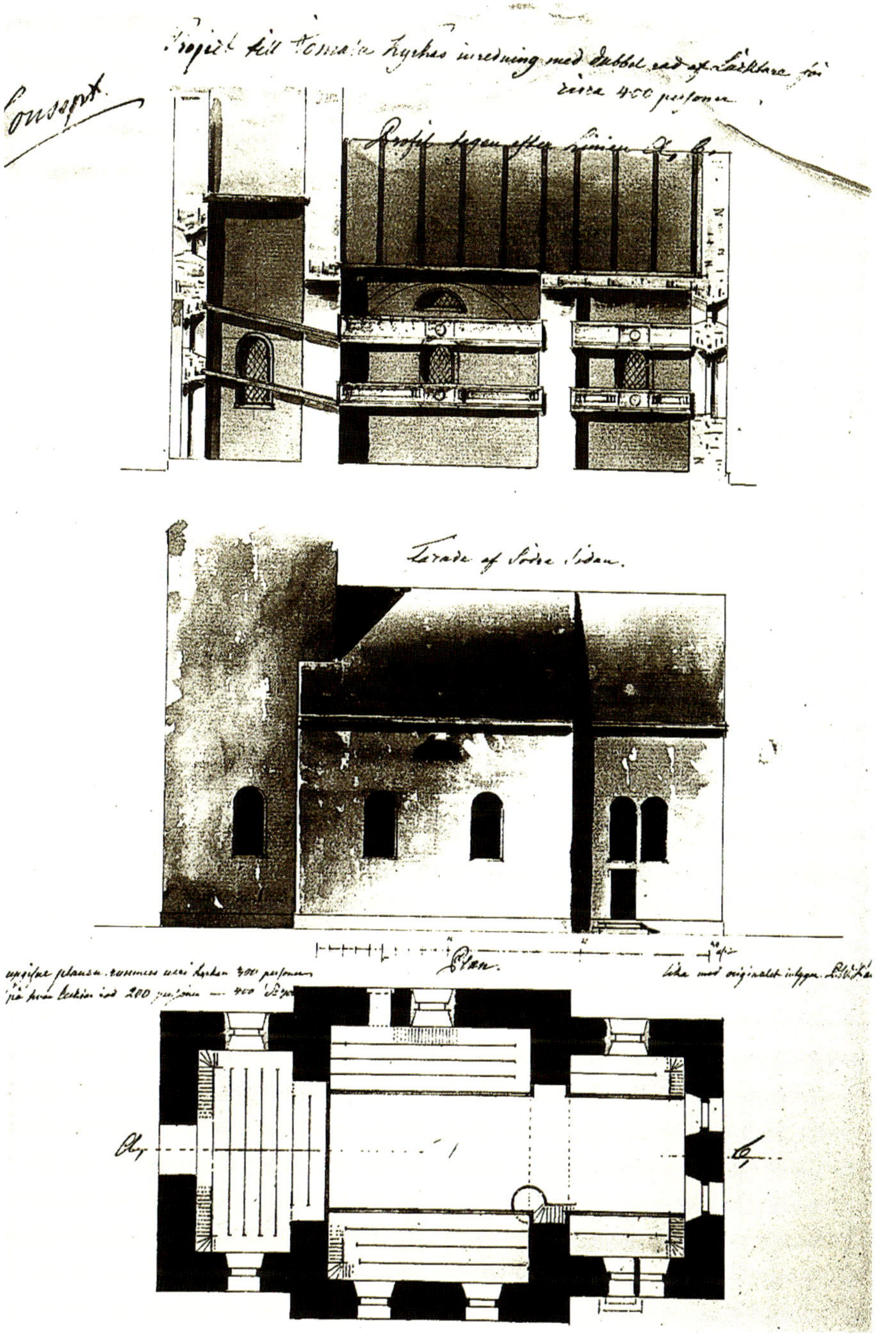

▲ Fig. 110. Jomala church. Alteration drawing from 1808.

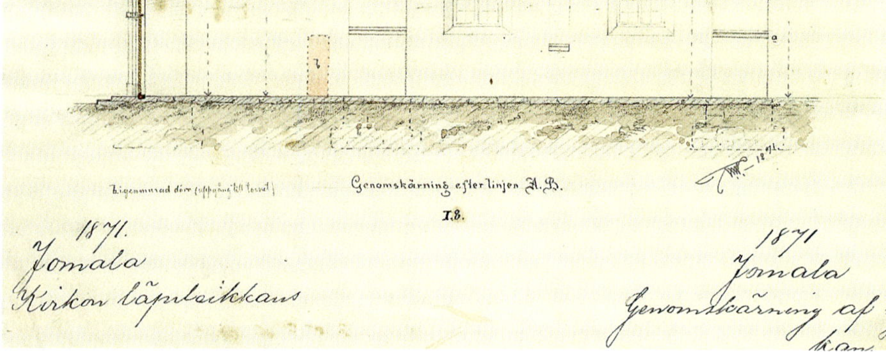

▲ Fig. 111. Jomala church. Longitudinal section, documentary drawing from 1871.

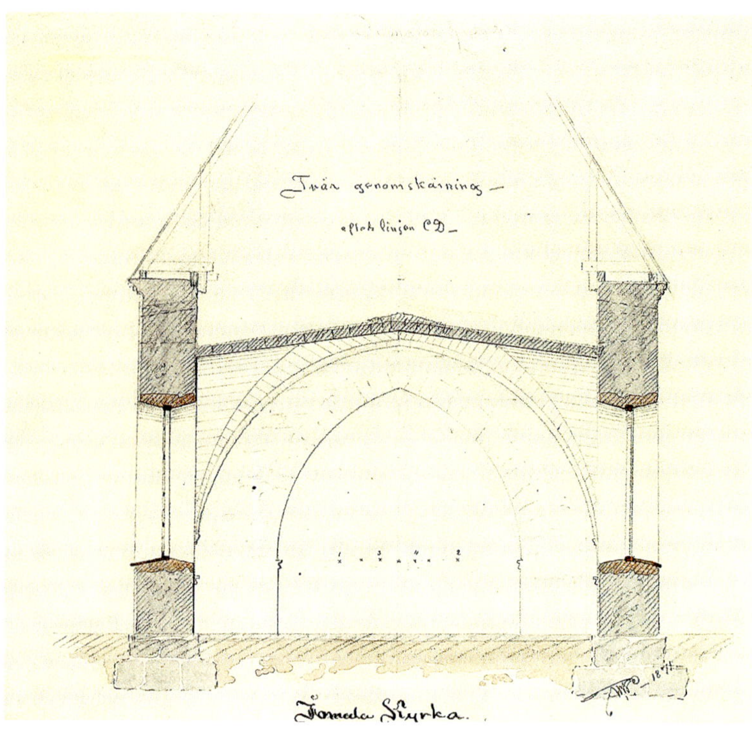

▲ Fig. 112. Jomala church. Transversal section, documentary drawing from 1871.

We see a unique solution where tower and chancel together with the nave form a symmetrical and well-proportioned architectural body. The nave has unusual dimensions, with a width exceeding the length. It is flanked in the east by the chancel, with a straight eastern wall, and by the tower in the west. The chancel and tower have almost identical proportions, being also wider than they are long. In spite of the drawing, the chancel was probably lower than the nave, and we know that the shoulders of the tower really formed a continuation of the roof of the nave.

Important details, not evident from the 1808 drawing, are well complemented in the documentary drawings made during the First Art Historical Expedition in 1871, conducted by the Finnish Antiquarian Society. The architect Woldemar Westling made his documentary drawings for the transversal section and for the longitudinal section of nave and tower in the last minute, at a stage when the vaults of the nave, the triumphal arch, and the attic of the nave were still intact. All of this was demolished in the 1880s.

We can see that the triumphal arch in the east repeats the same shape as the tower arch between tower and nave. The nave is divided into two wide and short bays. Two vaults cast in fieldstones with exceptionally wide spans, rest on low profiled brackets of limestone. Above the nave is shown an intact attic, with three large openings facing north. Because of the demolition of the vaults mentioned above, this attic is today severely damaged. Yet one can still see fragments of the preserved openings, also towards the south.

So far the connection between tower and nave remains unclear. A cavity from the westernmost roof truss of the nave is seen in the outer east wall of the tower, which indicates that the tower at this stage is part of the construction of the demolished roof. A couple of mortar samples do however suggest that the attic floor may have belonged to the original Romanesque stone church, from the beginning of the 13th century. More mortar samples should therefore be analyzed, especially from the socle level of the nave. Nor is the original function of the attic floor clear, but there were for instance corresponding defense attics in Romanesque churches in Öland, Sweden. It is also possible that the space above the vaults was used for fireproof storage.

The documentary drawings from 1871, by Woldemar Westling,

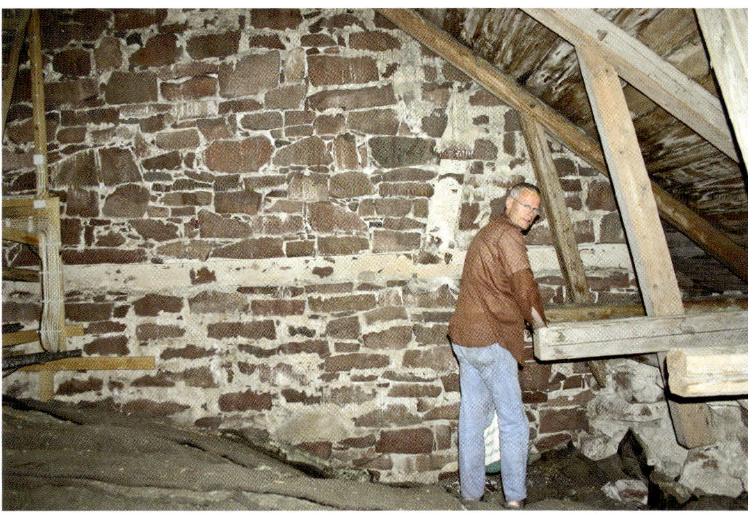

▲ Fig. 113. Jomala church. Interior from the attic of the nave, towards the tower in the west.

facilitate a reconstruction of the church interior (cf. Fig. 10). Towards the chancel in the east and towards the tower in the west, the nave was limited by identical high-pointed arches, both resting on limestone support. The main entrance of the church, facing south, was located in the western side of the nave, axially opposite the northern portal of the church. A priest door led directly to the low chancel, with a straight east wall. The chancel had plenty of light openings, towards the east a so called Trinity window with three narrow windows placed tightly together, and two coupled windows towards the south.

Limestone elements were conspicuous in the architecture: portals as well as windows were framed by limestone. But Jomala is also the only church in Åland where limestone sculptures have been part of the ornamental program. The Åland Museum today houses a limestone sculpture found in a closet in the church at the beginning of the 19th century: a lion head, with a human face in its mouth (Fig. 6). The sculpture is Romanesque, that is, it belongs stylistically to the time before 1250, and it might have been suited as a gable ornament on the separate chancel torn down in the 19th century. The human face on the northern shelf of the tower arch is also Romanesque in style. The limestone sculptures and certain building details point to the possibility that the nave and the chancel might have been somewhat older than the west tower. The west tower was erected in the 1280s, contemporary with the painting program on the walls. The Crucifix from the end of the 13th century was probably hanging in the Triumphal arch, resting on a rood beam.

Up to the 1830s the medieval church seems to have been preserved more or less intact. To prepare space for "another nine farmers" in the 17th century, the two side altars at the chancel were torn down. As far as window openings and portals are concerned, the preserved drawing from 1808 includes planned changes, in Empire style. In this case a drawing from the 1840s gives a more accurate picture of the original south façade.

Considerable changes were initiated by the Imperial Intendent's Office in Helsinki in 1824, to be finished after many sorrows in 1844. The demolished original chancel was substituted by the broad transept with a sacristy in the east. By mistake the transept became too low. To form a uniform silhouette, the roof above the nave was lowered as late as 1884. That did not only destroy the defense floor, but the magnificent fieldstone vaults of the nave were also demolished, together with the triumphal arch between nave and transept.

THE WALL PAINTINGS

The interior of Jomala Church was originally covered by early Gothic wall paintings from the 1280s. These paintings were strongly polychrome, in yellow, blue, green and red. At least three different pictorial sequences on top of each other were separated by ornamental friezes. The actual sequence of the events described can be discerned only in the tower arch and in the western gable of the nave. The tower arch (cf. Fig. 8a-b) probably represents scenes of a courtly nature from the biblical parable of the prodigal son. The main figure is dressed in a tunica striped in white and yellow. Uppermost to the south the enthroned and crowned father distributes his legacy, uppermost to the north the son proudly rides out with a falcon, a hound and a splendid retinue in order to conquer the world as a knight. Down towards the south we can see a fragmentary scene from a brothel where the son is enjoying himself, while the damaged scene down towards the north probably represents his homecoming.

The western gable towards the nave represents the Day of Judgment, with the Throne of Grace (the crucified son in his father's arms) as the executing judge. Down to the north the damned walk in towards the gap of hell, while the blessed walk southwards towards the gates of heaven. On the northern wall of the nave a "Wheel of Fortune" can be fragmentarily seen, marked with the four ages of man (childhood, youth, manhood, old age). Fragments of a Romanesque ornamental frieze, sporadically preserved along the walls of the nave, show that the walls here too have been covered by polychrome mural paintings in several friezes on top of each other. This probably also goes for the vaults in the nave and the chancel.

INVENTORY

• Crucifix.

Jomala still has a rich treasure of sculpture preserved in the church. The first to be noted is the crucifix to the left of the altar. It is probably from the latter half of the 13th century, imported from Gotland. In the 14th century it was subjected to some modernizations, when for example the clusters of blood were added, to express the new philosophy of suffering of the time. The cross itself has unfortunately been lost.

• Saint Anne

A Mary sculpture from the early 14th century, north of the tower arch facing the nave, has later been altered to Saint Anne (Fig. 54). Another sculpture of Mary with the infant Christ standing in her arms (south of the tower arch), is of unknown date. Fragments of the late medieval triptych (from the 15th century), representing the Deposition of Christ from the cross, are found on the southern and northern walls of the tower. Originally all sculptures were strongly colored and gilded.

• The medieval baptismal font.

Even the medieval font, of Gotland limestone from the middle of the 13th century, has been richly painted in different colors. Today all traces of color are missing.

During archaeological excavations in 1961 a large number of glass splinters were found (cf. Fig. 12). They date from the 1280s and are of Gotland origin. Probably all the windows were equipped with precious stained glass. A large number of coins were also found during the excavations. The great majority of these were from the end of the 13th century, but in the nave eighteen coins from the beginning and middle of the 13th century were found.

The modern stained glass window in the porch represents Saint Olof and was made by the American artist Thure Bengts, a Jomala native. It was donated by Professor Bengts and was unveiled in 1968. ■

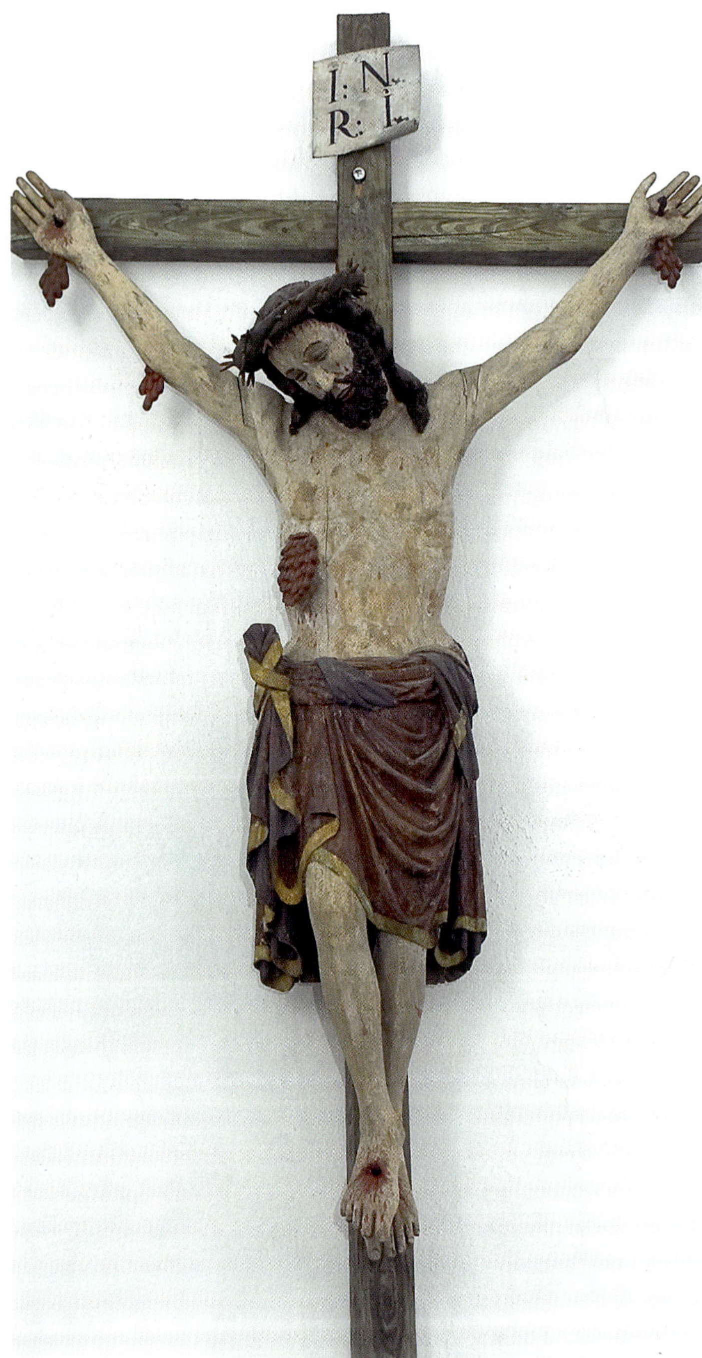

▲ Fig. 114.Jomala church. The crucifix.

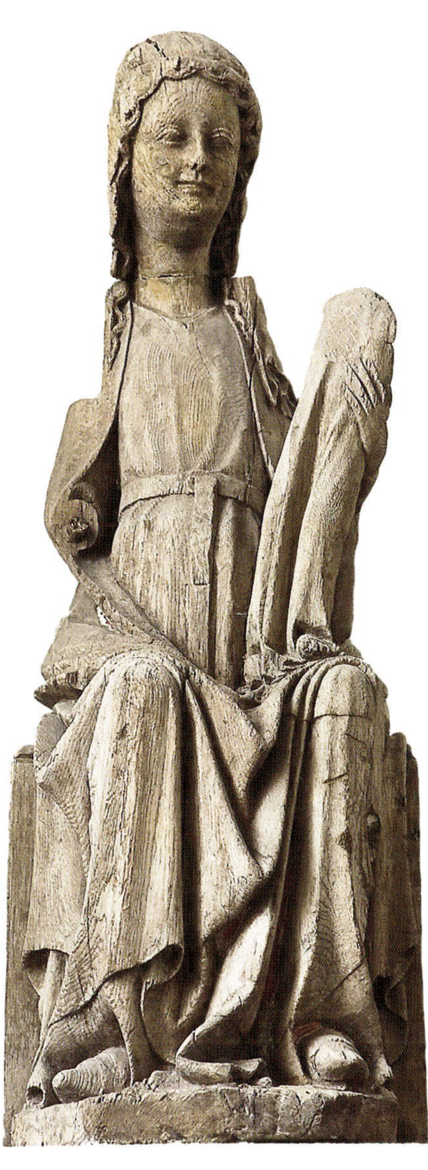

▲ Fig. 115. Jomala church. Sculpture of the Madonna, oak.

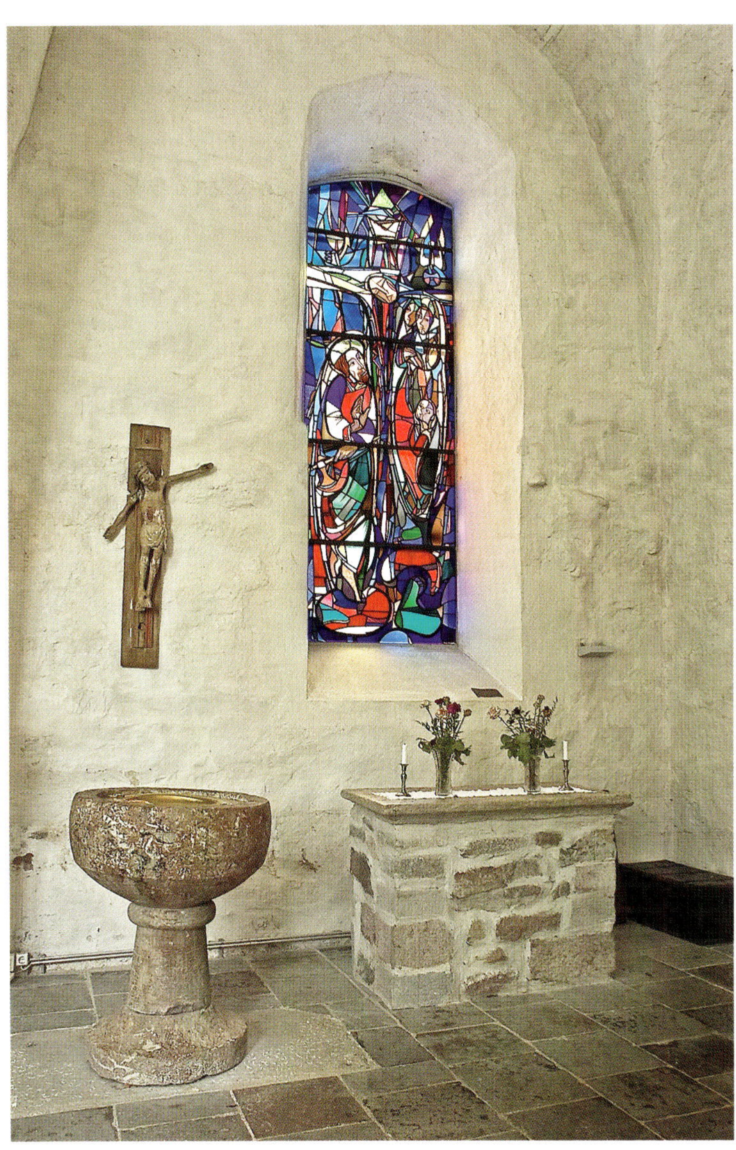

▲ Fig. 116. The medieval font of the church and a stained glass window from 1968. On the wall a detail of the "Deposition from the Cross" a fragment from the medieval altarpiece.

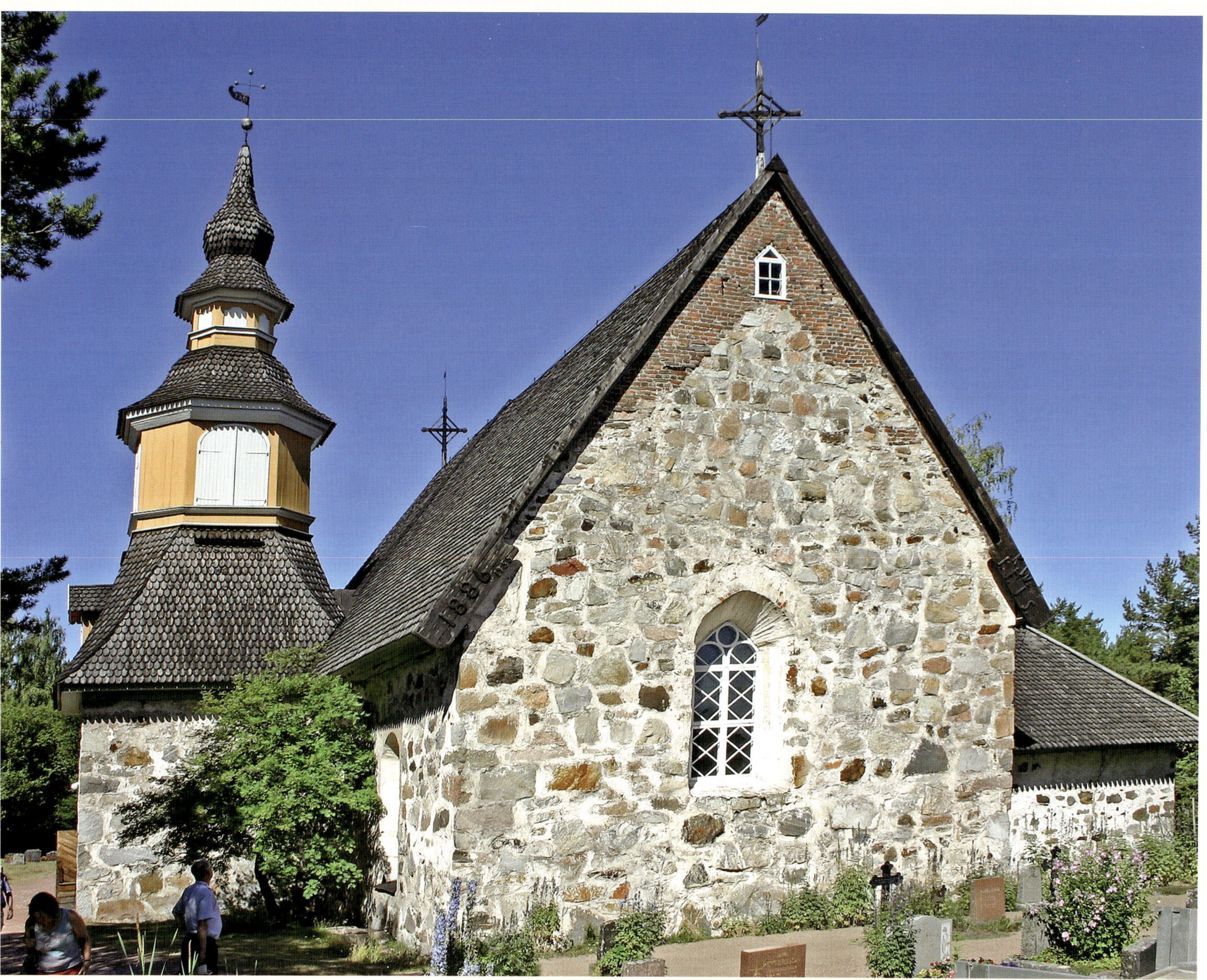
1886

KUMLINGE CHURCH

In medieval sources Kumlinge is mentioned as chapel under the mother church of Sund, but already in 1478 the church in Kumlinge appears as a church in an independent parish.

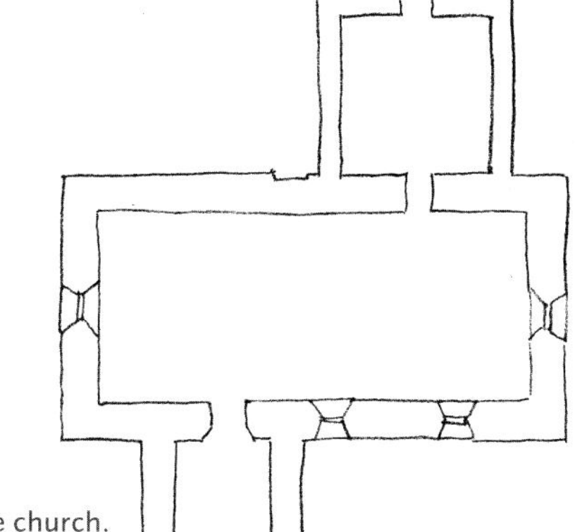

▲ Fig. 118. Kumlinge church. Ground plan.

According to the will of Kort Hartvigsson, from 1484, the church of Saint Anne in Kumlinge was to receive donations. The church has a strangely isolated location centrally on the main island of Kumlinge, separate from the village and today also far away from the sea.

THE EXTERIOR

Different from other Åland churches, the church in Kumlinge is not built in red granite. Instead the exterior is dominated by rough and irregular walls executed in differently colored fieldstones. Both gables reveal secondary heightening of the roofs. The year 1785 is inscribed in one of the eaves-boards towards the west. The south façade shows that two enlarged round arched window openings have been moved from their original places. The gable walls have one window each. The chancel window in the east has a pointed arch, while the west gable window is round arched.

A tower south of the rectangular nave is crowned by a Baroque swollen spire with an onion cupola. The lower part of the tower, the porch, is not in alignment with the nave. Like the nave, it is erected in fieldstones, without obvious shifts. The roof of both nave and tower consists of tarred wooden shingles. The bell stage is painted yellow with white sound openings. A spacious sacristy has been erected against the northern wall of the nave. West of the sacristy one can see traces of a walled-in northern window.

GROUND PLAN

The ground plan consists of a single nave, divided into three bays, and in the nave and the south tower the walls are thick. The inner measures of the nave are 17.11m x 7.37m and the porch against the southern wall measures 4.17m x 3.85m. The sacristy towards the north, with walls of a thinner construction, consists of a square with inner measures 6.23m x 6.23m. In all, the nave has four window openings, two facing south and one in each gable. The portal of the porch is the only entrance to the church. The sacristy has a northern window. The attic of the nave can be reached through the walled-in staircase in the west wall of the tower.

THE INTERIOR

The vaulted room is dominated by wall paintings covering vaults and walls. Three rib vaults in brick form richly modeled vaults, where the intersection points are marked by five rings, forming *ring vaults** (Fig. 120). The inner walls lack supporting arches for the vaults, which instead rest on brackets in the walls and in the inner corners. The inner height from floor to head of the vault measures 7.42m. The high altar, erected against the eastern chancel wall, has a deep paneled niche in the south. Dendrochronological dating places a pine plank from the niche in the 14th century. The altar is covered by a wide limestone slab with an inscribed ring cross. An identical ring cross is repeated in the semicircular limestone slab forming a step in front of the altar.

An early medieval Mary shrine dominates the altar. Two niches in the eastern wall flank the altar on both sides. North of the altar stands a small limestone font, with a tree trunk as a base. The crucifix hangs high up in the room. The pulpit, close to the sacristy portal by the northern wall, has a polygonal basket divided into mirrors. It is adorned with paintings of Salvator Mundi, the evangelists Matthew, Luke, Mark and John, and Peter, the apostle. An organ, built by the Wirtanen

◀ Fig. 117. Kumlinge church. Exterior from the east.

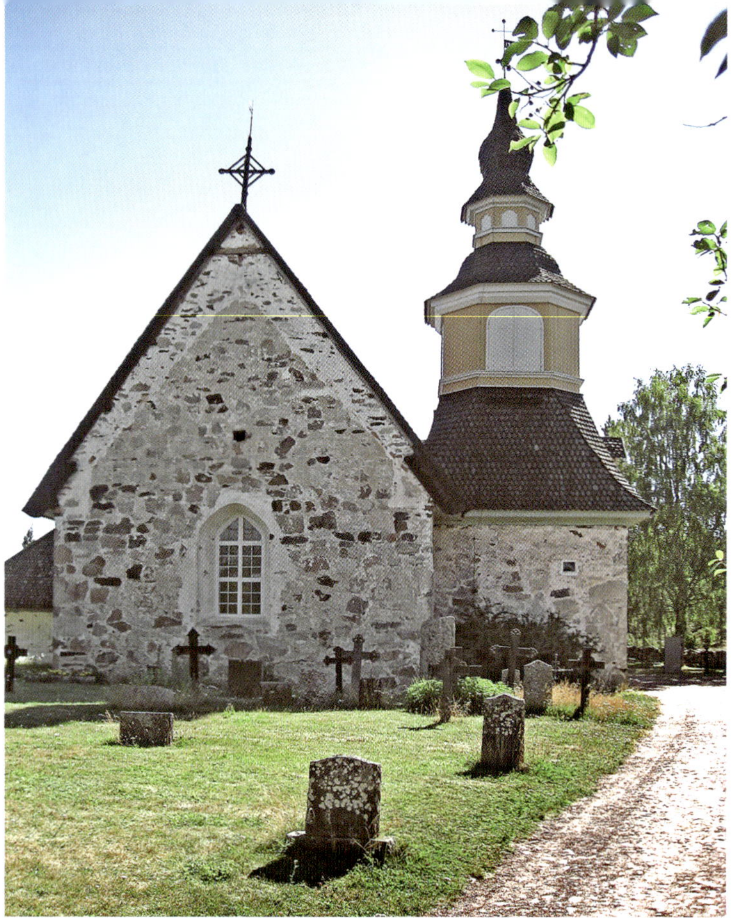

▲ Fig. 119. Kumlinge church exterior, from the west.

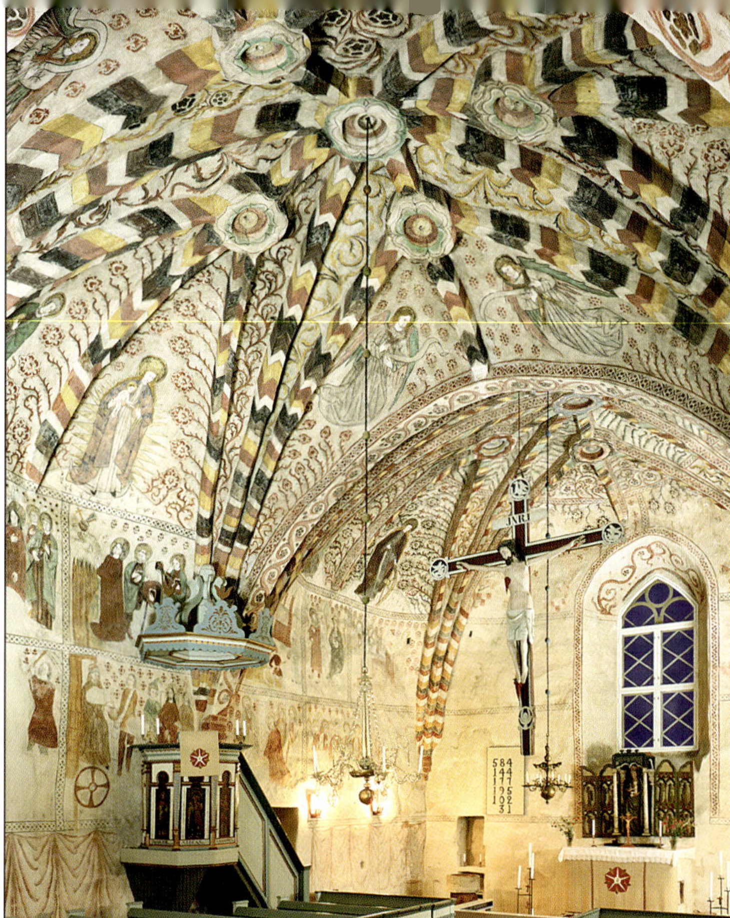

▲ Fig. 120. Kumlinge church, interior towards the east.

firm in 1963, occupies the south east corner of the nave.

The ceiling of the porch has a barrel vault in fieldstones. For the ringing of the bells the vault is penetrated by three holes, lined with wood. Thus the combined function of porch and bell tower seems to be an original arrangement. A walled-in stone slab, protruding from the eastern wall of the porch, further indicates that the porch may have served as a chapel with a side altar. The ceiling of the sacristy has flat wooden paneling.

THE WALL PAINTINGS

Stylistically, the wall paintings in the nave of Kumlinge church belong to the end of the 15th century, or to around 1500 (Figures 46 and 47). The paintings have covered the entire interior in three horizontal friezes along the walls of the nave. The uppermost two friezes are filled with a rich program including scenes from the Childhood of Christ, the Passion, and images from the New Testament. The lowest frieze depicts simple textile hangings. The paintings on the walls have suffered from later whitewash and from secondary window openings and enlargements. They were uncovered and carefully restored by conservator Veikko Kiljunen in 1961. The vaults however, are filled with angels and female saints and framed in by decorative foliage and stenciled patterns on the surfaces, and with zigzag lines along the ribs. They were never covered by whitewash. Immediate parallels to the Kumlinge paintings are lacking, this goes for both style and painting program. A painting representing the face of Christ, or the Sudetarium of Veronica, above an original south window, indicates a connection with the Birgittine nunnery church at Naantali, where the motive is repeatedly occurring.

THE ALTARPIECE

A Mary shrine, dated to around 1250 on stylistic grounds, is placed on the altar. It was probably imported from South Scandinavia or from Northern Germany. The corpus at the center of the shrine consists of a rectangular piece, filled with a sculpture representing Mary and Child, which during the late Middle Ages was exchanged for a more modern

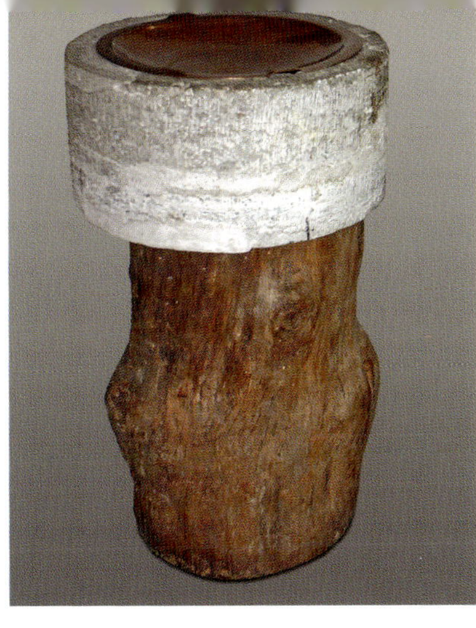

◀ Fig. 121. Font from the church of Kumlinge.

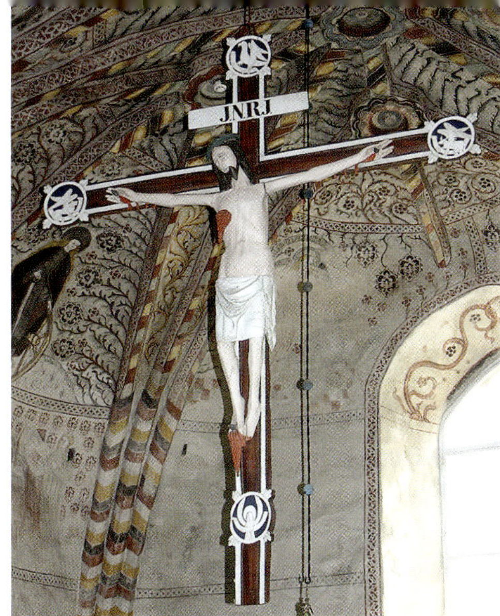

◀ Fig. 122. The crucifix, marking the border between the chancel and the congregation, originates from the beginning of the 15th century.

version of the Madonna. The side wings can be closed around the corpus, so that the trefoil shaped doors can fit into the baldachin roof of the corpus. The cut-through wings are decorated by elegantly carved reliefs of the Nativity of Jesus and his early childhood. The style is courtly, typical of early Gothic. The head of the Jesus child from the original Madonna sculpture was discovered in archaeological excavations in 1961.

BUILDING HISTORY

No traces were found of an earlier wooden construction on the site. Still, inventories which could belong to a predecessor to the present church have been identified. To these belong the Mary shrine with the adjoining head of the Child Jesus, and the little limestone font, both on stylistic grounds dated to the 13th century (Figures 21 and 22). According to earlier archives, there was a monastery in Kumlinge. Archaeological investigations in 1961 revealed the remains of an older building in the churchyard, immediately close to the northwest corner of the church. Until this enigmatic ruin has been analyzed for dating, only speculations on its function can be presented.

Mortar analysis from the original, fire-damaged, east gable and some isolated samples from dendrochronology imply that this stone church in Kumlinge derives from the 14th century. A fire leaving traces in the eastern gable above the vaults probably occurred in the Post-Reformation period. The western gable shows no sign of fire. It belongs to the early 15th century.

Joints in the walls show that the porch is a secondary addition erected against the south wall, and preliminary results from mortar analysis suggest that the porch, including the staircase to the attic, is late medieval. Thick walls in nave and porch indicate original plans for vaulting the interior. The medieval church also included a small sacristy behind the sacristy portal in the north.

During the 15th century the nave was vaulted in three bays, with ring vaults where ribs form a star pattern. The church was completely decorated with wall paintings in a unique iconographic program. Among the medieval wall paintings, two different stages can be identified: the older consists of seven preserved inauguration crosses, including a few fragments in the arch of the chancel window and around the brackets of the vault.

In the 17th century, after the Reformation, the church was redecorated according to the new Lutheran liturgy. It meant new pews, a new pulpit, and a gallery towards the west gable with images of the apostles painted on the screen.

During the Northern War the church suffered great damage, when it served as stables for the Russian soldiers, among other indignities. The paintings were sooted, the inventory destroyed, and both church bells were lost. Both silver vessels and money were embezzled during the flight to Stockholm. In 1767 the wooden part of the clock tower was renewed. Responsible building master was Anders Hartlin-Piimänen, who also built the new sacristy in 1784. He was also responsible for the heightening of the gables and the roof, and also for covering the roof with new wooden shingles.

In the 19th century all the window openings were enlarged, and the location of the south windows was adjusted. In the 1870s a north window was opened, only to be walled in again in the renovations in 1961, when the central heating was installed. In the 1960s the wall paintings were also cleaned. ■

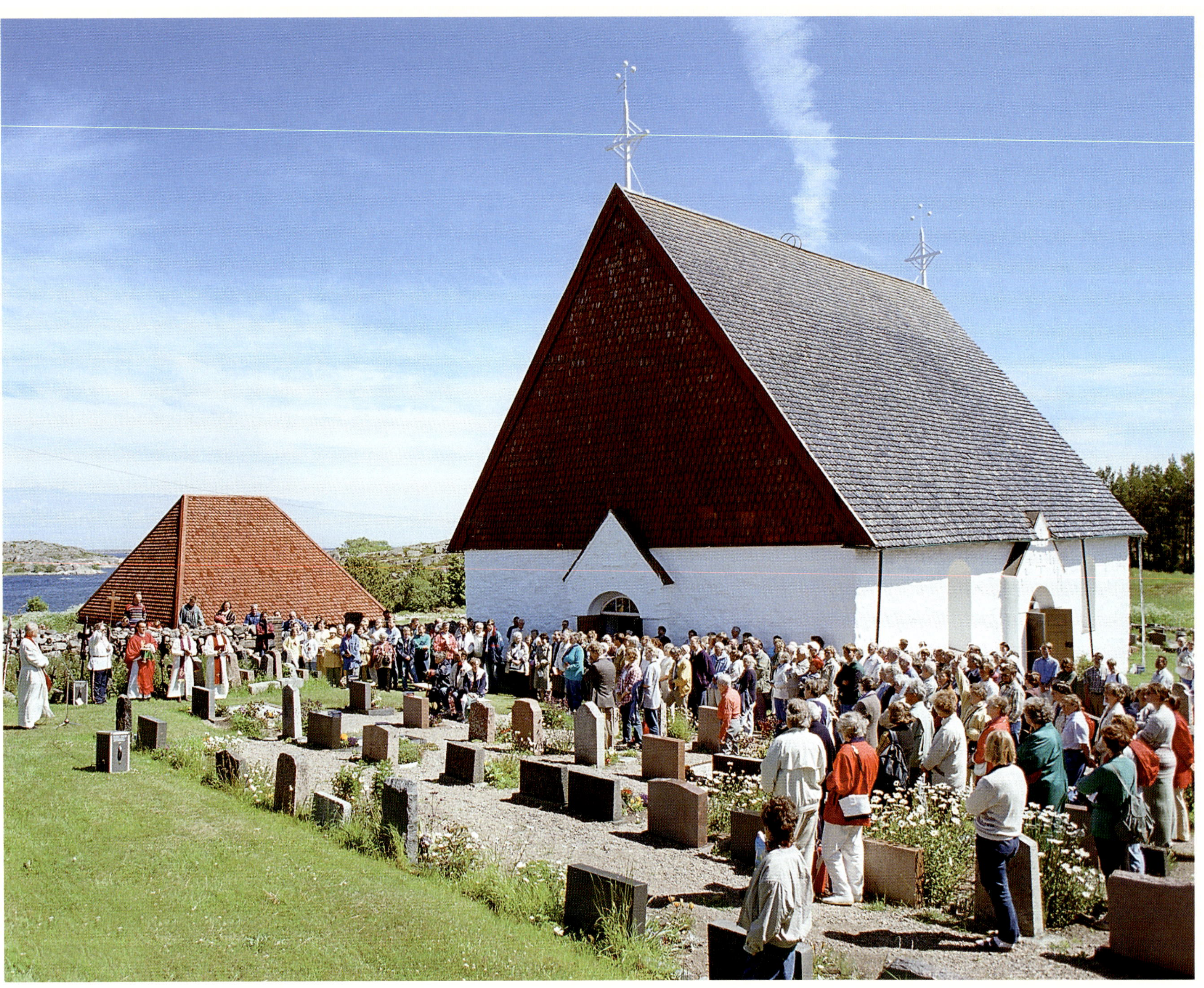

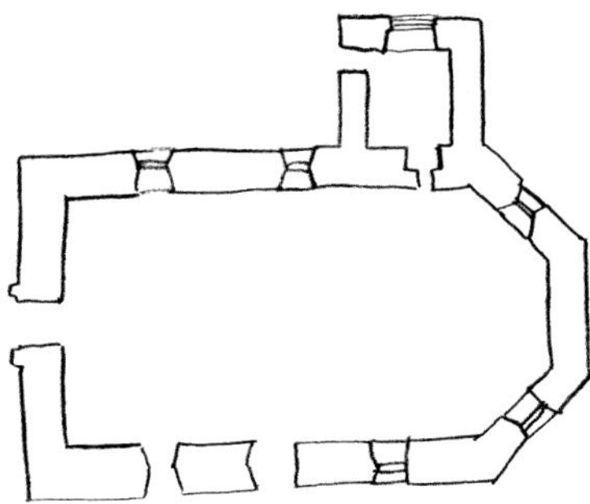

▲ Fig. 124. Kökar church, ground plan.

KÖKAR CONVENT CHURCH

The present church in Kökar stands on the foundations of the old convent church. The convent church in turn, seems to have been a normal Åland parish church.

THE EXTERIOR

The church is built of stone and has relatively low walls under a high roof covered with red shingles. The western gable is high, partly covered with shingles, while the chancel in the east is semi hexagonal. The church has two identical entrances, in the western gable and in the middle of the southern long wall. In the northern long wall there is a stone sacristy. The wooden campanile lies on the western side of the churchyard, and has the additional function of a landmark for seafarers, with electric lighting of the channel installed on the wall.

GROUND PLAN

The ground plan forms a rectangular, fairly wide nave, with its characteristic semi hexagonal chancel in the east. Externally it is about 23.5m long and about 14m wide. There is neither porch nor hall in the church. The sacristy on the north side measures 7 x 5.5m externally and has two coupled windows to the north.

THE INTERIOR

The single nave interior is light thanks to six windows of equal size: two in the chancel, two on the south side and two on the north. The impression is further strengthened by the whiteness of both walls and the inner wooden barrel vault, with a few details in ultramarine blue. The pulpit is situated against the northern wall, while the chancel has a bench for the parish organist and a bishop's bench on either side of the altar circle. The altarpiece depicts the Last Supper. It was painted by G.G. Sveidel in Turku and acquired in 1803. There is an organ gallery against the western gable, built for the first organ 1910-11. The present organ was installed in 1992. Among other inventories may be mentioned two votive ships, one of which from the 18th century, a glass chandelier and two brass crowns.

The most remarkable object is, however, the bowl of a baptismal font, dating from the early 13th century, made of Gotland limestone. According to tradition it had been walled into the medieval church preceding the present one.

HISTORICAL BACKGROUND

The site of the church has a long history which is difficult to interpret. It is perhaps best known for the foundation of one of the three Franciscan monasteries in medieval Finland. Extensive excavations on the site, however, point to some kind of activity as early as the end of the 13th century. The mention of the name Kökar in the Danish Hedeby Itinerary from the end of that century indicates that the region, above all

◀ Fig. 123. The church of Kökar, exterior from the southwest.

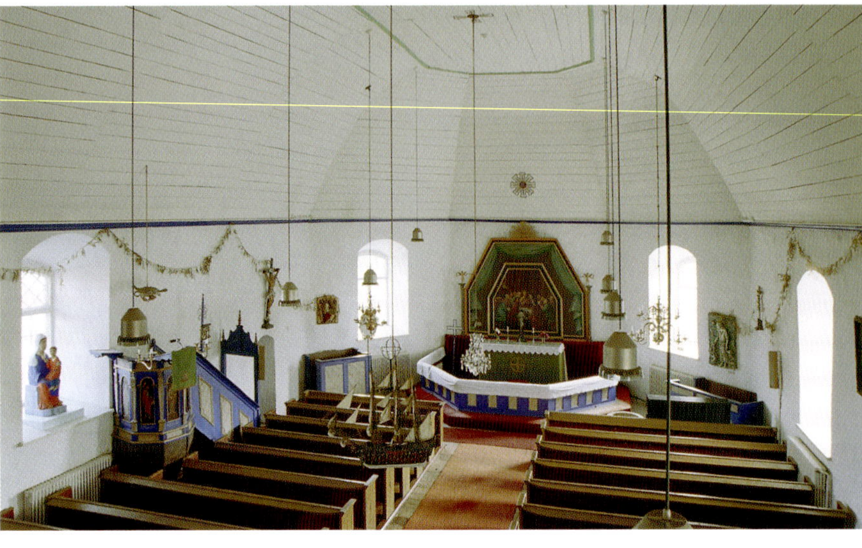

▲ Fig. 125. Interior towards the east.

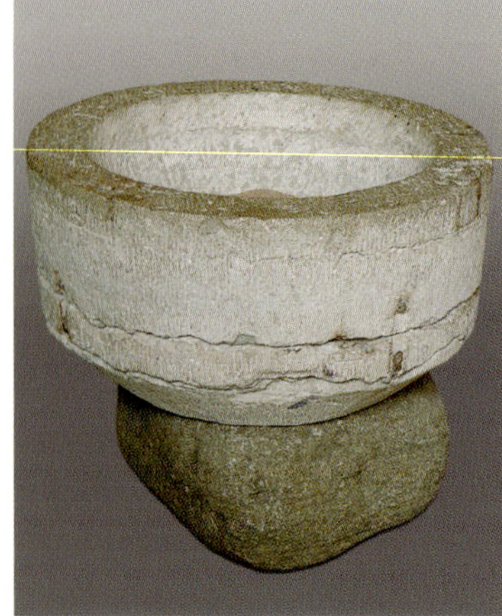

▲ Fig. 126. The font of the church.

Hamnö, was already a well-known harbor along important routes.

The excavations also point to the latter part of the 14th century, possibly even earlier, being the probable date for the erection of the first stone church on the site. The church had one nave, with a narrower rectangular chancel, but otherwise had almost the same dimensions as the present one. Around 1400 a solid part of the building was added against the western gable, which is most likely to be seen as a west tower. The medieval church had seven windows. At least the chancel window had stained glass in mullions of limestone. There were also five door openings and a larger opening between the tower and the nave. The roof had u-shaped pantiles of so called monk- and nuntype. It has been possible to investigate minor parts of the building, above all the chancel and the supposed tower, and here a number of graves have been found, giving ^{14}C dates to both the 14th and the 15th century. The fact that the relatively large church building was placed on a small island, separated from the three main inhabited islands of Kökar, indicates that the church was not exclusively intended for the needs of the Kökar people.

The Franciscans probably settled in Hamnö as early as the 14th century, but a proper convent seems not to have been founded until the middle of the 15th century, when they took over the church. There are several relevant background factors for the settlement: the strategic situation along important routes, the harbor of Hamnö with its long traditions, and not least the very extensive fishing that took place in the Kökar waters. Few details are known about the activities of the Kökar monastic establishment, but judging by sparse documents from 1472 up to 1526 it seems to have been a complete convent. The simple lodgings lay north of the church and extensive excavations have revealed foundations of kitchens, refectories, cellars and precinct walls. A rich assortment of finds has also been revealed, among others large numbers of late medieval silver coins, especially Swedish bracteates but also Baltic coins.

The activity in the Middle Ages was, however, not restricted to the monastery area. A little south of the church two larger areas of habitation have been investigated, with finds dating from the end of the 14th century up to the Reformation. There had been large wooden buildings on strong stone foundations, all of them having lavish roofs with u-shaped pantiles, a clear division of rooms with fireplaces, and in part floors with carefully made stone paving. The real functions of the buildings and their relations to the monastery are, however, still rather unclear. Otherwise, Hamnö has remains of at least two harbors with simple quay constructions, and in the south the foundations of a little seafaring chapel described below.

In the 1530s the convent was closed due to the Reformation, and the buildings soon began to decay. A hundred years later the former convent church was a ruin with collapsed vaults, and the Kökar people were for-

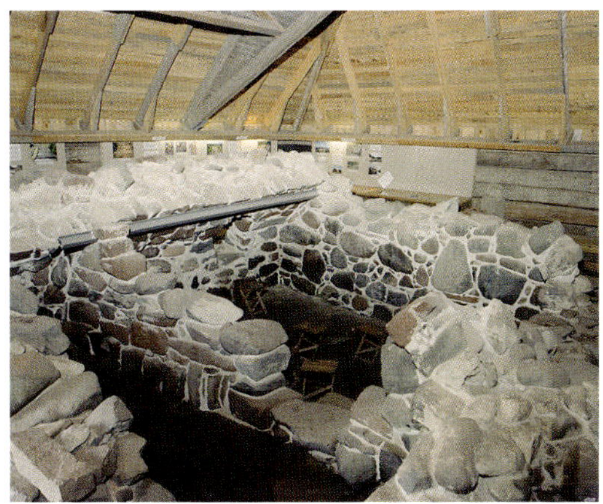

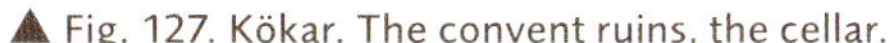
▲ Fig. 127. Kökar. The convent ruins, the cellar.

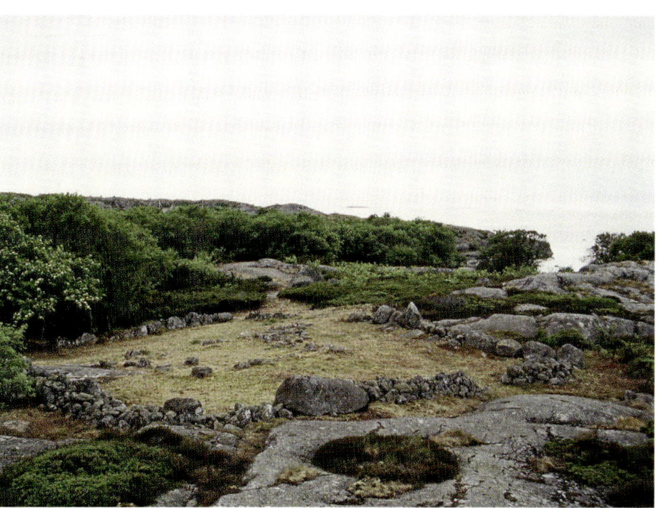

▲ Fig. 128. "Kappalskatan", a medieval chapel ruin in Hamnö.

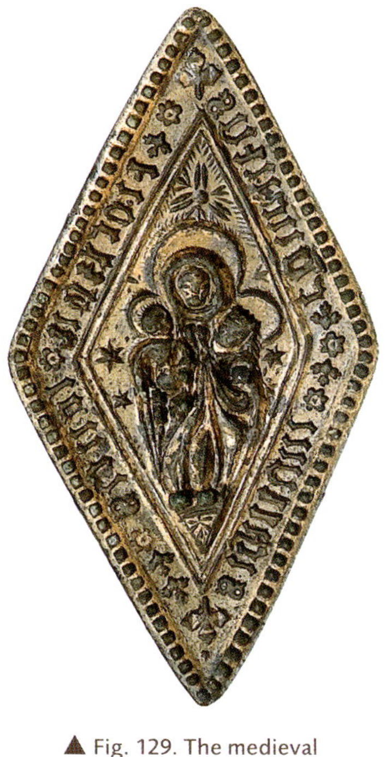

▲ Fig. 129. The medieval seal of the convent at Kökar.

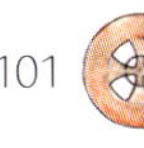

bidden to have their services in it. Instead a little wooden chapel was erected in 1645 on the churchyard. The following year an altarpiece depicting the Crucifixion was acquired which is still preserved.

After only one century the chapel, too, was in bad shape. After discussions continuing for many years the parish finally decided to build a new stone church on the foundation of the old one. Large parts of the remaining walls were torn down, and with the help of two national collections and a large donation from the Stockholm fish buyers, the new church was ready in 1784. Originally, the idea had been to preserve the old rectangular chancel form (cf. Fig. 61), according the plan of Anders Hartlin-Piimänen, but after a change of architects a more modern three-sided chancel was chosen. After that the church has remained largely unaltered to the present day. The only changes have been to tear down a little wooden sacristy in 1876 and replace it by the present stone sacristy. At the same time a little wooden hall was pulled down in front of the southern entrance. Internally the organ gallery was added in 1910-11 and in the 1930s new benches were installed.

THE CHAPEL

On the south side of Hamnö, in Kappalskatan, there are remains of what has been thought to be a little medieval seafaring chapel. The building was wooden, erected on a stone foundation filled with mortar, measuring 5 x 7m. In the east there was a chancel window with glass intarsia in leaden window bars. Isolated pieces of u-shaped pantiles are indications of a tiled roof. Outside the foundation there is a precinct wall nearly a meter high measuring 19 x 24m, with clear openings to the west, north and east pointing to possible harbors. It has long been thought that this chapel, like corresponding buildings in the archipelago, could be linked to the Danish Itinerary route and the early Middle Ages. Recent findings of glass intarsia and possible tile roofs, however, rather point to the late Middle Ages. Preliminary ^{14}C datings even seem to indicate that the chapel was used as late as the beginning of the 16th century. The real age and activity of the chapel, and its links to the convent church nearby are thus still unsolved problems.

On the northern side of the present church there is today a modern chapel. Inside are remains of a stone cellar which was part of the monastery grounds, the so-called Klosterkällaren. The cellar was excavated in 1974, and two years later a protective roof was built over the ruin. In connection with the first ecumenical Franciscus Festival the building was consecrated as a Franciscus Chapel. Inside on the northern side there is an altar with an altarpiece in stone mosaics, and on the southern side an exhibition with finds, pictures, and texts from recent archaeological excavations. ■

(Kenneth Gustavsson wrote this section on Kökar).

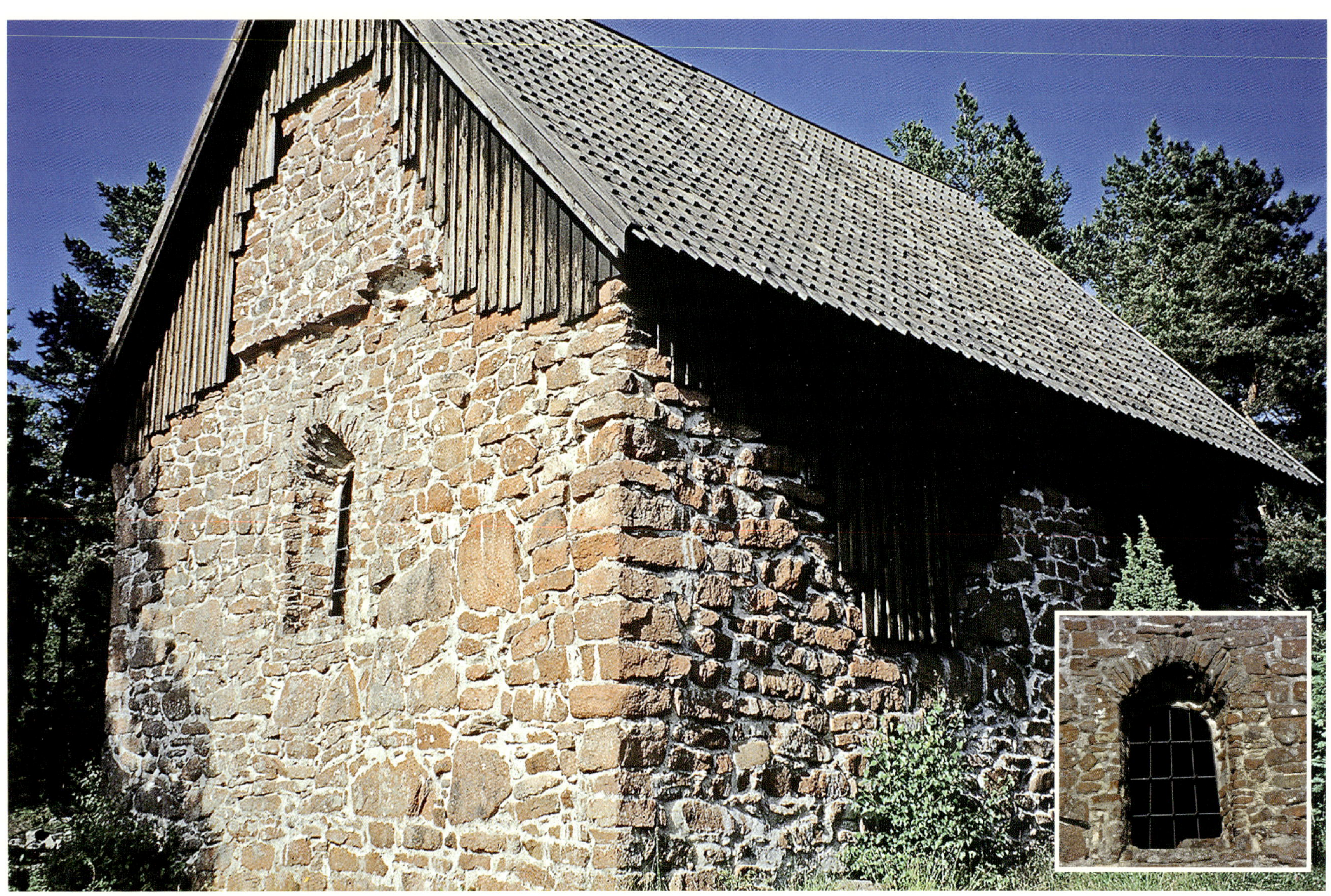

LEMBÖTE CHAPEL

Lemböte chapel stands high up on the Lemböte mountain on the eastern shore of Slemmern, the stretch of the sea east of present-day Mariehamn.

"Linaboete" is mentioned in the so-called Danish itinerary, written down some time in the middle of the 13th century, but there is no mention of a chapel. Thus Lemböte lies along the old sailing route which according to the Danish itinerary started at Utklippan in Blekinge (a part of Sweden which was part of Denmark in the Middle Ages), to Tallinn in Estonia. The chapel, consecrated to Saint Olof, of medieval origin, was situated at a natural well-sheltered harbor called the Western Harbor, or the so called Chapel Bay.

THE EXTERIOR

The chapel, erected in rapakivi, is partly in ruins. A highly placed window in the east gable is fairly well preserved, with a crowning arch lined with granite chips. A 20cm long piece of the original limestone framework, with a groove for the window glass, is still wedged into the top of the window. The east gable also has a cavity from a now lost tie-beam. Another window opening can be discerned in the eastern part of the south wall. Centrally in the west gable is the entrance to the chapel. Like the rest of the ruin it has gone through a substantial restoration. The walls of the chapel are sheltered by a wooden roof. Missing parts in walls and gables have been substituted by wooden constructions.

GROUND PLAN

The chapel consists of only one room measuring 7 x 5.3m. The spacious church yard is surrounded by a circular dry wall of fieldstones. It has two openings, one to the west, and the other to the southwest.

THE INTERIOR

In the stripped interior a niche in the east gable wall catches the eye. The altar arrangement is a late reconstruction.

BUILDING HISTORY

Mortar samples, taken in the summer of 1996 in the cavity on the eastern gable, indicate that the chapel either belongs to the end of the 13th century or to around 1370. Both these dates correspond to a hoard of coins discovered in October 1840, "on the western side of the partly preserved eastern gable", i.e., immediately close to the eastern wall. Some sources even mention that it was found under the altar. A few weeks later the treasure was published in Åbo Tidningar. It included 270 coins in total. They were numismatically checked by Bror Emil Hildebrand in Stockholm, after which they, alas, partly disappeared into the unknown. Another 273 coins have been registered from Lemböte chapel, 55 of these were of medieval origin. Among those that could be identified twelve coins belonged to the first half, and five to the latter part of the 13th century. Fourteen of them date to the 14th century. The oldest coins may be interpreted as artifacts from an earlier wooden chapel, since the results of mortar dating do not reach to the beginning of the 13th century.

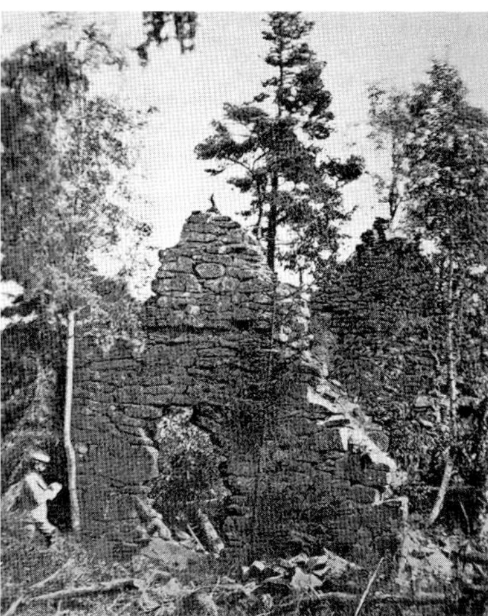

▲ Fig. 131. Lemböte chapel ruin, photographed by Reinhold Hausen in 1871.

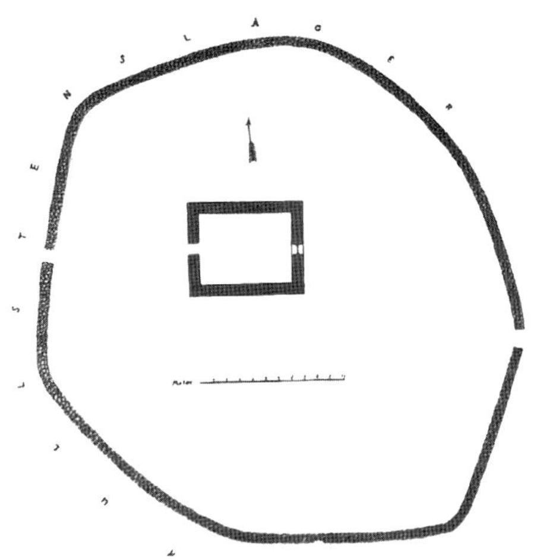

▲ Fig. 132. Lemböte chapel, ground plan by Reinhold Hausen in 1871.

After the Reformation the chapel was closed, and the liturgical vessels were confiscated. The decay started immediately. In a report from 1674 the vicar of Lemland, Mathias Benedictij Hedemorus, described the situation as follows:

From the mother church ½ mile, at a village called Lemböte, is a stone chapel, which old people call Saint Olof's chapel. It is said to be 12 ells long and 8 ells wide: The altar can still be seen, but the roof has long since fallen off; inside and outside surrounded by birches.

In 1871 the ruined chapel was photographed by Reinhold Hausen, and the restoration works were initiated in the 1880s under direction of the architect Allan Schulman. The chapel has repeatedly been restored, and is used today both for worship and for concerts. ■

◀ Fig. 130. Lemböte chapel, exterior from the northeast, and detail of the chancel window.

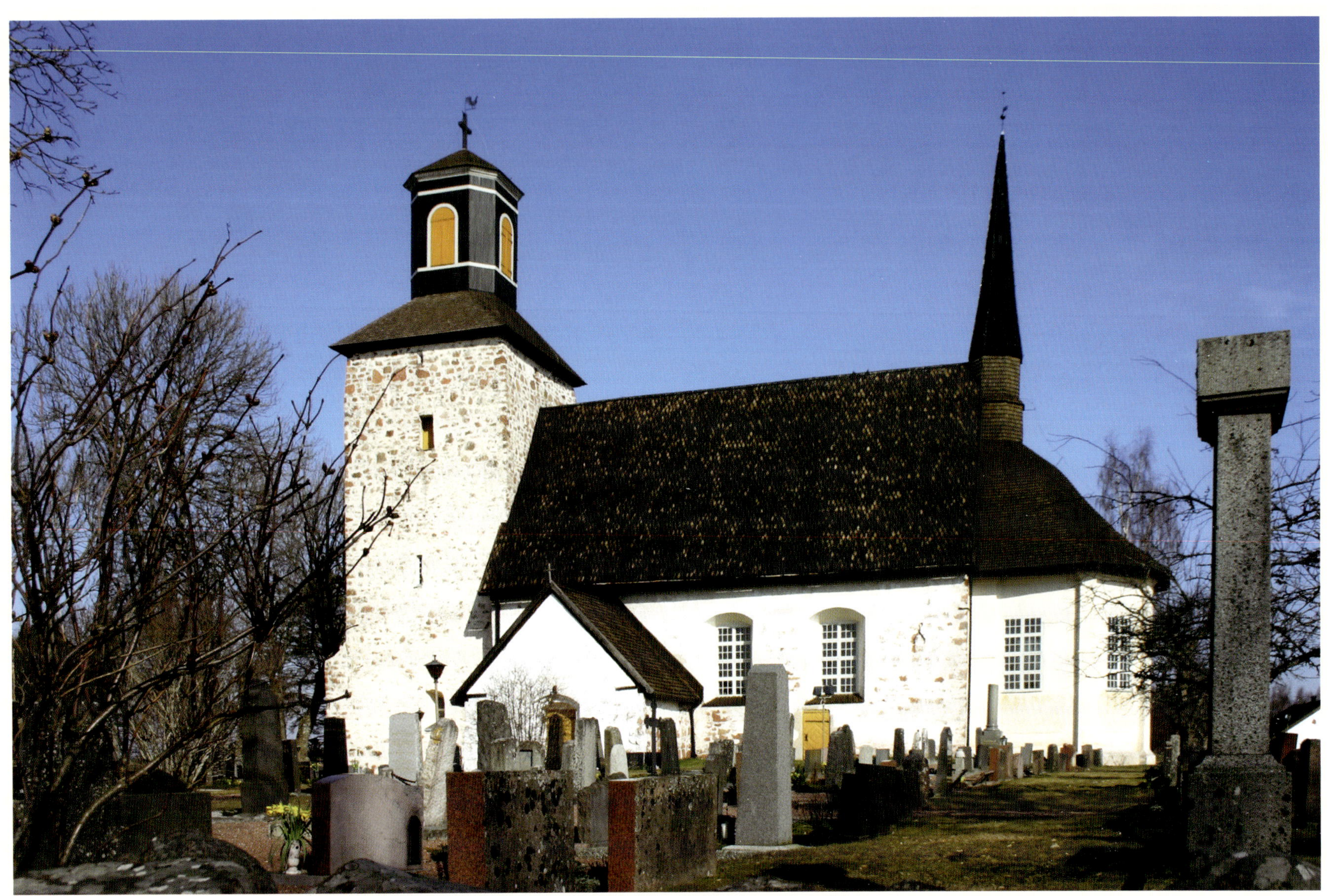

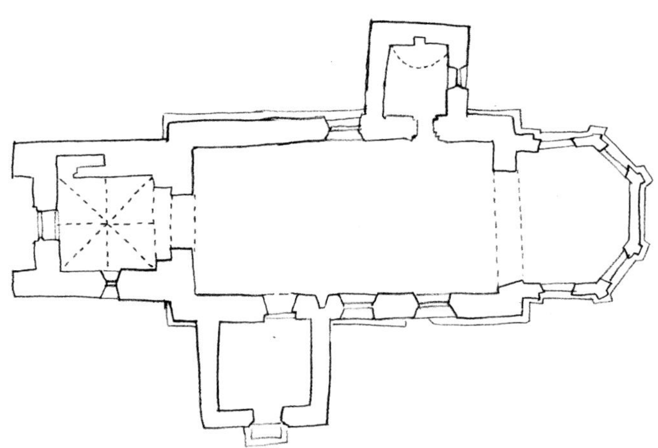

▲ Fig. 134. Lemland church, ground plan.

LEMLAND CHURCH

Lemland church lies in Söderby, adjacent to the largest Iron Age grave field in the parish, not far from a sheltered harbor towards Lumparn, the inland sea of Åland. It was long thought that the church was consecrated to Saint Birgitta and that it dated from the 15th century, but archaeological excavations and a renovation in the 1950s revealed a much older church, with an earlier wooden predecessor.

 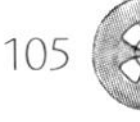

The chapel of Lumparland was subordinated to the Lemland mother church, while the relation to the seafaring chapel of Lemböte cannot be clearly established.

THE EXTERIOR

Like other Åland mother churches, Lemland church is built of Åland red granite, or rapakivi. The simple stepped socle surrounding the rectangular nave clearly shows that the nave is the oldest part. Joints in the walls and the lack of a socle confirm that the west tower, porch, sacristy and a polygonal chancel towards the east are of a later date. An impressive tower has been erected against the west gable of the nave, and a little sacristy is added to the eastern part of the north wall. The porch is situated to the west of the south wall, towards the original main portal. Towards the east of the same wall a priest door to the chancel has been blocked up. Big windows break through the walls to south, north and east. Because of the ***ridge turret**** placed on the joint between the nave and chancel the church has an unusual silhouette. Today the entrance to the porch serves as the main portal to the church.

GROUND PLAN

The rectangular nave measures 18.6 x 11.4m. The walls are around 1 m thick. Several different building units have been successively added to the nave, such as the tower in the west, the porch in the south and the sacristy in the north east. The nave opens towards a polygonal chancel in the east through a wide opening. The outer walls of the chancel are broken up by large window openings. The southern entrance of the porch is the main portal. The other entrance in the west wall of the tower is of subordinate importance.

◀ Fig. 133. Lemland church. Exterior from the southwest.

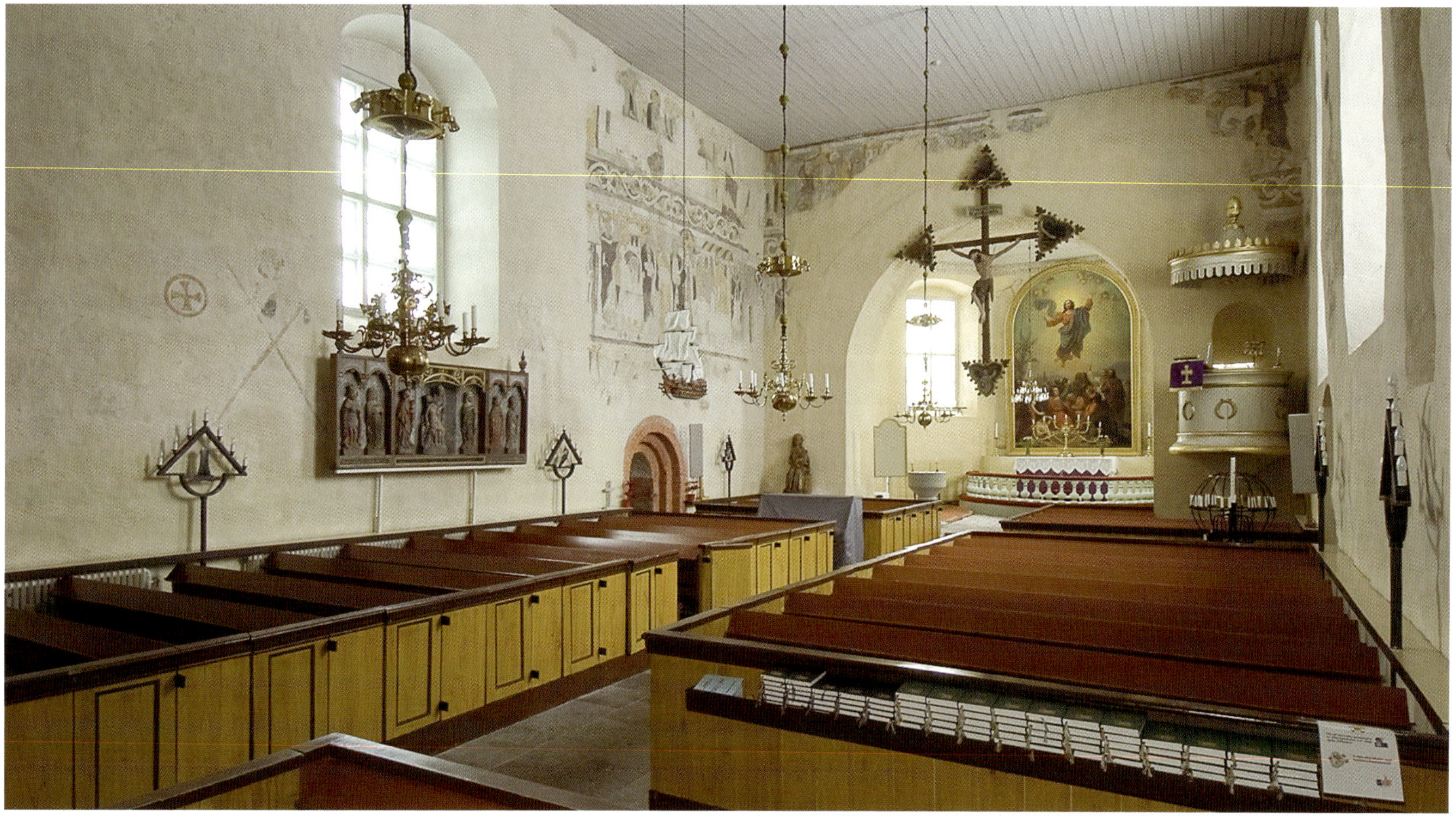

▲ Fig. 135. Lemland church. Interior towards the east.

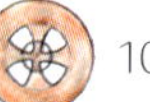

THE INTERIOR

The high nave, a rectangular hall church of around 136m², has a horizontal ceiling of white-painted wooden panels. The nave and the chancel are joined by a high arch, while a lower arch opens the nave to the ground floor of the tower in the west. The original division of the nave into a chancel part and a congregational part appears clearly: the wall paintings of the chancel, in many horizontal layers on top of each other, are abruptly broken off where the congregation part starts. The chancel formed a little more than a third of the nave

An original window opening is visible high up on the south wall. The tall and narrow window, with a pointed arch and framed in limestone, has been blocked by the later porch. Similarly, towards the west, another smaller window is blocked by the secondary tower.

The south entrance of the nave, the original main portal into the church, is finished by a triangular arch, with a rounded shape at the top. The use of bricks is restricted to the sacristy portal, which is framed by three recessive rounded arches. The present altarpiece representing 'The Ascension of Christ' was made by the court painter R.W. Ekman in 1876. The pulpit, attached to the southern part of the triumphal wall, dates from 1852.

BUILDING HISTORY

The foundation of a wooden church was discovered during archaeological excavations of the church in the 1950s, a little obliquely close to the northern long wall. The age of the wooden church is uncertain, but the oldest coins excavated point to the early 13th century. One result from

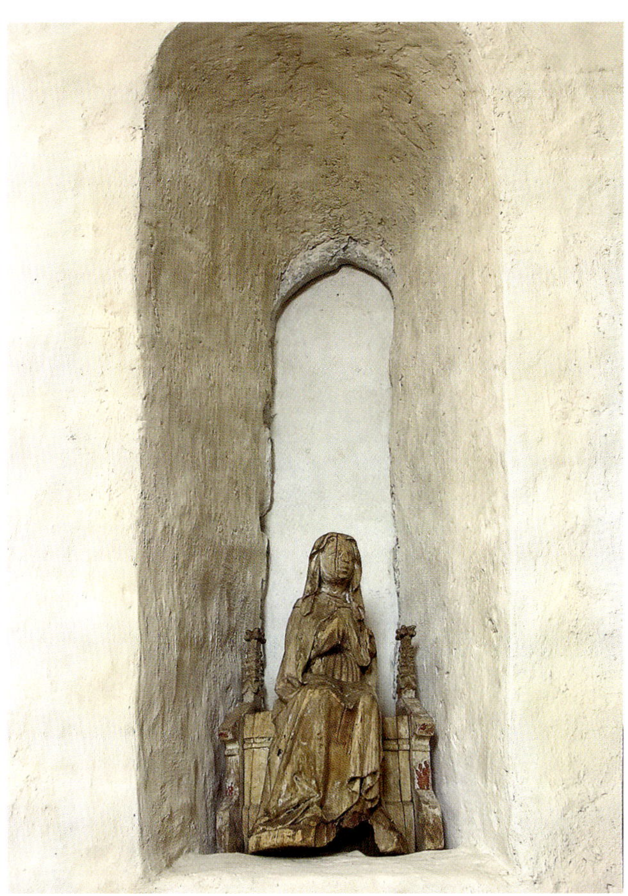

▲ Fig. 136.Lemland church. Walled-in original window on the south wall.

dendrochronological analysis yields the 1240s, but otherwise dendrochronology indicates 1290 or thereabouts for some of the wooden beams.

The wooden ceiling of the nave and its decorative ornamentation can dendrochronologically be dated to the end of the 13th century, which corroborates the dating of the Gothic wall paintings of the chancel (see reconstruction drawing Fig. 20). Only five fragmentarily preserved planks remain of the original ceiling (Fig. 19), but the paint is clear enough to show that the ceiling had been covered by fine medallion painting. The insignificant thickness of the walls and the wall paintings reaching up to the horizontal ceiling demonstrate that vaulting was never intended for this nave.

Two or three high and narrow windows, framed in limestone, faced

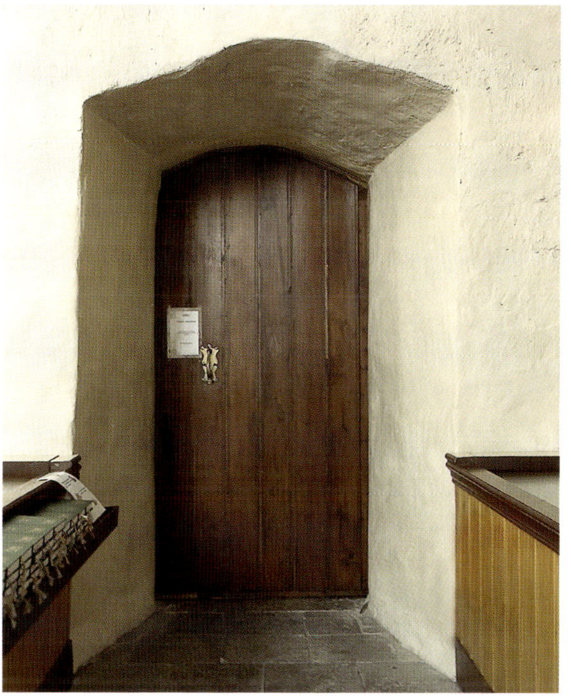

▲ Fig. 137. The south portal of the church, from the interior.

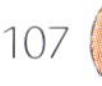

south. One of them is preserved. The chancel window on the eastern wall of the nave was a double window in limestone.

Fragments of the chancel window, found during archaeological excavations, are preserved in the porch. Dendrochronological analysis and mortar dating have further shown that the west tower was built around 1317, and that it reached up to the spire in the first building stage. The original shape of the spire is unknown, but in all likelihood it was formed as a pyramid. Single wooden samples from the wall plates of the sacristy and the porch have been subject to dendrochronological analysis. Both seem to belong to the beginning of the 14th century.

THE POST-REFORMATION PERIOD

Immediately after the Reformation the interior was renewed with a pulpit, pews, a bishop's throne, and the lectern. All this was, however, due for repairs as early as 1637, in connection with a new chancel screen. The interior was whitewashed for the first time in the 1660s. The altarpiece, the crucifix, the lid of the font, and the built-in chairs were also improved. Dean Boetius Murenius who made visitations to the church, remarked on the votive ships that "the many ships should be removed

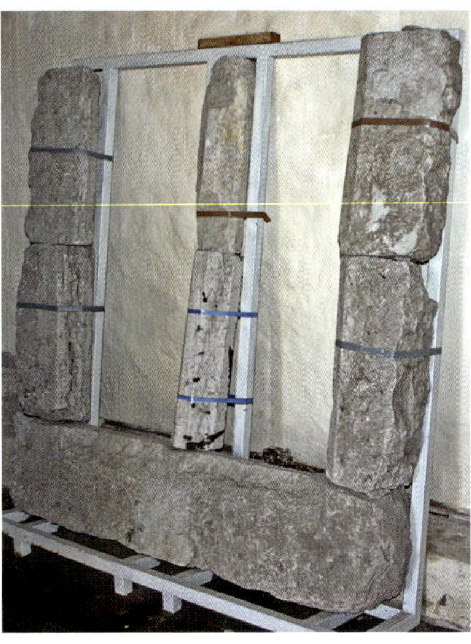

▲ Fig. 138. Lemland church, fragmentarily preserved limestone window.

and the biggest one should be painted and kept clean."

The lower polygonal extension to the east was built in the 1670s as burial chapel for Admiral Johan Bergenstjerna and his wife Kirstin Persdotter from Haddnäs Estate. This burial chapel was transformed into the main chancel of the church in 1775. The original east chancel wall was demolished to be replaced by a high arch towards the new chancel. A gallery screen, decorated with pictures of the apostles, probably also dates from the 18th century. During the 19th century a number of changes were made. The spire of the tower was renewed in 1817, according to designs from Stockholm. In the 1840s the southern windows were enlarged, at the same time as the priest door was walled in. These alterations also involved the opening of a window to the north.

THE WALL PAINTINGS

The medieval wall paintings of the church were uncovered by Veikko Kiljunen during the renovation of the church in 1957 (Figs. 17 and 18). Originally the chancel had richly colored wall paintings in three horizontal sequences, separated by ***palmette friezes**** in an archaic style (cf. Fig. 16). High up to the north successive narrative scenes represent the Last Supper. Underneath follow scenes from the life and miracles of Saint Nicholas, bishop of Myra. The top of the eastern wall depicts the Passion Series, of which it is still possible to discern the Flagellation, the Crucifixion, and Mary Magdalene in the scene of Noli Me Tangere.

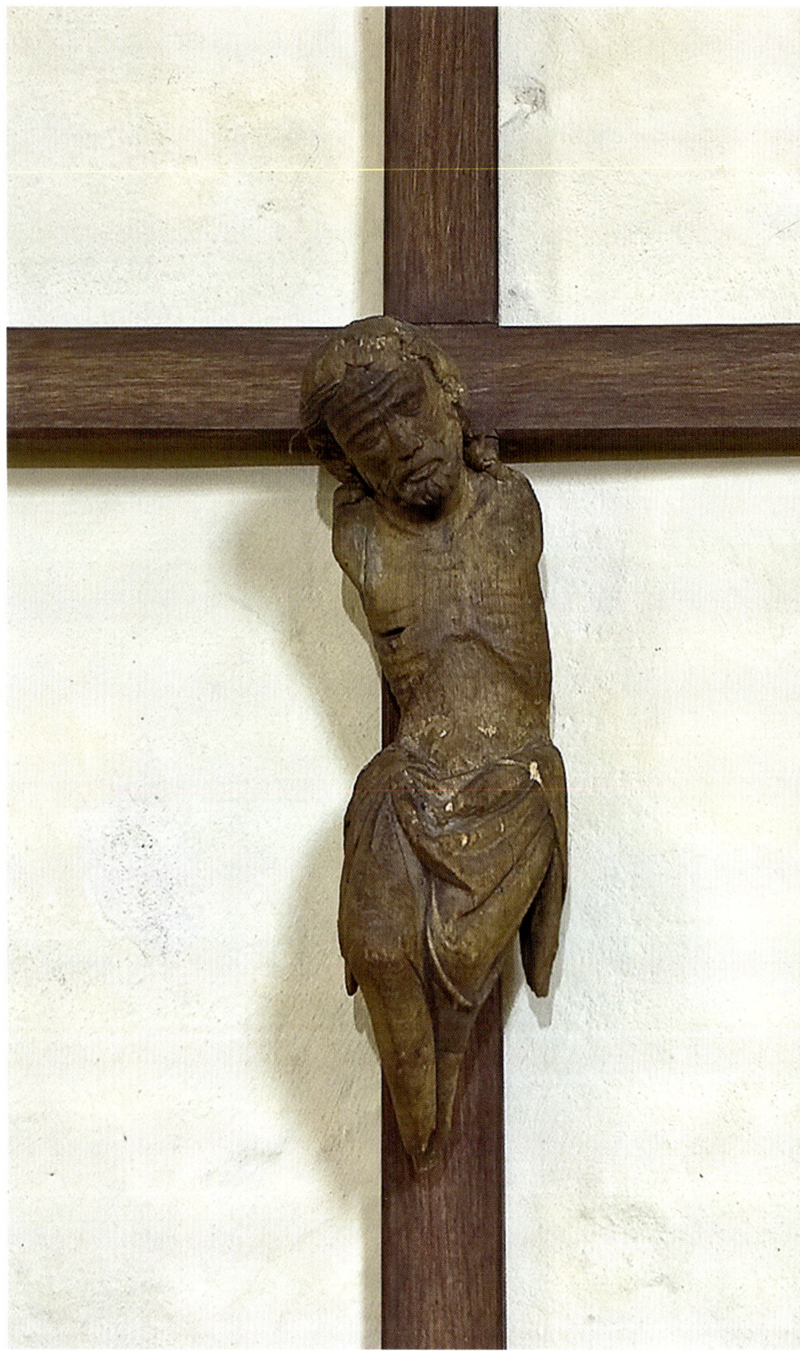

▲ Fig. 139. Lemland church. The smaller crucifix, oak.

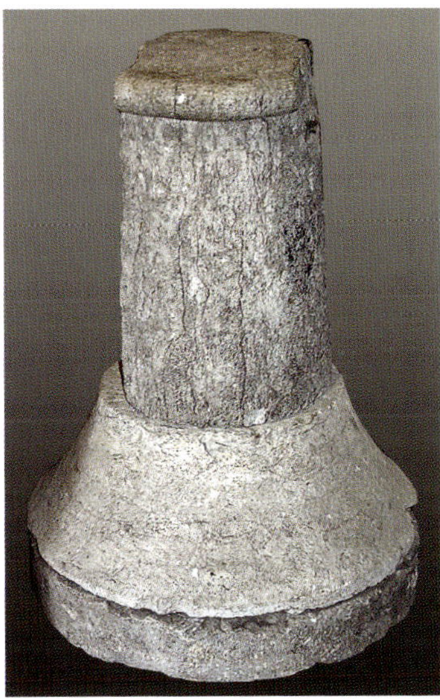

▲ Fig. 140. The base of a baptismal funt.

The miracles of Saint Nicholas in the middle sequence on the eastern wall were demolished by the opening of the new chancel in the 18th century. Due to secondary window openings, only a few details of a saint's legend can be discerned on the south wall of the chancel. The inscription CATERINA indicates scenes from the life of Saint Catharine of Alexandria. The series probably started south of the chancel window.

The wall paintings in the congregational part of the nave are very different. Here solitary apostle figures are depicted close to inauguration crosses (Fig. 29). The figures are elegantly painted in red against the white plaster. Only Andrew has been identified through his symbol, the X-shaped cross.

SCULPTURES

- **Madonna Enthroned, with the Child Jesus,** from the 1320s is the oldest preserved wooden sculpture of the church, and also one of the finest sculptures in Åland (Fig. 30). She originally had a golden crown and was brightly painted.
- **The crucifix** in the secondary triumphal arch is an excellent example of so-called suffering crucifixes from the Cologne area in the middle of the 14th century (Fig. 34).
- **The little crucifix** in the niche by the walled-in priest door in the south may possibly be a Gotland work from the mid-14th century.
- **Two small sculptures, one representing Saint James as a pilgrim, and the other a bishop,** possibly Nicholas, are late medieval.
- **The sculpture of Saint Birgitta,** in the walled-in western window of the nave, is from the 15th century, when, apparently to conform to the prevailing fashion, the church was consecrated to the popular Swedish saint (Fig. 53).
- **The altarpiece,** now hanging on the northern wall, dates from the middle of the 15th century (Fig. 59). Its niche skewing inwards represents East Prussian traditions. In this reredos, probably acquired for the new inauguration of the church with Birgitta as a patron saint, Birgitta is honored together with the older patron saints: The Pietà in the middle is surrounded in the corpus by John the Evangelist and Mary Magdalene. The west wing includes the Swedish saints Erik and Birgitta, and the left wing Saint Catharine of Alexandria and Saint Nicholas, i.e. identical to the saints in the painting program of the chancel. On behalf of Admiral Bergenstierna from Haddnäs the altarpiece was equipped with a new crowning piece, representing the Last Supper at the same time as it received a new layer of color.

The foot from a medieval font of Gotland limestone was discovered in archaeological excavations in the churchyard. ■

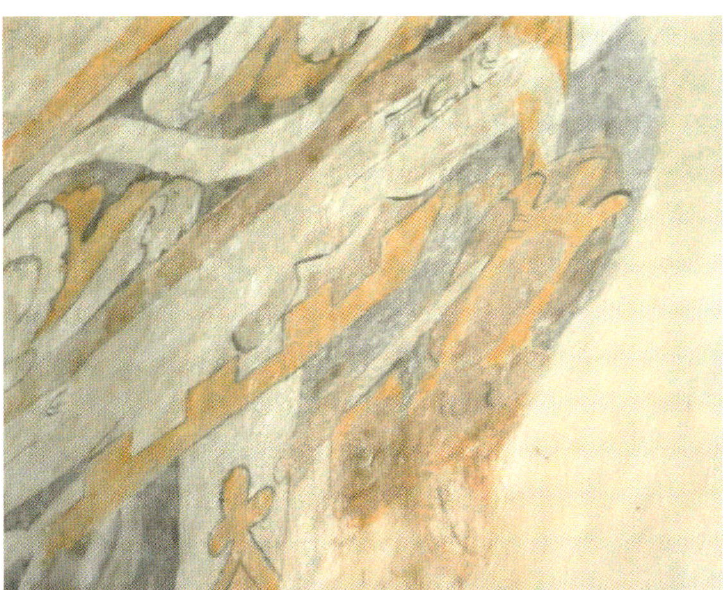

▲ Fig. 141. The martyrium of Saint Catherine. Detail from the south wall of the chancel depicting scenes from her beheading with the sword against her throat.

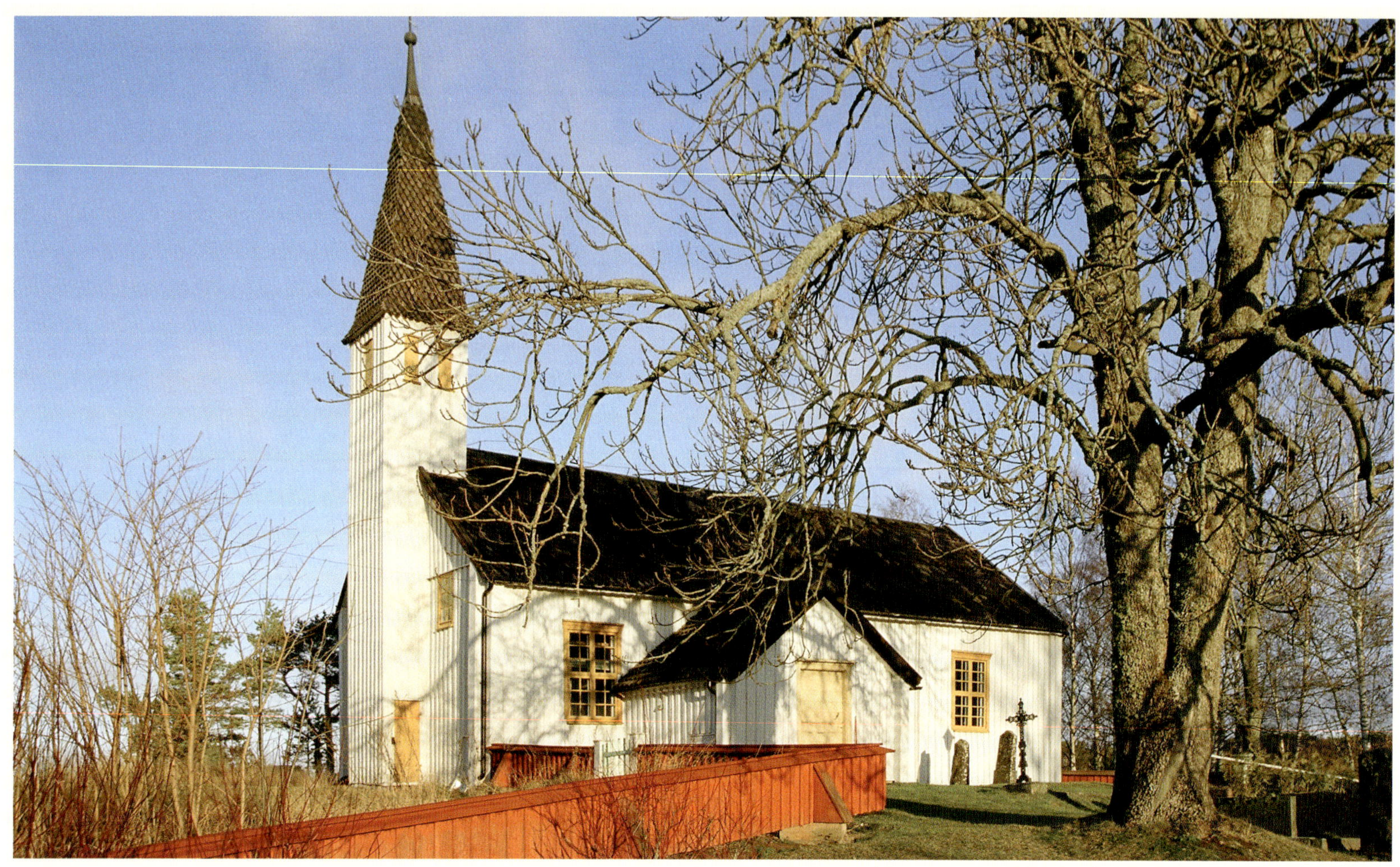

▲ Fig. 142. Lumparland chapel church. Exterior from the southwest.

LUMPARLAND CHAPEL

The chapel church of Lumparland, is centrally situated in the parish, on a high hill in Klemetsby. At the same time it is accessible by sea via Kapellviken bay, which opens up towards the inland sea Lumparn.

It is consecrated to both Saint Andrew and Saint Birgitta, and it belongs to Lemland mother church. The churchyard is enclosed by an old style wooden precinct wall, covered by a wooden saddle roof.

THE EXTERIOR

The low, white-painted wooden chapel disguises the underlying horizontal timber construction by vertical boarding with laths. The chapel is covered by a tarred shingle roof. The eastern gable is divided into three sections, while a slightly protruding narrow belfry, 9.64m high, rises at the western gable. The tower is crowned by a steep pyramidal spire. Eight large windows, with small windowpanes, are symmetrically arranged along the northern and southern walls, and the chancel. A porch is erected against the western part of the south wall.

GROUND PLAN

The chapel has a rectangular plan, with a semi-hexagonal chancel towards the east. The interior measures 18.15 x 7.2m. The south porch measures 3.6 x 4.1m, which is roughly equivalent to the inner measurements of the sacristy, which are 4.1 x 3.4m. The tower, only about two m wide, protrudes one m out of the western gable.

THE INTERIOR

The interior of the church is light, thanks to the numerous windows (size 118 x 103cm) and the light color scheme of inner walls and ceiling. The church has a wooden barrel vault. The interior is dominated by the big altar-painting on the eastern chancel wall, signed by Victor Westerholm in 1887, with the motif 'Come unto me'. In 1842 an older pulpit without sculptural decoration was replaced by another, simply paneled one. The gallery, with a screen where the panels depict Salvator Mundi surrounded by the apostles, was painted by Klas Lange (Claes Langh) in 1760. An older altarpiece representing the Last Supper was donated by Merchant Captain Anders Andersson Edberg of Klemetsby in 1736. The votive ship was donated to the church in 1835 by the shopkeeper Carl Gustaf Löthman.

BUILDING HISTORY

The present chapel church has had many predecessors:

A) The chapel is first mentioned in 1544, when it lost a bell weighing about 25 kilos. In 1637 worrying reports indicate that the chapel stood on a marshy meadow, that nothing was locked, that the windows were broken and that the chapel had been seen full of goats. The complaints were considerable: The church roof had rotted, the altar was too low, the floor uneven with untidy benches. Lacking were also the altar desk, a bishop's chair and the lectern. By 1642, barely adequate repairs had been made: windows, roof, and floor had been fixed. The roof of the chapel, measuring 9.5 x 7.9m, was covered by birch-bark and roof timber. In 1647 it was suggested that the altar should be raised in order to bring the altarpiece to the same level as the windows, the pews should be repaired, and a pulpit should be installed by the window. A porch of about 3 x 3m was also mentioned. In 1651 the repairs of the interior were considered to be finished. The altar had finally been raised, and the chapel had received a new altar desk, a new pulpit, and a baptismal font. It was stated that "the interior was excellently and lawfully decorated". The only thing which remained to be done was to construct a door for the built-in chair, a lid for the font, and a back for the bridal chair. A belfry was mentioned in 1655. In 1660 a church bell was donated by the married couple John Olofsson Berg and Kirstin Persdotter from Haddnäs. It was cast in Stockholm. The belfry was renovated in 1666.

B) As early as 1659 there were discussions about moving the chapel. Various options were mentioned, with the result that the chapel was

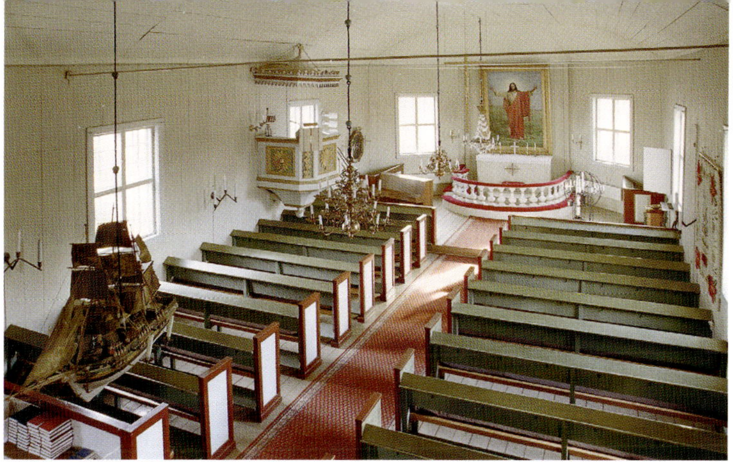

▲ Fig. 143. Interior towards the east.

moved in 1666. It was also recommended that the altarpiece should be gilded. The place chosen was a hill close to the marshy meadow, the previous place for the chapel. Eight windows were acquired to the new chapel, but there is no information about its ground plan or proportions. Only a chancel door was mentioned. This second chapel was demolished during the Northern War, when it was burnt down by Russian soldiers. The church bell was saved from the fire.

C) Rebuilding gradually started on the foundation of the old chapel after the Uusikaupunki peace treaty in 1721. In 1728 it was time to lay the roof of the new chapel. It measured 11.3 x 7m, with an inner height of almost three m. The porch of the chapel faced south and the sacristy north. The altarpiece representing the Last Supper was donated by Anders Andersson Edberg in 1736. A new bell, paid for by the parish, was cast in Stockholm in 1745. Both bells probably hung in the little belfry still decorating the western gable. A women's gallery was added in 1781, probably along the northern wall, next to the earlier gallery, which had been painted by Claus Langh. In 1804 it was stated that the porch needed to be shingled, but that "there was no particular wish for an extension of the cramped church". Despite this, costs and drawings were discussed already in 1806.

D) After the extension of the chapel, it got its present ground plan in 1812. A three-sided chancel to the east was added, 11 ells long and 12 ells wide. The plan was clearly inspired by Kökar Chapel. That stone church from the 1780s also influenced the chapel of Sottunga, which went through a similar extension of its chancel some twenty years later. Externally, the chapel was paneled and red in color. The roof covering consisted partly of tarred shingles, partly of tarred planks. A new pulpit with an internal panel and external boarding was acquired in 1842. The votive ship was donated in 1847. In 1886 Victor Westerholm, the artist who lived by the Lemström Canal and who had founded an Impressionist artists' colony, the so-called Önningeby Colony, offered to produce a new altar painting inexpensively. The offer was gratefully received. Externally the chapel was whitewashed in 1896. ■

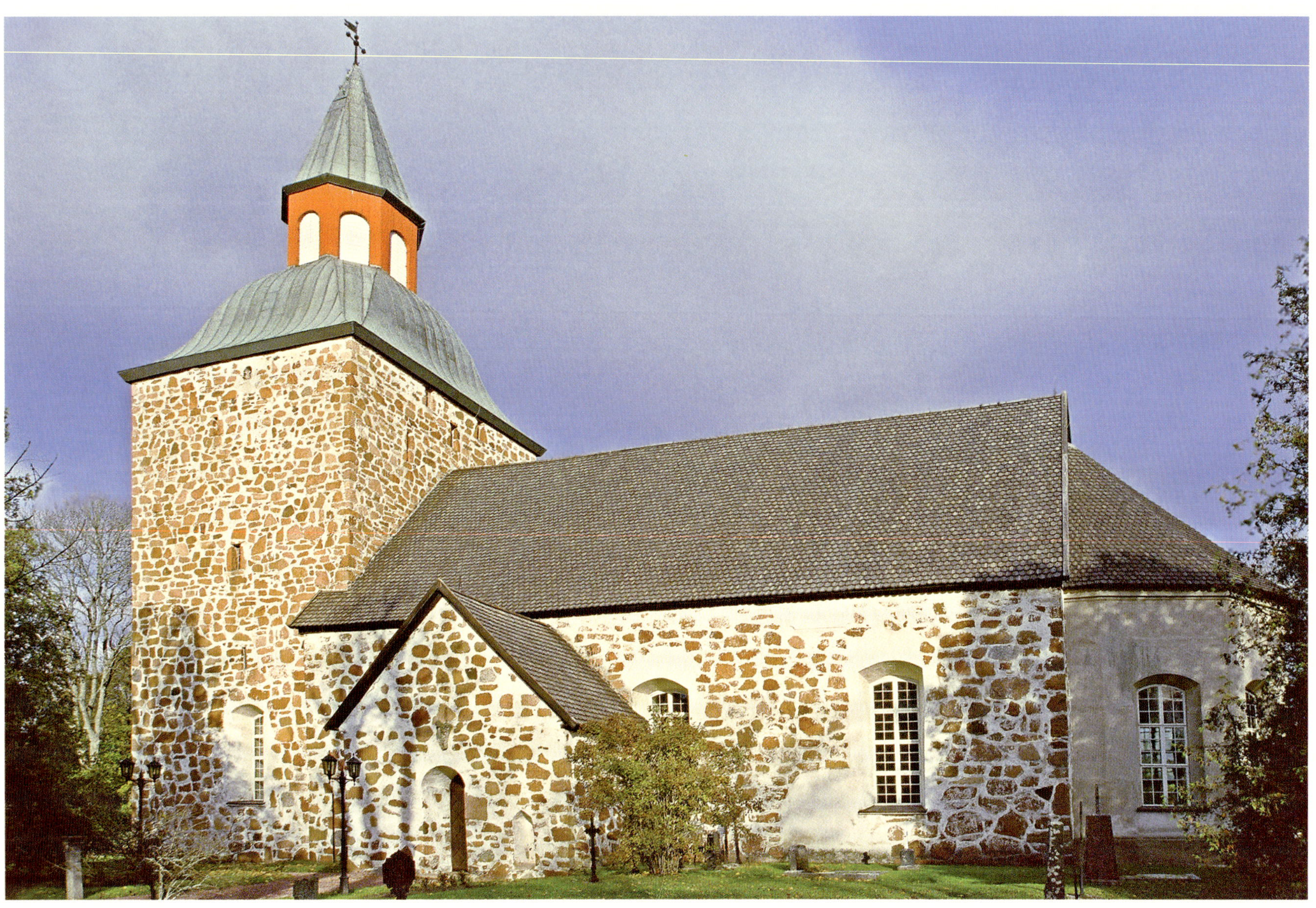

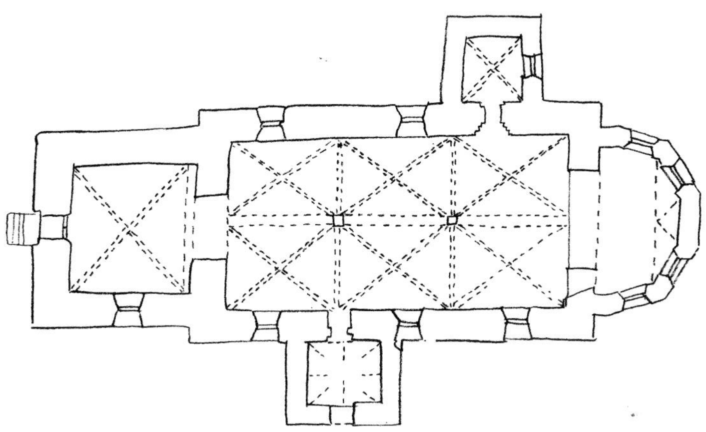

▲ Fig. 145. The ground plan of Saltvik church.

SALTVIK CHURCH

Saint Mary's Church in Saltvik is situated by the rivulet Kvarnbäcken in Kvarnbo, in the middle of the richest Iron Age area of Åland, surrounded by several large graveyards.

The adjacent largest Iron Age graveyard, Johannisberg, shows that Kvarnbo was the central place in Åland during the Viking Age. It also indicates unbroken continuity of settlement and cult well into the medieval period. The settlement connected to Johannisberg was probably situated in the middle of the great area of black earth where the church stands. Traces of houses from the Viking era have been found in this area, both in the churchyard and below the church.

THE EXTERIOR

The church of Saltvik is built of red granite (rapakivi), with large window openings to the north and south. It has no visible outer socle. A small sacristy is joined to the nave. There is also a porch in the south and a tower in the west. Joints in the walls show that the porch and the tower are secondary additions to the nave, while the relation between sacristy and nave is not obvious from the exterior. With its light plaster coating, the polygonal apse facing east differs from the other façades. East of the porch a walled-in priest door leading directly into the chancel is visible. The middle window of the southern façade is partly concealed by the porch. The nave has a total of five large window openings, two facing north and three facing south. Four more windows belong to the apse. A south window forms the only light opening to the high west tower, crowned by a Baroque spire from the middle of the 18th century. The church has two entrances: one in the south gable of the porch and another in the tower portal in the west.

GROUND PLAN

The rectangular ground plan, with inner measures ca 19.3 x 9.7m includes *double naves**. Six cross-vaulted bays are resting on two pillars along the central axis. A polygonal chancel was added as a continuation of the central axis towards the east. Similarly, towards the west tower the room opens through a wide and low arch. In front of the southern portal stands a porch. The sacristy can be reached through a portal in the eastern part of the north wall. Towards the south and the north, large window openings cut through the walls of the nave.

THE INTERIOR

The interior of the church gives a disparate impression, with traces of innumerable alterations. High white ***rib vaults****, cast in modern concrete, rest on slender pillars with square cross sections. The nave opens through a high pointed nave towards the polygonal chancel in the east, and towards the west tower through a lower arch.

Various traces of destroyed vaults and fragmentarily preserved wallpaintings make it difficult to interpret iconography and chronology. Thanks to a number of large window openings, the interior is bathed in light. A recessed round-arched framework of brick surrounds the sacristy portal towards the north. It is still possible to discern the traces of an earlier vault lower down on the west gable wall.

The inventory, with medieval artifacts from different centuries, reflects the same variations but the 17th century really dominates the interior. Large areas of the medieval wall paintings were whitewashed to leave space for a total Post-Reformation iconographical program, directed by Dean Boetius Murenius (vicar at Saltvik, 1636-1666). In turn, these 17th century paintings have been destroyed. The grand altarpiece from 1662 is a donation from the Footangel family at Germundö Manor (Fig. 58), the Footangel family decorated the church with their coat of arms at the same time. Nowadays the pulpit from 1829 is placed in the

◀ Fig. 144. Saltvik church, exterior from the southeast.

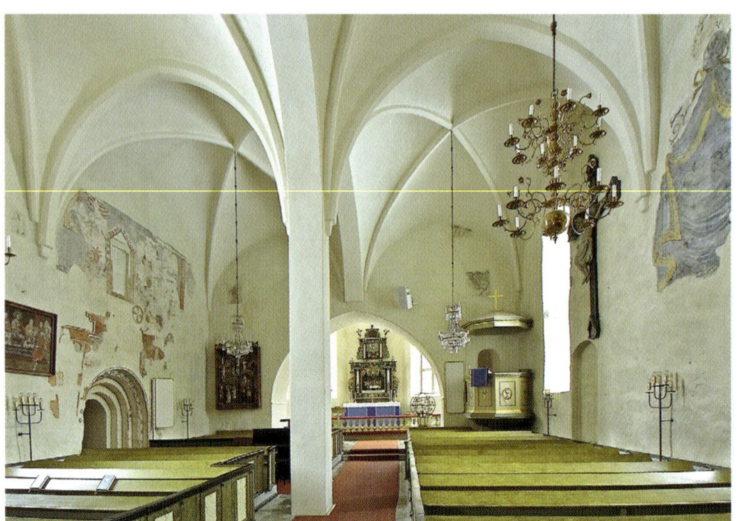

▲ Fig. 146. Saltvik church, interior towards the east.

▶ Fig. 147. Saltvik church, detail of the northern chancel wall, with Post Reformation wall paintings.

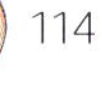

south east corner of the nave. It can be reached through a wall passage from the chancel.

BUILDING HISTORY

The remains of a skeleton were found under the northern wall of the present nave during excavations in the 1950s. Thus the site was used earlier as a burial ground and we therefore have to presuppose an older wooden church on the site, although nothing is known about this. The remains of a stave construction, earlier thought to be the remains of a stave church, are more likely part of the earlier Viking Age settlement in the area. Innumerable heavy-handed secondary interferences make the building history of Saltvik church complicated and hard to interpret. Scientific analysis, however, has thrown some light on the problems:

About 1270-1296 the rectangular nave and sacristy were erected. The church was probably vaulted as soon as the walls had hardened. Remains of this first vaulting along the walls demonstrate that these vaults were not very high. Narrow and highly placed windows formed light openings, three towards the south and two towards the east. The northern wall lacked windows. The main altar stood free from the east wall, further towards the middle of the chancel. To begin with, the church had at least two side altars, one for Mary in the north, west of the sacristy portal, and another in the south, immediately west of the priest door leading into the chancel.

Dendrochronological analysis shows that large architectural alterations were performed at the end of the 14th century. For reasons unknown, the original fieldstone vaults of the double naved construction were now torn down, only to be replaced by other vaults a few decades later, this time in brick. Among other changes was the erection of the porch in front of the main portal of the nave in the 1370s. Soon after, in 1381, the west tower was constructed in one singular building phase up to the pyramidshaped wooden spire. A rounded arch was opened between nave and tower in connection with the building of the tower. Large side altars were added in front of each central pillar. Walls and vaults were covered by paintings in the 15th century.

THE POST-REFORMATION PERIOD

In the beginning of the 16th century, following the Reformation, the church was left in disrepair. Probably most of the medieval wooden sculptures of the church were lost during this period, among others the Madonna sculpture which must have adorned the northern side altar in this church devoted to Mary. According to the Lutheran liturgy, the interior was completely renewed with a new pulpit, pews, and a gallery

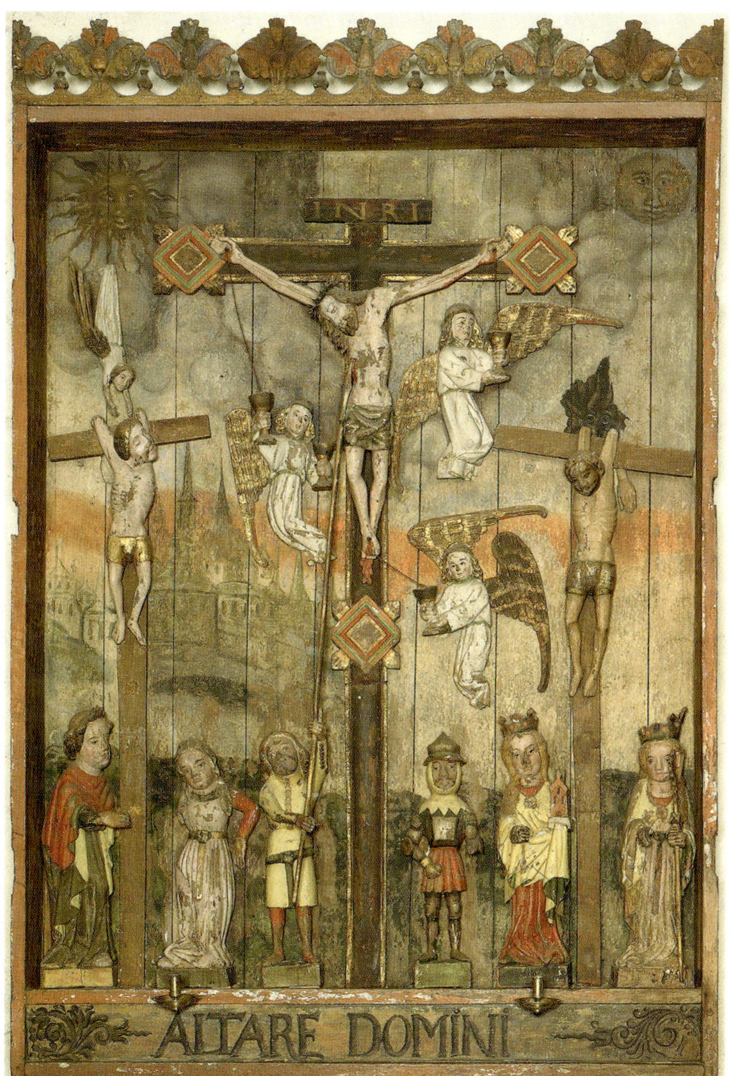

▲ Fig 148. Saltvik church. Altare Domini, corpus of an altarpiece from the 15th century.

along the west wall. From the 1630s onwards the books of accounts and the visitation records provide evidence of what was done. All the side altars were removed and the earlier free standing high altar was moved against the eastern wall. Large parts of the medieval wall paintings had to give way to a Lutheran painting program, executed by Master Mårten Johansson. The initiative came from Boetius Murenius.

Minor architectural alterations were made in the 17th and 18th centuries. A window towards the north was opened in the 1830s to improve the readability in the gallery. But truly radical changes were not made until the 1850s, when the medieval brick vaults were torn down and replaced by a flat wooden vault. The polygonal chancel was added in the east at the same time, and large parts of the eastern gable were torn down, including the original chancel windows. A triumphal arch through the former chancel wall was opened up to the new chancel. Further, all the windows were enlarged, conforming to the windows in the new chancel. A new altarpiece representing "Christ in Gethsemane" acquired in 1862 was painted by the court painter Robert Wilhelm Ekman.

After archaeological excavations, the church was once more extensively renovated and rebuilt in the 1950s. Yet another demolition of the inner ceiling was performed when the wooden barrel vault was replaced by new double-naved vaults cast in concrete. Whatever was left of earlier wall paintings was uncovered and restored, and the altarpiece from 1662 was moved back to the high altar. The architect in charge was Ruben Lindgren.

INVENTORY

There are only random survivals of the medieval inventory of the church.

• **The crucifix** on the south wall has a rare shape. The little aediculae at the end of the cross arms have only one parallel: the crucifix from nearby Sund, from the middle of the 13th century. Like in Sund the cross consists of local wood, this time of poplar. Dendrochronological dating of a pine board supporting the back of the cross-center yields the 1250s. (Fig. 23).

• **The font**, quatrefoil from top to bottom, is a piece of high quality imported from Gotland in the middle of the 13th century. Even if there are several parallels to the font in Sweden, it is unique in Finland. It is well-cut and highly polished and carved from so called Hoburg marble (Fig. 24).

• **"Altare Domini"**, the corpus of an altarpiece from the 15th century, hangs today on the north side of the triumphal arch. Side wings, with sculptures in double rows, are missing. Single figures from the wings were integrated into the corpus, when it received its present appearance in the 17th century. The motif is the crucifixion of Christ, including the two robbers and the mourning Mary and John.

• The painting representing **Saint George and the Dragon**, 2.38 x 3.10m, was painted in oil on panel in 1659 by Mårten Johansson. The initiative came from Boetius Murenius. Today the painting hangs on the northern wall of the tower's ground floor. (Fig. 57). The model is the well known Equestrian group in the Great Church of Stockholm, with the same motive. This group from 1489 honors Sten Sture, Senior, for the victory at Brunkeberg, when he defeated an invading force led by Christian I of Denmark. ■

Signilskärs Kapellruin

uppmätt och planlagd
år 1890
af
Reinh Hausen

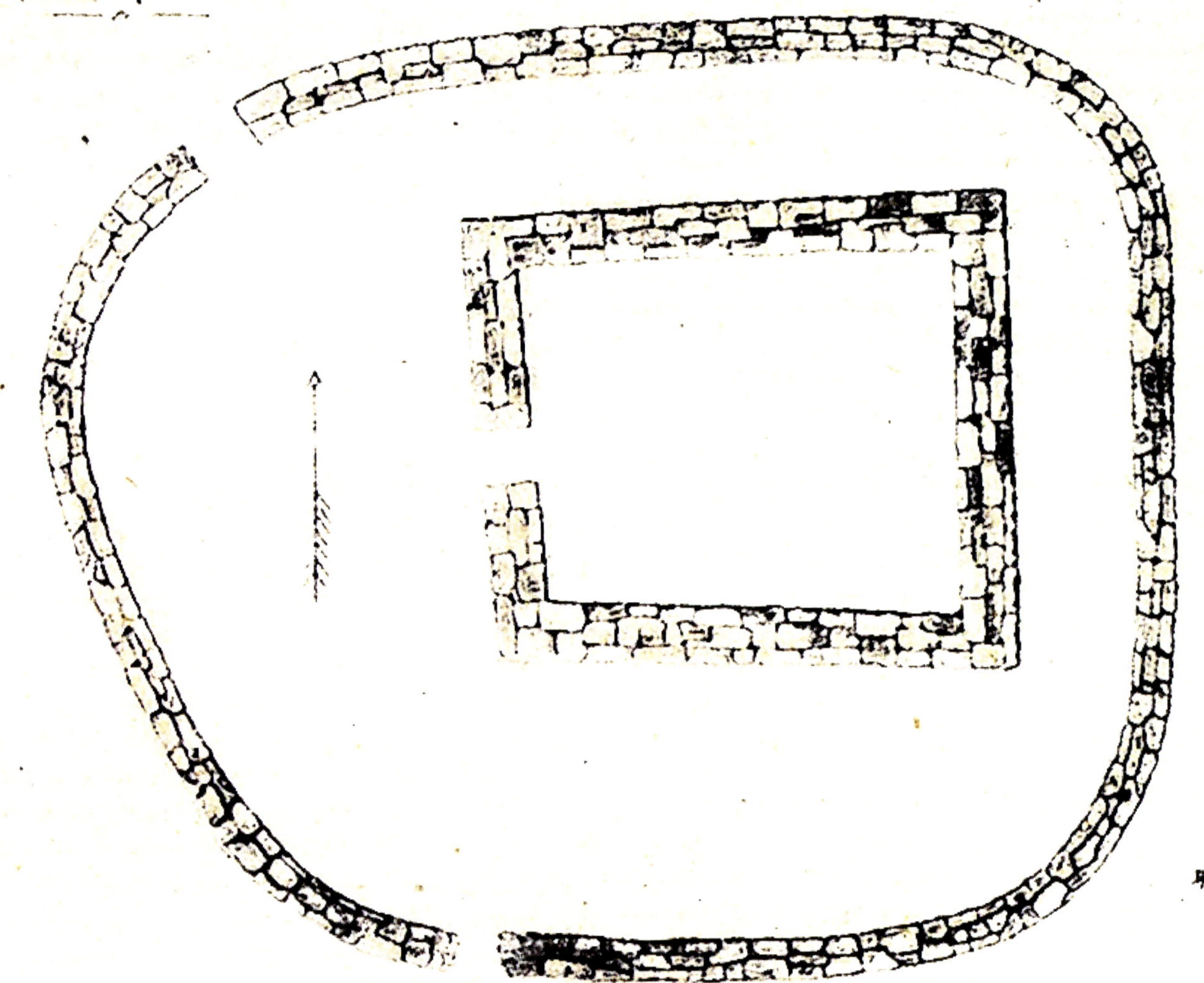

Fyrkantens östra mur
1,70 meter hög.
0,80 met. hög.

meter

SIGNILDSKÄR CHAPEL RUIN

This mystery laden chapel lies on one of the islands in the group called Signildskär far out in the west in the Åland Sea, and the place has always been an important anchoring point on the sea route between Grisslehamn in Sweden and Eckerö in Åland.

Exactly when a chapel was erected on the island is not known. To secure the delivery of post and the sea traffic Gustavus Vasa ordered the island to be inhabited all the year around. In 1538 "Sancte Signildskär" is mentioned for the first time in written sources, without actually mentioning a chapel. By the 18th century there is mention of a ruin in the place. The chapel is surrounded by myths. According to the legend it is connected to an English princess called Signel, or Signella, who escaped to the island from her enemies, and here built a chapel in gratitude of her salvation. To the same legendary group of islands belongs another island with the enigmatic name "Heligman" (Holy Man).

A detailed documentation of the ruin, written by the vicar at Hammarland, P.U.F. Sadelin, was published in "Finlands Allmänna Tidning" in 1853.

When this island first received an inhabitant can, as no sources are available, not be recorded. Due to its position it was probably visited early, maybe already by the Romans. At least, since the Viking Age it has often been called upon by seafarers, who maybe then erected the so called chapel on the island, of which there are still ruins. This chapel consists of a building in gray stone, with a thickness of 2½ ells without any mortar between the stones. This building measures 12½ ells in length, 10½ ditto in width and it is 3 ditto high and it has probably been covered by boards. The same building is surrounded by a courtyard with a low grey stone wall, which on the north side is laid at a distance of 11½ ells from the house itself, while the distance on the other walls measures only 3 ells. On the western side, under this enclosure, runs a ditch for draining water from the closed courtyard. In olden times this building was probably used by seafarers for worship, and the courtyard as a burial place for those deceased during the journey. Discoveries of bones have been made on the latter. According to an old tale on the island this chapel was built by a queen who was escaping from an enemy.

◀ Fig. 149. "Signilskär's chapel ruin" measured and "planned" in 1890 by Reinh. Hausen.

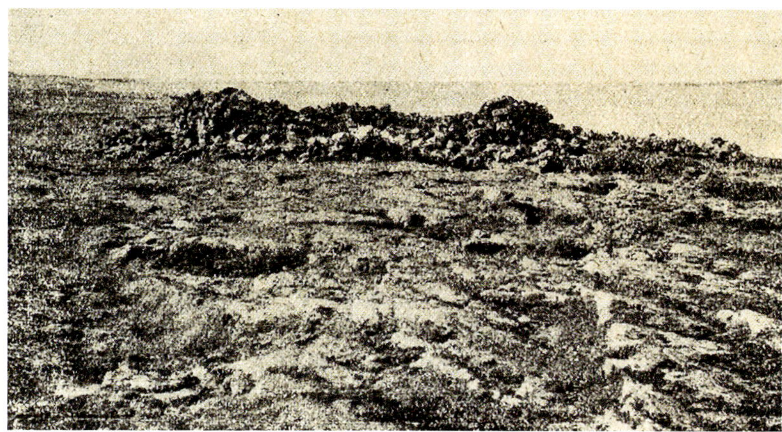

▲ Fig. 150. Chapel ruin at Signildskär. Photographed in 1923, before the reconstruction in 1948.

When translated into meters the measures above are approximately as follows: the thickness of the walls 1.5m, the length 7.7m, the width 6.5m and the height 1.8m. There is interesting information on the lack of mortar and on the enclosed courtyard functioning as a burial place for those who had not survived the voyage. Reinhold Hausen did a documentation drawing of the site in 1890, and confirmed the information given by Sadelin. In the ruin there was only one opening, towards the sea in the west.

Unfortunately, a Finnish patrol leveled the ruin in 1940, when the fortifications from the Winter War were to be destroyed. Matts Dreijer archaeologically investigated the chapel in 1948, whereupon the ruin was reconstructed. The excavations confirmed that the chapel was erected on top of a cleft in the rock running in the north northwest-south southeast direction. The remains of two skeletons were discovered at the clearing of the cleft. Odontological investigation of the teeth showed that the skeletons belonged to two elderly men buried in the cleft. ^{14}C AMS analysis of the chin bone of one of the men showed that the burial took place some time between 1470 and 1655. In the cleft were further found around 40 coins, most of them Swedish. Two of them belonged to the 13th century although the great majority of the coins dated from the 14th century.

Even if the chapel does not follow the more significant sailing route of the Danish Itinerary, it is still of medieval origin, possibly from the end of the 13th century. A medieval pilgrims road is the likely predecessor to the Post-Reformation postal road, which from Signildskär continued to Eckerö and further straight across the main Åland island to Vårdö, Kumlinge and Brändö, and across the waters to Kustavi in Finland Proper. ■

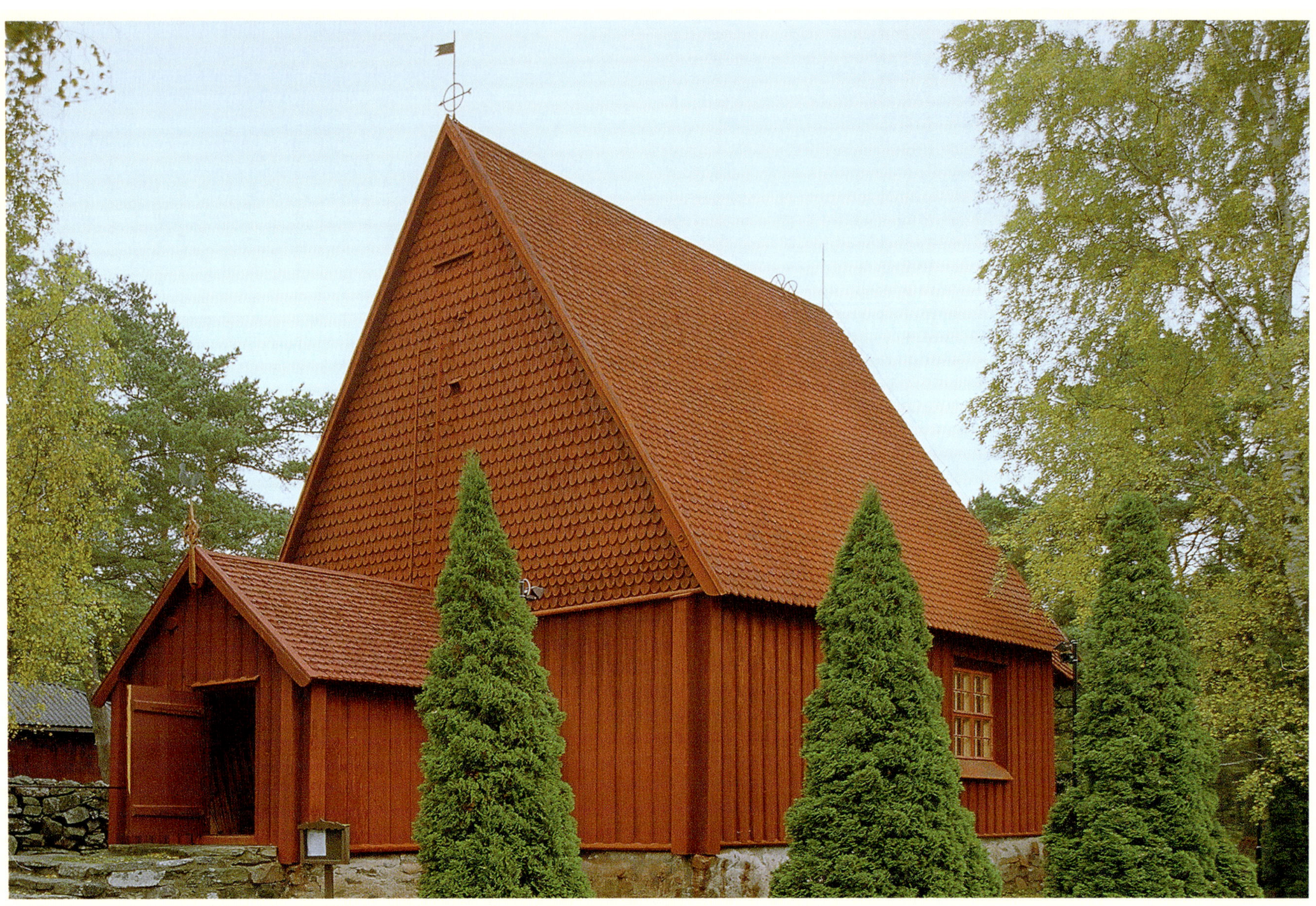

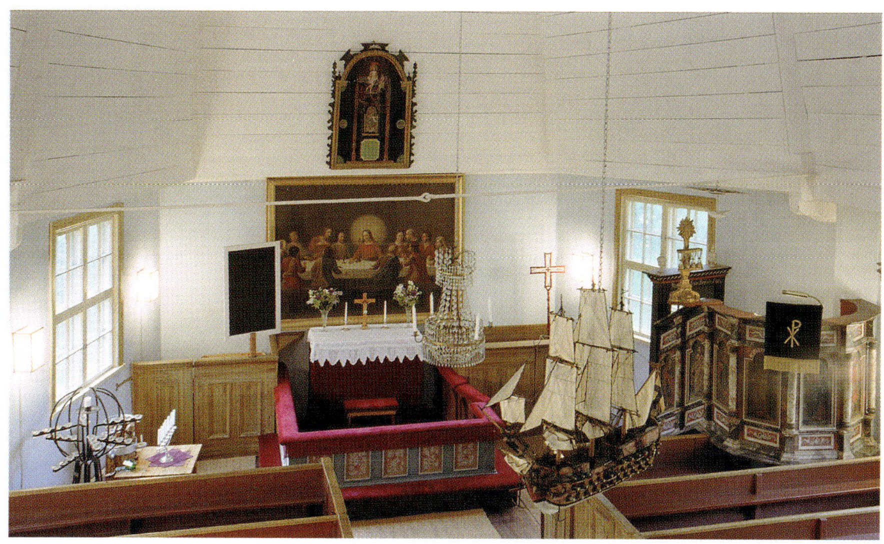

▲ Fig. 152. Sottunga church, interior towards the east.

SOTTUNGA CHAPEL

The red-painted wooden chapel, belonging to Föglö mother church, lies on the southern tip of Sottunga island far from the other habitation.

 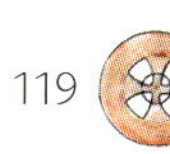

Outside the churchyard the belfry stands isolated on the other side of the road running from the ferry harbor in the south to Sottunga village further north.

THE EXTERIOR

The red little chapel is a short wooden building with an unusually high gable in the west. The top of the gable is shingled. The same red shingles cover the steep high roof. A low porch, or rather a hall, forms the entry in the middle of the west gable. In the north a little windowless sacristy connects to the church. Towards the east the chancel wall forms a three-phased conclusion to the rectangular plan. Six uniform windows face east, south, and north. A three-phased, or semi-hexagonal, chancel in the east forms a special ground plan for the single nave measuring about 12.7 x 7.8m. The windows are uniformly placed around the walls. Only the west gable and the sacristy lack fenestration.

THE INTERIOR

The interior of the church is quite light. The unusual proportions are enhanced by the inner barrel vault. Its height of eight meters doubles the height of the surrounding walls. The pulpit in the south, signed by Jonas Bergman in 1753, has paintings of the apostles. Christ is flanked by Peter and Paul. The altarpiece representing the Last Supper, painted by P. Berggren in Stockholm, was acquired in 1845.

BUILDING HISTORY

The chapel is first mentioned in 1544, in connection with Gustavus Vasa confiscating its copper bell. Vague information from 1658 that income was needed from the offertory boxes to finance the chapel has been interpreted as referring to new building activity. Three years later Dean Boetius Murenius in his visitation records describes a medieval interior, with much to criticize. According to him a log stretched across

◀ Fig. 151. Sottunga chapel, the exterior.

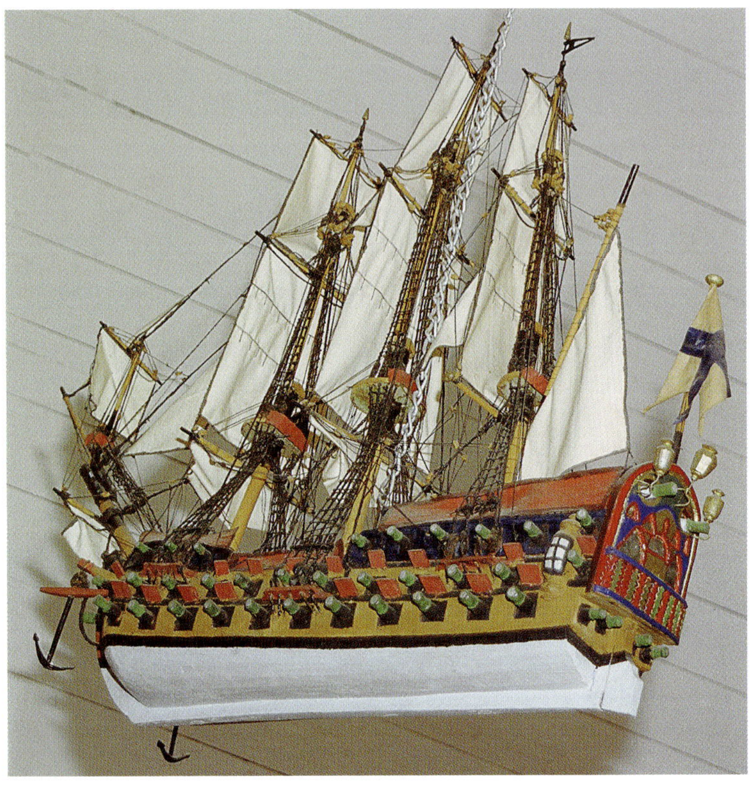

▲ Fig. 153. The votive ship from Sottunga.

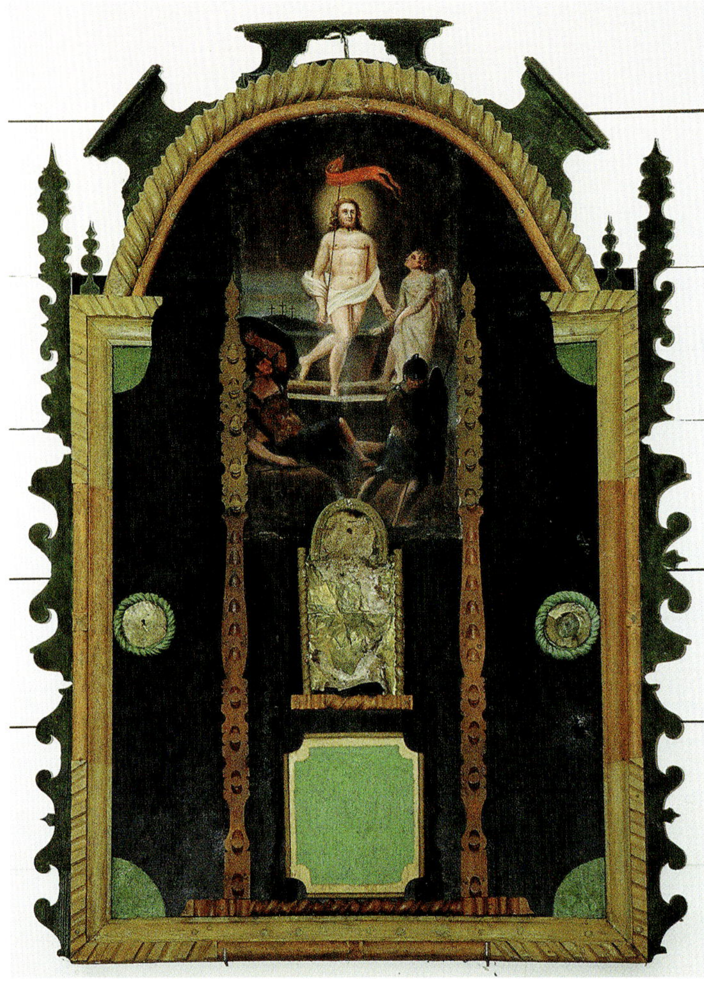

▲ Fig. 154. Older altarpainting, donation from the pilot student Petter Nordberg from Mosshaga.

the entire church. Over the altar "there were many old and broken superfluous images", and "The log and the ugly images must be removed, except for the crucifix," etc. The citation implies a medieval arrangement with a trabes, a cross log above the church space, to mark the transition between chancel and congregation.

According to Murenius the log carried a crucifix flanked by other wooden sculptures – an obvious Calvary group, with the crucified Christ surrounded by Mary in mourning and John, the apostle. Everything had been left in disrepair: the windows by the altar, the book stool and the pulpit were badly carved and awkwardly fitted into the wall, the altar too low. Carpenters were to be called in to make a new church door, the desk for the altar, a pulpit with stairs, and an altarpiece below the window. Murenius further ordered the windows by the lectern and the pulpit to be enlarged and the altar raised.

The churchyard had no gate, and in 1692 it was time to change the window frames. An old altarpiece was procured from Geta chapel in 1709 at a cost of 6 "riksdaler".

In 1711 there was a complaint that the road from the village to the chapel was wet, rocky, and marshy. The chapel was in a state of decay and needed considerable repair. Preferably it should be moved closer to

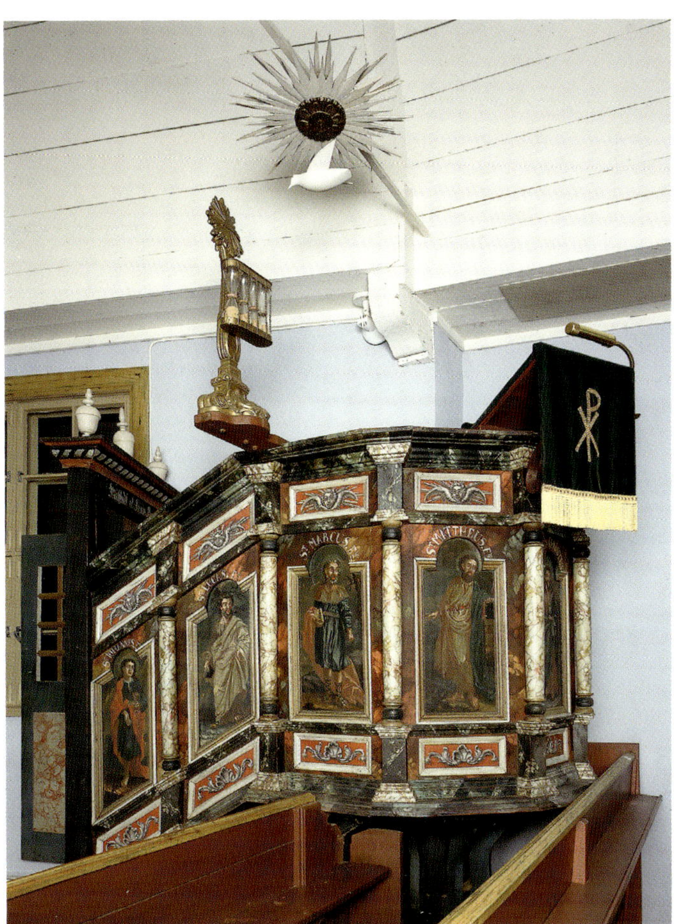

▲ Fig. 155. The pulpit from Sottunga chapel church, signed by Jonas Bergman in 1753.

the village, to a place called Källnäs. The move should be made in the wintertime when sledges could be used.

Everything however points to the move never taking place, and that the chapel still stands on its original site. The accounts state that the only thing happening was that the crucifix was painted and gilded the following year. Also, boards were acquired to repair the roof, at the same time as the windows of the chapel were seen to.

All plans to renovate and move the church came to nothing because of the Northern War, when inhabitants from Sottunga, like other Ålanders, fled to Sweden from the enemy. Two independent sources from 1726 confirm that the chapel had burned. In a commentary to the inventory list after the homecoming it is said that the altarpiece as well as the chapel had been burned by the enemy. The money for a new building was, however, in safe keeping in the chapel chest. "Vicar Stålbohm must ensure that the chapel with its loans is secure in the chapel chest, kept by the vicar, which money they intend to use for building a new chapel instead of the former chapel, burnt by the enemy."

In 1730 it is said that "the new chapel, which had been built on its former site, had been installed and its doors, windows and floor renewed." What remained was the hall with the chapel door, i.e. the main entry, as well as the fixtures: pulpit, priest benches, the top desk for the altar, and pews. The repairs should be financed by collects from the offertory box on Finnö. The chapel should be tarred and painted red. In 1735 timber was acquired for the campanile. According to F.W. Radloff in 1795, the chapel was almost square-shaped, 14 ells long and 13½ ells wide (8.25 x 8m). The belfry was considerable in size and contained two bells, the bigger with the following inscription: "This bell was bought for Mary Magdalene Chapel in the parish of Föglö in 1769 and it was recast in November 1781".

It was once more time to decide whether to replace the decayed church with a new building, or whether a renovation would be sufficient. For financial reasons the latter option was chosen, "with the addition of new timber". Carpenter Eric Lindström was in charge of building a new chancel, which had previously been lacking. In 1802 the chapel was elongated by 7½ ells (a little more than 4 metres), thus receiving its definitive ground plan with its three-phased finishing to the east. At the same time the high wooden barrel vault was built. In 1843 the old wooden wall around the church yard was replaced by a wall in stone. The belfry was extensively repaired in 1853. ■

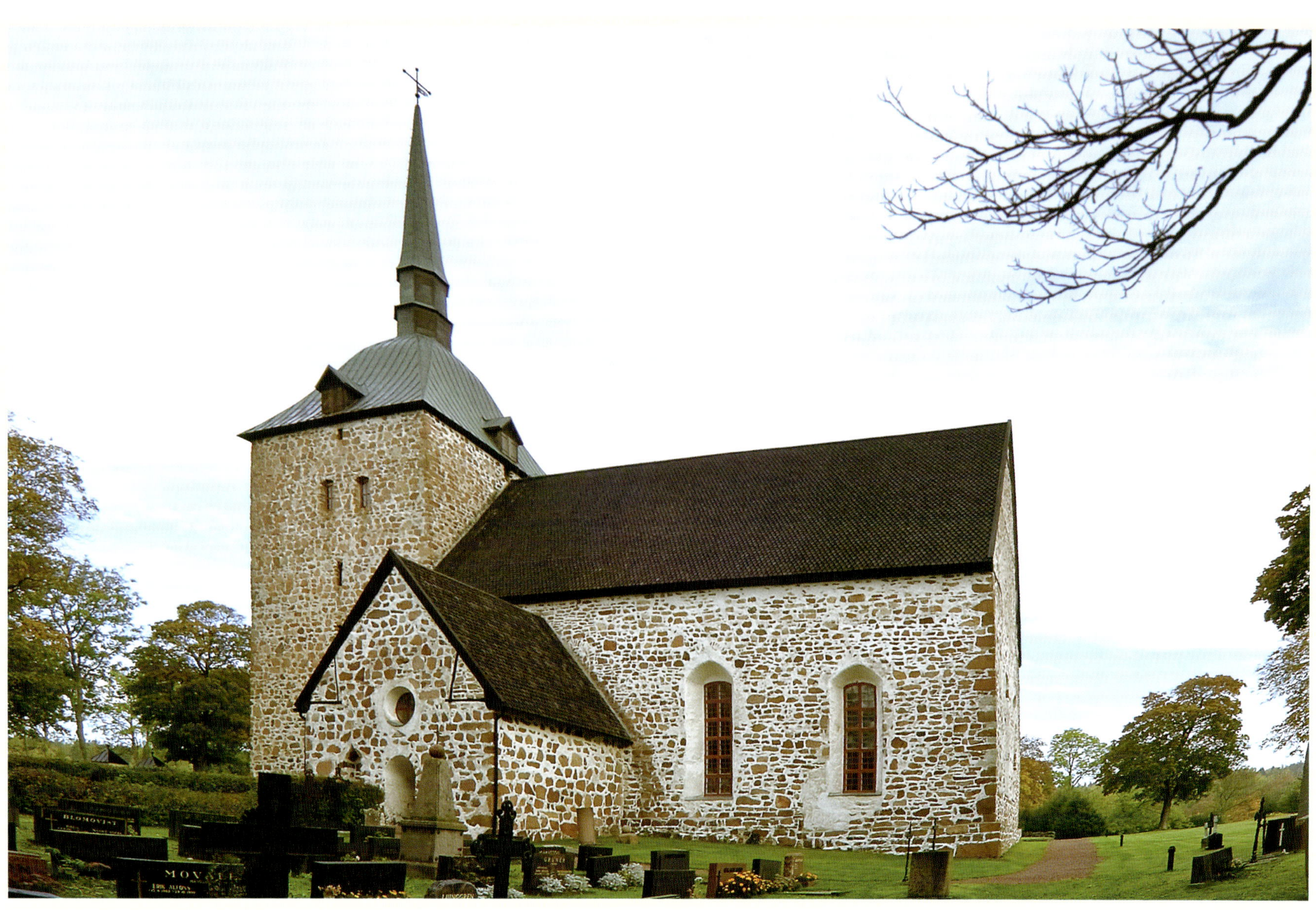

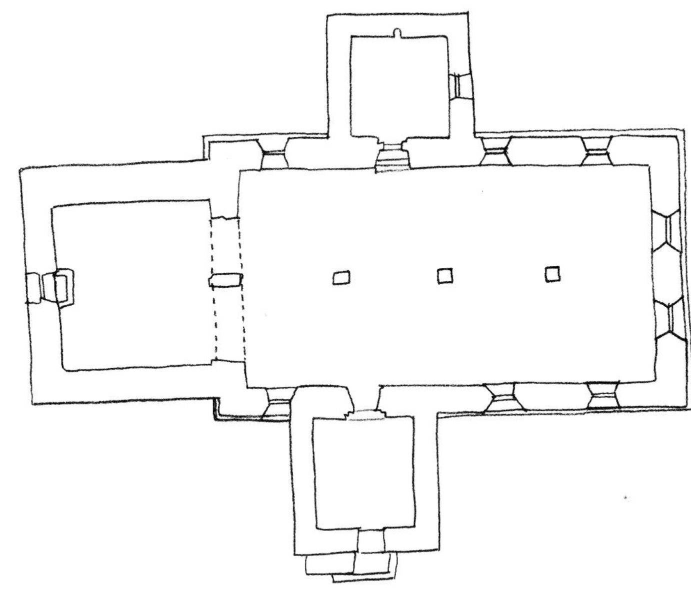

Fig. 157. Sund church, the ground plan.

SUND CHURCH

Sund is the largest medieval church in the Islands. Like other mother churches, the church in Sund was erected in connection to an Iron-Age graveyard, which here lies north of the church.

The area was mentioned as a tourist attraction in the 17th century, with now lost spectacular mounds, and medieval house foundations which await further investigation. The church is beautifully situated on the slope down towards Kyrksundet, which earlier was a sailable route, giving the parish its name (sund meaning 'strait'). The church, consecrated to St. John the Baptist, has never been archaeologically investigated. It was mother church to Vårdö chapel, and until the beginning of the 15th century also to the chapelry of Kumlinge.

THE EXTERIOR

Sund church, built of selected small-sized red granite, with larger blocks of granite in the corners, is high and impressive. The primitive socle, built up in different levels following the sloping topography, underlines the differences in the levels and adjusts smoothly to the terrain. It also marks the secondary building units, as it disappears behind the porch, the tower, and the sacristy. The tower was erected later against the west gable of the nave. Further additions were the porch towards the south built in front of an older southern portal, and the sacristy built against an existing northern portal. Traces of a walled-in priest door leading directly to the chancel can still be seen east of the porch on the southern façade, as can the arches of two original narrow and high-placed windows. Otherwise the exterior of the nave is characterized by big and high window openings to south, east, and north. The west tower, crowned by a high and narrow spire, is the biggest in Åland. Its solid walls are broken up by a few highly placed light openings.

GROUND PLAN

The rectangular nave (interior measures 23.47 x 12.17m, about 288 square metres), is vaulted into two naves, resting on three pillars along the central axis. Against the nave are later additions such as a west tower, a sacristy, and a porch. Both sacristy and porch have been erected in front of earlier portals. Today, the main entrance into the church is in the tower, in the central axis of the west wall. Large windows break through the walls towards the south and the north. The two east gable windows reflect the double vaulting of the nave.

THE INTERIOR

High vaults and large windows in all directions make the interior light and spacious. Three stone pillars with square cross sections along the central axis create four bays in each nave. The vaulting in local stone has been cast with considerable professional skill. The bays are separated by elegantly formed longitudinal and transverse arches, resting on limestone columns and limestone brackets fitted into the walls of the nave. The vaulting in two naves and the portals with triangular finishings in towards the church, show Gotland influence. By the southern portal one of the original windows, blocked by the secondarily built porch, has been recovered. Another recovered window is a circular light opening asymmetrically placed in the northern part of the western gable. Brick imitation, painted immediately after the vaulting, covered all transverse and longitudinal arches. Fragments of the imitation can

◀ Fig. 156. Sund church, exterior from the south.

still be seen on the column closest to the chancel. The floor of the nave slopes towards the chancel in the east. The interior in blue and white leaves a somewhat cool impression.

BUILDING HISTORY

THE 13TH CENTURY

The first stone church in Sund, i.e. the nave, was built in 1250-1275. The age has been determined by mortar dating, and the chronology agrees with the dendrochronological analysis of the crucifix and the Mourning Mary. The double naves were part of the original plan. The church is facing south, i.e. three windows and two portals cut through the south façade. Of these, the main portal further west was framed by a recessive pointed arch in limestone. The priest door further east led into the chancel. In the north wall, almost axially against the main portal there was a portal, but no windows. Because of the two naves the portal of the west gable was asymmetrically placed south of the central axis. This west portal was blocked by a beam anchored deeply into the wall. The asymmetry of the portal was compensated by the circular window high up north of the west gable and another opening framed in limestone farther up still.

Of all Åland churches, Sund shows the clearest marks of Gotland influence. This can, for instance, be seen in the triangular arches finishing the portals and in the double naves. The three southern windows were of different sizes and placed at different levels. But they probably all had the same shape, that is, they were sitting deep into the walls and had rounded arches, with simply profiled limestone mullions. The eastern wall of the chancel was broken by two windows, probably a little bigger than the southern windows but otherwise of the same type. The Calvary group was fixed onto a horizontal and transverse beam, the trabes, along the dividing line between the chancel and the congregation.

As soon as the walls had hardened the nave was vaulted. Transverse and longitudinal arches were immediately covered by brick imitation on the first layer of plaster. The earliest wall painting is probably on the wall between the chancel windows, where the Calvary group motif was repeated in a painted version (cf. Figure 15). Originally this wall painting was fully visible behind the free-standing altar. Today it is hidden behind the big altarpiece dominating the eastern wall. Along the walls brackets of limestone to carry the vaults are identical to those in Hammarland and Jomala. The other wall paintings of the nave are a little later, around 1280-1300, and here further influence from Gotland can be seen in isolated figures of saints framed in by aedicules.

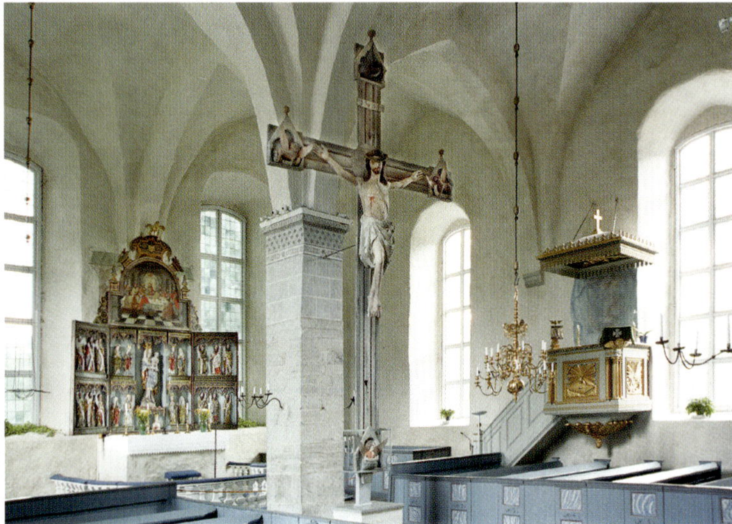

▲ Fig. 158. Sund church, interior towards the southeast.

THE 14TH CENTURY

At the beginning of the 14th century the sacristy and the tower were added. At this stage there was no western portal at ground level. Nor was there any vaulting of the ground floor of the tower. Instead it was divided into two storeys by an intermediate wooden floor. The bottom floor of the tower could thus be reached only through the nave portal in the original western gable. A staircase inside the northern wall secured internal communication from the ground floor up to the tower. The staircase provides further confirmation of initial plans of vaulting the tower. The west tower of Sund is roughly contemporary with the towers in Hammarland and Lemland. Originally the tower was probably crowned by a simple pyramidal spire. A few light openings penetrated the massive walls of the tower.

At the beginning of the 14th century a wooden sculpture of Saint Olof was ordered from Gotland, probably to adorn a side altar by the long wall. At about the same time the Gothic crucifix was remodeled to enhance the suffering, which was the prevailing spirit of the time. The mouth section was re-carved to emphasize the pain, and blood clusters were added to the elbows, wrists, and to the side wound in the chest.

Sculptures representing the apostles John and Paul were ordered from northern Germany in the 1380s. They are sculpted from the same oak trunk. These sculptures are among the finest in Scandinavia with their excellent fold treatment and their psychologizing portraits. The

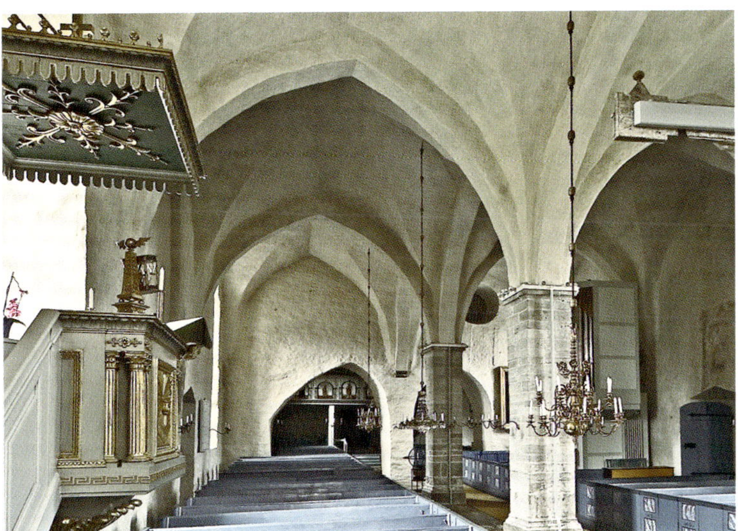

▲ Fig. 159. Sund church, interior towards the west.

apostles were richly painted and they had back plates indicating that they may have been freestanding. Still, the original arrangement of these sculptures in the church remains unknown. (cf. Figures 36 and 35).

THE 15TH CENTURY

In the 15th century the ground floor of the tower received its high vaulting. The primitively cast tower vault was immediately provided with strange abstract foliage ornamentation. The porch, with a carelessly executed vault similar to that of the tower, was probably built at the same time. During the process one of the southern windows of the nave was blocked. The big church bell was inscribed with a dedication to Saint John the Baptist, and acquired by the church in 1480. Possibly the tower also got a new up-to-date pyramidal wooden spire, surrounded by four smaller turrets, identical to the spire in Finström.

During the 15th century some new wooden sculptures were acquired, above all an altarpiece from northern Poland. It is a very large triptych with the Madonna surrounded by the four crowned virgins and four other female saints in the margins. On the side wings are the apostles representing the Credo series. Other more modest sculptures represent Saint George and the Dragon and Saint Barbara.

The churchyard of Sund must have acquired the octagonal form in the 15th century at the latest. It was first documented in the 1650s and can still be seen on an enlargement map from 1872.

THE 16TH CENTURY

At the reduction in 1547 a gilded silver monstrance weighing a little more than 3 kilograms was confiscated, together with two small bells and three candlesticks of pewter. Otherwise the Post-Reformation liturgy did not affect the Roman Catholic decorations of the church such as wall paintings and wooden sculptures. Still, neglect and general decay gradually reflects a changed attitude towards Catholic ecclesiastic art.

THE 17TH CENTURY

The great changes after the Reformation took place only during the 17th century. Visitation records from the 1630s revealed that church and sacristy were 'filled with rubbish and uncleanliness'. A new pulpit was now installed by the south wall. The pews, the chancel screen, and the bishop's seat were also renewed. The large, freestanding main altar was torn down and replaced by a new brick altar 'of moderate proportions' against the chancel wall. The wooden floor was renewed and successively provided with large stone slabs fitted in as covers for the new burial chambers. There was also a burial chamber in the sacristy, but the grave slab was lost at an early stage. During the 17th century all windows of the church were gradually enlarged. An entirely new window on the south wall improved the lighting in the western part of the church.

The west portal of the tower was not opened until 1658. At the same time the interior was whitewashed, thus covering the medieval wall-paintings. Mårten Johansson provided the crucifix and the altarpiece with new gilding and coloring. The earliest organ in the Islands was acquired for the church in 1672.

For the decoration of the organ gallery along the west gable of the nave, the painter Abraham Myra was engaged in 1662. The same painter was committed to paint an epitaph in 1671, representing the vicar Bryniel Kiellin with his family. Seven years later the church was devastated by fire, so intense that even the vaults were partly damaged. The medieval church bell melted down and the walls cracked. The inventory was saved, but was left for several days without shelter in the rain. The repairs involved replacing the medieval spire with turrets by the present one, which disregarding the 'flagpole' was estimated to be nearly five meters higher than the old tower.

THE 18TH CENTURY

As everywhere in Åland, the Great Northern War 1714-21 caused great destruction in the church. Though church silver, church archives, and church textiles were brought in safety to Stockholm, the vicar was forced

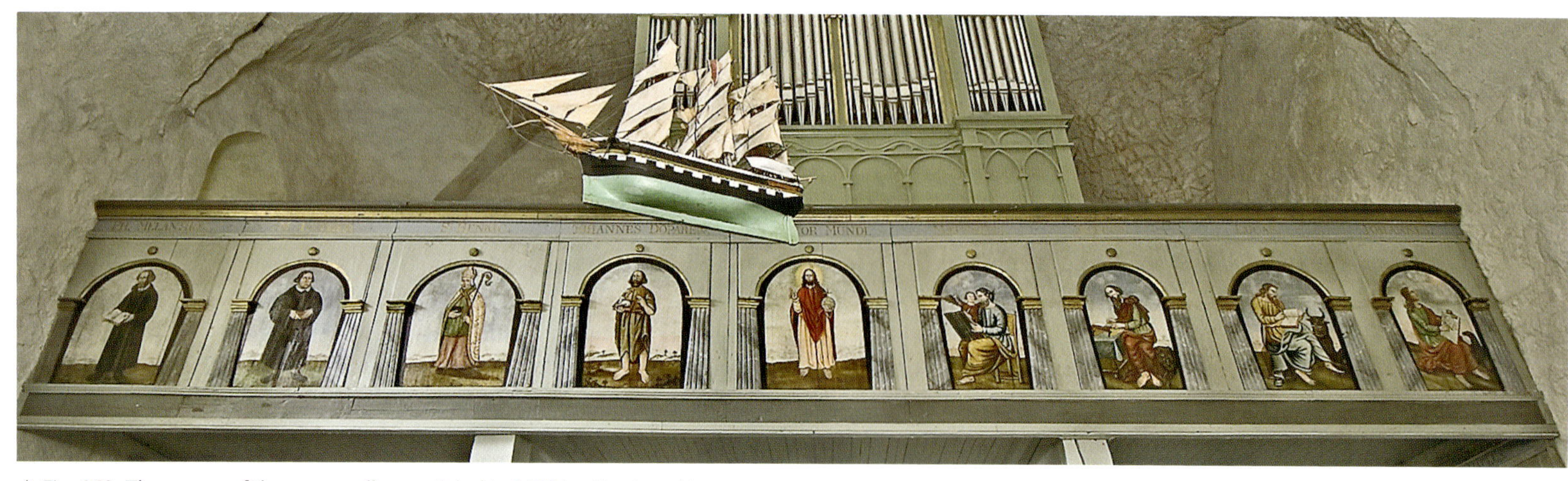

▲ Fig. 160. The screen of the organ gallery, painted in 1672 by Abraham Myra.

to sell both the medieval silver chalice and the textiles for financial reasons. Windows, doors, and textiles had been vandalized in the church.

THE 19TH CENTURY

The architectural alterations were relatively few. Focus was on light and new window openings according to the spirit of the time. In 1846 the priest door was walled in to prevent draughts. It was not until 1878 that the windowless northern wall was broken up by three new windows. At the same time the other windows were rebuilt to their present size.

The interior was also renewed. A new pulpit was acquired in 1838 and the altar railing and the pews were replaced. In 1880 a new altar painting, The Transfiguration of Christ, was ordered from the Finnish artist Alexandra Såltin. The church had its first heating system installed in 1897, when ovens of cast iron were placed in the sacristy and in front of the central columns in the nave.

THE 20TH CENTURY

Due to careless heating of the sacristy, the church caught fire in 1921. The entire wooden structure in the roof of all building units was destroyed. The damage was extensive inside the church, especially in the tower. In the renovations after the fire the brick imitations of the arches in the vault were whitewashed. The circular window, which had been walled in by bricks in the west gable, was re-opened. Central heating was introduced in the 1930s. The organ gallery, together with its valuable screen painted in 1670 by Abraham Myra, was moved out to the tower, and shortened. A new organ was acquired in the 1970s.

In 1998-99 the church of Sund was the object of a thorough and well-documented restoration program, with the intention of minimizing the alterations. Rather than a proper archaeological excavation, there was a documentation of parts under the church floor affected by new heating systems and electrical wiring. The walls and the ceiling were carefully cleaned, and the paintings were competently conserved.

- **Wall paintings** (cf. Figures 15 and 161).

SCULPTURES

- **The crucifix, and other sculptures** (Figures 13, 14, 31). Several fine medieval sculptures from the church of Sund were sold to the Historical Museum of Turku in the 1880s. Among them is one Mary in Sorrows, earlier presumed to have come from Gotland, but which by closer analysis is shown to have been carved of oak from Schleswig-Holstein. Mary was dendrochronologically dated to the 1260s. Saint Olof enthroned, a work made in Gotland at the beginning of the 14th century, is also in Turku (Fig. 31).
- **Sculptures** representing **Saints Paul and John** (Figures 35, 36).

INVENTORY

- **The altarpiece** (Fig. 52).
- **The organ gallery** in the tower, originally placed against the west gable of the nave, where it carried the organ acquired in 1671. The gallery screen was painted in 1672 by Abraham Myra.
- **The epitaph, or the votive painting** (cf. Figures 15 and 161). ■

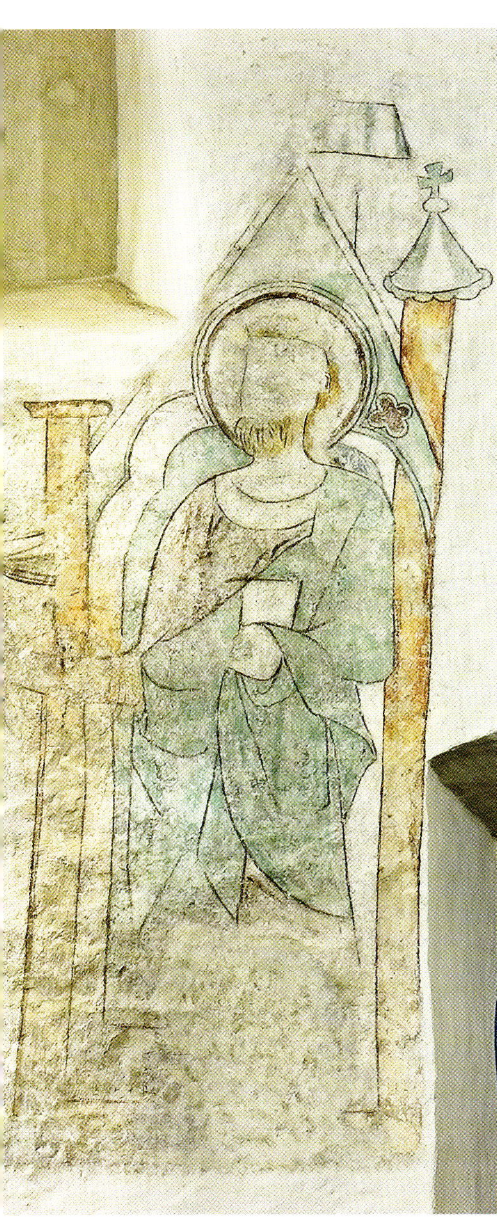

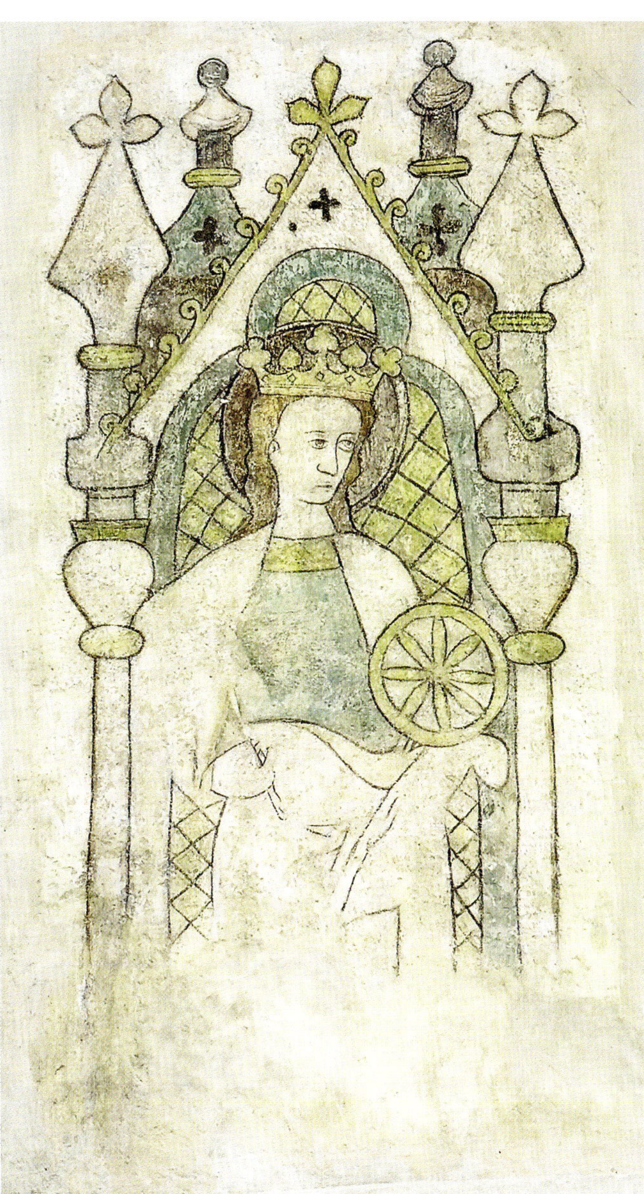

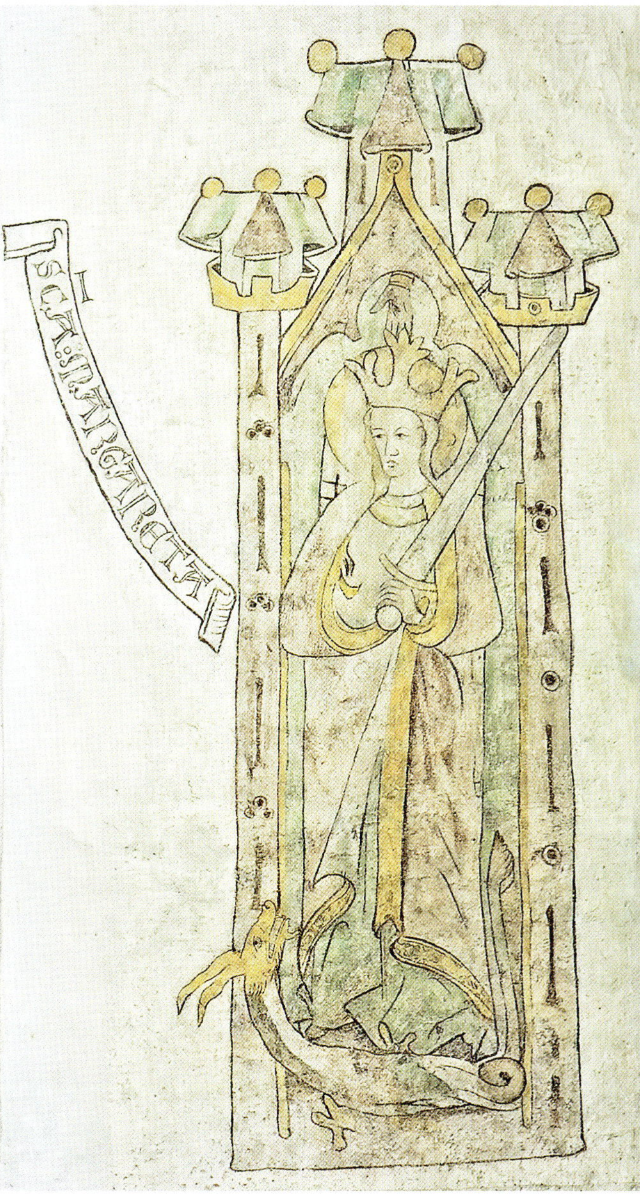

▲ Fig. 161 a-c. Wall paintings from the end of the 13th century in the church of Sund, representing an anonymous male saint, Saint Catherine of Alexandria and Saint Margareth. (cf. Figures 15).

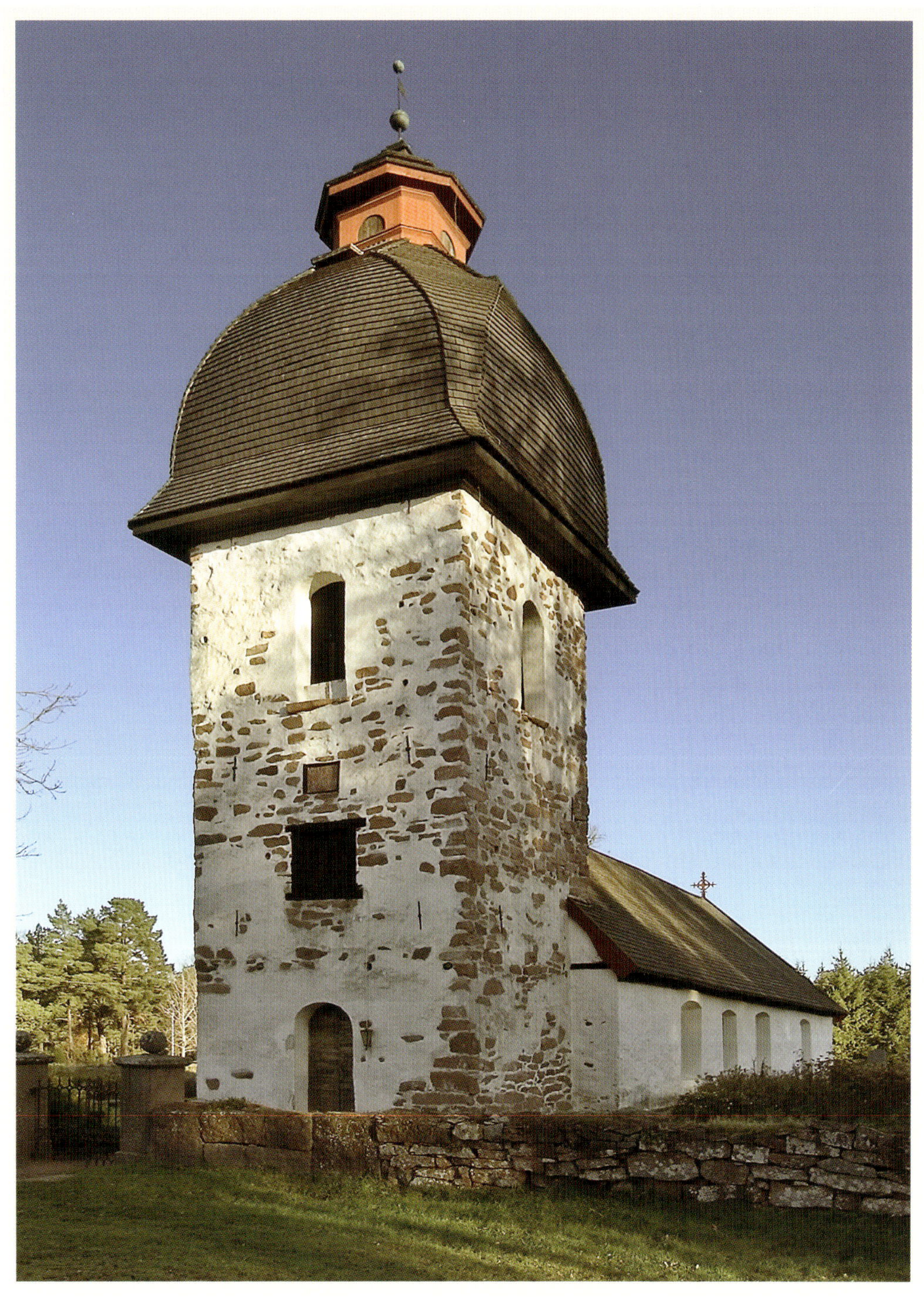

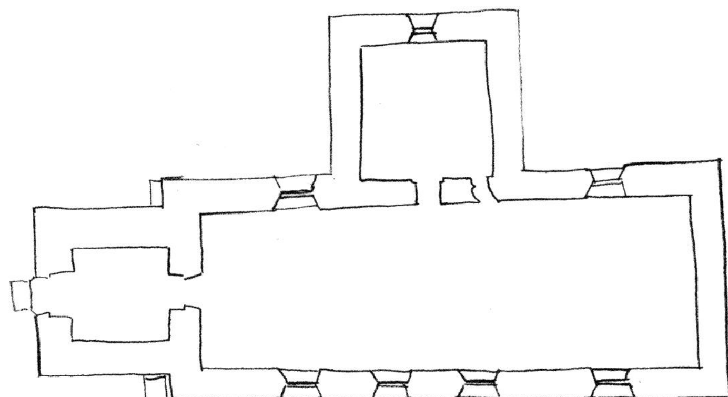

▲ Fig. 163. The ground plan of Vårdö chapel.

VÅRDÖ CHURCH

The stone chapel in Vårdö, or Sundsskären, consecrated to Saint Matthias, belongs to Sund mother church. It is situated on the main island of Vårdö a little bit away from other habitation.

It was built just south of the Åland postal road, in the middle of the triangle between Vargata, Vårdöby, and Listersby. During many centuries the chapel has gone through considerable changes and enlargements. Today it is possible to reconstruct the different stages of the building. The place name Vårdö is first mentioned in 1347.

THE EXTERIOR

The western part of the low, oblong and whitewashed chapel has a later narrow tower, roughly built and with a disproportionally large spire, the result of a radical enlargement and rebuilding in the 1780s. The spacious sacristy approximately in the middle of the northern façade, with the year 1786 inscribed in the gable, is not joined with the nave. The chancel wall towards the east has no windows. Four large and widely arched windows face south. Two identical window openings flank the sacristy towards the north. There is no separate porch. Instead the entry to the chapel functions as a porch in the ground floor of the tower. The main entrance sits centrally in the west gable of the tower, continuing the central axis of the nave. The northern wall plate has been elongated immediately west of the sacristy.

GROUND PLAN

The long rectangular ground plan has a vaguely trapezoid shape, where the chancel wall towards the east is somewhat wider than the corresponding west wall (inner measures around 19.5 x 7/6.3m). The sacristy is not joined with the north wall of the nave. The bell tower was added later to the west gable of the nave.

THE INTERIOR

The single nave interior is flooded in light thanks to many large window openings, light inner walls and a high barrel vault. The color scheme is a cool white and blue. The nave, with an inner space of 198 square meters, reveals no traces of medieval wall paintings. The altarpiece with the theme 'Christ in Getshemane' was ordered from the court painter Robert Wilhelm Ekman in Turku in 1852. A vaulted passage from the sacristy leads up to the pulpit from 1794. The organ gallery along the western gable was installed in its present location in 1785, just after the nave had been enlarged. Zachariasson in Uusikaupunki built the organ in1889. The lower part of the tower functions as a porch.

BUILDING HISTORY

THE 15TH CENTURY

Many different types of scientific analyses confirm that the chapelry of Vårdö got its stone chapel towards the end of the 15th century. The medieval origin is also indirectly shown in many ways: The big bell from Saint Matthias' chapel was confiscated in the 1540s. Reports from 1590 revealed a crack in the dilapidated eastern gable wall showing

◀ Fig. 162. Vårdö church, exterior from the southwest.

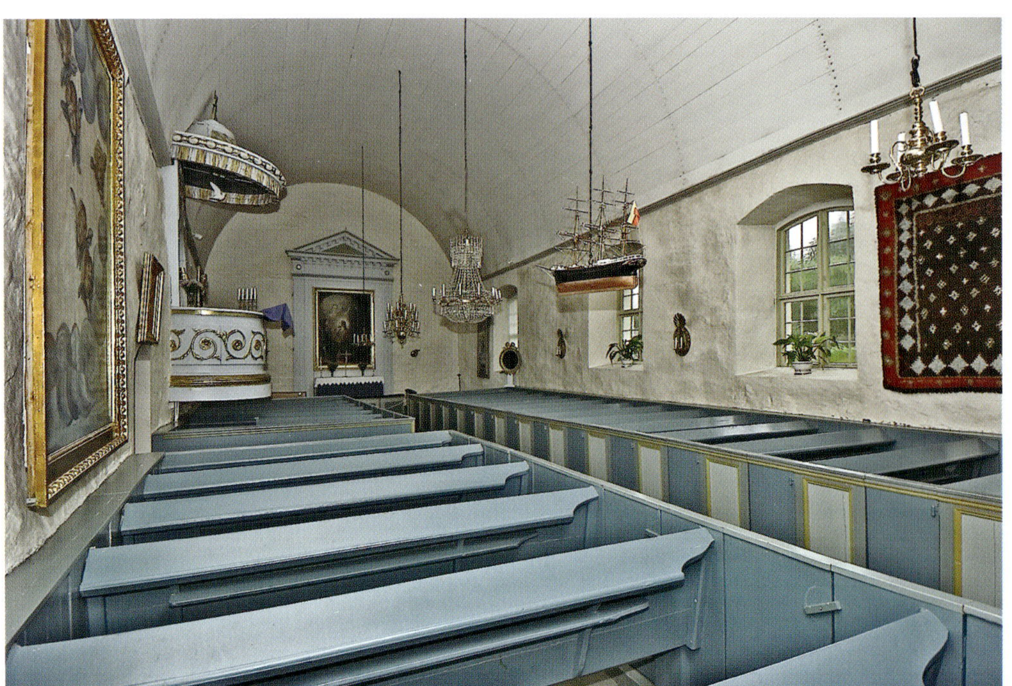

▲ Fig. 164. Vårdö church, interior to the east.

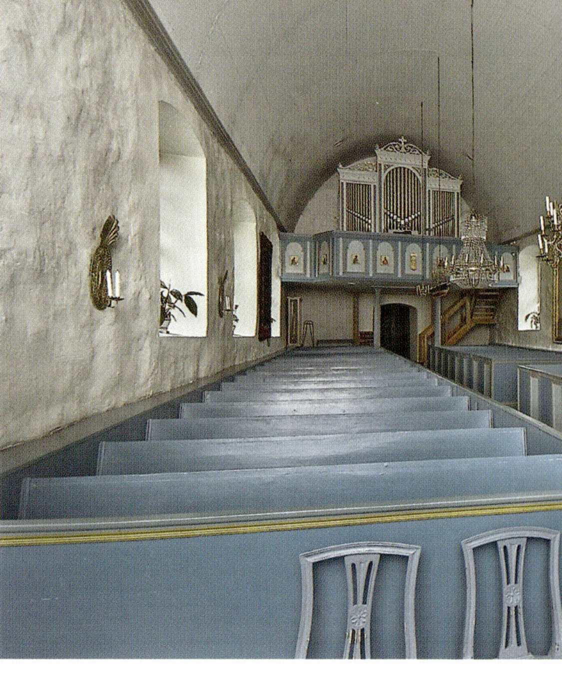

▲ Fig. 165. Vårdö church, interior to the west.

that the chapel needed maintenance and that it was built of stone. The visitation records from 1644 indicate that disputes on how much the chapel should contribute to the maintenance of the mother church had been going on for a long time. Nobody knew how old the chapel really was, but 'it seems that the mother church must have been built long before the chapel.' But the reason for building the chapel was beyond doubt. Since the distance to the mother church was far, and the journey in wintertime could be arduous, the "Christian authorities" had given the parishioners the freedom to build their own chapel, as "it was difficult for old and sick people and for the young to travel the long distance".

At first the chapel was much smaller than it is today (13.57 x 8.8m, inner floor space about 120 square meters) (cf. Fig. 51). The walls were low, even if exact measures are unavailable. Whitewashed exterior walls contrasted against the low saddle roof, covered by tarred and chopped boards on birch bark. A bell hood crowned with a spire and resting on four poles, sat centrally like a ridge tower. The chapel had in total three windows: the chancel window on the eastern gable, divided into four sections, and two window openings on the southern wall with three sections each. There were no windows facing north. It is possible that the chapel had a wooden porch from the very beginning, while there was still no sacristy. The main entrance was placed in the western gable. The horizontal inner ceiling was paneled. Contrary to medieval canon law the main altar was made of wood, and adorned by a 15th century altarpiece.

When Boetius Murenius initiated his visitations in the chapelry in 1637, he met a chaotic Catholic medieval interior. The chapel was filled with "rotten old papal tawdriness". "Miss-shaped images were installed instead of an altar painting, and junk rags were hanging along the walls". A big crucifix –"a large body"– hung across the nave, on a crossbeam.

THE POST-REFORMATION

THE 16TH CENTURY

One of Gustavus Vasa's confiscations in 1544 was a big bell from Vårdö, together with two small bells. The big bell would have weighed about 200 kilos. The Reformation did not bring about any great chang-

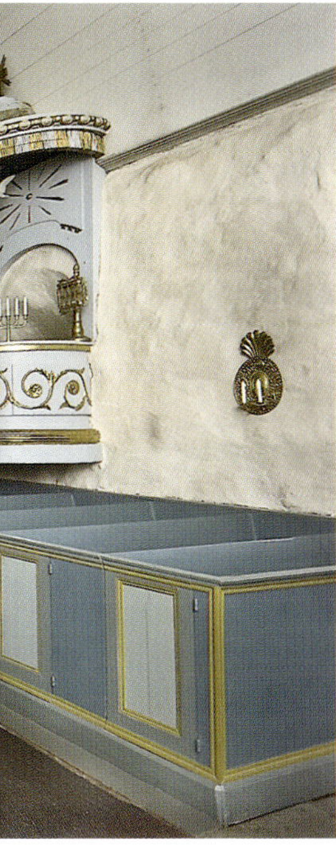

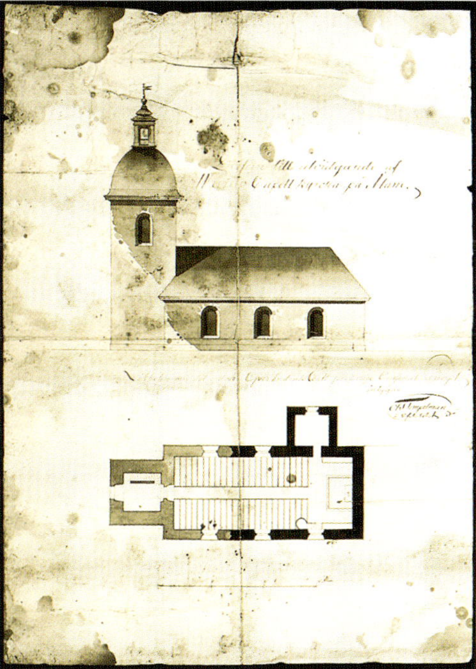

▲ Fig. 166. Drawing for an enlargement of Vårdö church, signed in the 1780s by the court architect Olof Samuel Tempelman, Stockholm.

es for the church building. On the contrary the Catholic interior was left more or less intact. Still it can be assumed that a simple pulpit and pews for men and women had been acquired as early as the 16th century, in accordance with the new Lutheran liturgy. In 1590 it was necessary to repair a crack in the wall of the eastern gable.

THE 17TH CENTURY

The church was subjected to new alterations when Boetius Murenius ordered a third window to be hewn up in the southern wall, to facilitate readability at the pulpit. He also wanted to remove the old ridge tower on the chapel roof, where the poles contributed to rot in the roof joists. The parishioners, who liked the picturesque ridge tower, objected to the plans and it was left in its place for the time being. The ceiling got horizontal paneling in 1672. The wooden porch in front of the western portal found its form in the 1640s. Approximately at the same time, in 1645, the old wooden altar was torn down and substituted with a new brick altar. Since there was still no sacristy at this stage, a cupboard was furnished in the chancel for the sacramental vessels and vestments. In the middle of the 17th century the pulpit was renewed, as well as the pews for men and women. In 1659 a new wooden sacristy was finally built against the northern wall of the nave, which was broken through for an opening. Since the small chapel was overcrowded, a new gallery along the western wall was built in 1664. A new altarpiece with 'painted gold and silver' was ordered from the painter Mårten Johansson in 1666, but its motif is unfortunately not known. In the 1690s a new wooden bell tower finally replaced the old ridge tower. The tower was built against the western gable, probably with the earlier wooden porch as ground floor.

THE 18TH CENTURY

The chapel was badly damaged during the Great Northern War 1714-21, and the following decades were mainly devoted to subsequent reparations. The congregation felt that the chapel was much too small and themselves took the initiative to plans for enlargement. These were to be executed in the 1780s, according to drawings by the architect Olof Tempelman at the Royal Super Intendent's Office, Stockholm. But the enlargements were only partly realized. After the old western gable with its adjacent wooden tower had been torn down, the nave was prolonged by 12 ells westwards. The porch also disappeared during the enlargement. The eastern gable with the whole ridge was raised by 68 centimeters and the nave got a new high wooden barrel vault. New large window openings were broken through the nave walls, three to the south and two to the north. Daylight came in to a newly built gallery through a round window high up in the western gable. A spacious stone sacristy was erected against the middle of the northern long wall, but it did not follow the drawings. In the 1790s the chapel acquired its present pulpit, designed by Carl Fredrik Adelcrantz of the Super Intendent's Office in Stockholm, and constructed by Eric Fällström. A simple, new altarpiece was framed, also according to Adelcrantz' design.

THE 19TH CENTURY

In 1804 the west tower of stone was constructed, and thus Vårdö acquired its characteristic tower hood. The builder responsible was Mikael Hartlin Piimänen from Turku. He was severely criticized for not keeping to the proportions of Tempelman's hood design from 1783. A porch was included on the bottom floor of the tower. To improve readability in the gallery a garret was constructed in the southern slope of the roof. A fourth window, identical with the others, was opened on the southern façade in 1852. The barrel vault was again raised in 1872, after which it was painted with zinc white. Iron stoves were acquired for both sacristy and nave in the 1890s, when the old shingled roof was replaced by asphalt felt covering.

THE 20TH CENTURY

After a longer period of deterioration during the first half of the 20th century a well needed restoration was initiated in the 1950s. It lasted until 1970. The bulky gallery, which had occupied more than one third of the room, was diminished and received new stairs. The aged heating system with iron ovens was replaced by electric heating. The interior was painted and the armatures entirely renewed.

Chapter 3

THE ÅLAND CHURCHES PROJECT AND THE NECESSITY OF INTERDISCIPLINARY RESEARCH

ABOUT THE ÅLAND CHURCHES PROJECT

An important aim of the project was to put an end to all speculation about the age of these significant churches. New approaches are needed this time. It is not enough to use traditional humanistic methods, instead the churches themselves should provide the historical sources. Archaeological artifacts and coins do not necessarily date stone churches, as they can derive from older buildings on the site, and they may also belong to later periods. The lack of written sources must be compensated by all available methods. All experts should be consulted.

Now was finally the time to establish the true dates of the churches. To reach an objective chronology, I was prepared to employ systematic implementation of scientific methods of analysis on a large scale. This priority of the natural sciences has come as a surprise to many art historians. Scholars have even expressed concern that such an approach might overshadow humanistic aspects such as architecture, art history, and style. Yet interdisciplinarity and the implementation of scientific methods in fact often provide the very basis for archaeological, architectural and art historical analyses. Only with reliable results is it possible to draw conclusions concerning the medieval history of the Åland Islands, about the building activity, and about the art of the churches.

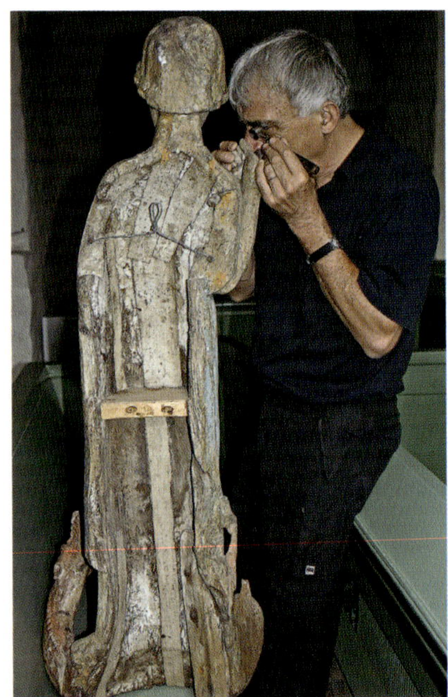

▲ **Fig. 167. Peter Klein analyzing a wooden sculpture in Finström church, July 2005.**

Ideally this chapter should function as a guide through the large numbers of complicated scientific processes. Above all through the different steps of developing mortar dating, which have been taken within the Åland Churches project. Other methods used are also described, as is the interdisciplinary collaboration and the result of this approach.

^{14}C analysis of fragmentarily preserved wood

Less well preserved wood, not datable through dendrochronology, such as fragments from wooden scaffolding or organic fragments embedded in the mortar, has systematically gone through radiocarbon analysis. Together with the results from dendrochronology, this material has provided an important databank with age control for comparative research.

Dendrochronology

To begin with, everything seemed straightforward and easy. Dendrochronology was the method to solve all problems. It was to be implemented on all the churches, on all building stages. Of all scientific dating methods dendrochronology is the most reliable. The sample is drilled from the sapwood to the inner core, if possible with all annual rings included. When comparing the pattern of the annual rings with the pattern of the master curve individually developed for different geographical regions, it is in principle possible to establish the exact year when the timber was felled. So far the method has primarily been used for oak and pine.

Thus dendrochronology was the first scientific method implemented by the project, and all available timber in the Åland churches was tested. The analyses were performed in 1991-1992 by Thomas Bartholin, from the National Museum of Copenhagen and the University of Lund. Of a total of 283 samples 159 yielded results, and out of these 107 were of medieval origin. This material was to form the basis for an Åland master curve. However, a large part of the samples were of spruce, a timber which is not easily dated by this method. Often, it would also show that the annual rings were too few for a determination of the age.

It was also demonstrated that well preserved timber mainly derived from secondary building stages, or from later repairs. Due to rot and fire, many parts of the roof constructions had been renewed. Dendrochronology can provide an exact date for the wood in question, but not necessarily for the original building stage. Therefore, the initial results were somewhat disappointing.

Although dendrochronological analysis could not always determine the date for the first building stage of the construction, the benefits of the implementation were soon evident. Dendrochronology could determine the ages for secondary building stages, such as towers, vaults, porches, and sacristies, which meant that we had valuable material for comparative analysis, and for the interpretation of an internal building history of the churches.

Peter Tångeberg, the Swedish conservator and art historian, was consulted about the wooden sculptures in Åland; he suggested that I should contact Peter Klein from the University of Hamburg, in order to complement stylistic analysis with dendrochronological dating of the sculptures. Klein has developed an important non-destructive method for wooden sculptures, where a nailbrush and a loop replace the drilling into the wood. The analysis of individual wooden sculptures is described in their respective contexts.

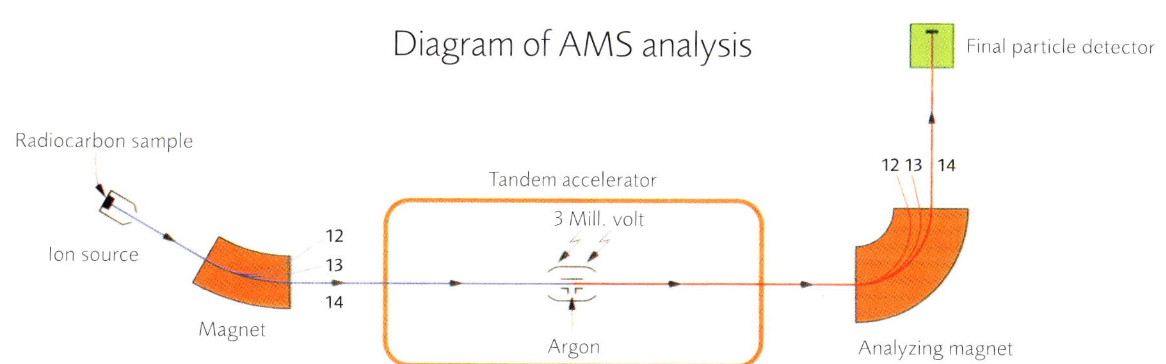

Radiocarbon dating

As a method radiocarbon dating (^{14}C analysis) was developed at the end of the 1940s by Willard F. Libby, who received the Nobel Prize for this discovery in 1960. In the atmosphere of the earth, carbon exists primarily as carbon dioxide (CO_2). In the inner circulation of the carbon, carbon dioxide is bound to the earth through the photosynthesis of plants. From the plants it is further spread to animals and to different living organisms in the food chain.

The amount of ^{14}C stored in plants and animals, in the oceans and in the global carbon reserves, remains rather constant through the ages, which means that the ^{14}C contents of living organisms is largely the same as in the atmosphere. Radiocarbon dating is based on the ratio between radioactive ^{14}C and the stable isotope ^{12}C, a relation that mirrors the atmospheric concentration of the isotope in living organisms. Isotopes of an element stand for atoms with the same number of protons (6 for carbon), but with different numbers of neutrons in the nucleus. There are three different naturally occurring carbon isotopes: the ^{12}C isotope, which in addition to 6 protons includes 6 neutrons (a total of 12 nuclear particles), the ^{13}C isotope with 7 neutrons, and finally the ^{14}C isotope which has 8 neutrons. By far the most common is the stable isotope ^{12}C which represents 98,9% of all carbon isotopes. The ^{13}C isotope, equally stable, amounts to 1.1%. Thus, together the two stable isotopes form about 100% of all carbon isotopes. Unlike the other carbon isotopes, however, the ^{14}C isotope is unstable, and is only a minimal part of the entire whole. That is, only one of a million million carbon atoms is a ^{14}C isotope. It is radioactive, and therefore characterized by radioactive decay, which starts when the living organism dies. The decay has a half life of 5730 years, which means that after less than 6000 years the organism contains only half of the original amount of ^{14}C isotopes. Furthermore, a Beta particle is triggered for each decaying atom.

At the beginning, the measurements were done conventionally, by Beta counting, or measuring and detecting of Beta emissions from ^{14}C atoms over a period of time. Conventional dating requires large samples. One kilogram raw-material (mortar) is needed to get the necessary amount of 1-2 grams of pure carbon. Since only isotopes decaying during the period of analysis are measured, the conventional method is less precise and the statistical uncertainty becomes larger for small samples.

For radiocarbon dating the introduction of accelerator mass spectrometry (AMS) in 1977 meant considerable improvement. The system requires a tandem accelerator, which includes two separate phases of acceleration. The diagram demonstrates the process: the prepared graphite sample is placed in an ion source, after which the ionized carbon isotopes pass through two angled magnets on each side of the accelerator. Already by the first magnet a number of ^{12}C and ^{13}C isotopes are thrown out of their course. The remaining isotopes (^{14}C) reach the tandem accelerator, which they pass with accelerated (hence the name) speed, only to force the remaining ^{12}C and ^{13}C isotopes off course at the next magnet. Thus only the ^{14}C isotopes reach the final detector, where every single ^{14}C isotope is counted: the fewer the ^{14}C isotopes that reach the final particle detector, the older the sample. Radiocarbon dating is a statistical method, with built in error margins presented as ± values.

Calibration

A basic fact concerning all ^{14}C dated materials, not only mortar, is that the result is presented as a BP ("Before Present") age. Paradoxically "present" in this case is identical to the year 1950, since after that the amount of carbon dioxide was disturbed by repeated atomic tests and nuclear power stations. Since the ratio of the isotopes in the carbonate of the sample reflects the carbon dioxide at the time when the mortar hardened, this BP age is converted to calendar years using a calibration curve. This calibration curve is based on ^{14}C dating of annual rings in trees of known age, and it observes the continuing changes in the concentration of atmospheric ^{14}C. Therefore the curve falls irregularly, which affects the precision of the results. Where the curve is falling steeply, the margin of error is only a few years, but where the curve is largely horizontal, or when it wiggles and turns upwards, the measurement becomes less precise. For medieval Scandinavia in general, and for medieval Åland especially, the irregularity during the 14th century is a greatly disturbing factor. Where the chronology has been a matter of disagreement, however, it is still very valuable to be able to place individual buildings within the right century.

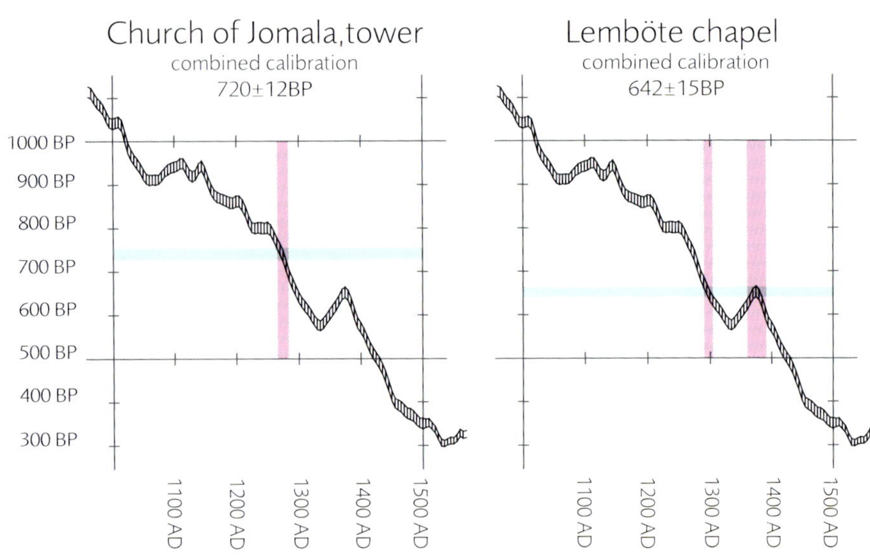

▲ **Example of calibration uncertainties during the 14th century.**

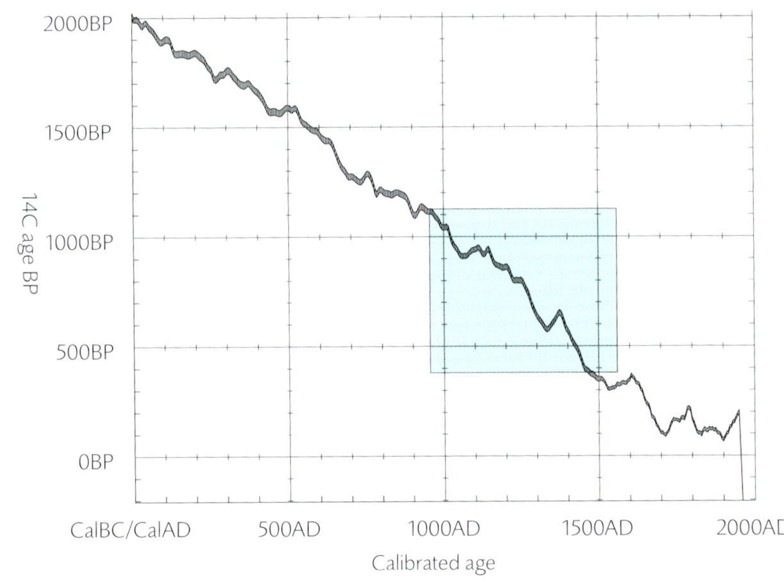

▲ **The calibration curve between the birth of Christ, and 2000 AD. Oxcal.**

The irrationality of the calibration curve

Two Åland examples are presented to demonstrate the effects of calibration on dating: to the left, the tower in Jomala, with the BP age of 720±12, to the right, Lemböte chapel BP 642±15. In both cases the margin of error is relatively small. The BP age is marked horizontally in blue. The vertical line in mauve marks the calendar age defined when a BP age cuts the calibration curve. In Jomala the BP age hits the calibration curve in a position where it is falling steeply. In this case the cutting is sharp and obvious and results in an exact age, 1270-1285AD. When it comes to Lemböte chapel, the BP age cuts the calibration curve when it is irregular and occasionally turning upwards, which means that the BP age cuts the calibration curve in two different places. Regardless of the error margin in the BP age being relatively small, the dating result is broad and uncertain. This time the calibration results in two different ages, that is, 1295-1310 and 1360-1387.

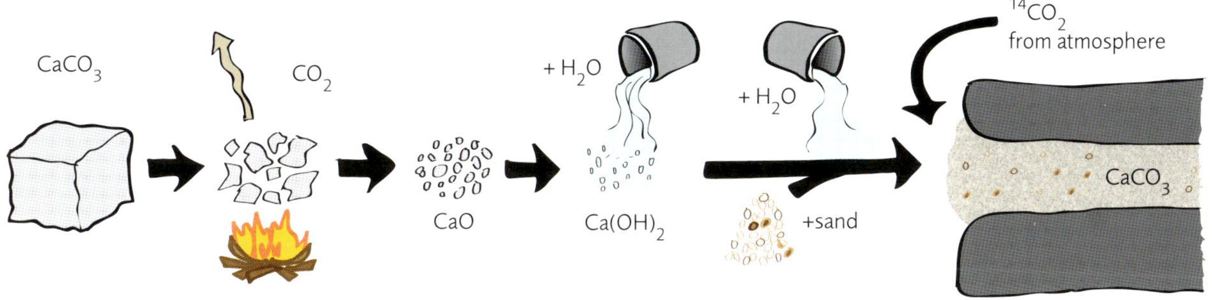

▲ **Fig. 168. The chemical process of mortar (Pia Sonck-Koota, modified version of Hale et al. 2003).**

^{14}C ANALYSIS (AMS) OF MORTAR

Mortar – unlike other materials– is the only one to be found in large quantities and from every stage of construction in its original composition. Therefore mortar dating has a great potential for archaeology. The first time I heard of the method was in 1989, when Högne Jungner, head of *the Laboratory for Radioactive Dating* at Helsinki University, presented the results from conventional ^{14}C dating at a Franciscan conference at Källskär, Kökar, in the outer Åland archipelago. I immediately realized the great potentials of the method, and the need to distance myself from all earlier theories and speculations. From now on mortar dating was to be implemented on a large scale. It would, of course, be done parallel with other methods, both archaeological and scientific. In August 1989 an interdisciplinary group was immediately formed, consisting of the physicist Högne Jungner, the archaeologists Kenneth Gustavsson and Milton Nuñez, and me, an art historian and archaeologist.

Mortar is not an organic material. Yet the chemical process in the hardening in principle makes it into an ideal matrix for ^{14}C dating (Fig. 168). To make mortar, limestone has to be heated up to at least 900°C. After the carbon dioxide has been released in the process, calcium oxide (unslaked lime) remains. Later, when this calcium oxide is slaked with water, slaked lime occurs. In the next stage, slaked lime is mixed with water and aggregate, usually sand. In the hardening process the slaked lime reacts with atmospheric carbon dioxide, and calcium carbonate is produced. Thus the mortar absorbs the carbon dioxide from the atmosphere and thereafter behaves as if it were organic.

The principle behind mortar dating was known as early as the 1960s, but it involved well-known risks, with a negative effect for the development of the method: The mortar could contain unburned limestone, due either to insufficient burning, or contaminating carbonate in the sand. These yield ages that are too ancient. Mortar can also result in ages that are too recent, which happens if the lime has gone through re-crystallization. If the mortar sample is taken deep within the construction, a delayed hardening occurs, with equally rejuvenating effects.

New procedures, new collaboration in 1994

Mark Van Strydonck, at the ^{14}C Dating Laboratory, Royal Institute for Cultural Heritage, Brussels, has been one of the pioneers in dating mortar. He abandoned the method in 1993, believing it was too complicated. Before that, however, he declared that ^{14}C analysis of mortar could be developed as a method, provided that AMS-analysis was implemented. He based this on experiments of his own. Some of the first experiments with AMS analysis of mortar were done already in 1990 by L.E. Tubbs and T.N. Kinder. They, however, only analyzed small fragments of charcoal within the mortar, not the mortar itself.

In 1994 Högne Jungner and Jan Heinemeier (from the AMS ^{14}C Laboratory at the University of Aarhus, Denmark) received promising results from implementing ^{14}C AMS analysis on mortar from the so-called Viking Tower in Newport Rhode Island, in the United States. After some sleepless nights, I decided that the Åland Churches project should also transfer to ^{14}C AMS analysis of mortar. From now on, all earlier results from conventional ^{14}C analysis were to be disregarded, and the entire process was to start all over. Hereafter, only AMS analysis of mortar would be considered. The samples were analyzed at the AMS ^{14}C Dating Centre at Aarhus (Fig. 169), which meant that the project became more interdisciplinary and international in character.

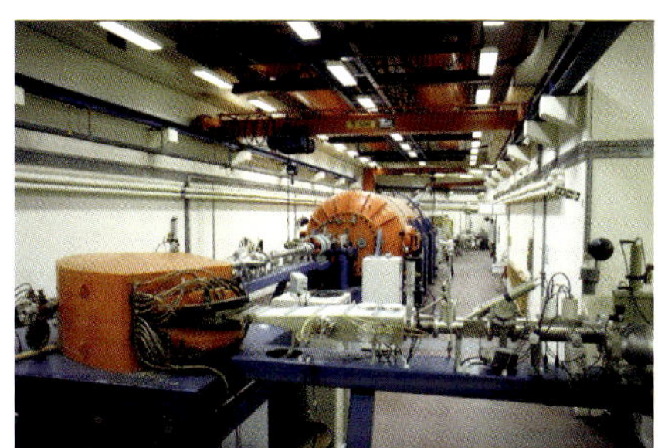

▲ **Fig. 169. The tandem accelerator at the University of Aarhus, Denmark.**

A great advantage of AMS analysis, compared to conventional analysis of mortar, is that smaller samples are required. For the AMS-analysis a handful of mortar per sample is sufficient, and as little as one milligram of the prepared sample will be enough for the analysis (Fig. 170). In addition to the material analyzed, the remaining part of the sample is collected for any possible re-dating, and for different types of chemical and geological analyses.

The results from the transition to AMS analysis meant that such Åland mortars as had earlier been analyzed conventionally were now corrected. Within individual building units the results were more coherent and more recent, with the margins of error diminishing.

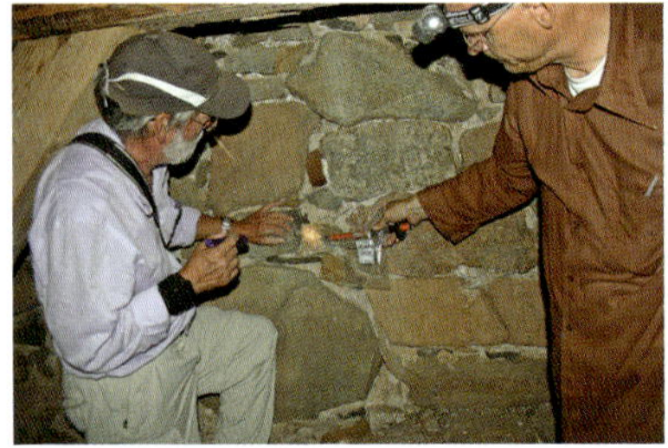

▲ Fig. 170. Jan Heinemeier and Alf Lindroos sampling mortar in the church of Kumlinge in 2007.

The geologist Alf Lindroos joined the project in 1994, marking another important step forward for the project. Since then he has been the central figure of the team, in charge of the scientific development of the method. To solve problems with contamination and re-crystallization, he focused on preparatory procedures. Since then the Åland Churches project has been the only team to systematically develop the method internationally.

International cooperation and challenges in 1997

In the autumn of 1996, I was invited to be a guest professor in architectural history at the University of Louisville (UofL), in Kentucky, with far reaching consequences for our project. In 1997 Stephanie Maloney, professor of Art History at UofL, invited me to join their excavations at Torre de Palma, Portugal, the largest Roman Villa on the Iberian peninsula. Thus the project expanded to include also Classical Archaeology. Help was needed to establish the chronology of the site. At Torre de Palma, the mortar is like Åland mortars in principle - it is a matter of non hydraulic lime mortar. With the aid of mortar analysis a chronology could be established for the site, from the first century AD until ca 639 AD. At the same time preliminary experiments were done on Spanish mortars from Merida and Barcelona. John R. Hale, classical archaeologist from UofL, became an active member of the international research team. He suggested that we should try the method in Rome, to see how it worked on well-known buildings, firmly dated by historical sources.

Sampling Roman pozzolana concrete in Rome thus began in 1998, which meant a real challenge for the development of the method. Chemically, hydraulic Roman pozzolana mortar is entirely different from lime mortars in Åland and in Portugal. "Hydraulic" in this case means that the mortar includes volcanic ash, which makes it possible to harden under water. Roman pozzolana mortar is stronger than other concrete-like materials, and so it became one of the prerequisites for the architectural revolution, when the Romans could liberate themselves from old rules of masonry and create freely. Even if we have had remarkable successes in testing AMS analysis on pozzolana mortar from well known buildings of firmly documented ages, such as the Colosseum and Trajan's Market, and buildings in Ostia, harbor and holiday retreat for the Romans, we already now know that pozzolana mortar is much more complicated to date than non hydraulic lime mortars. Lynne Lancaster, from Ohio University in Athens, Ohio, an expert on Roman building technique, has been our guide in Rome.

So far, all dating analyses connected to Åland have been done at Aarhus, as have many samples from our international projects. Other dating laboratories involved in our international collaboration are since 2005 the Oxford Radiocarbon Accelerator Unit, England and, since 2006 the NSF (Natural Science Faculty) - Arizona Accelerator Mass Spectrometry (AMS) Laboratory, Tucson, United States.

Development of the mechanical and chemical separation

To avoid risks from contamination of unburned lime-stone and from the effects of re-crystallized calcite, the mortar samples have to go through different types of preparatory processes, including both mechanical and chemical separation.

Mechanical separation: For an optimal collection and enrichment of the datable, soft and porous mortar carbonate, every single sample is carefully crushed in a mechanical separation. The process aims at excluding or at least minimizing the hard and unburned limestone, which contains old carbonates and therefore can yield ages too ancient in the analysis. Then the samples are sifted in a sieving system that varies in grain size from 20 to 500 microns (1 micron is 1/1000mm). The finer grains of the mortar pass through the rougher sieves, where they are separated from the larger grains of the aggregate, which can include both calcite crystals from re-crystallizations and contaminating, unburned limestone. For the final AMS analysis we normally choose a grain size window of 39/46-75 microns. The prepared powder is then subjected to cathodoluminescense microscopy, which reveals any possible remains of unburned limestone.

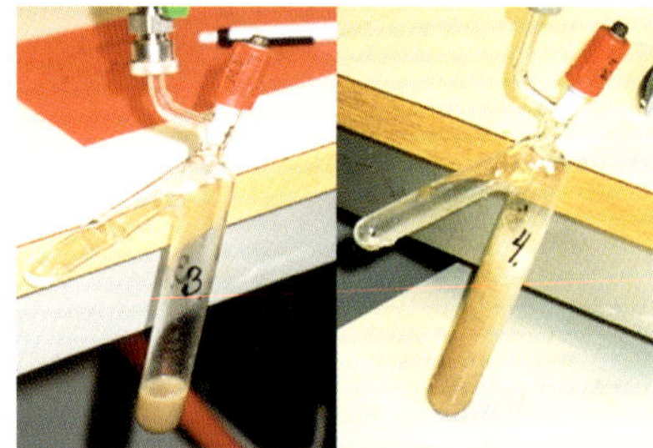

▲ Fig. 171. Chemical preparation using phosphoric acid in two carbon dioxide fractions. On the left the phosphoric acid is still isolated, on the right it reacts with the mortar carbonate.

Chemical separation: In the subsequent chemical separation an 85% solution of phosphoric acid is poured under vacuum over the mechanically separated mortar, at this stage a fine powder of approximately one mg. A chemical reaction occurs, which begins very fast. The mechanically separated sample is still isolated from the phosphoric acid in the side arm of the vial (to the left in Fig. 171). To the right in Fig. 171 it bubbles in the vial when the phosphoric acid reacts with the binding carbonate. Thus, the carbon dioxide is liberated from the sample in the form of gas. The carbon dioxide from this first reaction is identical to the first carbon dioxide fraction, a term frequently used in this text. This gas is collected in vials at different stages of the dissolution process. The first carbon dioxide fractions are isolated within seconds, whereas the second takes a few minutes. The next fractions are isolated during the subsequent hours. Since the mortar carbonate dissolves so much faster than unburned limestone, the carbonates from the mortar dominate the beginning of the dissolution process. The first carbon dioxide fraction is therefore expected to be less influenced by slowly dissolving unburned limestone, and thus these first carbon dioxide fractions are supposed to come closer to the hardening of the mortar than the later ones. Until 2002, the mortar samples were separated and analyzed in two carbon dioxide fractions.

One big step forward in the chemical separation was taken in 2002, when our experiences from Roman pozzolana mortar had demonstrated the importance of following the dissolution process in the interpretation of the results. To maximize this information, all samples from then on went through a chemical separation in five successive fractions (Fig. 172). The process results in age profiles that illustrate all stages of the dissolution process. For Åland in general, the first CO_2 fractions reveal the correct age (cf. Fig. 180a).

Exceptionally, as with mortars that have been damaged by fire, the conclusive age is revealed later in the age profile.

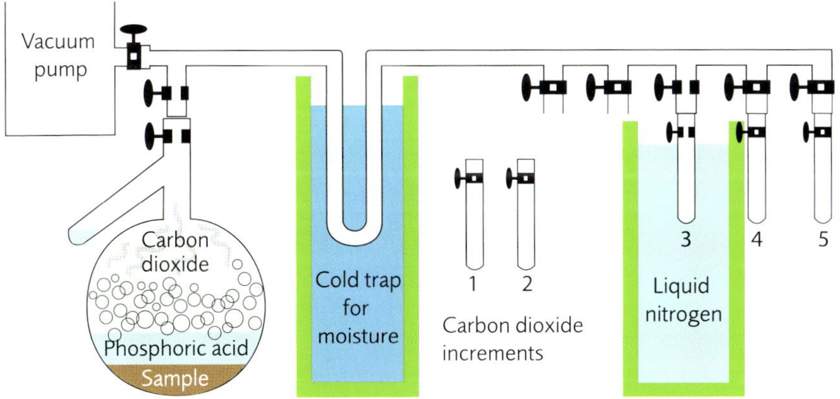

▲ Fig. 172. Chemical separation in five successive carbon dioxide fractions. In this case the process has lasted a few minutes and two CO_2 fractions have already been isolated. The third fraction is being chilled by fluent nitrogen, while the two last ones, which take hours, have not yet been isolated.

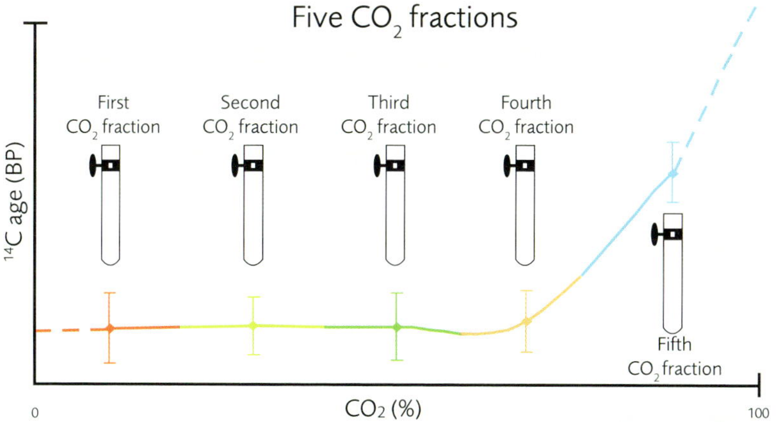

▲ Fig. 173. Example of an age profile with the individual CO_2 fractions marked. In this case the correct age is identified in the horizontal plateau at the beginning of the profile. (CO_2 fractions 1-4). The contamination does not affect the result until the last fraction.

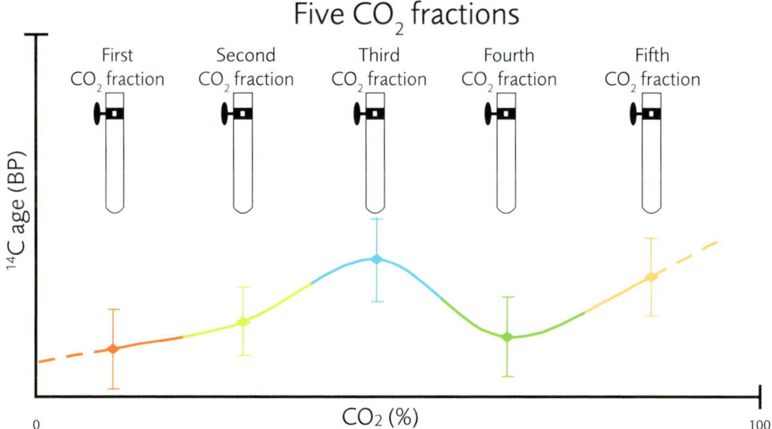

▲ Fig. 174. Example of an age profile where the first CO_2 fraction reveals the right age, while a slight contamination can be traced already in the second CO_2 fraction.

Eckerö

Dendrochronological analysis from the church of Eckerö presents results typical of the Åland churches – rather than revealing the age of the first nave, we see a large spread of results varying from around 1554 and 1650 (Fig. 175).

Obvious marks of secondary repairs, partly confirmed in the archives, can be seen. In this case the real age of the nave is based on scientific dating methods of different materials, such as mortar, charcoal, and wood (Fig. 176a).

Combined calibration of eight mortar samples from the nave yields the age 1275-1300AD, which agrees with the ^{14}C analysis of the fragmentarily preserved scaffolding and the northern wall plate. This time the results coincide with the ^{14}C analysis of a charcoal particle embedded in the mortar. A fourth wooden sample, partly outside the margins of error for the other samples, may depend on a secondary replacement of the wood. The other uniform samples were later confirmed in a renewed analysis in a complete age profile of Eka 030 (cf. 176a).

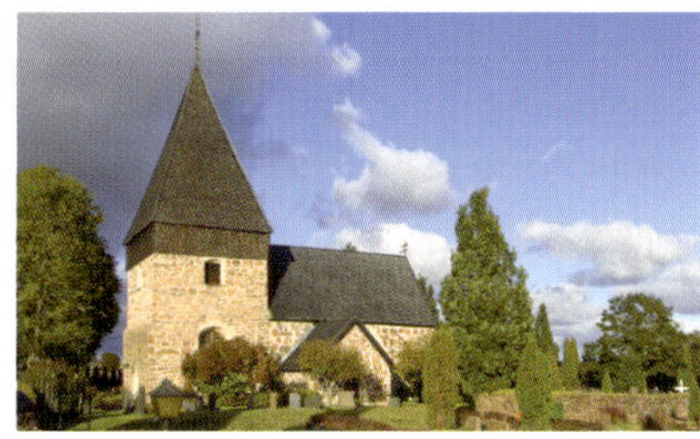

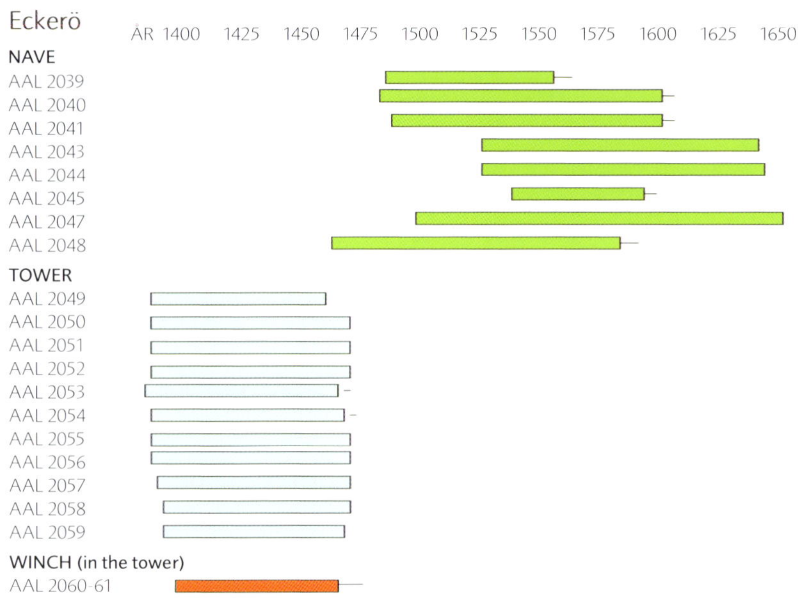

▲ **Fig. 175. Dendrochronological analysis from the church of Eckerö.**

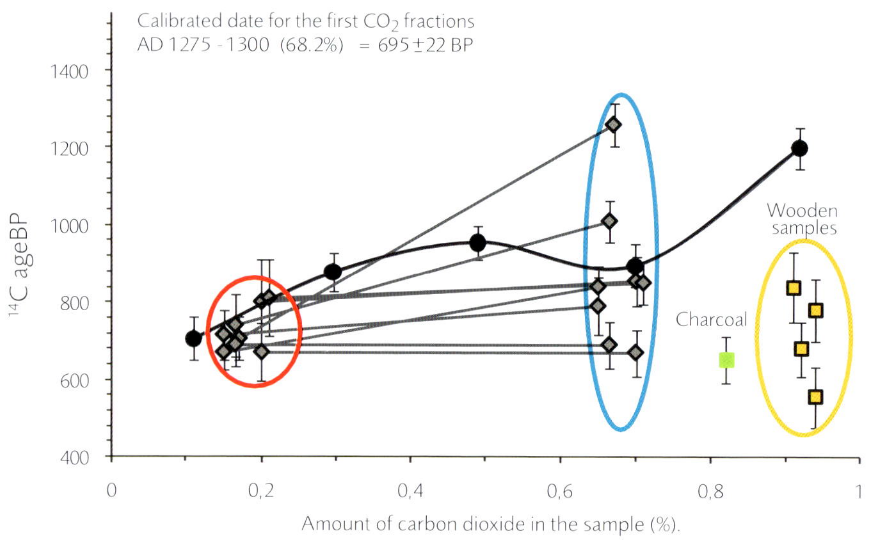

▲ **Fig. 176a. Results of scientific dating of the nave at Eckerö: mortar dating in two carbon dioxide fractions and ^{14}C analysis of poorly preserved wooden constructions. The first carbon dioxide fractions of eight mortar samples are inscribed in a red circle, the second fractions in a blue circle. One of the samples has further been analyzed in five fractions to form a full age profile.**

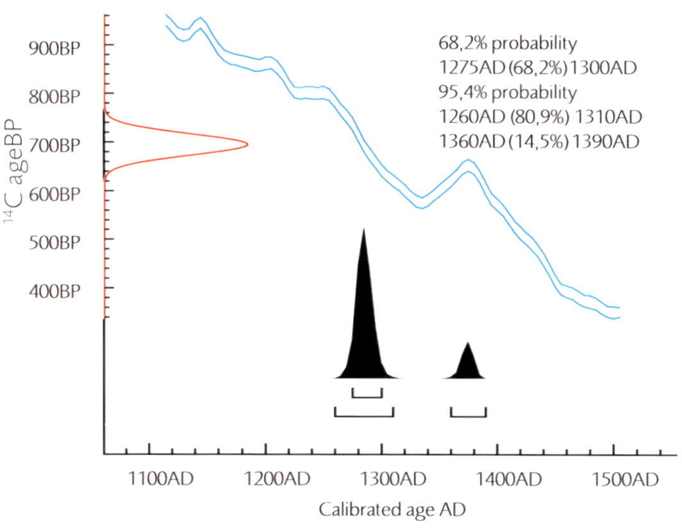

▲ **Fig. 176b. Combined calibration of all first carbon dioxide fractions (encircled in red) yields the age 1275-1300AD, at a probability of 68,2%.**

Geta

In Geta church, the results from dendrochonological analysis were confusing. Every second roof truss seemed to belong to the 1590s, whereas the rest of the timber was felled in the 1820s (Fig. 177).

Only one timber, the northern wall plate, suggests a medieval origin, sometime after 1450. This was a case which only mortar dating could solve.

In this case the three age profiles are unusually convincing (Fig. 178a). All first carbon dioxide fractions converge within the range of the same error margins. In addition all four introductory fractions in one of the age profiles (Geka 002) form a horizontal line. We see an almost ideal profile, without contamination from either ageing or rejuvenating effects. A combined calibration from all first fractions yields the age 1435-1455 AD. The result is additionally supported by a wooden splint, embedded in one of the samples, falling within the same error margins. Thus, in the church of Geta mortar dating confirmed that the only dendrochronologically established sample from the Middle Ages really belongs to the original construction. In this case the implementation of different methods and different materials yields uniform results.

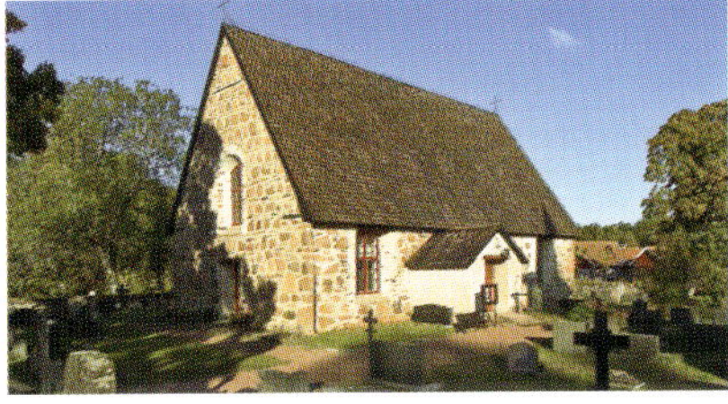

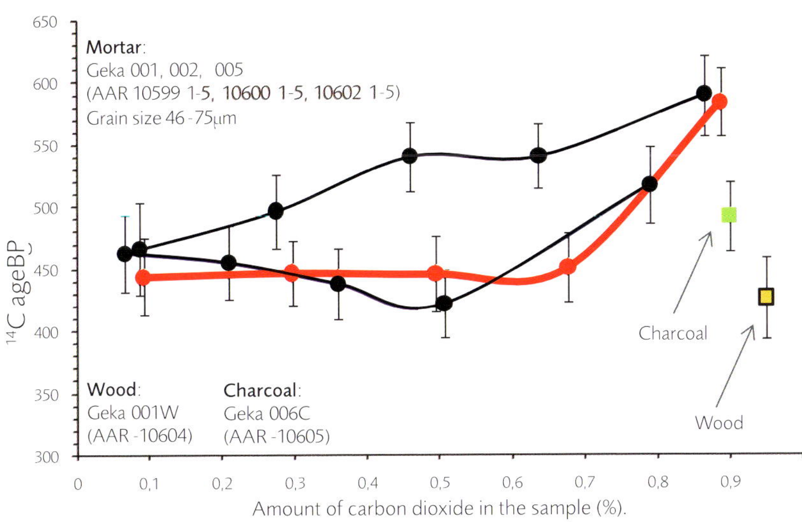

▲ **Fig. 178a. Three age profiles of mortar analysis in the church of Geta. Especially important is the horizontal age profile of Geka 002, enhanced in red. Within the same error margins also fits a wooden splint embedded in the mortar.**

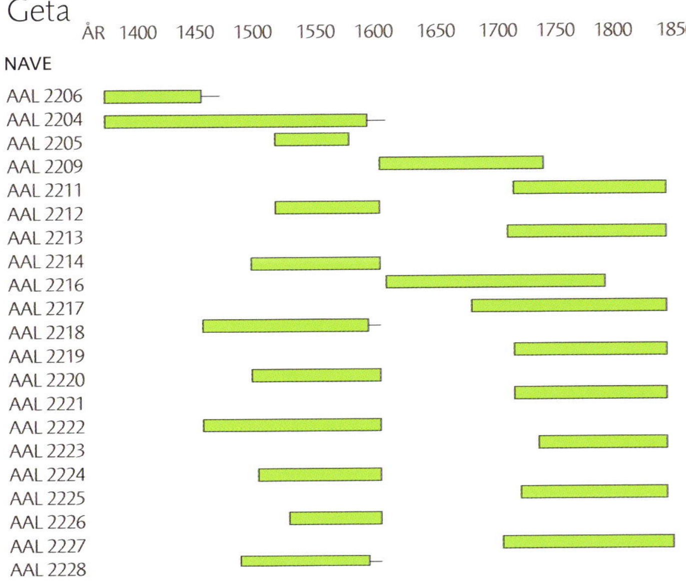

▲ **Fig. 177. Dendrochronological analysis from the church of Geta.**

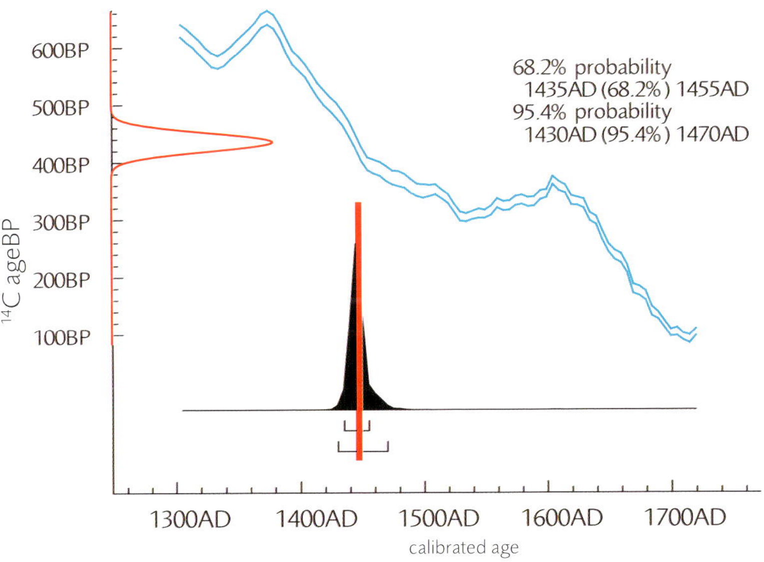

▲ **Fig. 178b. Combined calibration of the first carbon dioxide fractions from individual age profiles, 436 ±16 BP, yield the age 1435-1455AD, which is in complete agreement with the dendrochronology (vertical in red).**

Finström

The church of Finström is one of the best preserved medieval buildings in entire Finland, but the building history of the church is confusing.

Dendrochronology seems to provide explicit results from different building units. The sacristy from the 1440s is oldest, closely followed by the nave around 1450, the porch from the 1450s, and finally the tower, which was erected in 1467 (Fig. 179). Such a late date for the entire building is surprising. Therefore a number of mortar samples were taken from the walls of the nave. It was important to test the dendrochronology.

Four of the samples were analyzed in complete age profiles (Fig. 180a). From a technical point of view the results were extremely well disciplined, all of them reaching identical results at the first carbon dioxide fractions. The results are in complete agreement with the dendrochronology of the nave.

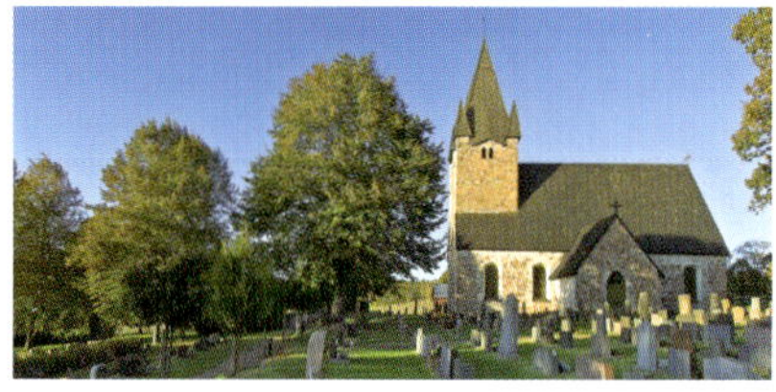

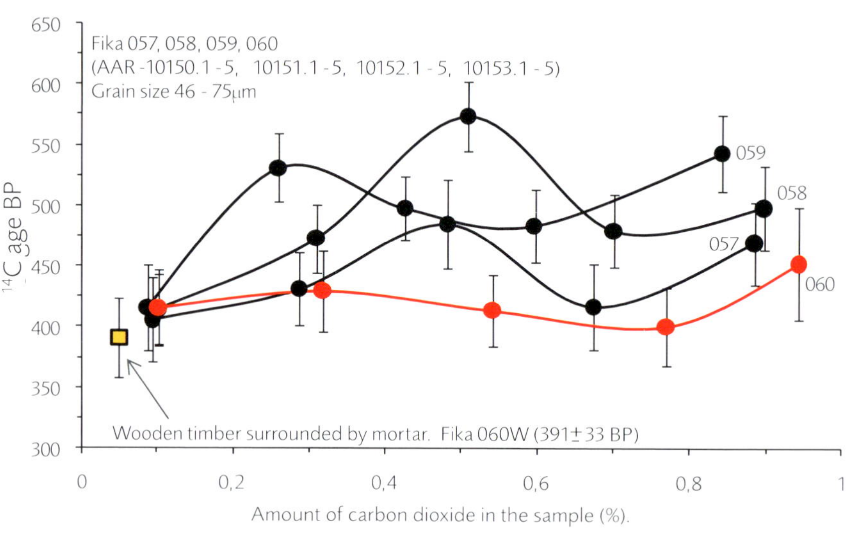

▲ **Fig. 180a. The first carbon dioxide fractions in four age profiles converge at the 414±16 BP age. Yet once more, one of the age profiles, Fika 060, is almost horizontal and completely free from contamination. The embedded wooden fragment, Fika 060W, fits well into the picture with the age 391±33 BP.**

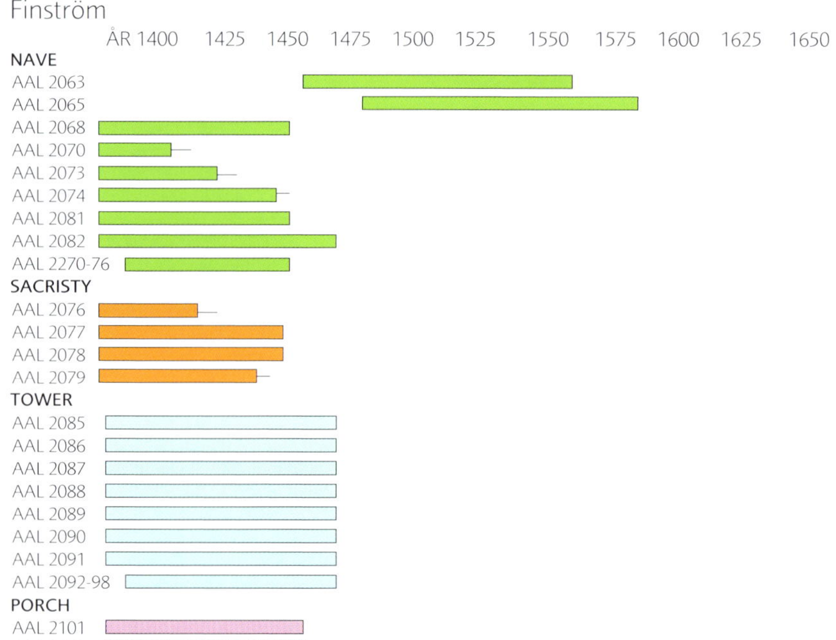

▲ **Fig. 179. Dendrochronological analysis from Finström.**

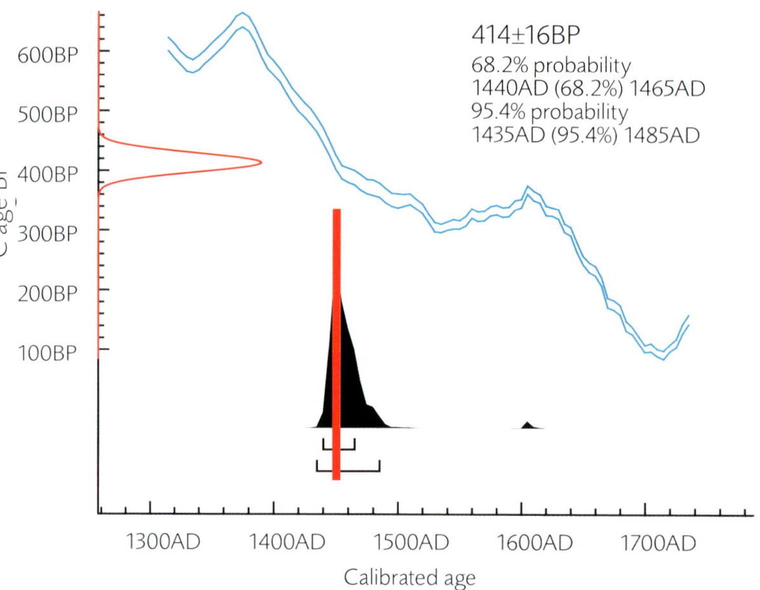

▲ **Fig. 180b. Combined calibration of the first fractions yields 1440-1465AD, at a probability of 68,2%, which is in agreement with the dendrochronology, 1450AD.**

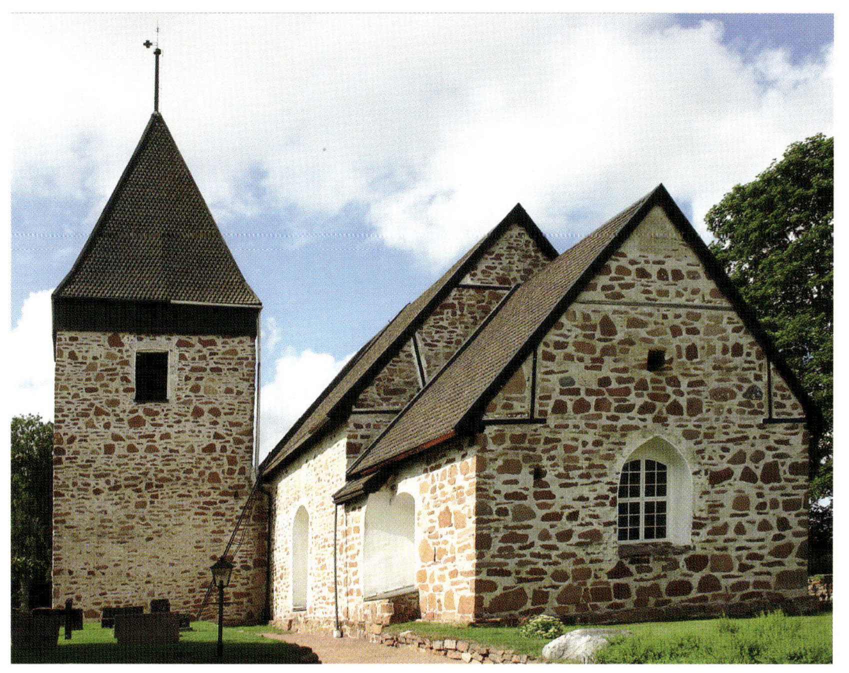

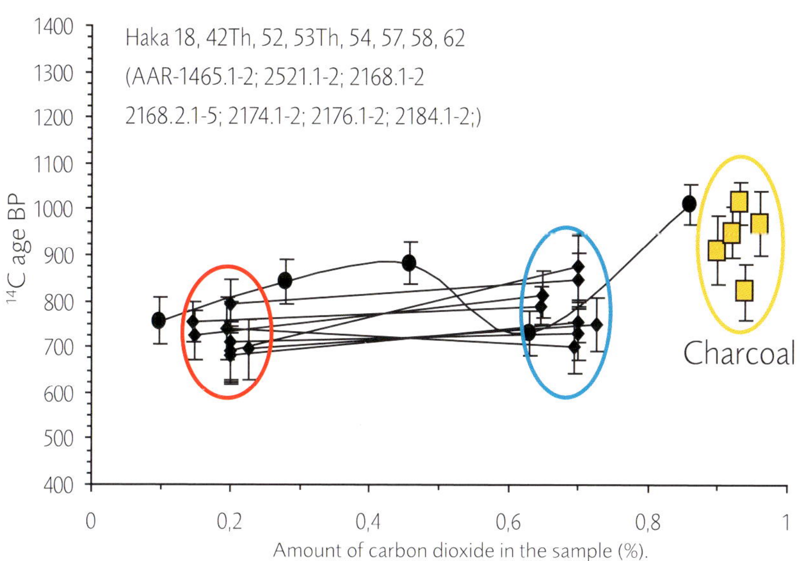

▲ **Fig. 181a. The church of Hammarland. The results from mortar dating from the first building stage of the nave, analyzed in two carbon dioxide fractions. One of the samples was later analyzed in five successive fractions. The first fraction of the age profile confirms the earlier results.**

Hammarland

In Volume I of the *Åland Churches*, covering Hammarland and Eckerö, four different ages were presented for the nave in Hammarland, based on mortar analysis and ^{14}C dated wooden samples, depending on the age difference between the individual results being uncomfortably large. It is now obvious, however, that eight mortar samples from the nave, all of them representing CI, differ from the others in a remarkable way (cf. Fig. 181a). It has gradually become clear that the results actually represent two different stages – the nave and a later secondary stage, which among other things includes the vaulting of the nave. The first stage of the nave was erected 1265-1285, while the following stage belongs to the 14th century.

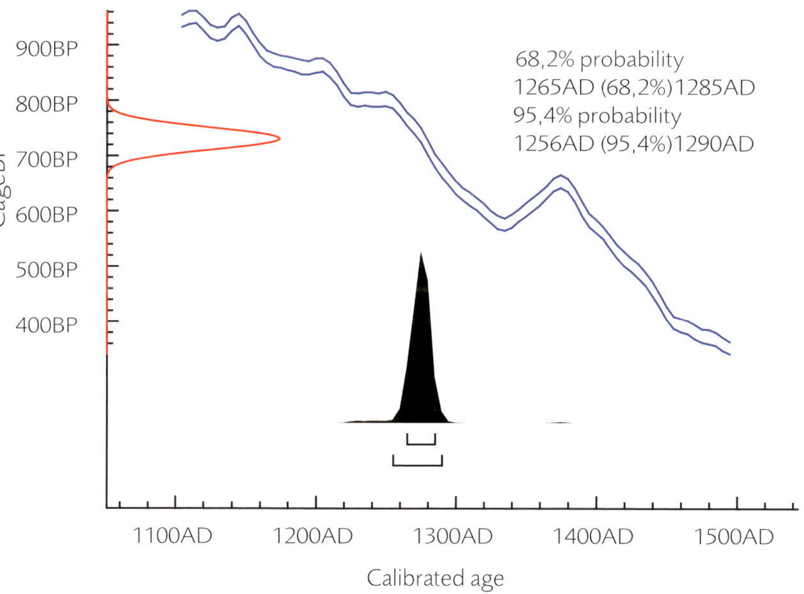

▲ **Fig. 181b. A combined calibration from the first fractions (encircled in red Fig. 181a) yields the age 730±20 BP, or 1265-1285AD, at a probability of 68,2%.**

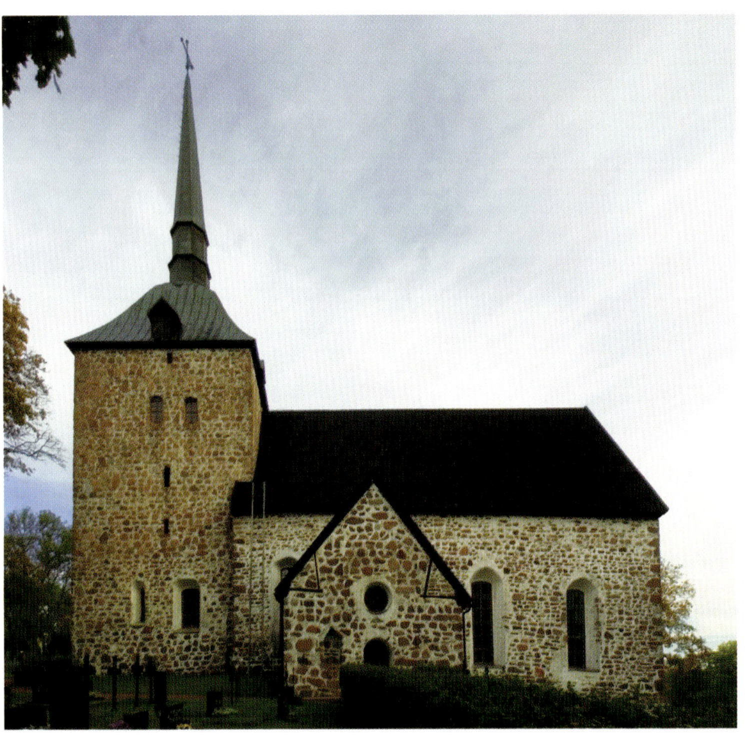

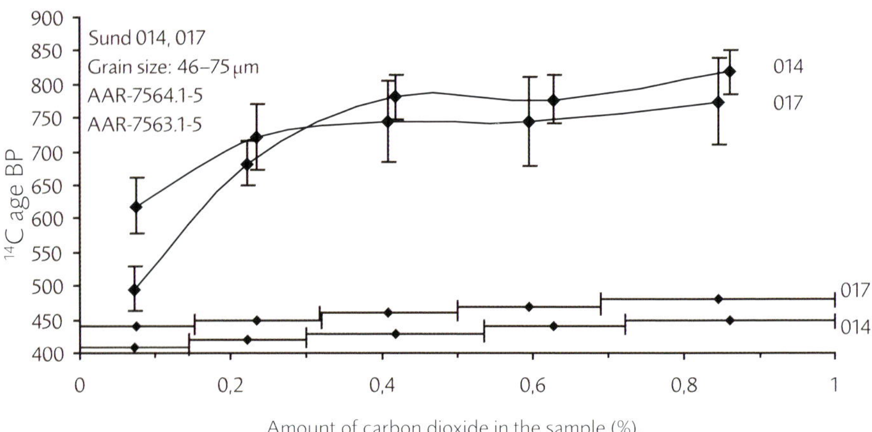

▲ **Fig 182a. Two age profiles from fire damaged mortars from the nave coincide within the same error margins on the horizontal platfoms formed later in the profile.**

Sund

There are, unfortunately, no results from dendrochronology at Sund. All available wood from the nave has repeatedly been damaged by fire. The only wooden material left was a couple of charred fragments of the moulding forms from the tower staircase. These were also ^{14}C analyzed.

Thus the only remaining way to ascertain the age of the nave was by analysis of mortar badly damaged by fire. From the nave, including the vault, there are a total of five age profiles, all of them radically different from other Åland samples. Two of the profiles remind us of the profiles from hydraulic Roman pozzolana mortar, where the horizontal platform of the age profile often reflects the known age. A combined calibration yields 1255-1280AD at the highest probability (Fig. 182a-b).

These atypical age profiles have to be interpreted critically and carefully, since real age control is lacking. Still, our experiences from other fire damaged constructions where age control is available have supported our hypothesis that the correct age in case of fire, is reached later in the profile. Our experiences from Sund have given important insights into the identification, interpretation and dating of buildings damaged by fire.

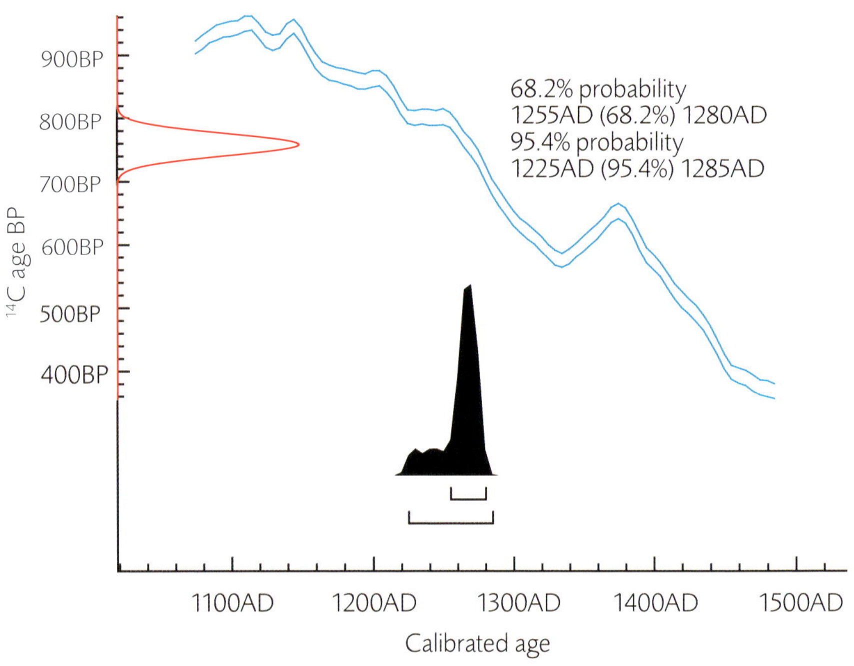

▲ **Fig. 182b. Combined calibration of the platforms yield 758±17 BP, or 1255-1280AD, at a probability of 68,2%.**

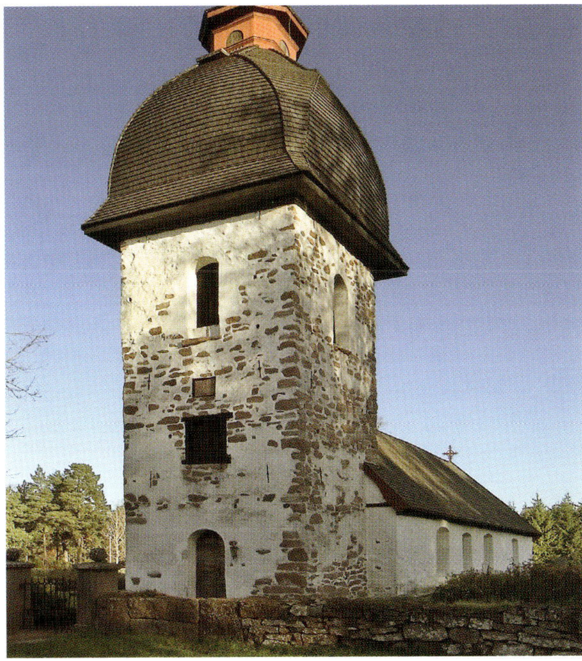
▲ **Fig. 183a. Vårdö church, the exterior.**

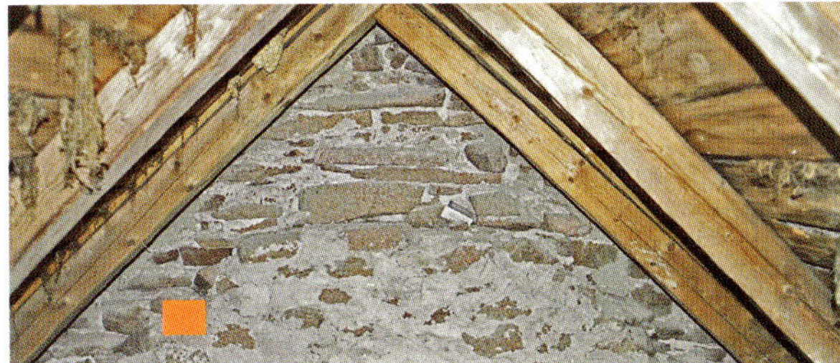
▲ **Fig. 183b. Vårdö 005, mortar sample taken from the original east gable of the nave.**

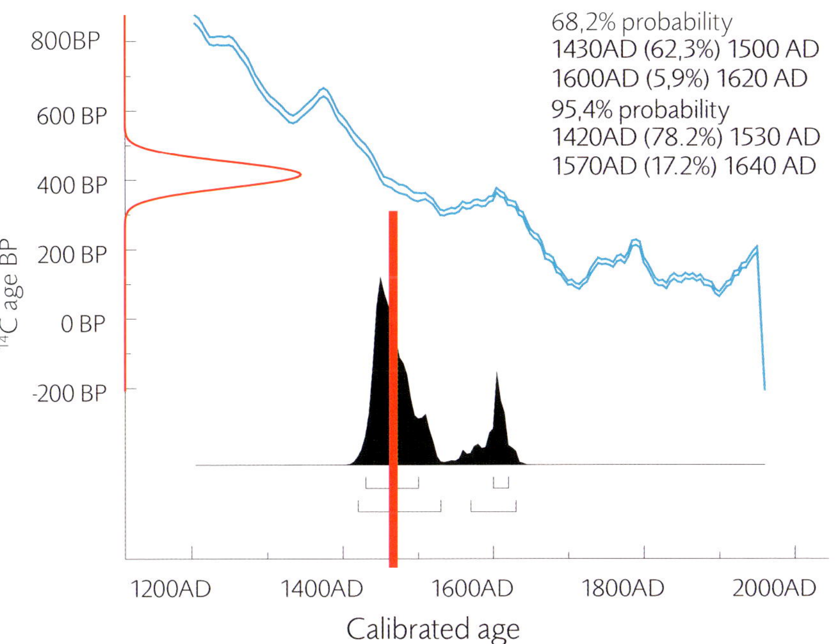

▲ **Fig. 183c. AMS analysis of mortar (Vårdö 005) yields 415±37BP, that is, after calibration 1430-1500 at the highest level of probability, in agreement with the dendrochronological analysis (vertical in red).**

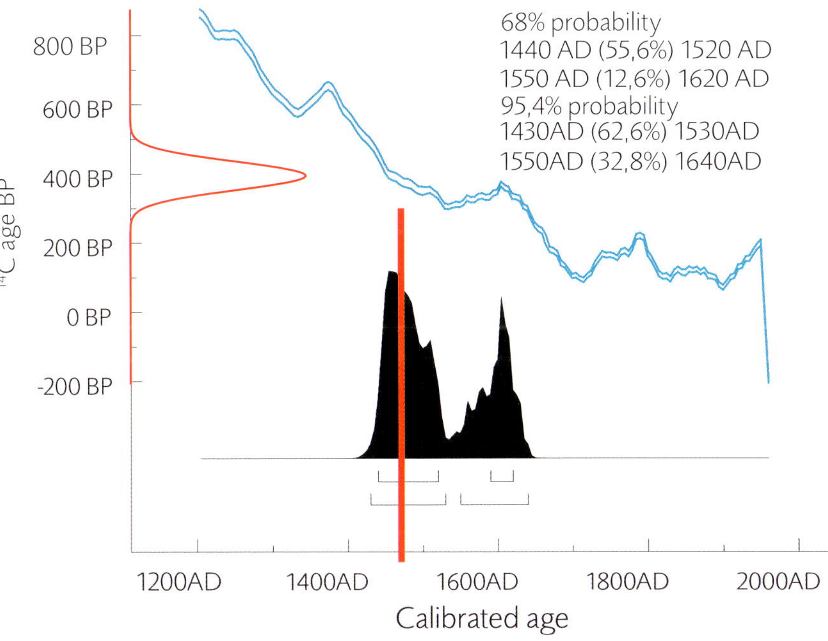

▲ **Fig. 183d. AMS analysis of charcoal particle embedded in the mortar (Vårdö 005). This is a rare case where the charcoal, 394±41BP, yields the same age as the dendrochronology.**

VÅRDÖ

Fig. 183b above, shows an interior from the attic of the nave at of the church at Vårdö, where the original east gable has been preserved. The red square indicates the sampling of Vaka 005, a mortar sample which also included an embedded particle of charcoal. The calibrated age in Fig. 183c represents Vaka 005, a mortar sample where the first fraction (415±37BP) after calibration coincides with the dendrochronological analysis of the northern wall plate. Exceptionally, in this case the embedded charcoal particle of Fig. 183d, (394±41) yields the same result as the mortar. Usually, as is well known, the charcoal particles are older than the mortar, but in no case could they be younger.

COMPARISON BETWEEN MORTAR ANALYSIS AND OTHER SCIENTIFIC DATING METHODS

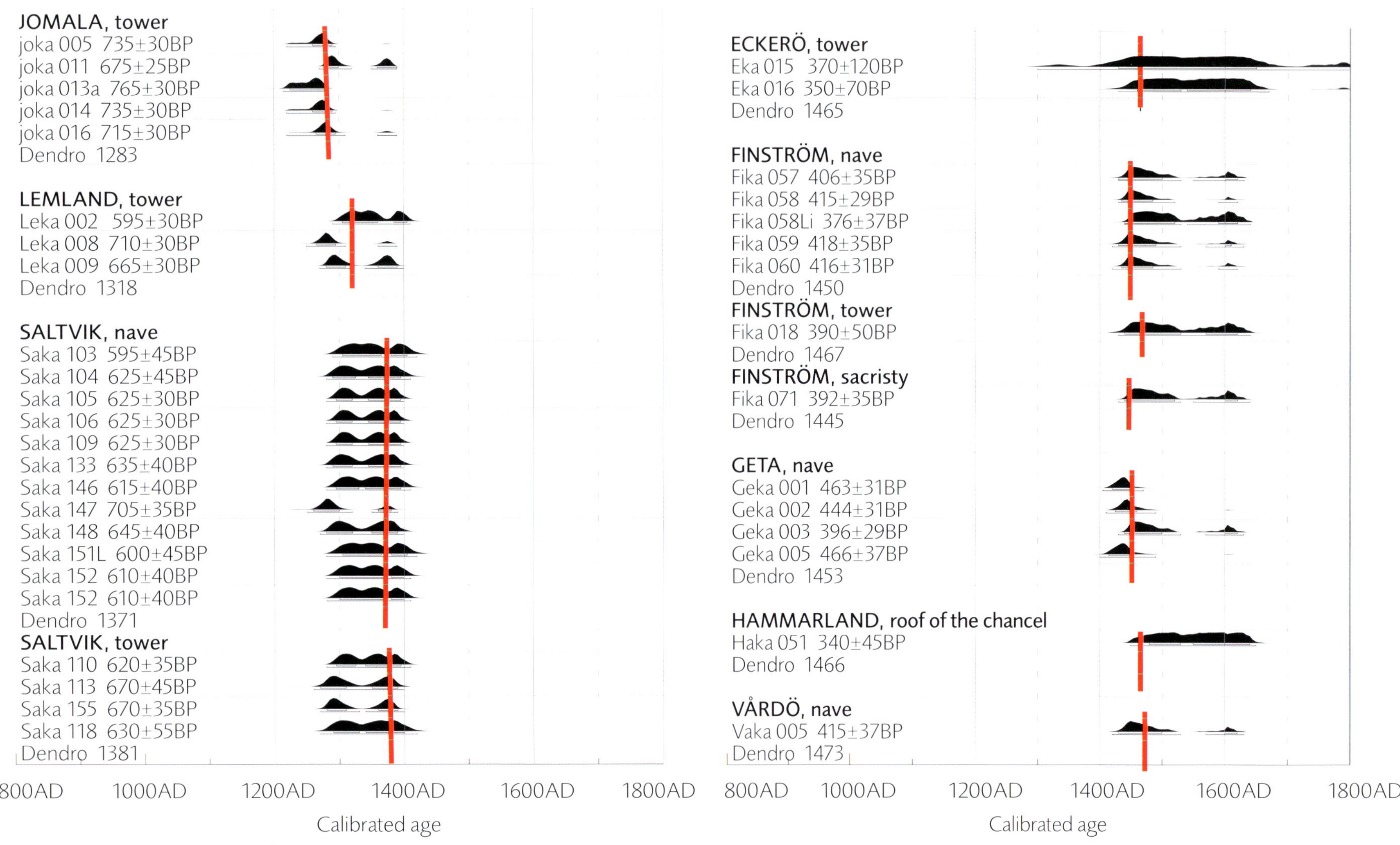

▲ Fig. 184. Mortar samples from Åland (calibrated dates from the first CO_2 fractions marked horizontally in black) confirmed by dendrochronologically dated wooden structures (vertical in red).

The time has come to submit the samples from mortar dating to comparative analysis. Constructions which have been firmly established by dendrochronology of course have the highest priority. Of all Åland mortar results, 38 can be weighed against dendrochronology, of these 36 mortar samples agree with dendrochronology (Fig. 184).

RELIABILITY CRITERIA

Our experiences from Åland lime mortar, so far covering 150 samples analyzed, has made it possible to formulate four criteria of validity. Simultaneously they serve as criteria for different degrees of reliability and as auxiliary tools in the interpretation of cases where age control from other methods and other materials are lacking, in short – when mortar dating is the only option. To avoid misinterpretations the criteria have been kept as strict as possible on purpose.

Valid for independent mortar analysis, without age control:

Criterion I (CI)

When the first two carbon dioxide fractions in the analysis coincide (in this case one single sample per building unit is sufficient). In principle Criterion I is thus void of disturbing contamination, and shows only a minimal gradient between the first two CO_2 fractions. In cases where the samples have been analyzed in full age profiles, a horizontal platform at the beginning of the profile is expected to show the same minimal gradient, if at all.

A subdivision of Critierion I is made up of age profiles where the correct age is revealed by a horizontal platform later in the profile. This can occur when hydraulic pozzolana mortar is analyzed, and when the mortar is damaged by fire.

Criterion II (CII)

When the first CO_2 fractions coincide in a series of three or more samples from the same building unit.

Not valid for independent mortar analysis, requires age control:

Criterion III (CIII)

When the first CO_2 fractions coincide in two samples from the same building unit.

Criterion IV (CIV)

When the first CO_2 fraction in one single sample from a building unit results in an age which is acceptable compared to other building units within the same construction.

The Åland mortar samples with age control versus no age control are divided 52% to 48% (Fig. 185). 75 out of 79 samples with age control agree with the known age, which means that they have to be regarded as conclusive. Thus 95% of all samples with age control are in agreement with the known age. The requirements for Criterion I have been so strictly formulated that they only match 33% of all conclusive samples with age control. Only four samples deviate from the age control. So far we don't know why.

Of the remaining 71 samples without age control, the majority, or 45 samples, follow the strict requirements for Criterion I and II. The results in the blue staple are therefore conclusive, which means that the total percentage of conclusive results amounts to 80%, regardless of age control.

In regard to non-hydraulic Åland mortars, we generally find that only 57 samples meet with the strictest of all criteria, Criterion I, which means 38% of all conclusive results. Criterion II represents the majority of the conclusive results. 92 samples, or 62% of all samples, belong to series where three or more samples from the same building unit reach identical results with the first CO2 fractions. In this case we have contamination from unburned limestone, but it has been successfully eliminated with the aid of mechanical and chemical separations. 42 samples (28%), which represent both Criterion I and Criterion II simultaneously, must be seen as especially reliable.

The staple to the far right represents 26 inconclusive results. These results are not uniform, but we normally know the reason why. They often represent Criteria III and IV, which means that too few samples have been analyzed per building unit. Even if several of the results indicate a certain age, it is not conclusive enough without age control. This category also includes fire damaged samples from the church in Sund, samples which result in age profiles without horizontal plateaus, and therefore impossible to interpret.

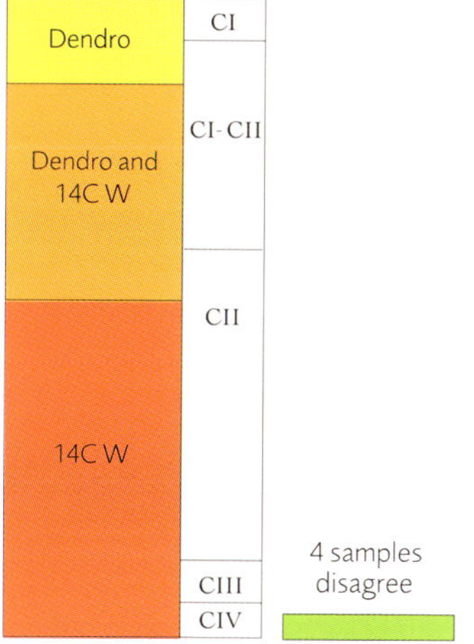

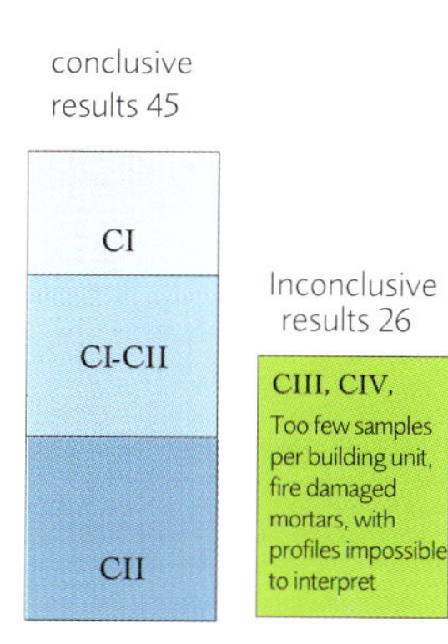

▲ Fig.185. Classification of results from Åland mortars. The staple in red and yellow to the far left represents samples with age control, based on dendrochronology and/or ^{14}C dated wooden structures. 75 samples out of a total of 79 agree with the known age. The adjoining narrow white staple reveals the proportions of the different validity criteria. Four samples in green deviate from the known age. In the staple with different shades of blue represents 45 mortar samples without age control. They can still be considered conclusive, since they represent only Criterion I and Criterion II. Another staple in green to the far right represents 26 inconclusive results.

COMPARISON BETWEEN ÅLAND MORTAR SAMPLES, ¹⁴C SAMPLES OF WOOD AND DENDROCHRONOLOGY

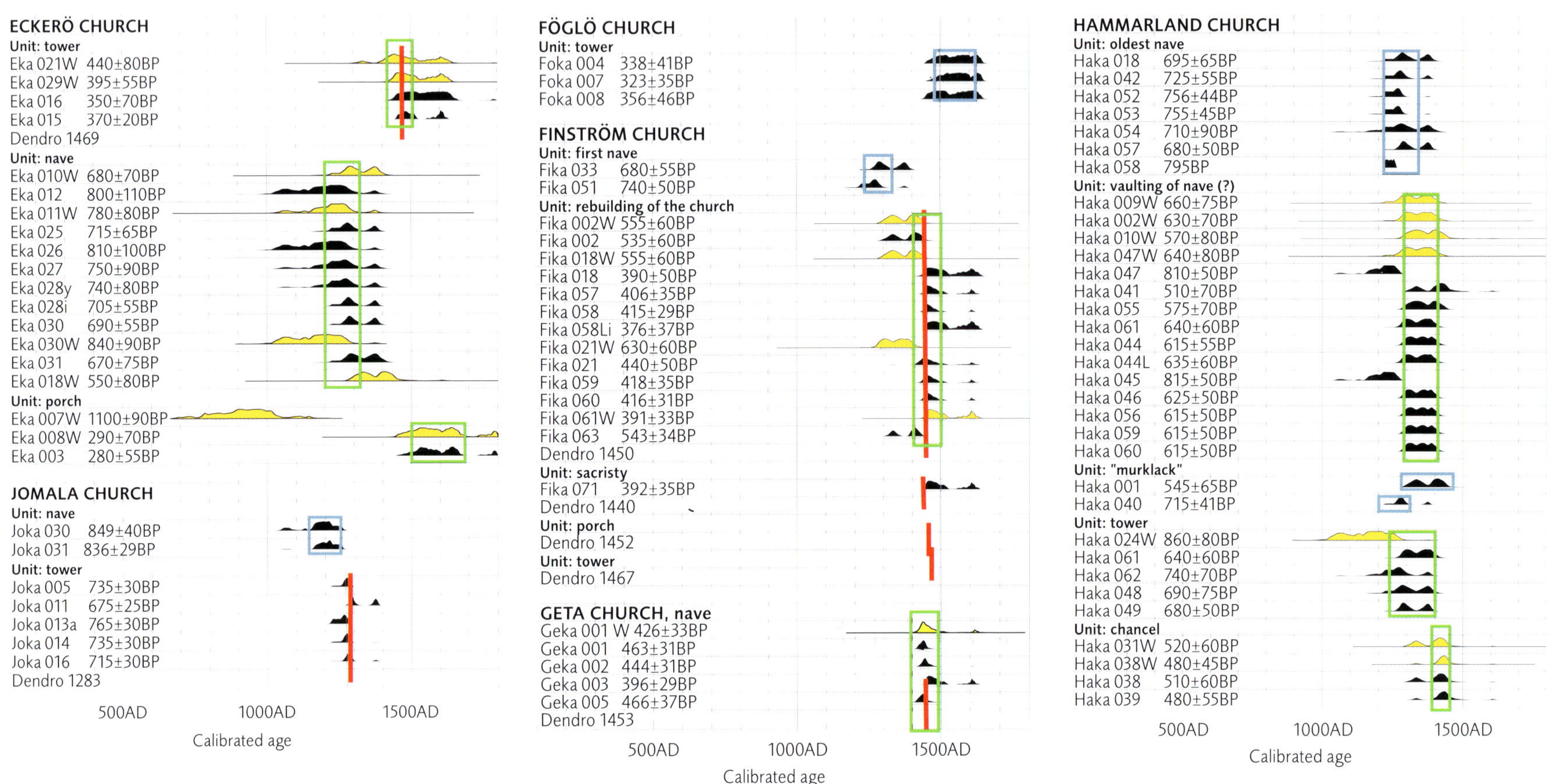

▲ Fig. 186a-c. Comparative results of all conclusive Åland samples that have been scientifically analyzed. Calibrated results of ¹⁴C analysis of wood is marked horizontally in yellow, mortar horizontally in black, and dendrochronology vertically in red. Green rectangles frame building units that have been dated with both ¹⁴C analysis of wood and mortar. Rectangles in blue mark building units where mortar dating has been the only option.

Results of different scientific dating methods implemented in the Åland churches are presented in Fig. 186a-f. With the exception of the fire-damaged church in Sund, and the fire-damaged east gable in Kumlinge, it is always the result of the first CO_2 fractions that counts. Note that where age control is available, i.e., either dendrochronology or ¹⁴C analysis of fragmentarily preserved wooden constructions and wooden fragments embedded in the mortar, the results from mortar and wood agree with one another. In some rare cases the wooden fragments deviate. They can be considerably older (Eka 007W, Haka 024W) or just a little older (Fika 018W, Fika 21W and Fika 063W). Where the odd wooden sample, in an otherwise homogeneous series, exceptionally is more recent (Eka 18W) secondary repairs can be suspected. In two cases, the mortar samples show considerably older results (Haka 047 and Haka 045) in an otherwise very uniform line. They are therefore included in the 5% that deviates from age control. Further, note that results of dendrochronology, when available, coincide with both mortar and ¹⁴C analysis of wood. Results from dendrochronology for the nave at

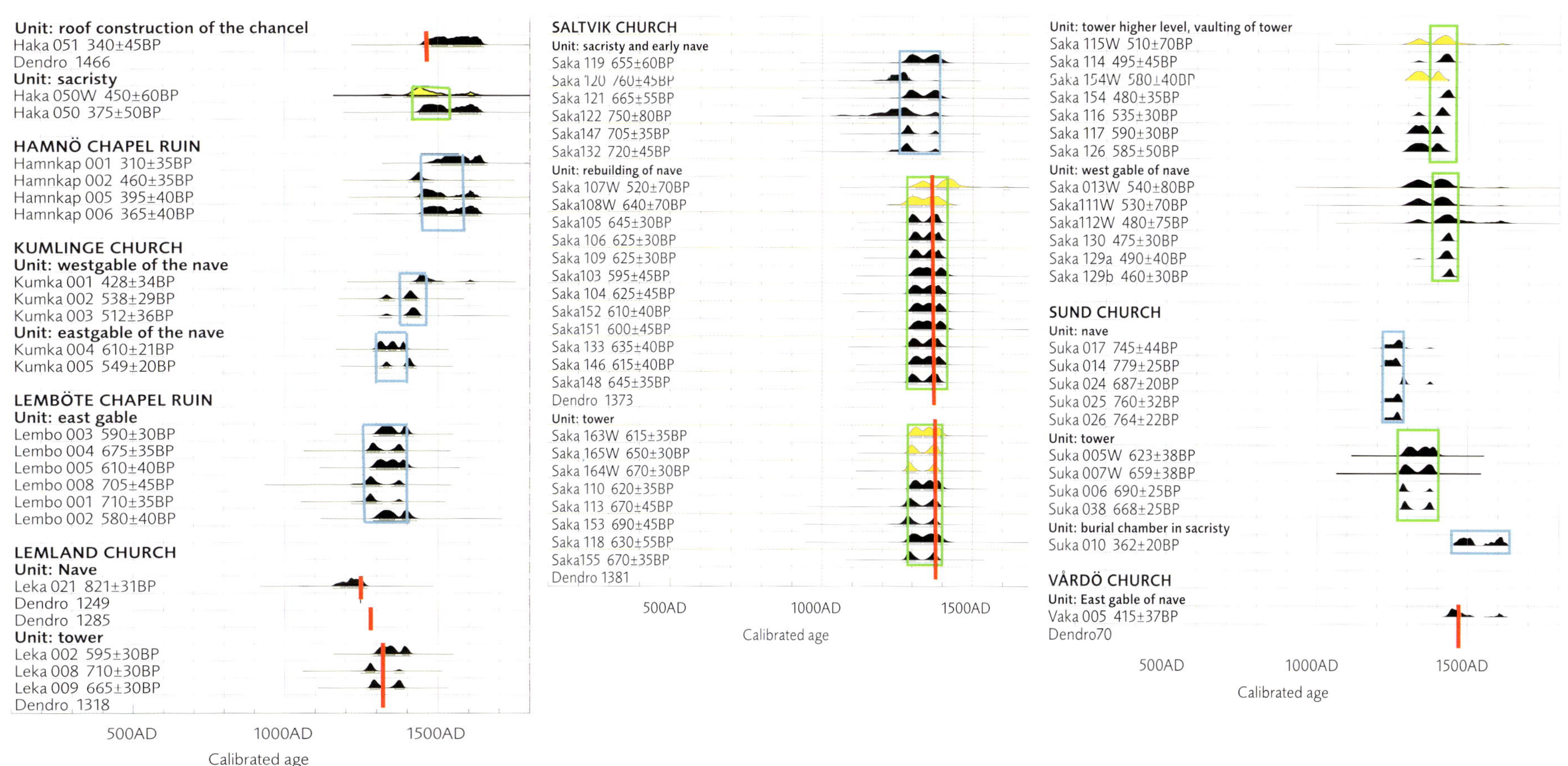

▲ **Fig. 186d-f. Comparative results from all conclusive Åland samples analyzed scientifically (continuation from previous page).**

Hammarland, which represent repairs after a fire in the 1440s, are not included in the diagram.

Regarding mortar analysis and the first stone church in Finström, we still have to be cautious. The samples Fika 033 and Fika 051 indeed both meet the requirements of Criterion I, and therefore, in principle, they should be independently valid for the dating of the church. More samples, however, should be taken before a scientific analysis can show the existence of an early stone church in Finström. The same thing is true for the nave at Lemland.

Charcoal particles embedded in the mortar are missing in the survey. This is because they usually yield old and uneven results, depending on the old wood effect. Such an effect arises when only the inner core of a timber remains after the fire. Yet, for the sake of comparison charcoal particles are also analyzed. They can be contemporary with the mortar, but obviously they must not be more recent.

Green rectangles framing the results of individual building units mark the age indicated by mortar dating and age control from ^{14}C analysis of wood and dendrochronology. Rectangles in blue are especially important, since they date structures where mortar has been the only material available suitable for scientific dating.

A CHRONOLOGY TAKES SHAPE

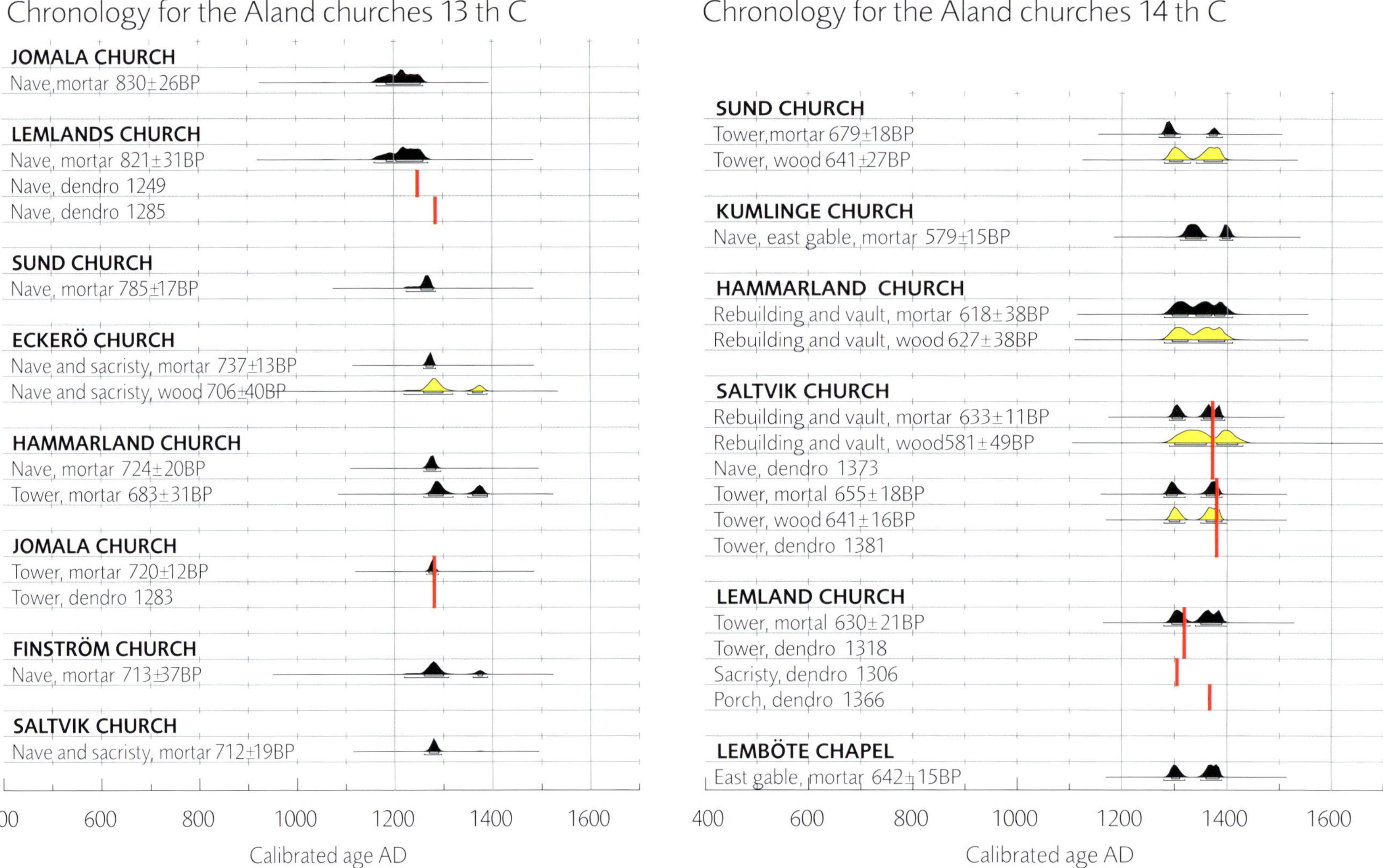

▲ **Fig. 187a. The chronology for medieval stone churches in Åland, the 13th and 14th centuries.**

The chronology of the Åland stone churches consists of a combined calibration, partly of mortar samples, partly of wooden samples (Figs. 187a-b). Note that the chronology remains the same, regardless of whether it is based on mortar dating or scientific dating of wood. In the analyses mortar and wood generally come close to one another.

Once more it has to be stressed that analysis of mortar often is the only way to reach the oldest building stages. We can further see how the building activity spreads relatively evenly from the 13th century onwards. Even if it is possible to find that building activity has been more intensive in some periods than in others, no hiatus in the building activity can be discerned.

The naves of the main churches, the so called mother churches, on the main island (Jomala, Lemland, Sund, Eckerö, Hammarland and Saltvik, probably also Finström) were erected more or less simultaneously during the 13th century. Of these Jomala and Lemland seem to be more ancient that the others, but as

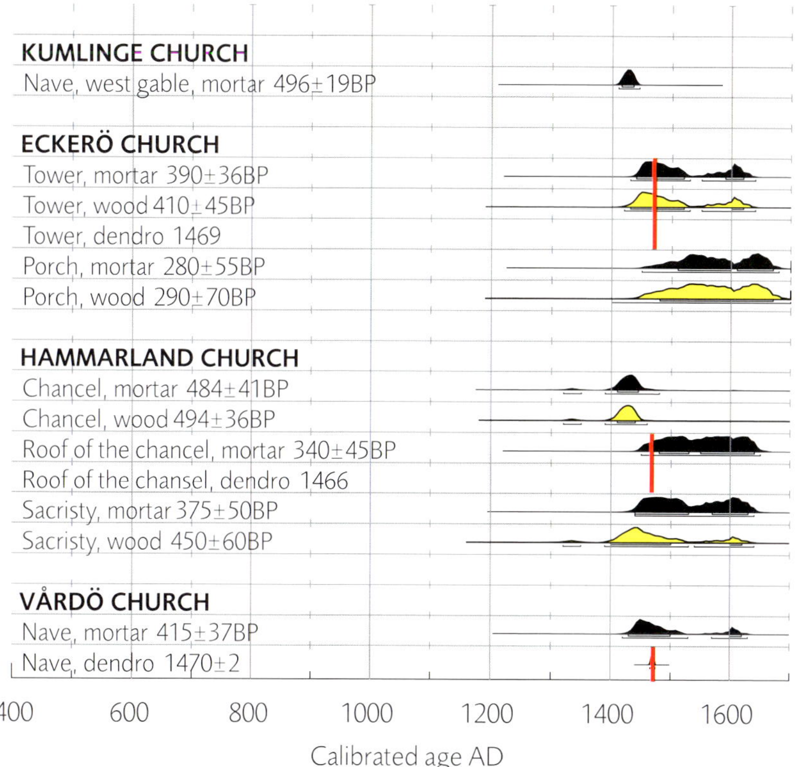

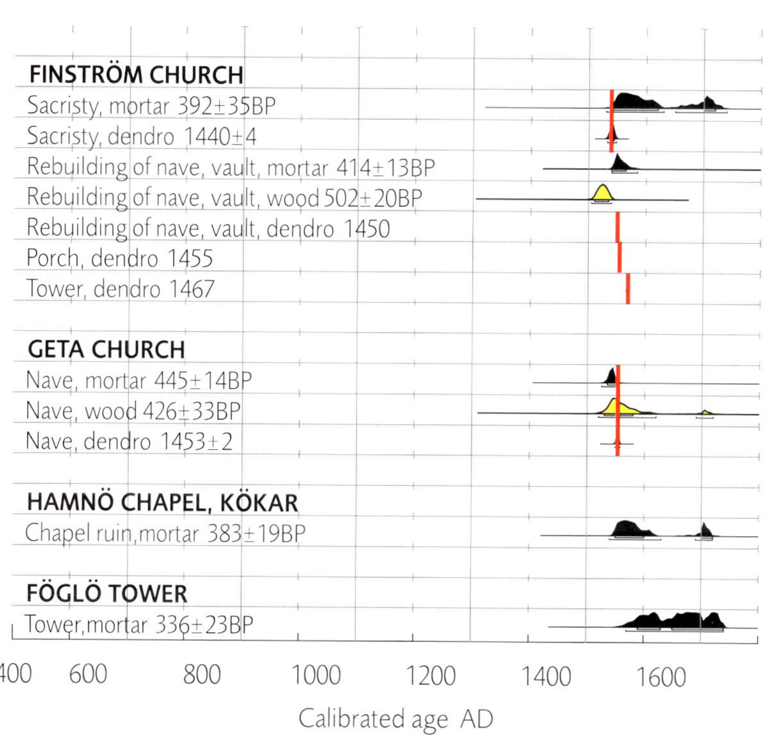

▲ **Fig. 187b. The chronology for medieval stone churches in Åland, the 15th century.**

with Finström, these results so far rely on too few samples analysed.

Most early datings are based on mortar analysis alone. The results fulfil the strict demands of Criterion I and II, often in combination of the two. The nave of Lemland is so far the only one to be dated to the 13th century by dendrochronology, even though only few samples are available. The dating of the west tower in Jomala to the 1280s is very convincing with uniform series of both dendrochronology and mortar analysis. Further, the campanile in Jomala seems to be the only one dated from the 13th century, with the possible exception of the tower in Hammarland.

The chronology of the 14th century is not quite clear. As already mentioned, it is a century which cannot easily be established through ^{14}C analysis. We are still waiting for results from the archipelago churches in Föglö and Kökar. Therefore, they are not yet included in the different surveys (Figs. 186a-f; Figs. 187a-b). But other, non-scientific evidence such as coins and preliminary mortar results, indicate that Föglö also can belong to the 14th century. We still lack results from mortar dating in Kökar, but other materials that place the complex in the 14th century have been scientifically confirmed. The stone chapel of Lemböte, on the old sailing route between Denmark and Estonia, and described in the so-called Danish Itinerary, was either erected at the very end of the 13th century, or in the 14th century. In this case, the uncertainty depends on the wiggles in the calibration curve for the 14th century. But thanks to dendrochronology we now know that this century also was a dynamic period for Åland church building. That was the time for an intensive period of tower building, and many secondary building units such as porches and sacristies take shape. At Saltvik radical rebuilding and vaulting takes place in the nave at the end of the 14th century.

The period 1450-70 means another intensive building period in Åland. We can now witness an almost total rebuilding of the church of Finström. In this case scientific dating indicates a more substantial rebuilding than just the vaulting of the nave and the erection of the west tower. It also involved the heightening of the nave and the sacristy. A porch was added to the nave, and the impressive new tower, surrounded by four turrets reflecting influence from the Turku Cathedral completes the rebuilding.

Three other towers were erected relatively late, at the end of the 15th century, i.e., in Eckerö, Föglö and probably also in Kumlinge. The west gable of Kumlinge church was built in 1410-30. The only completely new buildings from this century are the stone chapels in Geta and Vårdö, belonging to the mother churches of Finström and Sund respectively. Very surprising is the late date of "Kappalskatan", the little wooden chapel at Hamnö, Kökar. Here no wooden material remained, but mortar from the socle level indicates that it could, together with the tower at Föglö, belong to the very latest medieval ecclesiastic constructions in Åland, erected around 1500.

From the chronological survey (Figs. 187a-b) one might get the idea that the 15th century was the most dynamic period as far as activity in building churches in Åland is concerned. It is therefore important to complement the picture with a map focusing on the vital points, the naves (Fig. 188). With different centuries marked in different colors a clear pattern can be discerned.

It is quite obvious that the 13th century is the most intensive building period, with at least six mother churches, marked in orange, erected close to one another on the main island. Finström, which remains unclear, is marked with diagonal orange lines. The 14th century meant that stone church building reached the archipelago parishes, with naves marked in green. For Föglö and Kökar, the dating so far depends on analyzing other materials than mortar. On the main island the focus was on secondary additions to existing naves. The 15th century is dominated by the vast rebuilding of the church in Finström, marked in blue, in addition to secondary building units added to several of the naves. Completely new are the stone chapels of Geta and Vårdö, likewise marked in blue. Furthermore, wooden chapels of unknown age but most probably medieval, have been traced to Lumparland, Sottunga and Brändö.

Conclusion

A long time has passed since my longing to get an answer to the enigmatic and fascinating past of the Åland Islands was triggered. I had hoped that one day it might be possible to understand the larger context, and to take part in comprehensive interdisciplinary research– collaboration resulting in an objective and reliable chronology for the medieval stone churches in Åland. Developing new tools to compensate for the lack of written sources was to be of great importance. At an early stage it became clear that mortar dating, together with the implementation of all other possible scientific methods, would provide an important opening. In retrospect we can claim that it was more than fortunate that the big challenge - to develop an objective dating method for archeological questions – was initiated in the Åland Islands. Here mortar was very well behaved, and there is plenty of comparative material available from other methods. Regardless of whether Åland mortars are analyzed in two or five CO_2 fractions, it is generally the first fraction that counts. The results are easy to interpret and they generally yield distinct dates.

Exciting and enjoyable collaboration within our research team has had fruitful results. Even if details certainly will be refined, and results will become more precise, we have come close to our ultimate aim: a chronology for the medieval stone churches in Åland. We have seen that mortar dating is often the only way to reach the first building periods of the churches. Hopefully our experience from scientific dating in Åland can inspire future research. For us, such an interdisciplinary approach has provided the necessary basis for reliable results.

The scientific community has followed our research with great interest. Internationally, the response has been positive. The most prominent researchers and laboratories in the field are now actively participating in the development of our method.

In Finland, however, our work has been continuously criticized from the beginning by one researcher in the field of medieval stone churches, who has reached very different results in his estimation of a chronology for the Åland churches.

The project *International Mortar Dating* marks an important opening nationally, and as part of our international project, sponsored by the Academy of Finland since 2007, the method is being tested on Turku Cathedral and on a number of churches in the Åboland archipelago outside Turku.

The comparative research and the development of the method also continues on an international level, and here the corpus of Åland mortars is an important source of information. The discussion concerning the different credibility criteria, which has been of fundamental importance for the interpretation of the results, so far concerns Åland mortars especially. A complete table covering all Åland samples has recently been published (Heinemeier et. al. 2010, see also www.kyrkor.ax). We also know that the criteria work outside the Åland Islands, in Portugal and in Gotland in Sweden, where the lime mortar is non-hydraulic. We aim at a general refinement of the method, where we will define the limits for mortar dating and map areas where the method works.

The mortar dating study of the churches of the Åland Islands represents a significant development in medieval archaeology in recent years. And while much research remains to be done, it is hoped that this study will serve as a new basis for further development in the field.

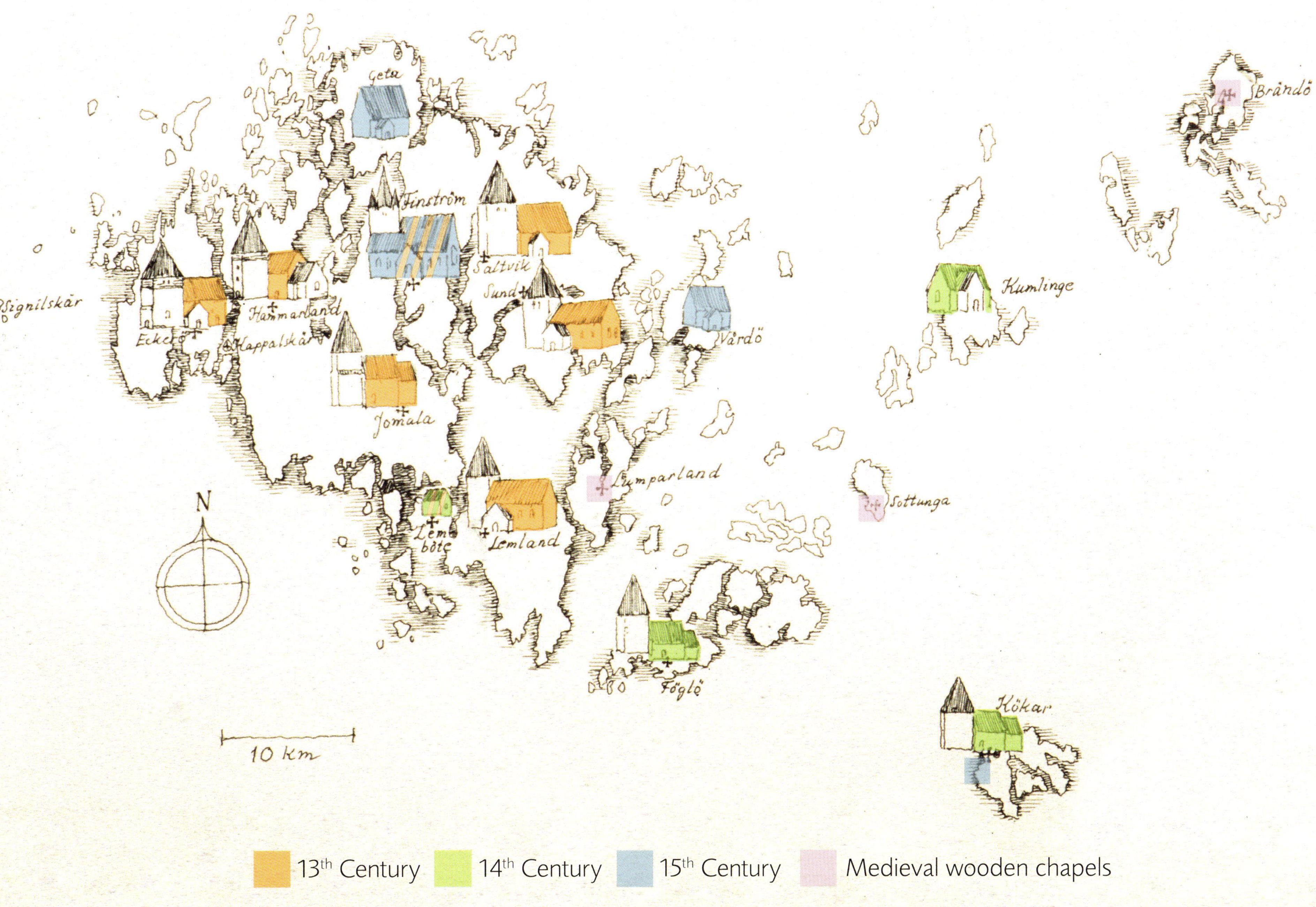

▲ **Fig. 188. The Åland churches, the chronology of the naves marked on the map.**

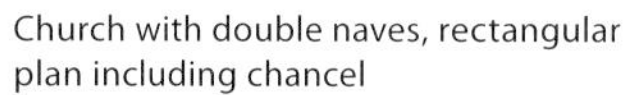
Church with double naves, rectangular plan including chancel

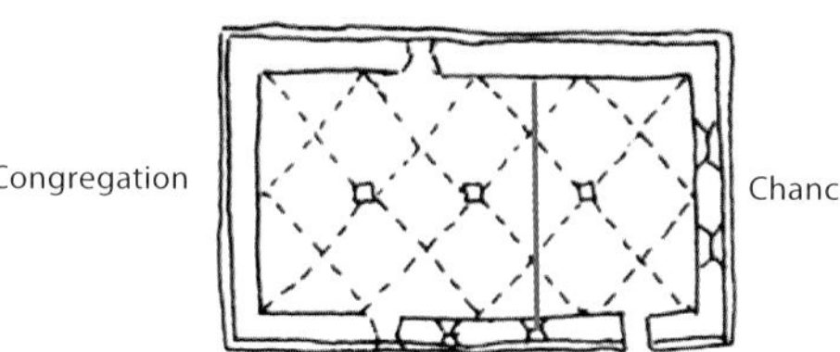

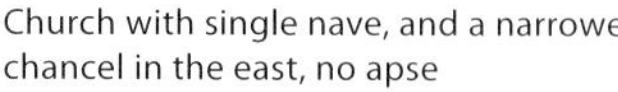
Church with single nave, and a narrower chancel in the east, no apse

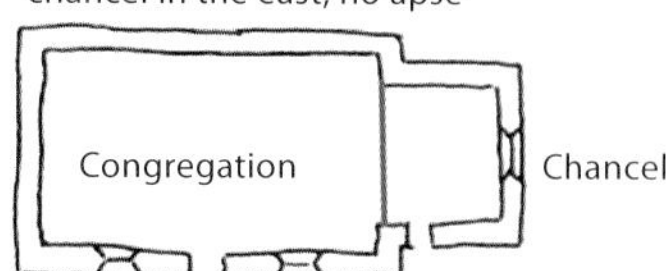

GLOSSARY

Aisles part of the church, passageways on either side of the nave, often lower than the nave

Ambo medieval pulpit

Apse semicircular addition to provide space for the high altar, usually placed at the eastern end of the nave, generally lower than the nave

Axis in architecture a straight line, along which elements of the plan are symmetrically or systematically disposed

Baldachin decoration in the form of a sheltering roof placed above wooden sculptures in an altarpiece, usually openwork, protruding and fastened on to the back wall of the altarpiece, see Fig. 66.

Barrel-vault barrel-like, formed as a half-cylinder with a semicircular cross-section

Bay regular and uniform structural subdivision of a church, the space enclosed by the two transverse arches and the two wall arches in a single nave, or by the transverse arches and longitudinal arches in a church with double naves, or a church with one nave and two aisles

Bracket projection from a wall with a carrying or supporting function, used as base for vaults and protruding building units

Calvary group a scene from Golgotha where Christ Crucified is flanked by Mary in mourning to the left and John, mourning apostle to the right, see Fig.15.

Chancel (often also called Choir) in a hall-church, without an apse, the space in the eastern part of the rectangular plan reserved for the clergy, with the high alter for the liturgy of the mass. Can also be a separate narrow building unit, either with a straight eastern wall or finished by an apse towards the east

Choir (often also called Chancel) in a hall-church, without an apse, the space in the eastern part of the rectangular plan reserved for the clergy, with the high alter for the liturgy of the mass. Can also be a separate narrow building unit, either with a straight eastern wall or finished by an apse towards the east

Choir-screen a screen wall or partition dividing the choir or chancel from the nave

Column freestanding vertical support, consisting of base, shaft and capital. The shaft usually has a circular cross section. Usually forming the division between the nave and the aisles in a church

Corpus central part of an altarpiece, flanked by wings which can be closed against the corpus for certain liturgical feasts, such as Lent, etc

Course horizontal level range of stones or bricks in the construction of the wall, laid evenly

Cross arm as the shorter parts of a cruciform plan

Cross vault intersecting barrel-vaults forming a groin-vault

Dendrochronology scientific dating method based on the master curve of the annual rings in the felled timber in building constructions or in wooden sculptures

Double nave church consisting of two parallel naves, divided by columns or pillars along the central axis. Can have a rectangular ground plan without an apse, or a rectangular ground plan with an apse

Eaves-board board fixed under the overhanging of the roof shingles

Groin sharp crease-like edge formed by the salient between two intersecting vaults, as in two barrel-vaults joined in right angles

Hall church 1. Church with aisles but without a clerestory, approximately uniform height throughout the interior (in German Hallenkirche). 2. A single nave church, where the interior forms a uniform space within the rectangular ground plan, with chancel or choir included in the rectangle not forming separate building units (in Swedish Salkyrka)

Iconography art historical terminology for the interpretation of images and symbols

Iconoclasm conscientious destruction of images, often connected to the Reformation

Jamb vertical support for an arch or a vault, carrying the weight of the arch or the vault

Joint meeting point of two building units. If bonded at the joint, they were probably built at the same time. A **vertical joint** without bonding may suggest different building stages

Man of Sorrows Christ rising from the dead, demonstrating all his wounds. Often with the arms of passion

Molding any continuous projecting or inset architectural member with a

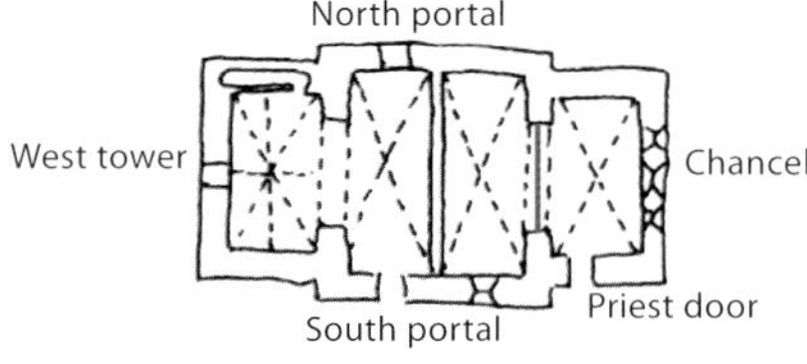

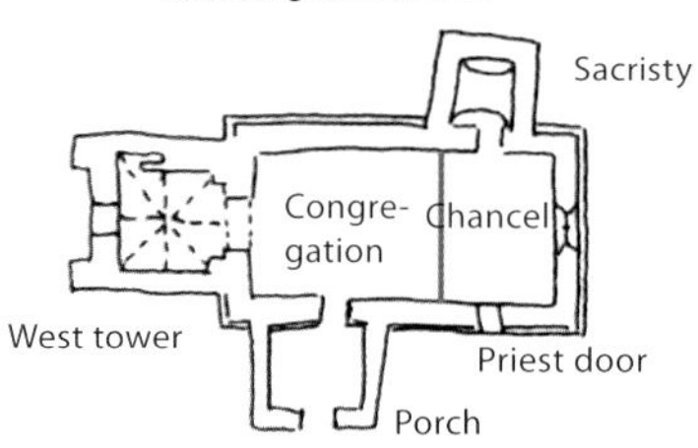

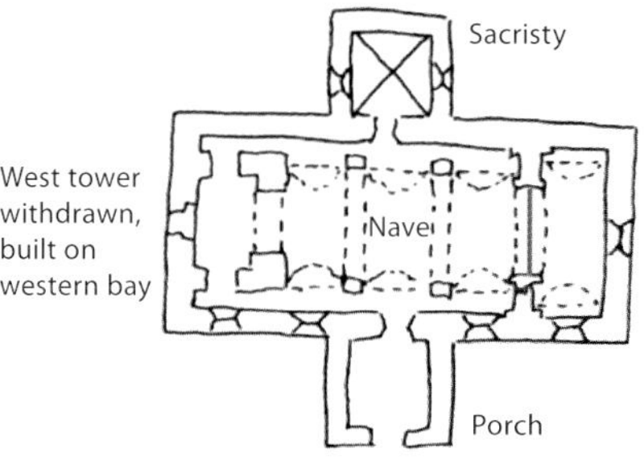

contoured profile defining and separating architectural details

Nave the main body of the church between western wall and chancel, whether aisled or not, used by laity or the congregation.

Ordovician geological term for limestone found in Åland, Öland (Sweden), and in Estonia

Palmette frieze ornamental dividing frieze, see Fig. 16.

Paten plate for the oblates, see Fig. 33.

Patron Saint a church is dedicated to a patron saint

Pillar vertical support with square section, with or without base and capital, dividing nave and aisles, or the parallel naves in double nave churches

Pietà presentation of Mary in mourning, holding her deceased son in her arms, see Fig. 43.

Predella horizontal and narrow lower part or base of an altarpiece, see Fig. 43.

Priest door separate entry from the south for priests directly into the chancel

Porch southern entrance hall to church, usually later addition in front of original main portal

Rapakivi easily split Åland red granite

Reliquary casket for or holder of relics, see Fig. 37.

Rib vault carried by a structural skeleton of ribs

Ridge turret little tower riding on the ridge of the roof, see Fig. 133.

Ring crucifix the cross-arms united by a ring, with the center of the circle in the intersection of the cross, see Fig.15.

Ring vault in a stellar-vault the intersection of the ribs are circumscribed by rings, see Fig. 120.

Rood beam cross beam between chancel and nave, or across the nave, for the carrying of the crucifix, synonym for trabes, see Fig. 15

Roof-beam horizontal beam in a roof truss uniting the rafters

Roof-truss triangular structure carrying the roof. Consisting of roof-beam and rafters, resting at regular intervals on the wall-plates

Sacristy separate space towards the north, for keeping vestry and church silver etc., also used as changing room for the clergy

Side-altar in addition to the high altar, medieval churches had at least two side-altars, one in north devoted to Mary and the other to the patron saint

Shell structure outer and inner shell of larger fieldstones, with the smoother side facing the exterior, filled with mortar and aggregate

Socle foundation wall, protruding from the wall

Spandrel wedge shaped downwards narrowing parts in the inner corners of the vault

Springing of vault the lowest course of a vault, supporting structure

Stellar vault late medieval development of rib-vaults, with the ribs arranged in the pattern of a star

Transverse arch placed at regular intervals across the nave, and the aisles, supporting the vaults

Triptych tripartite construction, for instance an altarpiece consisting of corpus, flanked by two wings

Triumphal arch between chancel and nave, to mark the separation between clergy and the congregation

Triumphal crucifix hanging in the triumphal arch

Transept in a cruciform church the transepts are the wings perpendicular to the nave that complete the cross form; a transept is often of the same section as the nave, and may have no aisles

Turrets miniature towers

Wall arch inside the wall, or parallel to a wall, anchoring for the vaults

Wall–pier pillar erected against the wall, often a later construction

Wall plate longitudinal timber set on top of a brick and masonry wall, on which roof trusses, joists and rafters are resting

INDEX OF NAMES

BIBLIOGRAPHY

Unprinted sources

The provincial Archives of Turku
- The Archives of the Diocese

The National Board of Antiquities, Helsinki
- The Department of Cultural History, The Topographical Archives of the History Unit
- The Cultural History Image Archives
- The Building History Unit

The Provincial Archives of Åland
- The Archives of the Dean
- Archives for the Respective Parishes

Åland's Museum
- The Archives
- The Collections

Printed sources

Acta Visitatoria, Boetius Murenius 1637-1666. Finska kyrkohistoriska samfundets handlingar VI, Porvoossa 1905-1908.

Analecta Hymnica Medii Aevi, Herausgegeben von Clemens Blume S.J. LV. Thesauri Hymnologici Prosarium, des Thesaurus Hymnologicus H.A. Daniels und anderer Sequenzenausgaben. Des 2. Teiles zwetier Band. Leipzig. 1922 (Minerva G.m.b.H., Frankfurt am Main, Unveränderter Nachdruck 1961).

Finlands medeltidsurkunder samlade i tryck I-VIII. Utgifna af Finlands Statsarkiv genom Reinhold Hausen, Helsingfors 1910-1935.

Hallborg, Laurentius O. *De Alandia I*. Dissertatio Academica, Algot Scarin (praes.) Aboæ 1730.

Källström, O. *Medeltida kyrksilver från Sverige och Finland förlorat genom Gustav Vasas konfiskationer*, Uppsala 1939.

Nervander, Emil, *Sommarresor på Åland*, Mariehamn 1983, (nytryck).

Radloff, F.W. 1795, *Beskrifning öfver Åland*, Åbo, Mariehamn 1998 (nytryck).

Rannsakningar efter antikviteter. Bd. 1/Häfte 1, Uppland, Västmanland, Dalarna, Norrland, Finland: text/på Akademiens uppdrag utg. under red. Av Carl Ivar Ståhle et.al. Kungliga Vitterhets-, Historie- och Antikvitetsakademien, Stockholm 1960.

Tärnström, Christophorus, *De Alandia, Maris Baltici insula*, Partem priorem, Elias Frondin (praes.) Upsaliae 1739.

Ålands medeltidsurkunder, H1-1400, (red. Johannes Sundwall), Helsingfors 1954.

Ålands medeltidsurkunder, H2-1400-1450, (red. Johannes Sundwall), Helsingfors 1958.

Literature

Andersson, Aron, En medeltida nattvardskalk från Kökar, Åland, *Åländsk Odling*, Mariehamn 1980, 40-44.

Andersson, Aron, *Silberne Abendmahlsgeräte in Schweden aus dem XIV. Jahrhundert*, Stockholm 1956.

ARS Suomen Taide 1. Toim. Salme Sarajas-Korte et al., Espoo 1987.

Bennett, Robert, Kumlinge kyrka, Ålands medeltida kyrkor, *Stockholm Studies in History of Art, 25*, Lund 1973, 135-143.

Berggren, Lars, De gotländska dopfuntarna i den medeltida östersjöhandeln: lyxartiklar eller barlast? *Songs of Ossian, Festschrift in Honour of Professor Bo Ossian Lindberg, Taidehistoriallisia tutkimuksia, Konsthistoriska studier 27*, Helsinki 2003, 59-73.

Bonnier, Ann Catherine, Hammarlands kyrka, Ålands medeltida kyrkor, *Stockholm Studies in History of Art 25*, Lund 1973, 84-102.

Bonnier, Ann-Catherine, *Kyrkorna berättar, Upplands kyrkor 1250-1350*, Uppsala 1987.

Bonnier, Ann-Catherine, Medeltidens kyrkor. *Uppland, Landskapets kyrkor, Sockenkyrkorna, kulturarv och bebyggelsehistoria*, 2004, 28-57.

Breide, Henrik, Itinerariet. Det historiska dokumentet – en översikt, *Kung Valdemars segelled*, huvudred. Gerhard Flink, Stockholm 1995, 11-23.

Dreijer, Matts, En undersökning av Lemlands kyrka, 1957, *Åländsk Odling*, Mariehamn 1961, 20-43.

Dreijer, Matts, *Det åländska folkets historia, I:I. Från stenåldern till Gustav Vasa*, Mariehamn 1983.

Dreijer, Matts, Då Sottunga fick egen kyrka, *Åländsk Odling*, Mariehamn 2000, 88-92 (nytryck från Sanct Olof, 1949).

Dreijer, Matts, Finströms St. Mikael – en problemkyrka, *Sanct Olof*, Mariehamn 1969, 15-25.

Dreijer, Matts, Jomala kyrka, *Åländsk Odling 1963*, Mariehamn 1963, 3-52.

Dreijer, Matts, Kalkstenskorset i Sunds kyrka, *Sanct Olof*, Mariehamn 1953, 48-59.

Dreijer, Matts, Kalkstenslejonet i Jomala, *Åländsk Odling*, Mariehamn 1957, 25-64.

Dreijer, Matts, Kumlinge kyrka. Några anteckningar vid en undersökning i samband med kyrkans restaurering sommaren 1961, *Åländsk Odling*, Mariehamn 1962, 142-158.

Dreijer, Matts, Lumparlands kyrka, *Åländsk Odling*, Mariehamn 1961, 90-98.

Dreijer, Matts, Medeltidskyrkan i Föglö, *Åländsk Odling*, Mariehamn 1967, 3-31.

Dreijer, Matts, Relik-krucifixet från Föglö. *Sanct Olof*, Mariehamn 1967, 14-16.

Dreijer, Matts, S. Mikael i Finström, *Åländsk Odling*, Mariehamn 1973, 23-67.

Dreijer, Matts, St. Nicolaus i Lemland, *Sanct Olof*, Mariehamn 1957, 16-26.

Dreijer, Stig, *Det åländska folkets historia. 3. Frihetstiden och den gustavianska tiden 1721-1808*, utgiven av Ålands kulturstiftelse, Mariehamn 2006.

Dreijer, Stig, Relik-krucifixet från Föglö Sta Maria Magdalena kyrka, *Sanct Olof*, Mariehamn 1988, 19-32.

Fagerlund, L.W. *Signildskär*, Åland VIII, Helsingfors 1923, 1-55.

Flink, Gerhard ed. *Kung Valdemars segelled*, Riksantikvarieämbetet, Stockholm 1995.

Folk, R.L., Valastro, S. Jr. Successful technique of dating of lime mortars by carbon -14. *Journal of Field Archaeology* 3, 1976, 203-208.

Gallén, Jarl, Kökar, Klosterbröderna och havet, *Maritima medeltidsstudier, Jungfrusund 2*, Åbo 1989.

Gardberg, Carl Jacob, Lemlands kyrka, Ålands medeltida kyrkor, *Stockholm Studies in History of Art 25*, Lund 1973, 65-83.

Gustavsson, Kenneth, Franciskanerklostret på Kökar. Nytt ljus over medeltiden i Skärgårdshavet, *Historisk Tidskrift för Finland, 3. 1994. årg. 79*, 494-518.

Gustavsson, Kenneth, *Hamnö En medeltida klostermiljö i ytterskärården. Sevärt 6*, Mariehamn 1997.

Gustavsson, Kenneth, Kökar, kyrka, kloster och fiskeläge, *Kung Valdemars segelled*, ed. Gerhard Flink, Stockholm 1995, 121-134.

Gustavsson, Kenneth, Kökars kyrka 200 år, *Sanct Olof 38*, Mariehamn 1984, 121-128.

Gustavsson, Kenneth, Medeltida gravar vid Kökars kloster, *Sanct Olof 42*, Mariehamn 1988, 149-157.

Haapanen, Toivo, *Verzeichnis der mittelalterlichen Handschriftenfragmente in der*

Universitätsbibliothek zu Helsingfors, I, Missalia, Helsingfors, 1922.

Hale, John R., Jan Heinemeier, Lynne Lancaster, Alf Lindroos & Åsa Ringbom: "Dating Ancient Mortar", *American Scientist* Volume 91, 2003, 130-137.

Hausen, Reinhold, *Finlands medeltidssigill i afbild utgifna af Finlands Statsarkiv*, Helsingfors 1900.

Hausen, Reinhold, Ur Ålands forntid. Kökars kloster, *Åland. Bidrag till kännedom af hembygden utgifna af Föreningen Ålands vänner IV*, Helsingfors 1916, 56-71.

Hausen, Reinhold, Ur Ålands forntid. Lemböte kapell, *Åland. Bidrag till kännedom af hembygden utgifna af Föreningen Ålands vänner IV,* Helsingfors 1916, 51-55.

Hausen, Reinhold, Ur Ålands forntid. Sankt Knuts gille. *Åland. Bidrag till kännedom af hembygden utgifna af Föreningen Ålands vänner IV,* Helsingfors 1916, 91-95.

Hausen, Reinhold, Ur Ålands forntid. "Landsens signet". *Åland. Bidrag till kännedom af hembygden utgifna af Föreningen Ålands vänner IV*, Helsingfors 1916, 85-90.

Helgeränet, från mässböcker till munkepärmar, Abukhanfusa, Kerstin (red.), Borås, 1993.

Hellberg, Lars, Ortnamnen och den svenska bosättningen på Åland, *Skrifter utgivna av Svenska Litteratursällskapet i Finland, nr 517,* Helsingfors 1987.

Heinemeier, Jan, Högne Jungner, Alf Lindroos, Åsa Ringbom, Thorborg von Konow & Niels Rud: "AMS 14C dating of lime mortar", i: Beam interactions with materials and atoms, *Nuclear Instruments & Methods in Physics Research, Section B, volume 123, Nos 1-4, March (II)* 1997, s. 487-495.

Heinemeier, Jan, Åsa Ringbom, Alf Lindroos, Árny E Sveinbjörnsdóttir: Successful AMS ^{14}C Dating of Non-Hydraulic Lime Mortars from the Medieval Churches of the Åland Islands, Finland. *RADIOCARBON*, Vol 52, Nr 1, 2010, 171-204.

Hiekkanen, Markus, *The Stone Churches in the Medieval Diocese of Turku, A Systematic Classification and Chronology*, SMYA-FFT 101, Helsinki 1994.

Hiekkanen, Markus, *Suomen keskiajan kivikirkot*, Suomalaisen Kirjallisuuden Seuran Toimituksia 1117, Helsinki 2007.

Immonen, Visa, Golden Moments. Artefacts of Precious Metals as Products of Luxury Consumption in Finland c. 1200-1600. I text, II catalogue, *Archaeologia Medii Aevi Finlandiae XVI*, Turku 2009.

Kakkuri, Juhani ja Hanna Virkki, Maa nousee. *Jääkaudet*, toim. Marjatta Koivisto, Porvoo 2001, 168-225.

Karlsson, Marita, *Åländska husgrunder från yngre järnålder-tidig medeltid*, Mariehamn 1987.

Karlström, Gisela, S. Maria Magdalena i Föglö, *Sanct Olof*, Mariehamn 1986, 163-172.

Klackenberg, Henrik, Moneta nostra. Monetariseringen i medeltidens Sverige, *Lund Studies in Medieval Archaeology 10*, Stockholm 1992.

Klemetti, Heikki, *Suomalaisia Kirkonrakentajia 1600- ja 1700-luvuilla*, Porvoossa 1927.

Konsten i Finland. Från medeltid till nutid. Red. Bengt von Bonsdorff et al. Ny bearbetad upplaga 1998.

Källström, O., *Medeltida kyrksilver från Sverige och Finland förlorat genom Gustav Vasas konfiskationer*, Uppsala 1939.

Lagerlöf, Erland, Gunnar Svahnström, *Gotlands kyrkor, en vägledning*, fjärde omarbetade utgåvan, Visby 1991.

Laitinen, Anu, Fynd av kalksten från Lemlands och Föglö kyrka, *Åländsk Odling*, Mariehamn 1974, 97-102.

Laitinen, Anu, Sottunga kyrka, *Åländsk Odling*, Mariehamn 1974, 103-112.

Lamm, Jan Peder, Historiola Metallica Alandica, *Festskrift tillägnad Matts Dreijer på hans 80-årsdag 31.01.1981*, Mariehamn 1981, 160-182.

Lancaster, Lynne C., *Concrete Vaulted Construction in Imperial Rome, Innovations in Context*, Cambridge University Press, 2005.

Langley M.M., Maloney S.J., Ringbom Å, Heinemeier J, Lindroos A. 2010. A Comparison of Dating Techniques at Torre de Palma, Portugal: Mortars and Ceramics. In: Ringbom Å, Hohlfelder R, editors. Assistant editors Pia Sjöberg and Pia Sonck-Koota, Building Roma Aeterna, Current Research on Roman Mortar and Concrete, Proceedings of the conference March 27-29 2008, *Commentationes Humanarum Litterarum 128, 2011*, Societas Scientiarum Fennica, Ekenäs 2011, 242-256.

Lindgren, Mereth, *Att lära och att pryda: om efterreformatoriska kyrkmålningar i Sverige cirka 1530-1630*, Kungl. Vitterhets historie o. antikvitets akademien, Stockholm 1983.

Lindgren, Mereth, *Bilden av Birgitta*, Höganäs 1991.

Lindroos, Alf, *Carbonate Phases in Historical Lime Mortars and Pozzolana Concrete: Implications for ^{14}C Dating*, Department of Geology and Mineralogy, Åbo Akademi University, Diss. Åbo 2005.

Lindroos, Alf, Jan Heinemeier, Åsa Ringbom, Fiona Brock, Pia Sonck-Koota, Miia Pehkonen, Juhani Suksi, Problems in Radiocarbon Dating of Roman Pozzolana Mortars, Editors Åsa Ringbom and Robert L. Hohlfelder, Assistant editors Pia Sjöberg and Pia Sonck-Koota, Building Roma Aterna, Current Research on Roman Mortar and Concrete. Proceedings of the Conference, *Commentationes Humanarum Litterarum 128, 2011*, Societas Scientiarum Fennica, Ekenäs 2011, 214-230.

Lindroos, Alf, Åsa Ringbom, Jan Heinemeier & Árny Sveinbjörnsdóttir: "Mortar dating using AMS ^{14}C and sequential dissolution: Examples from Medieval, non-hydraulic lime mortars from the Åland Islands, SW Finland", *RADIOCARBON Volume 49*, Nr 1 2007, 47-67.

Lindroos, Alf, Åsa Ringbom, Riikka Kaisti, Jan Heinemeier, Gregory Hodgins and Fiona Brock, The oldest parts of the Turku Cathedral. C-14 chronology of fire damaged mortars, *Proceedings from the Symposium about archaeology and history of churches in the Baltic region*, Visby 8-12.6.2010, in print.

Markus, Kersti, *Från Gotland till Estland, Kyrkokonst och politik under 1200-talet*, Kristianstad 1999.

Nilsén, Anna, *Program och funktion i senmedeltida kalkmåleri. Kyrkmålningarna i Mälarlandskapen och Finland 1400-1534*, Stockholm 1986.

Nilsén, Anna, *Kyrkorummets brännpunkt. Gränsen mellan kor och långhus i den svenska landskyrkan, Från romanik till nygotik*, Stockholm 1991.

Nordman, C.A., Medeltida skulptur i Finland, *Suomen muinaismuistoyhdistyksen aikakauskirja-Finska fornminnesföreningens tidskrift 62*, Helsingfors 1965.

Nyman, Valdemar, Anteckningar om Geta kapellkyrkas äldre skick, *Åländsk Odling*, Mariehamn 1960, 57-93.

Nyman, Valdemar, *Det åländska folkets historia I:2*, Ålands medeltida kyrkokonst, Mariehamn 1978.

Nyman, Valdemar, Vårdö kyrka, *Åländsk Odling*, Mariehamn 1972, 43-92.

Nyman, Valdemar, 1200-tals målningarna i Jomala kyrka, *Åländsk Odling*, Mariehamn 1963, 53-86.

Palamarz, Piotr, *Kastelholms slott: från medeltida borg till byggnadsminne*, Mariehamn 2004.

Pegelow, Ingalill, *Helgonlegender i ord och bild*, Kristianstad 2006.

Pirinen, Hanna, Luterilaisen kirkkointeriöörin muotoutuminen Suomessa: pitäjänkirkon sisustuksen muutokset reformaatiosta karoliinisen ajan loppuun (1527-1718), *Suomen Muinaismuistoyhdistyksen aikakauskirja - Finska Fornminnesföreningens tidskrift, 103,* Helsinki 1996.

Pooth, Ernst, Zur Baugeschichte der Kirche von Jomala, Ålands medeltida kyrkor, *Stockholm Studies in History of Art, 25,* Lund 1973, 9-24.

Propper, Gerold, Sunds Kyrka, Ålands medeltida kyrkor, *Stockholm Studies in History of Art 25,* Lund 1973, 40-64.

Ramsdahl, Carl, Jomala kyrkas ombyggnad 1828-1844, *Åländsk Odling,* Mariehamn 1956, 3-31.

Réau, Louis, Iconographie de l'art chrétien, T. 1-3, Paris 1955-1959.

Remmer, Christina, Mårten Johansson målare, *Sanct Olof*, Mariehamn 1995-96, 100-119.

Reutersvärd, Oscar, De medeltida dopfuntarna på Åland, *Ålands medeltida kyrkor,* Acta Universitatis Stockholmiensis, Stockholm Studies in History of Art 25, Lund 1973, 144-165.

Ringbom, Åsa, Hemsida för projektet Ålands kyrkor *www.kyrkor.ax* (uppdateras kontinuerligt)

Ringbom, Åsa, Altarskåpet i Hammarland – rekonstruktion och ikonografi, *Det ikonografiske blik, Festskrift til Ulla Haastrup,* København 1993, 111-118.

Ringbom, Åsa, *Boetius Murenius – en åländsk ikonoklast?* Tro og bilde i Norden i Reformasjonens århundre, Oslo 1991, 253-267.

Ringbom, Åsa, "Mortar Dating and Dolphins: Santa Costanza reconsidered", Songs of Ossian", *Festschrift in honour of Professor Bo Ossian Lindberg, Taidehistoriallisia Tutkimuksia-Konsthistoriska Studier, 27,* Helsinki 2003, 22-42.

Ringbom, Åsa, "Motivics and Mariology: Maria in Sole in St. Michael's Church of Finström", *Icon to Cartoon. A Tribute to Sixten Ringbom, Taidehistoriallisia tutkimuksia , Konsthistoriska studier 16,* Helsingfors 1995, 273-287.

Ringbom, Åsa, Reflections on Liturgical Drama in Mediaeval Scandinavian Art. *Roma, magistra mundi. Iteneraria culturae medievalis. Meilanges offerts au Père L.E. Boyle*, Louvain-la-Neuve 1998, 737-757.

Ringbom, Åsa, Sundskorset – ett medeltida minneskors? *Väster om Skiftet, uppsatser utgivna av Historiska Institutionen vid Åbo Akademi,* Åbo Akademi Historiska Institutionen meddelanden 8, red. Sune Jungar och Nils Erik Villstrand, Åbo 1986, 11-35.

Ringbom, Åsa, Alf Lindroos, Jan Heinemeier, John R. Hale, Lynne Lancaster & Fiona Brock: "Radiocarbon Dating of Mortar". *Poster presentation at the Archaeological Institute of America, Annual Meeting 3-6 January 2008, Chicago.*

Ringbom, Åsa, Christina Remmer: *Ålands kyrkor, Volym I, Hammarland och Eckerö,* Mariehamn 1995.

Ringbom, Åsa, Christina Remmer: *Ålands kyrkor, Volym II, Saltvik*, Ekenäs 2000.

Ringbom, Åsa, Christina Remmer: *Ålands kyrkor, Volym III, Sund och Vårdö,* Mariehamn 2005.

Ringbom, Åsa, Jan Heinemeier, Alf Lindroos, & Árny Sveinbjörnsdóttir: "Projektet Ålands kyrkor och murbruksdatering – rapport från en metodutveckling. *Nordisk Kirkearkeologi 9, Kalundborg, Danmark 2007, hikuin 36,* Viborg 2009, 129-158.

Ringbom, Åsa, Jan Heinemeier, Alf Lindroos & Fiona Brock: "Building Roma Aeterna, Mortar Dating and Roman Pozzolana, Results and Interpretations". Building Roma Aeterna, Current Research on Roman Mortar and Concrete, Proceedings of the conference March 27-29 2008, Editors Åsa Ringbom and Robert L. Hohlfelder, Assistant editors Pia Sjöberg and Pia Sonck-Koota, *Commentationes Humanarum Litterarum 128, 2011*, Societas Scientarum Fennica, Ekenäs 2011, 187-208.

Ringbom Åsa, John Hale, Jan Heinemeier, Alf Lindroos & Fiona Brock: "Mortar dating in Medieval and Classical archaeology", *CHS (Construction History Society) Newsletter 73*, 2006, 11-18.

Ringbom, Åsa, John Hale, Jan Heinemeier, Lynne Lancaster & Alf Lindroos, When did the Mortar Harden? A new method for dating buildings and other structures through AMS radiocarbon analysis. *Poster presented at the XVI International Congress of Classical Archaeology, Associazione Internationale di Archeologia Classica, Harvard University August 24*, 2003.

Ringbom, Åsa, Alf Lindroos, Jan Heinemeier and Kenneth Gustavsson, Dating stone churches in the outer Åland archipalgo. *Proceedings from the Symposium about archaeology and history of churches in the Baltic region*, Visby 8-12.6.2010, in print.

Roeck-Hansen, Birgitta, Township and Territory, A study of rural land-use and settlement patterns in Åland c. AD 500-1500. *Acta Universitatis Stockholmiensis, Stockholm Studies in Human Geography, 6,* Stockholm 1991.

Sárkány, Tamás: "Finströms kyrka", *Ålands medeltida kyrkor,* Acta Universitatis Stockholmiensis, Stockholm Studies in History of Art 25, Lund 1973, 115-134.

Schiller, Gertrud, *Ikonographie der christlichen Kunst, Band 4,2; Band 5,* Gütersloh 1980, 1990, 1991.

Sjöberg, Pia, Åsa Ringbom, Alf Lindroos, Pia Sonck-Koota, Radiocarbon dating of the medieval churches of the Åboland archipelago. *Proceedings from the Symposium about archaeology and history of churches in the Baltic region*, Visby 8-12.6.2010, in print.

Svanberg, Jan & Anders Qwarnström, *Sankt Göran och draken,* Stockholm 1993.

Tuhkanen, Tuija, *"In memoriam sui et suorum posuit" Lahjoittajien muistokuvat Suomen kirkossa 1400-luvulta 1700-luvun lopulle*. Åbo 2005.

Tångeberg, Peter, Mittelalterliche Holzskulpturen und Altarschriene in Schweden. Studien zu Form, Materiel und Technik, Stockholm 1986.

Sárkány, Tamás: "Finströms kyrka", *Ålands medeltida kyrkor,* Acta Universitatis Stockholmiensis, Stockholm Studies in History of Art 25, Lund 1973, 115-134.

Ullén, Marian, *Dädesjö och Eke kyrkor*, Sveriges kyrkor, Stockholm 1969.

Walker, Mike J.D. *Quaternary Dating Methods*, Chichester 2005.

Wienberg, Jes, *Den gotiske labyrinth. Middelalderen og kirkerne i Danmark*, Lund Studies in Medieval Archaeology II, Stockholm 1993.

Voionmaa, V. Studier i Ålands medeltidshistoria. *Finska Fornminnesföreningens tidskrift* XXVII, Helsingfors 1916.

Young, Karl, *The Drama of the Medieval Church I-II*, Oxford 1933.

Ålands medeltida kyrkor, Acta Universitatis Stockholmiensis, Stockholm Studies in History of Art 25, Lund 1973.

Åland. Bidrag till kännedom af hembygden I-VIII. Utgifna af Föreningen Ålands Vänner, Mariehamn 1910-1926.

www.kyrkor.ax

www.mortardating.com

Sources of Illustrations

HELSINKI

The National Board of Antiquities, the Cultural History Image archives, the History Unit, 111, 112

Helsinki University Library, 28

The National Archives, 51

ÅLAND

Åland's museum, 80, 93, 94, 96, 171

AARHUS, DENMARK

AMS 14C Dating centre, University of Aarhus, 169, 135, sketch

INDIVIDUALS

Lars Berggren, back cover portrait

L.W. Fagerlund 1923, 150

Kenneth Gustavsson, 128

Reinhold Hausen 11, 131, 132, 149

Bo Ossian Lindberg, 10, 15, 20, sketches 37, 188

Alf Lindroos, 172, 176a, 178a, 180a, 181a, 182a

Augusto Mendes, 2, 3, 4, 6, 7, 8a-b, 9, 12, 13, 14, 16, 19, 21, 22, 23, 24, 25, 26, 29, 30a-b, 31, 32, 35, 36, 37, 39, 41a-b, 43, 44, 45, 46, 47, 48, 53, 54, 55, 56, 57, 58, 59a-b, 60, 63, 64, 65, 66, 67, 70, 71, 72, 73, 74, 77, 78, 79, 82, 83, 84, 85, 86, 87, 92, 95, 101, 104, 105, 107, 114, 115, 116, 116, 119, 121, 122, 123, 125, 126, 129, 130, 133, 135, 136, 136, 139, 142, 143, 144, 145, 146, 148, 151, 152, 153, 154, 155, 156, 158, 159, 160, 161a-c, 162, 164, 165, 167, 169

Anna-Maaret Pitkänen-Darmark, 2. inauguration cross, plans and façades in 1, 5, 27, 38

Åsa Ringbom, 17, 18, 33, 34, 40, 49, 62, 75, 88, 90, 91, 97, 98, 99, 100, 103, 106, 113, 117, 119, 130 detail, 138, 140, 141, 167, 170, 171, 175, 176b, 178b, 179, 180b, 181b, 182b, 183b-d, 184, 185, 186a-f, 187a-b

Pia Sonck-Koota, 173, 174, and the maps pp 12, 26, 34. The reconstructions based on information from the National Land Survey of Finland in combination with the present coastline, and Fig. 6. Ringbom & Remmer 1995, 19.

Kjell Söderlund, front cover